Agirre's Diaries

Basque Classics Series No. 13

Series Editors

William A. Douglass
Gregorio Monreal
Pello Salaburu

AGIRRE'S DIARIES

Edited by Iñaki Goiogana

Center for Basque Studies
University of Nevada, Reno
2018

This book was published with generous financial support obtained by the Association of Friends of the Center for Basque Studies and from the Government of Bizkaia.

Basque Classics Series No. 13

Series Editors:
William A. Douglass,
Gregorio Monreal,
and Pello Salaburu

William A. Douglass Center for Basque Studies
University of Nevada, Reno
Reno, Nevada 89557

Translation by Jennifer Ottman
Introduction by Iñaki Goiogana
Originally published: José Antonio Agirre Lekube : diario 1941-1942, (Bilbao: Sabino Arana Fundazioa, 2010).

http://basque.unr.edu

ISBN: 978-1-949805-00-0
Copyright © 2017 by the Center for Basque Studies and the University of Nevada, Reno
All rights reserved. Printed in the United States of America

Library of Congress Cataloging-in-Publication Data forthcoming

Contents

Prologue: 7

1941 Diary 21

2nd Trimester 79

3rd Trimester 135

4th Trimester 191

A Page a Day for 1942 249

Index 311

Prologue

Iñaki Goiogana

The diary that this prologue introduces is a unique work by a no less unique author. It is a unique work because José Antonio Agirre kept no other diaries, as far as we know, and because as the first *lehendakari* of the Basques, he represented and incarnated his country's desires for many years, from his election in Gernika on October 7, 1936, to his premature death in Paris on March 22, 1960. This diary, then, is a historical document. However, it also has a special place even among all the documents that have Agirre as their protagonist or author. It is special and unique because it covers a number of months of his life for which, due to the war and the fact that he was living in hiding, we have very little documentation.

At the beginning of May 1940, José Antonio Agirre could be satisfied with the situation in which his government found itself and with its management of the exile, making due allowances for the world war and Franco's dictatorship in Euskadi. The great wave of exiles had been directed into appropriate channels—the majority had returned home, some had succeeded in embarking for the Americas, and the remainder of the refugees were finding employment in the French economy with relative ease, given the labor shortages produced by the war. The shelters and aid centers were being closed, and the subsidies provided by the Basque government were on a clear downward trajectory, due to the fact that the exiles' need for assistance was diminishing. The Basque government did not have large financial reserves, but the decrease in spending and the new financial agreement reached with the Spanish Republican Board of Aid (*Junta de Auxilio a los Republicanos Españoles,* JARE), led by Indalecio Prieto from his base in Mexico, enabled it to move beyond the straitened circumstances it had been in before Christmas, when it ended its ties with the Spanish Republican Emigration Service (*Servicio de Emigración de los Republicanos Españoles,* SERE), headed by Juan Negrín and opposed to the JARE in all respects.

Once the social aspect had been handled, Agirre still needed to reach an agreement with the Socialist Party in order to decrease the government's aid apparatus still further and devote himself to the political work of opposing the Spanish dictatorship and developing a deeper treatment of the demands for self-government. The Basque nationalists' aim was for the Basque parties, both the nationalists and those that gave their obedience to the state, to recognize their national essence. The socialists had opposed this request during 1939 and the first months of 1940, but an agreement was not far away.

On May 8, 1940, after months of conversations, José Antonio Agirre met with the Basque socialist leaders, including Julián Zugazagoitia, and they agreed on the basis on which the Basque government would be established going forward. Nevertheless, the agreement was not signed, since the definitive text had to be drawn up, and the Agirre-Zabala family already had plans that day to travel to the Belgian locality of La Panne to see their relatives who had taken refuge in Flanders. The parties set the *lehendakari*'s return as the date for the ratification of the document.

For this reason, and due to the events that immediately followed, we do not have the agreed text, but we do have two working drafts. The later of the two drafts states:

> The Basque government is obligated to defend the freedom of Euzkadi and those spiritual and social values that have been definitively consecrated by the blood of the patriots who have fallen in the struggle.
>
> In consequence, the Basque government will develop its future policy on the basis of the following fundamental principles:
>
> a) Action directed toward placing Euzkadi in a position in which, taking its national personality into account, it may be able to democratically express its will and obtain Basque freedom to the degree and extent that the free will of the Basques may determine.
>
> b) In Basque solidarity and fraternity both among individuals and among the regions of Alaba, Gipuzkoa, Nabarra, and Bizkaya, to which territories the Basque will expressed through a plebiscite, historical solidarity, and current Basque political aims extend.[1]

---

1   *Un nuevo 31: Ideología y estrategia del Gobierno de Euzkadi durante la Segunda Guerra*

This, or something like it, was what the exiled Basque politicians were going to sign in the middle of May when the German armies attacked the Netherlands, Belgium, and Luxemburg and went on to enter France through this corridor, just as they had done in August 1914, at the start of World War I. However, this time luck was against the Allies, and the German armies did not stop at the gates of Paris.

Agirre, as already noted, was with his family enjoying a few long-awaited days of vacation. All the influence that the Basque leaders could bring to bear through their friends at the International League of Friends of the Basques (*Liga Internacional de Amigos de los Vascos*, LIAV) had been necessary to obtain a special pass to go to Belgium, since even though before the offensive, the war did not seem real—these first months of the war are known as the *drôle de guerre*, the "phony war"—the French were at war with the Germans, and passes to travel to border areas were restricted.

This dangerous coincidence was the start of the itinerary that, having begun on the beaches of Flanders, would end in New York. The *lehendakari* could scarcely have imagined what was awaiting him on what was supposed to be a long weekend with his family.

From the time of the German offensive in May until Christmas 1940, Agirre hid in various places—a Jesuit school, a boarding house, and so on—but he needed to leave Belgium, not only for his own good, but also for that of his government. The French disaster meant that the majority of the Basque leadership was either in occupied territory or in territory administered by the collaborationist Vichy regime. In democratic countries, prominent Basques with political influence and ties to the Basque government could be found only in the delegations in London and Buenos Aires. Manuel Irujo was in the United Kingdom, along with some members of the national executive of the Basque Nationalist Party (*Partido Nacionalista Vasco*, PNV), and Ramón María Aldasoro was in Argentina. There was also the delegation in New York, headed by Manu de la Sota. In this situation of a power vacuum, Irujo stepped forward and established the Basque National Council (*Consejo Nacional Vasco*), but neither the physical distance between the Basque politicians

---

Mundial a través de la correspondencia de José Antonio Agirre y Manuel Irujo, ed. Iñaki Goiogana, Xabier Irujo, and Josu Legarreta (Bilbao: Sabino Arana Fundazioa, 2007), 215.

nor the lack of economic resources were much help in smoothing over the differences between the New World delegates and London.

Agirre remained in Belgium from May to December 1940. He was not cut off from his comrades in Paris and in southern France, but contact with them was very difficult. In addition, insistent rumors about his possible location in Belgium were circulating. Even before they knew where he might be, his comrades in the Americas and in London were already speculating about who might be able to provide assistance to the *lehendakari* in Belgium. And they were not mistaken. If Manu de la Sota or Irujo could come up with the idea that the Basque Jesuits resident in Belgium might be helping Agirre, Franco's agents could imagine the same thing and, sooner or later, figure out where he was. He needed to leave Belgium, but how? and by what route?

The first question was quickly answered. He would leave as a South American—Panamanian—citizen who wanted to return to his country. With the help of a Panamanian consul in Belgium, Germán Gil Guardia Jaén, Agirre was able to obtain a false identity that shared his initials, José Andrés Álvarez Lastra.

The route was more difficult. The logical route for a South American who wanted to return to his country was to cross the Atlantic after embarking in a Spanish or Portuguese port. This escape route, for obvious reasons, was not open to Dr. Álvarez Lastra, and so it was necessary to opt for the opposite direction. If it was impossible to reach the Western Hemisphere by going west, there was no alternative but to head east.

Consequently, the first step in the itinerary that the *lehendakari* sketched out was to enter Germany, to be followed, once in the territory of the Reich, by a stop in the Soviet Union, reached by way of a third country—for example, Greece. Finally, after arriving in the Soviet Union, Agirre proposed to travel across that country to the Pacific and embark there for the west coast of the Americas. It must be remembered that when Agirre began his wanderings in January 1941, Germany and the Soviet Union were not at war, but rather the reverse. They were at the peak of their mutual collaboration following the Molotov-Ribbentrop Pact of August 1939.[2] In the end, this route also turned out to be

---

2   See the diary entry for February 17, 1941, in which the *lehendakari* notes the arrival that day at the boarding house where he was staying of "a dozen Russian aviators," undoubtedly the fruit of an exchange between Germany and the Soviet Union.

impractical, because it was blocked by the German-Soviet war that broke out in June 1941, when the Agirre-Zabala family was in Sweden.

The *lehendakari*'s second plan, after the war in the East had impeded access to the Soviet Union, necessarily had to resemble the route that went by way of a Spanish or Portuguese port, but avoiding those dangerous locations. Agirre had no alternative but to cross the Atlantic, but avoiding the Iberian Peninsula. In reality, there was another possible way to flee the Nazis, and that was to fly from Sweden to Great Britain. The *lehendakari* always considered this possibility a last resort for escape, only if the maritime route became impossible or would entail great delays. His reasons for preferring a ship to a plane were probably related to the goal he had set for himself of reaching the Western Hemisphere, and perhaps also to the possibility that the air route would be expensive, it would be difficult to obtain passage, or it might not be possible to include the entire Agirre-Zabala family. The fact is that Agirre preferred the maritime route and that, with Manuel Ynchausti's help from New York, he succeeded in embarking on the Vasaholm on July 31, 1941, arriving in Rio de Janeiro on August 27.

In the Americas, his difficulties did not disappear, but however great those difficulties were, the possibilities opened to the *lehendakari* were infinitely greater. His false Panamanian passport posed an obstacle for entering the United States, but the solution proposed—changing identity in Uruguay and continuing the journey under his true name—meant Agirre's first mass welcome in Uruguay and Argentina. In the Southern Cone, Agirre had the chance to realize that his political significance was not limited to the community of political emigrants and that he had some influence with the authorities and the general public in that region.

The American insistence that he enter the United States incognito annoyed the *lehendakari*, but the opportunity to teach at Columbia University, even if it was only as a lecturer, was something that he welcomed as a divine blessing. At the same time, residing in the United States meant a certain distance from the bulk of the exiles, but to the same degree, it implied proximity to the authorities of the most important country in the world. The contacts he made upon arriving in New York demonstrated the rightness of the choice of the United States as his destination in exile. The city of skyscrapers was the place of refuge for a small minority of exiles who, both during the war and in the postwar period, would become an influential and important group. We are referring to the European democratic Catholic exiles.

The diary is a day-by-day account of seventeen months in the life of a fugitive, an exile, but it is not a travel account. Agirre recorded both personal and public affairs in it. It shows very well how at the most difficult moment of the war, when it seemed that the Axis troops had no rivals who could stand against them, the *lehendakari* threw in his lot unequivocally with democracy. This was not a choice based on circumstances, but one that had been pondered and accepted from before the war. In this diary, there are numerous criticisms of the totalitarian regimes. In the same way, there are equally abundant phrases of admiration with regard to systems like the one Agirre was able to observe directly in Sweden, that is, the combination of representative democracy and the general wellbeing of the population. In every diary entry while he was in that Nordic country, Agirre found occasion to say something like "this is what I want for my country. Democracy and wellbeing." He did not limit himself to admiring the Nordic system, however, but rather, once in America, he joined with the Catholic social activists in exile in the United States for this purpose and, like all of them, offered his services to the British and the Americans, the only ones who would be able to guarantee the desired democracy and wellbeing in the postwar period. In the Basque case, there was also the national struggle, but this could not be presented as dissociated from the social struggle, and there are abundant references in Agirre's diary to the Basque struggle comparing it, for example, to South American independence.

This simple diary, then, enables us to become better and more deeply acquainted with the day-to-day experience of these months in the *lehendakari*'s life, but also to obtain information about what his plans were and to get a comprehensive idea of the nature of his ideology and thought.

All those who have studied the diary here presented have recognized its documentary value. Nevertheless, also without exception, there are questions that they have all posed in one form or another. Why did Agirre stop writing on an ordinary day, one without the least importance, after having kept up his notes day after day in situations of danger? Might he not have continued in another datebook or similar volume? It is strange, but it seems that there was no reason. He simply stopped. In reality, Agirre also did not explain what led him to start writing at the very same time that he began his wanderings through Germany, the day he caught the train to Hamburg—January 7—and not on New Year's or another day. It was not the most opportune moment to note down confidences on paper, since a simple police search could have caused him serious difficulties. Did he want to record his impressions of Germany, and then continued until he got tired? We do not know.

Independent of these questions without a clear answer, what is certain is that we have these notes that cover seventeen months from the years 1941 and 1942 and that they constitute an important document for learning about *lehendakari* Agirre's activities and Basque participation in World War II. It is a document that sheds some light on the actions of the Euzkadi government and of Basque nationalism after the world war, in the Christian Democratic and pro-European movement, for example.

All this led the Sabino Arana Fundazioa, taking advantage of the commemoration in 2010 of the fiftieth anniversary of the death of the diary's author, to propose the publication of a facsimile edition of the diary together with an annotated transcription and a selection of documents that would complete the information contained in the diary.

The first *lehendakari*'s handwriting is not especially difficult to read, but the small page size of the first volumes of the diary meant that in order to fit everything that he wanted to write, he had to reduce the size of his writing, so that while this diary is not difficult to read, it is also not very easy. At the same time, Agirre was writing for himself and did not worry about providing many explanations, with the consequence that some passages may seem obscure to readers today or to nonspecialists. In addition, when he was keeping this diary, the *lehendakari* knew neither English nor German and so transcribed some names with spelling errors, to the point that some names and surnames are almost unrecognizable.

In order to complete the information contained in the diary, an effort has been made to locate the letters and documents it mentions. Fortunately, the project was able to count on the cooperation of the Agirre-Zabala family, the first custodian of the diary itself,[3] which has made it possible to locate some of the letters written by the *lehendakari* and his wife Mari Zabala during their wanderings as they fled the Nazis. These personal letters have been supplemented by the publication of a series of documents—letters from the *lehendakari* to his collaborators, some of their replies, and press cuttings with interviews and statements by Agirre—that shed light on *lehendakari* Agirre's thinking and activities

---

3   The original volumes of the diary remained in the hands of the Agirre-Zabala family until they were deposited in the Archive of Nationalism, where they are preserved today and are available to researchers.

during this period. The documentary selection is not limited to the months covered by the diary. Rather, it extends to the news of the *lehendakari*'s return to Europe in 1945, thereby closing a circle opened some years before. In total, a set of thirty-one documents has been added to the diary's five original volumes.

In the transcription of the diary and of the other documents, changes have been kept to a minimum and have been made only when they were indispensable for a correct reading of the texts. Spelling errors and mistakes in the transcription of words in languages unknown to Agirre have thus been left as they appear in the original. The only alterations have been the addition of accents that were missing on some words, in order to facilitate the correct reading, and the transcription in bold type of some—rare—expressions that are underlined in the diary. Corrections have always been restricted to the notes, in order to enable a reading of the transcription that is similar as possible to the original and with a minimum of intervention by the editor. Since this is also a facsimile edition, readers can consult the facsimile directly and use the transcription as an aid for the more complicated passages.

In any event, this edition of Agirre's diary is a reedition of the original volumes, in fact a second or third reedition, depending on one's perspective. Taking a historical view for a moment, it can be said that the first edition of these notes was published even before the writing of them had come to an end, since a large portion of the diary was used, with various stylistic reworkings, in Agirre's *De Guernica a Nueva York pasando por Berlín* (From Guernica to New York by way of Berlin). Specifically, the entries written during Agirre's months in Germany were incorporated into chapter six, "Diario del Doctor Álvarez en Alemania" (Doctor Álvarez's diary in Germany).[4]

In addition to the passages Agirre incorporated into *De Guernica a Nueva York*, a complete edition of the diary was published in 1998.[5] That edition stated that the transcription was made on the basis of a microfilm copy deposited in the Library of Congress in Washington, and something close to a conspiracy theory was put forward to explain the presence of

---

4 The most recent edition in Spanish is José Antonio de Aguirre y Lecube, *De Guernica a Nueva York pasando por Berlín* (Madrid: Editorial Foca, 2004). In English, see José Antonio de Aguirre, *Escape via Berlin: Eluding Franco in Hitler's Europe*, intro. and annotations Robert P. Clark (Reno: University of Nevada Press, 1991).

5 José Antonio Aguirre y Lecube, *Diario de Aguirre*, ed. Iñaki Egaña (Tafalla: Txalaparta, 1998).

the microfilms in that major American library. A contributing factor in this theory was the link between the copies of the *lehendakari*'s diary and Jesús Galíndez, a delegate of the Basque government in New York and an FBI agent who disappeared in 1956 at the hands of assassins employed by Dominican dictator Leónidas Trujillo. The author of the prologue of the Txalaparta edition, the historian Iñaki Egaña, proposed that there might be a connection between the American authorities' seizure of the New York delegation's files following Galíndez's disappearance and the microfilm copy preserved in the Library of Congress.

We do not know all the details, but we do know the basic outline of how the United States Congress ended up with a microfilm copy of this diary. On August 20, 1954, Galíndez sent one of the hundreds of letters he wrote to the *lehendakari* during his time at the New York delegation, recounting his activities in the United States. He said in this letter, "I was working at the Library of Congress, and on several afternoons I went out in the car of the deputy director of the Hispanic Foundation. They're going to publish your diary for the library; they already have the permission."[6] Galíndez took advantage of the opportunity to visit the library in Washington whenever he had to visit a State Department official in the capital, since he was writing his doctoral dissertation on Trujillo's Dominican dictatorship.

Some weeks later, Galíndez wrote again to Agirre to tell him, "I have not received any comments about the diary and its microfilm, so I'm sending it without further ado to the Library of Congress, on the terms I told you about." We have not located the earlier letter with the conditions, but it was mentioned again later on in the correspondence between the *lehendakari* and his New York delegate, as discussed in the following paragraphs.

The next letter we have located with references to the microfilming is from January 29, 1955. By that date, the making of the copy had been completed. The delegate informed the *lehendakari* that the Library of Congress had returned the original volumes of the diary to him, along with two copies of the microfilm, one negative and one positive. The letter continued, "You will tell me what to do. If it seems alright to you, I suggest that the positive copy stay here and that I send the original and the negative to Paris; the Party wanted a copy, as I've already told you.

---

6   Letter from Jesús Galíndez to José Antonio Agirre, New York, August 20, 1954, Irargi-GE-78-1.

If you tell me to do so, I'll send it to you by certified mail, but it seems safer to me to wait for a trustworthy traveler."⁷ This is what Galíndez did, taking advantage of Eneko Belausteguigoitia's trip to the French capital to send the diary and the negative microfilm to Paris. In the letter in which he told Agirre that he was sending the diary, Galíndez said, "I remind you that Juan [Ajuriagerra] wanted to make a copy in Beyris."⁸

Agirre's first missive referring to the microfilming process that is preserved in the Basque government's archives, currently on deposit at the Centro de Documentación Irargi, is dated March 14 and informs Galíndez that he received the diary but does not remember "very well the conditions that you imposed on the library." Nevertheless, the *lehendakari* indicated that the material should not be used without his authorization. At the same time, Agirre authorized his delegate to send a copy to the PNV, whom the *lehendakari* would warn to make discreet use of it. Agirre's reticence was due to the fact that, even though "all its contents might be publishable," there were "two or three references that it is appropriate to reserve for the time being, given the current circumstances and the individuals designated in its pages."⁹

The conditions that Galíndez had agreed with the library were the "usual ones in these cases: that is, that the diary can be viewed, but it cannot be used either in whole or in part without the express permission of the author or someone duly authorized by the author."¹⁰ The *lehendakari* insisted that the contents of the diary not be used, but Galíndez expected that it would be difficult to change the conditions previously agreed.

> I am very concerned about the last pages of the diary, since there are direct references, with full names, to our captains who turned over Franco's secret codes. If someone got access to this diary, the situation of these courageous patriots could be terribly difficult, even today.... Since I didn't have

---

7   Letter from Jesús Galíndez to José Antonio Agirre, New York, January 29, 1955, Irargi-GE-78-1.
8   Letter from Jesús Galíndez to José Antonio Agirre, New York, February 24, 1955, Irargi-GE-78-1.
9   Letter from José Antonio Agirre to Jesús Galíndez, Paris, March 14, 1955, Irargi-GE-78-1.
10 Letter from Jesús Galíndez to José Antonio Agirre, New York, undated, Irargi-GE-78-1.

the diary here, I didn't remember that there could be such specific details. It doesn't matter that the rest of the diary is seen. It's a matter, then, of suppressing or withdrawing the last ten pages, while all the rest can remain intact. . . . The commitment that the diary cannot be quoted either in whole or in part without my permission does not eliminate the danger that someone could go to the library and read it, gathering the information I mentioned. I'm really afraid that if people have realized that this diary exists, Franco's embassy will send someone to take a look at it, with the first to be curious about it being Ambassador Areilza, with whom I've been joined by friendship since we were children.[11]

Galíndez's reply focused on getting the problem sorted out and taking responsibility for the mistake of not having read the diary in full before proposing it for microfilming: "I'm responsible for the idea of microfilming it; nevertheless, I'm confident that we'll be in time to solve the problem."[12]

The Basque delegate contacted the library again and agreed on conditions of use that we know from the *lehendakari*'s ratification of them:

In summary,

1) restrict access to the pages corresponding to the full month of May 1942 for twenty-five years, unless I give permission in writing, or our official representative for this matter does so on my behalf;

2) the rest of the diary may be examined, but I would like to know who the individuals are who use it, who should always have my permission to use the material in whole or in part for publication purposes.

If these conditions are not accepted, I will find myself forced to prohibit the use of the mentioned diary, pure and simple.[13]

---

11   Letter from José Antonio Agirre to Jesús Galíndez, Paris, March 31, 1955, Irargi-GE-78-1.
12   Letter from Jesús Galíndez to José Antonio Agirre, New York, April 2, 1955, Irargi-GE-78-1.
13   Letter from José Antonio Agirre to Jesús Galíndez, Paris, April 26, 1955, Irargi-GE-78-1.

On May 3, Galíndez wrote to the *lehendakari* indicating that he would write to the Library of Congress to inform them of his decision.[14]

Finally, as editor of the diary and of the documents in the appendices, I cannot fail to express my gratitude for the collaboration of a number of individuals in facilitating the comprehension of many passages and terms rendered obscure by the passage of time but successfully deciphered with their inestimable assistance. These individuals are Aintzane and Joseba Agirre Zabala, Javier de Lasa, Benito Ansola, Ander Manterola, José Julián Bakedano, Xabier Irujo, Kepa Ormaetxea, Edorta Jiménez, Koldo San Sebastián, Juan Carlos Jiménez de Aberasturi, Ingo Niebel, Luis de Guezala, Itziar Mendieta, and Aixa Gaztelu. *Mila esker.*

---

14 Letter from Jesús Galíndez to José Antonio Agirre, New York, May 3, 1955, Irargi-GE-78-1.

1941 DIARY

ADRESSES TO KEEP.

—Dr. Paul at Salvador de León 71, Box 1129—Tel. 92620.[1]
—Carlos Alfonso Guardia Jaén, Box 1175—Caracas.
—Don Constan—Piñango at Llaguno 2-1.[2]
—Rodolfo Arrigorriaga, Buenos Aires.
—Antonio Constantino Arrigorriaga, New York.[3]
—Insaust—12 East 86th Street. New York.[4]
—Manu—60 East 54th Street. Hotel Elysse—New York.[5]
—González Roa (Edmundo)—175 Boulevard de la Magdalena. Marseilles.

---

1   Address of José María Garate, the Basque government's delegate in Venezuela.
2   Constantino Zabala Arrigorriaga (1878–1958) was José Antonio Agirre's father-in-law. The address is that of his residence in Buenos Aires.
3   Antonio Constantino Arrigorriaga was the son of the famous tenor Florencio Constantino and of Luisa Arrigorriaga Larrazabal, Constantino Zabala's maternal aunt. Antonio Constantino was thus a relative of the *lehendakari's* wife.
4   Manuel Ynchausti (1899–1961) was a Philippine landowner who worked closely with the Basque authorities. The principal organizer of the International League of Friends of the Basques (*Liga Internacional de Amigos de los Vascos*, LIAB), he moved to the United States before France fell to the Germans. From New York, in contact with the state department and with the help of Manu de la Sota, he was José Antonio Agirre's chief source of outside support during his trip from Germany to America.
5   Manu de la Sota (1879–1979) was a writer and publicist. During the war, he represented the Basque soccer team and the Eresoinka musical group. In 1938, together with Antonio Irala, he was sent to the United States on a propaganda mission, and he remained there as a delegate of the Basque government until 1946. Inspired by his years in America, in 1946 he published a book in Argentina titled *Yanqui hirsutus: Pequeñas conversaciones sin importancia sobre los habitantes del nuevo mundo anglosajón* (The hairy Yankee: Brief conversations without importance on the inhabitants of the Anglo-Saxon New World) (Buenos Aires: Editorial Sudamericana, 1949).

—Trini—Rue du General Humbert n° 2, Paris XIV—Pont de Vaures.⁶
—Eduard⁷—87 Rue Saint Hubert. Tel. 950.51—Barchem—Antwerp.

ADRESSES TÉLÉPHONIQUES.
NOMS ET ADRESSES NUMÉROS

—Ecleston Square 14—Chicago. (L)⁸
—Consulate General of Panama, Ferdinandstr 56—Hamburg.
—José Sebastián da Silva Freitas—25 Rua do Amparo—2nd floor (Banco Lisboa y Açores), Lisbon.

---

6   Probably Trini Arrigorriaga, cousin of Constantino Zabala and wife of the sculptor Georges Bigeard.
7   Edouard (or Edward) Demarbaix was the director of the Compagnie Maritime et Commerciale S.A. José Antonio Agirre took refuge in his mother's house (Jan Moorkenstraat, Berchem-Antwerp) between July 1940 and his departure from Belgium for Germany. She is identified as Madame Tirlemont in the *lehendakari*'s book *De Guernica a Nueva York pasando por Berlín* (From Guernica to New York by way of Berlin); in English, see *Escape via Berlin: Eluding Franco in Hitler's Europe*, intro. and annotations by Robert P. Clark (Reno: University of Nevada Press, 1991). José Antonio de Aguirre y Lecube, *De Guernica a Nueva York pasando por Berlín* (Madrid: Foca, 2004), 118. For their part, according to Javier de Lasa, his father Martín Lasa, general director of liquids in the Basque government's Department of Trade and Supply, along with Juan Mari Agirre and Cesáreo Asporosa, created the Compagnie Maritime et Commerciale S.A. in Antwerp in order to channel part of the trade in non-military goods destined for the Spanish Republic and so obtain income for the Basque government. For the transport of these products they used the Mid Atlantic Shipping Company, directed from London by Marino Gamboa. Both companies were financed by the Basque government, but their official founders and directors included no one of Spanish nationality, out of fear that Franco's government might take legal action against them, ordering the seizure of the firms on the grounds that they were government agents and that Franco's new regime was the legal successor of the Spanish state. Correspondingly, Marino Gamboa was Filipino and therefore had a United States passport, and Edouard Demarbaix, as a Belgian citizen, served as the director of the Compagnie, but only as a figurehead. The real employees and executives were Cesáreo Asporosa and Juan Mari Agirre. Martín Lasa, for his part, was Mid Atlantic's representative in Antwerp. At the end of the Spanish Civil War, the Basque government liquidated its interest in the firm, leaving it and its activities in the hands of its creators, Martín Lasa and Juan Mari Agirre. The Compagnie Maritime et Commerciale S.A. continues operating today in the Flemish port where it began.
8   The (L) refers either to the Basque government's London delegation, headquartered at the address listed, or to José Ignacio Lizaso Ilarraza, the Basque delegate in the British capital.

—Hotel Majestic, Mexico (Tomás)[9] —Teres—Place Jean Jaurés 14—2nd floor (H. Pirines) Tarbes.[10]

—Harrazpi (Atalaya) Biarritz.

—Marie Thérèse—133-9.[11]

Dr. Rómulo Araujo—Avenue Luisse 244—1st floor[12]

Mr. Emmanuel de Berthier de Sauvigny.

P. nº 1832—Ofslag. va Deutshland.

Ramón María—[13]

Joaquín Viñas Calixto

73 Avenue de Mexique

---

9   Tomás Agirre Lekube (1912–1977), José Antonio's brother, was a soccer player and a member of the Basque soccer team. During the Basque team's Western Hemisphere tour, when they passed through Mexico, he went into exile in that country.
10 Probably Teresa Agirre Lekube, the *lehendakari*'s sister.
11 Address of the house where the *lehendakari*'s mother and siblings were living in Leuven.
12 Rómulo Araujo was the Venezuelan consul in Antwerp.
13 Ramón María Aldasoro Galarza (1897–1952) was a lawyer and a politician of republican convictions. When the war broke out, he formed part of the Bizkaia Defense Committee (*Junta de Defensa*), and when the Basque government was formed, he became a member with the post of counselor for trade and supply, representing the Republican Left (*Izquierda Republicana*) party. In 1938, together with Isaac López Mendizabal, Santiago Cunchillos Manterola, and Pablo Archanco Zubiri, he traveled to Argentina with the mission of promoting the Basque government through propaganda activities. The end of the Spanish Civil War and the start of World War II made his return to Europe inadvisable, with the consequence that he became the Basque government's delegate in Buenos Aires. He remained in this post and in Argentina until 1946, when he returned to Europe.

NOTES

—Mrs. Guardia Jaén.[14] Box 1075—Panama.

—Antonio Álvarez. Box 403—Panama (Cap)

—Baron Albert van den Branden de Reeth, 10 Aréve des Fumali, Boits Forts—Brussels.[15]

—Gamboa, Joaquín, Sarmiento 424, Buenos Aires[16]

—Orbe, Pedro and Jesús[17]

—Box 105 (Diocese), Camagüey (Cuba)

—15 Rue Bourla, Antwerp. Dr. Araujo.

—Lei Mikolei—Moorweiden 34.[18]

---

14 After Guardia Jaén's death, the Basque exile newspapers published an obituary that said, among other things, "In the early morning of Sunday, April 13, Dr. Germán Gil Guardia Jaén, known to all Basques for having been the Panamanian consul who saved our *lendakari*'s life, died in New York City. "Dr. Guardia Jaén served as Panamanian consul in Hamburg from 1931 to 1936, after which he went on to occupy the same post in the city of Antwerp. In the latter port, he had occasion to provide Lehendakari Agirre with the means to escape the Gestapo's persecution, furnishing him with a Panamanian passport under the false name of Dr. Álvarez Lastra and accompanying him to request the safe-conduct that enabled him to reach Berlin. When Panama declared war on Germany, Dr. Guardia Jaén was able to return to his country, from where he went to Montevideo as consul-general and secretary of the legation." "Fallecimiento del Dr. Guardia Jaén," *Euzkadi* (Santiago de Chile), no. 48 (April 1947), 3.

15 Albert van den Branden de Reth was a friend of the brothers Juan Mari and José Antonio Agirre, with whom he shared a house on Amerikalei Street in Antwerp.

16 Joaquín Gamboa Aurrecoechea (1892–1969), a prominent Basque nationalist, went into exile in 1938 in Argentina, where he participated in numerous Basque cultural organizations.

17 Pedro and Jesús Orbe Urquiza were two Basque priests living in exile in Belgium. They emigrated to Cuba in December 1939 and later moved to Mexico, where they had relatives who owned the well-known Euzkadi tire manufacturer.

18 Madame E. Mikolei was the owner of the boarding house where José Antonio Agirre stayed during his time in Hamburg. This boarding house, as noted in the diary, was located at 34 Moorweidenstrasse, in the Rotherbaum district. Nevertheless, the register of foreigners resident in Hamburg between 1939 and 1945 does not record the presence of either Agirre or Álvarez Lastra in the Hanseatic city. The *lehendakari*'s personal data are likewise absent from the *Hausmeldeunterlagen* (German residence registration documents) of Frau E. Mikolei's boarding house, but the same is not true for Guardia Jaén, who appears listed in the guest register as Jaén Herman Guardia, resident from November 27, 1940, to March 8, 1941.

NOTES

[In the upper margin:—His Excellency the Dominican minister.] Roberto Despradel.[19] Willand Strasse 25/26. Tel. 915524.

—His Excellency Dr. Villalaz—Berlin. Tel. 91.02.76[20]

—His Excellency Dr. Zérrega—Hotel Adlon, Berlin.[21]

—His Excellency Dr. Olivera—Embassy of the Argentine Republic—Berlin.[22]

—Victoria Boarding House—91-05-11.

JANUARY 1941
WEDNESDAY 1. *CIRCUMSISION OF JESUS*. 1-364

JANUARY 1941
THURSDAY 2. ST. BASIL THE GREAT. 2-363

JANUARY 1941
FRIDAY 3. ST. GENEVIEVE. 3-362

JANUARY 1941
SATURDAY 4. ST. RIGOBERT. 4-361

JANUARY 1941
SUNDAY 5. ST. TÉLESPHORE. 5-360

JANUARY 1941
MONDAY 6. *EPIPHANY*. 6-359

---

19 Roberto Despradel was the Dominican ambassador to Germany.
20 Villalaz was the Panamanian ambassador to Germany.
21 Alberto Zerega Fombona was a Venezuelan special envoy and minister plenipotentiary in Germany beginning May 4, 1939. He died in Paris in 1968 while serving as his country's ambassador to UNESCO. "Muerte del embajador Zerega Fombona," *OPE* (Paris), no. 5,077 (October 15, 1968), 4.
22 Ricardo Olivera was the Argentine ambassador to Germany from June 1939 until late 1941. He was later transferred to Vichy, where he would be the only accredited diplomat from the entire Western Hemisphere. Uki Goñi, *La auténtica Odessa: La fuga nazi a la Argentina de Perón* (Barcelona: Paidós, 2002), 38.

JANUARY 1941
TUESDAY 7. ST. MELANIE. 7-358

I got up at 4:15, had breakfast with Dr. Araujo, and left at 4:40 [Crossed out: 5:30] for the station. I arrived at 5:25, and the porter informed me that the train was ninety minutes late. Then it was another ten minutes later than that. I made the trip with three German officers who were coming from Paris. Kind and polite. I arrived in Cologne after crossing the border at 2:30. By a miracle, I caught the train for Hamburg, and I left my raincoat behind by mistake in the rush. At the border, politeness and ease. I traveled to Hamburg with a friendly naval officer decorated with the two military crosses. He knew French and was very helpful to me as an interpreter. I arrived in Hamburg at 9:50. Consul Guardia was kindly waiting for me. We arrived at the boarding house. Modest, but a good location. I slept very well. I gave thanks to God before going to sleep.

JANUARY 1941
WEDNESDAY 8. ST. LUCIEN. 8-357

Having gotten up a little late, we went out to walk around Hamburg for a bit. An attractive and handsome capital. We had lunch at the city hall (municipal restaurant); it was good and relatively economical.[23] We telephoned the minister in Berlin. He has not arrived yet; they expect him tomorrow. We reported to the police, in accordance with the law. They were kind and quick in attending to our business and issuing the residency document. The residency document is needed to get a ration book. We visited a German family who are friends of the consul. They gave us splendid afternoon refreshments. Cake, pudding, coffee, and pastries. Also a bottle of cider and one of liquor. The daughter, who is around forty-five, agreed to accompany me to the movies. A pleasant visit to a typical German family. Earlier, we had been to the station to report the lost raincoat. Home at 7:30. I read Plutarch, the vicissitudes of Themistocles and Camillus.[24] I slept peacefully.

---

23 The *Ratsweinkeller* located in the basement of the Hamburg city hall. It survived the destruction of World War II and is still open to the public today.

24 Plutarch of Chaeronea, Greek historian and moralist. His best-known work is *Parallel Lives*, precisely the one that Agirre mentions reading. The parallel lives that the *lehendakari* refers to in his diary are those of Themistocles and Camillus,

JANUARY 1941
THURSDAY 9. ST. MARCELLIN. 9-356

We spent the morning in our rooms. At twelve we went out for a walk. We went to the Panamanian Consulate, where they informed us that the minister will arrive in Berlin today.

They offered the consul a fish casserole with potato puree, and in anticipation of the repast consumed at the boarding house around three in the afternoon, we extended our walk. The fish was good, but the consul remains incorrigible in his bohemian disorder, and I maintained the opinion that it is better to eat sitting down in a restaurant than to get a casserole in the street and take it home. At four we went out to the UFA movie theater, where the young lady from yesterday was waiting for us at the door. With this kind and grateful lady we saw the magnificent film *Bismarck*.[25] Home at 7:15. I'm still reading Plutarch.

JANUARY 1941
FRIDAY 10. ST. ADALARD. 10-355

In the morning, we took a delightful walk through the port of Hamburg, which is truly grand, the third or fourth largest in the world. It's intensely cold. The Elbe is frozen, and the entire landscape is picturesquely white due to the frost and icy snow that fell overnight. We had a very good lunch at the Hotel Esplanade. In the afternoon, we attended a film showing and had dinner at the restaurant at the central station. It was a fish day, obligatory two days a week. The fish was good.

In the morning, the minister called from Berlin and gave us an appointment for Sunday, the 12th, when we were thinking of leaving for the capital.

Today I tried a classic Hamburg drink, suited to get rid of the worst possible cold.

Timoleon and Aemilius Paulus, Aristides and Cato the Censor, and Philopoemen and Flaminius.

25 Otto von Bismarck (1815–1898) was a Prussian politician and diplomat who served as chancellor of Germany between 1862 and 1890. He is considered the architect of German unification. The film to which Agirre refers is *Bismarck* (1940), directed by Wolgang Liebeneiner, starring Paul Hartmann, produced by Tobis Filmkunst, and distributed by UFA.

JANUARY 1941
SATURDAY 11. ST. HYGINUS. 11-354

In the morning, we went out late. We had lunch at the Alali restaurant, a club with decorations related to hunting. The food is very good. It's a distinguished place in Hamburg.

In the afternoon, we went to the movies. We saw a historical film about the musician Augustin of Vienna, who in his time filled the streets with music, conserved until today in popular songs.[26] Before dinner we went to the Alster Pavilion, where we spent a while listing to a quite refined orchestra. In the evening, we had dinner at a downtown hotel that was packed with people, as were two others where there was no room for us. We went to bed immediately afterward in order to rest, since we were to leave very early the next day, headed for Berlin.

JANUARY 1941
SUNDAY 12. *HOLY FAMILY.* 12-353

We arrived in Berlin after a long trip, at around one in the afternoon. The landscape is sad and arid. I remembered the episodes of Bismarck's childhood and youth; he spent his life in these locales. The train indicated by its carriage rates that we are at war. The minister, Dr. Villalaz, received us at a quarter to three. Attentive and very kind, he took an interest in my return and will intervene if there are difficulties, given the circumstances. At six we visited Dr. Zérrega, the Venezuelan minister, who listened very deferentially to the commissions we were bringing for him. At the Panamanian legation in the evening, we had the pleasure of greeting Dr. Despradel, the Dominican minister. Tomorrow we're planning to visit Dr. Olivera, the Argentine ambassador. For lunch we ate the single course with the state contribution of 1.20 marks, at an Italian restaurant.[27] Scanty and expensive.

---

[26] The mentioned film may be *Der liebe Augustin* (Dear Augustin) (1940) by the director E. W. Emo, produced by Wien-Film GmbH, written by Hans Sassmann, and starring Paul Hörbiger.

[27] Intended, like the Winter Relief (*Winterhilfswerk*; see note 90), to collect funds for social services and save the government the substantial amounts it was dedicating to that purpose, the *Eintopfsonntag* (One-Pot Sunday) on the first Sunday of each month consisted in each family cooking an inexpensive meal costing no more than fifty *pfennigs*. The difference between this amount and what the family normally spent on the day's food was turned over to SA or SS collectors. The *Eintopfsonntag* was also applied in restaurants, as the *lehendakari* indicates. Richard J. Evans, *El III*

JANUARY 1941
MONDAY 13. ST. LEONTIUS. 13-352

In the morning, we made arrangements at the American Express office, and after that we requested an appointment to greet the Argentine ambassador. He will receive us at five in the afternoon. We had lunch at the Panamanian legation as guests of the minister. In the afternoon, we visited the Argentine ambassador at five. An experienced and pleasant person. We spent an hour and a half in his company. He showed us the embassy and his private rooms, which are magnificently furnished, with great taste. We spoke about our mutual friends, both in Europe and in the Americas.

In the evening, we had dinner in the company of the Dominican minister. A pleasant interval, and we agreed to meet the next day at ten a.m. at the Panamanian legation. We went to bed immediately afterward, a little fatigued.

JANUARY 1941
TUESDAY 14. ST. HILARY. 14-351

In the morning, we met the Panamanian and Dominican ministers at the Panamanian legation. Since these two ministers were going to visit the United States legation, we took the opportunity to spend the morning looking up the price of tickets and fares for Panama by way of the United States at the American Express office, and we left a message at the Argentine embassy, as we had indicated to the ambassador.

We met the ministers in the street on their way back from the American embassy, and I was invited by the Dominican minister to have lunch at his house. He made me a present of a good cigar, one like I had not smoked for a long time. I took advantage of the time before returning to Hamburg to write a few lines to my friend Stevenson.[28] We left

---

Reich en el poder (1933–1939) (Barcelona: Península, 2007), 481. In English: *The Third Reich in Power, 1933–1939* (New York: Penguin, 2005).

28   Agirre sent the letter to which he refers to Moscow, thinking that Ralph Cornwallis Stevenson was still serving as a diplomat in that city. Nevertheless, the Foreign Office had withdrawn its former consul in Bilbao from the Soviet capital in July 1939, because he was married to a German woman. Subsequently, in October of the same year, the *lehendakari*'s British friend was dispatched to Rio de Janeiro, the Brazilian capital, where he served under the consul general until 1945, when he obtained that post himself. It would be there in Rio, as we will see later on in

Berlin at 3:30 and arrived in Hamburg at eight. We had dinner at the Hotel Esplanade and retired for the evening. The consul is leaving for Antwerp tomorrow.

JANUARY 1941
WEDNESDAY 15. ST. MAURUS. 15-350

Today we got up at six. The consul left for Antwerp. He will return next week. His arrival will be welcomed by my friends. I am left alone in Hamburg. It's intensely cold. It's snowing, not as much as in Berlin recently. I had lunch at the Hotel Splanade,[29] watching it snow and pondering a thousand things of today and tomorrow. After lunch, I went for a walk. I went into a church. I wasn't sure whether it was Catholic. I spent a good while praying. I left when I heard a noise like a door closing. I was alone in the church. I forgot my gloves. I went back to look for them. I found them, and the sacristan told me that it was a Protestant church. The image of the chalice and the host had made me think that I was in an orthodox place. In the end, God will have received my prayer.

I had dinner at the Splanade. Too many people and a long wait. I retired at ten and read Plutarch. During the afternoon, I read Rousseau.[30]

JANUARY 1941
THURSDAY 16. ST. MARCELLUS. 16-349

In the morning, I read Rousseau until noon, applying it to my country. I remembered Peñaflorida, Altuna, etc.[31] How little that period, which

---

this diary, that the old acquaintances from Bilbao would unexpectedly meet again. After his mission in the Brazilian capital, Stevenson continued his diplomatic career, serving in various locations until his 1955 retirement. He died in 1967. Juan Carlos Jiménez de Aberasturi, *De la derrota a la esperanza: Políticas vascas durante la II Guerra Mundial (1937–1947)* (Oñati: IVAP-HAEE, 1999), 372.

29   The *lehendakari* wrote down names as he heard them, and he frequently got the spelling wrong. In this case, the correct form is Esplanade.

30   Jean-Jacques Rousseau (1712–1778) was a Swiss writer, composer, and philosopher. He was one of the leading philosophers of the Enlightenment, and his work has powerfully influenced political thought and ideas up to the present.

31   Francisco Xavier Munibe Idiaquez, count of Peñaflorida (1729–1785), and Ignacio Manuel de Altuna (1722–1762) were two of the most distinguished representatives of the Basque Enlightenment.

is so interesting, has been studied! Something has been done thanks to Urkixo.[32]

I had lunch at the Splanade. It's still cold. In the afternoon I took a long walk of around two hours through the streets of Hamburg. I wanted to find a Catholic church, and although it sounds ridiculous, I couldn't find it. I will ask some people who can give me good directions. At 4:30, I went into a movie theater, where I saw an entertaining film. I had dinner at the Splanade. Today there were fewer people. The food is good, but the cost of living is very high. A trio plays music. Today they went in for tangos. May God forgive them. I went home at nine. I read the lives of Timoleon and Aemilius Paulus in Plutarch. Things are repeating themselves. It's still cold. The lakes and rivers are frozen. On the former, they've planted pine trees.[33] It doesn't look bad.

JANUARY 1941
FRIDAY 17. ST. ANTHONY. 17-348

I'm still reading Rousseau before rereading L'Europe tragique [Tragic Europe] by Gonzague de Reynold, since the quotations are sometimes a bit abbreviated, and the commentary exaggerated.[34] Rousseau says many excellent things, even if his principles are false. Not much that can disturb us Christians today. I suppose that the consul is in Antwerp. I'm following him in my thoughts. I went out into the icy cold. I think that it's more than fifteen below [under 5º F]. I had lunch at the same place as always. I took a long walk along the shores of the two lakes.[35] Finally, I found the cathedral. It was hermetically sealed. Like in our country!

Even my mustache froze. I again resorted to the movies in order to fill the time before dinner. The language problem makes it difficult for me

---

32 Julio Urquijo Ybarra (1871–1950) was an antiquarian and a scholar of Basque studies who founded the *Revista internacional de estudios vascos* (International review of Basque studies).
33 Probably a military measure intended to disorient British pilots on bombing runs against German targets.
34 Gonzague de Reynold (1880–1970) was a Swiss Catholic professor and writer. The book the *lehendakari* mentions is *L'Europe tragique, la révolution moderne, la fin d'un monde* (Paris: Éditions Spes, 1934).
35 The two lakes found in the center of Hamburg, really dammed sections of the Alster River before it flows into the Elbe, are the Binnenalster, or Inner Alster, and the Aussenalster, or Outer Alster.

to get to know the artistic and cultural establishments. I want to try tomorrow. I had dinner at the Splanade. They also went in for tangos today. "Since she left, I live in sadness…" are the lyrics of one of them. In the end, it's somewhat appropriate. Home at nine. I read the lives of Marcellus and Pelopidas.

JANUARY 1941
SATURDAY 18. FEAST OF CHAIR OF ST. PETER. 18-347

In the morning, I didn't leave the house. I read Rousseau's chapter on civil religion. How much prejudice, and how old-fashioned his considerations turn out to be! A child of his time, in the end. I started to read the famous letter to D'Alembert.[36]

I had lunch at L'Esplanade. They always ask for the ration stamps for fats (twenty grams per meal). Afterward, I took a long walk along the shore of the lakes, and I came back walking on the frozen lake. It's something to remember, like anything else. I passed the time however I could until seven, when I had dinner at the same hotel. The orchestra has finally given the tangos a rest. Home at nine. I read Cato the Censor in Plutarch. It's started to snow again, and the cold is still intense, even more so in Hamburg because of its maritime climate. I remember other similar climates in which life would certainly be bad with cold this intense.

JANUARY 1941
SUNDAY 19. ST. CANUTE. 19-346

Finally, the landlady of the boarding house told me where there is a small Catholic chapel. When she saw my rosary on the table, she confessed to me that she was also Catholic. It was a bit far—in view of the snowstorm that was falling—to the small church. Everything was seriousness and calm. Much more respectful—liturgy and worshippers—than in the Latin countries. I was at the church almost two hours. When I left, the snowstorm made the trip through the streets unpleasant. I ate lunch at the usual place. I spent a long time reading the newspaper (Il popolo d'Italia [The people of Italy]), and after that I went to the Alster pavilion, where I spent the rest of the afternoon nursing a large beer until it was

---

36 Jean le Rond d'Alembert (1717–1783) was a French philosopher, physicist, mathematician, and encyclopedist.

time for dinner (7:15).³⁷ Home at nine. When I left the hotel for the boarding house, the edges of the sidewalks were no longer recognizable, entirely smoothed out by the large amount of snow that had fallen. I was happy to reach my room. I'm still reading Plutarch. Today it was Philopoemen's turn.

JANUARY 1941
MONDAY 20. STS. FAB. AND SEB. 20-345

Today was a day devoted to meditating on a thousand projects for the future, the product of the ideas turned over during all these days of solitude and forced repose. Tomorrow I hope to have news of the consul, if he doesn't turn up suddenly, which is also possible. I had lunch at the usual place and in the usual way. I read Il lavoro fascista [Fascist labor] from cover to cover to kill time.³⁸ I then arrived at the church from yesterday at the exact moment when they were closing the doors. The person who was closing them, after discovering that I was Latin American, launched into a discourse on meridians, degrees, and longitudes, which since it didn't interest me and I barely understood it, I opted to cut off, courteously doffing my hat. The subject didn't seem very fitting to me. After that, killing time by wandering the streets and looking in store windows. I arrived at the Alster pavilion at six in order not to be out walking at night. I heard several flugelhorn solos that reminded me of my schooldays.³⁹ Dinner at seven and home at 8:30, to keep on making plans until sleep calls.

JANUARY 1941
TUESDAY 21. ST. AGNES. 21-344

A lot of snow fell overnight, which increased the transit difficulties from the previous days. In addition, it started to rain. The streets are a skating rink, they're so slippery. In the morning, I finished Rousseau's letter to

---

37 *Il popolo d'Italia* was a daily newspaper founded by Benito Mussolini in 1914—the first issue came out on November 15—to serve as a mouthpiece for the faction of the Socialist Party that supported Italy's intervention in World War I. In 1922, it became the organ of the National Fascist Party, publishing without interruption until its disappearance on July 26, 1943.

38 *Il lavoro fascista* was the organ of the National Confederation of Fascist Labor Unions. It was published in Rome between December 30, 1928, and July 25, 1943.

39 Agirre was a student at the Jesuit school in Urduña (Orduña), where he played the flugelhorn in the school band.

D'Alembert. Rousseau's morality is rigid, in contrast to his constant doctrinal evolution. Despite everything, there's a great deal that's useful, sane, and intelligent in what he says. I had lunch at the Hotel Esplanade, as always. Today a Spanish omelet. It wanted to be that, anyway. Eating it, I paid homage to the "motherland." I remembered what Manuel de Egileor[40] would say. Afterward, killing time, until at four I went to a movie theater until seven. They were ringing the bell for dinner. I saw a very entertaining comic film. Too bad that ignorance of the language made me lose half of it. Home at nine to read the interesting life of Quintus Flaminius. I learn something every day, even if nihil novum sub sole [there is nothing new under the sun]. The consul has not arrived. We'll hope for tomorrow.

JANUARY 1941
WEDNESDAY 22. ST. VINCENT. 22-343

The consul has arrived. He has brought me very good and interesting news from friends. Some of it indicates a certain emotional volatility, but in general, my friends are maintaining their health and their good common sense. I've spent a happy day. I read Consul Araujo's letter. How grateful I am to him for it! It touched me deeply. We ate lunch at the Esplanade, a little late, since the consul was tired from his overnight trip and rested during the morning. With the rain, the streets are impassable and dirty. I took refuge in a movie theater, since the consul was busy during the afternoon. The movies are a distraction and a pastime in the truest sense for me. At 7:15, I was already at the table in the hotel. The consul appeared a little later. We drank a bottle of Rhine wine to celebrate his fortunate return. I give thanks to God, who has promised to help men of good will. Home and to bed at nine.

JANUARY 1941
THURSDAY 23. ST. RAYMOND. 23-342

The streets yesterday were a series of puddles of water and snow. Because of that, or for some other, similar reason, I've caught a bad cold. I got up, or tried to get up, having entirely lost my voice and with severe bronchial congestion. At the same time, cigarettes help all this disturbance. I

---

40   Manu Egileor Orueta (1884–1970) was a prominent Basque nationalist activist. In June 1940, shortly before the complete occupation of France by Germany, he succeeded in embarking on a Breton fishing boat that took him to Ireland.

stayed in bed until noon, drank hot liquids, and began to feel better. In the afternoon, I stayed home. I wrote to Xabier, and at 7:15 I went to the Esplanade for dinner.[41] I returned home at 8:30 and lay down after another hot drink. Well wrapped up in the covers, I succeeded in sweating a good amount, and I slept.

I've continued discussing with the consul the news that he brought me. The minister sent word from Berlin asking us to go there Saturday. We'll see whether the travel arrangements are moving forward and whether the visas are being granted. We replied agreeing to make the trip to Berlin.

JANUARY 1941
FRIDAY 24. ST. TIMOTHY. 24-341

I got up fairly well recovered from my cold. I sweated well during the night. The minister sent word asking us to delay our trip until Monday. It's possible that we'll have to travel to Greece in order to sort out the matter of the Antwerp steamers. They'll decide in Berlin on Monday. We ate lunch at the Esplanade. After lunch, I retired to my room again, since I still have a cold. I worked all afternoon. I had dinner alone in the same place. The consul used the time to make various visits to his friends. I retired immediately after dinner. I went to bed early in order to be able to definitively get rid of my cold. It's started to snow again. The streets are excessively covered with snow. Various cars are unable to move because of the snow and the ice that forms. To sleep.

JANUARY 1941
SATURDAY 25. CONV. OF ST. PAUL. 25-340

I got up relatively late due to my cold, which has not quite disappeared. We went out at noon and had lunch at Alali, a very good restaurant in Hamburg. Afterward, we made various purchases, including a magnificent garment bag that could be bought without ration stamps. The same was not true of the dressing gown, thanks to there being someone who kindly gave us their stamps. We went to the barber shop. A simple haircut and a very simple price, 1.70 marks. We arrived home. To the movies at seven,

---

41 Francisco Javier Landaburu Fernández de Betoño (1907–1963) was a Basque nationalist parliamentary representative for Araba (Álava). After fleeing into exile from Vitoria-Gasteiz in 1937, he was a close collaborator of the *lehendakari*, as well as secretary of the LIAB. During World War II, he remained in Paris.

and at 9:30 we wanted to have dinner at a typical Hamburg restaurant from the seventeenth century, with period tapestries and paintings. We got there late (they don't serve after nine) and had a cold meal. Very interesting. We've agreed to go back tomorrow if, as we believe, we will be able to celebrate our farewell to Hamburg. To sleep at eleven.

JANUARY 1941
SUNDAY 26. ST. POLYCARP. 26-339

Informed now by personal experience of the mass times at the church in Saint Michael's Street, I went relatively early this morning. Quite a few worshippers. I received communion. A long mass, well sung. The sermon in German, around half an hour. I spent almost two hours in the church with great satisfaction, since I was feeling a need for it amid so wearisome and desperate a life.

We had lunch at the classic restaurant from last night. Very good and relatively economical. Our attention was attracted by a colossal stuffed snake, more than three meters long and more than thirty centimeters in diameter. In the afternoon, the consul was busy. I went to the movies—a great resource—until 7:15. Dinner at the Esplanade and home at nine. Tomorrow we leave for Berlin. We've sent our luggage to the station in order to be less weighed down.

JANUARY 1941
MONDAY 27. ST. JOHN CHRYSOSTOM. 27-338

We left Hamburg for Berlin at 8:30. We got up at seven, and our luggage was already at the station since the previous evening. A tedious journey with more than two hours delay, apparently because of the snow. A precious landscape, since the snow gave a luster to the aridity of the route, with its little pine trees all white. We arrived in Berlin at three in the afternoon instead of at 12:40. We arrived at the hotel by taxi. Centrally located and comfortable. We visited the minister. He received us with great friendliness, although he sees many difficulties for the trip. Afterward, we visited the Dominican minister. Kind as always, he agreed to make certain arrangements and invited us to visit him whenever we want. We arrived at the Panamanian legation, where the minister had invited us to dinner. He took us to the Restaurant Kranzler, where they fed us magnificently, and the minister treated us to a royal dinner. I didn't think that German oysters could be that good. An excellent duck. Good wine. Amid so many worries, it's not a bad thing to have an "oasis."

JANUARY 1941
TUESDAY 28. ST. JULIAN. 28-337

In the morning, I stayed in my room at the Hotel Victoria. I took advantage of the opportunity to write some letters while the consul went to the legation to take care of some matters with the minister. He came back around twelve and told me that the minister wants to go to Hamburg with us the next day, using the trip to apply for the Greek visa and the police exit permit there, since we're registered in Hamburg. It's the business of the Panamanian steamers that are in the port of Antwerp and that the Germans want to buy. They want me to give my advice as a lawyer. We ate lunch at a modest restaurant and asked Dr. Zérrega for a time to visit him. He gave us an appointment for seven. We retired to the hotel, and at seven we visited the Venezuelan minister, with whom we had an interesting and extremely cordial conversation. We talked about our mutual friend Dr. Araujo, who has received instructions to return to Venezuela. We had dinner and retired to the hotel at 10:30.

JANUARY 1941
WEDNESDAY 29. ST. FRANCIS DE SALES. 29-336

We got up at six. We went to meet the minister and were already on the train at 7:15. The cold is extremely intense, seventeen below [1º F]. We had a reasonably normal trip to Hamburg. At the end of the trip, the cold was intense inside the car. In Hamburg, they're at twenty below [-4º F]. We headed to the Greek consulate. The consul was not there, having been transferred. The vice consul cannot issue visas. We have to do it in Berlin. A trip in vain. We had a very good lunch at the Schuman Restaurant. If you have marks, this is easy to do. The reverential power of money, as poor Maeztu would say, knows no borders.[42] The minister

---

42   Ramiro de Maeztu (1875–1936) was a native of Vitoria-Gasteiz and an intellectual belonging to the Generation of 98. From initial leftist or liberal positions he shifted to the extreme right, becoming an activist in the Spanish Renovation (*Renovación Española*) movement during the Second Republic. He was one of the chief spokesmen for the idea of Hispanicity (*hispanidad*). He was killed in Aravaca on October 29, 1936, in one of the extrajudicial executions that took place in Madrid

ate lunch at the same restaurant with guests from Hamburg. We agreed to meet at the station to take the 7:20 p.m. train. We met at the station buffet. The train left around an hour late. We had dinner in the dining car. A tedious trip with an hour-and-a-half delay. We arrived at 1:15 in the morning. With the intense cold, we were glad to get to bed.

JANUARY 1941
THURSDAY 30. ST. ALDEGONDE. 30-335

As soon as we left the hotel, we headed for the Greek legation in order to obtain our visas. They were very kind about issuing one for the consul, who has a diplomatic passport. We're waiting for tomorrow to see what they'll do with me. We got a good impression. The matter of visas is very difficult with the war, which logically gets in the way of normal relations, especially with foreigners.

We had lunch at the Hotel Eden, where I saw an old friend.[43] We went as far as the Panamanian legation, where the minister gave us a note for the Greek legation, where they had asked us for it in order to facilitate the issuance of my visa.

In the afternoon, we entered a tea room at the same time that Hitler began his speech, which was listened to in silence and which interrupted the service to such an extent that having been there a good hour and a half, we left at the end of the speech without having had anything to eat or drink. The minister was waiting for us, and we had dinner with him. Home at ten.

JANUARY 1941
FRIDAY 31. ST. VERON. 31-334

This morning we visited the Greek consul to find out his decision with respect to my visa. He very courteously read us the text of the telegram that he was sending to Athens, since this is a requirement of the Greek

---

during the first months of the Civil War.

43 In *De Guernica a Nueva York pasando por Berlín* the *lehendakari* says about this encounter with an acquaintance in the German capital, among other things, "We left our interview with the Greek consul in such a good mood that we decided to have lunch at the Hotel Eden. An imprudence that cost me a nasty shock. From right at the door of the hotel dining room, I made out the silhouette of Mr. Espinosa de los Monteros, who was a monarchical representative in the same parliament I served in and who is now in Franco's service." Aguirre, *De Guernica*, 184.

government, assuring us that there would be a favorable response in a few days. We conversed for a good while about the affairs of the day. On the bus, I saw my old friend again. It seems that we have to meet everywhere. We had a very good lunch at the Hotel Esplanade. It's certainly a pleasant hotel. It has the same name as the one in Hamburg. The one in Berlin is superior. In the afternoon, we went to a movie screening. A very well-conceived German military propaganda film. We then had dinner at a popular beer garden. It was a fish day. A lot of people both at the movies and at the restaurant. Money gets spent, or better, money gets wasted. It's what happens. To the hotel at 9:30. I read the life of Marius. Everyone has his adventures.

NOTES

FEBRUARY 1941
SATURDAY 1. ST. IGNATIUS. 32-333

The consul went to the legation in the morning, as usual. I waited until lunchtime. We ate at a popular restaurant, 1.25 prix-fixe. They fed us well. We called the Dominican minister, who was just about to call me. We spent the afternoon with him very pleasantly. He invited us to a very good cognac. He wanted to invite us to dinner. We had a prior commitment with the Panamanian minister. We went to do that and had dinner at a beer garden. At 9:30 we went home. In general, people go to bed very early, but at restaurants, movie theaters, and theatrical performances a war psychology is evident, with a great deal of animation and heavy spending. The cold has decreased, since there isn't the biting wind of recent days. We're still at eight below [18º F], but in comparison to the previous temperatures, it seems normal to us. We're waiting for news about our visas on Monday. How much these formalities cost in wartime!

FEBRUARY 1941
SUNDAY 2. PRESENTATION OF THE LORD. 33-332

After we got up, we went to the church to hear mass. The church was packed. The worshippers with exemplary composure. The people sing during the whole mass. They do it well, and everyone sings, even the ones who are next to the doors. That type exists around the world, but in other places they talk instead of singing. And since they talk, they are often in the habit of saying that they are the best. On a different subject. We had lunch with a married German couple who are friends of the consul. Very friendly people, and a pleasant conversation. After dinner, we took a long walk along Unter den Linden. The Führer's Chancellery, ministries, imperial palaces. There's no taste, and above all, there's an agglomeration of buildings that takes away from the principal ones. Old houses next to grand monuments. Buildings of different and ugly styles next to, for example, the university. We visited the war museum. Very interesting. Afterward, we went to the Winter Garden, where we saw a variety show while having dinner, especially a magnificent troupe of Lilliputians. Home at nine to read and sleep.

FEBRUARY 1941
MONDAY 3. ST. BLASE. 34-331

This morning we had an interesting conversation with the Dominican minister, who was just coming from a meeting with the American chargé. He's always pleasant; we had an aperitif with him. Afterward, we had lunch at a restaurant on the outskirts of Berlin that I was not familiar with. Cheap and good. We went for a walk, and then at four we went to the screening of the film *War in the West*, a collection of episodes from the Polish campaign and especially from Holland, Norway, Belgium, and France.[44] Two [*Crossed out:* One] military bands played and did so very well—trumpets, drums, etc. We were invited by the married couple who are friends of the consul, and they then took us to have tea at a place downtown. We had dinner at eight, and home at 9:30, where I wrote to Insaust, and then to sleep.[45]

---

44 Svend Noldan's 1941 documentary *Sieg im Westen* (Victory in the West).
45 Manuel Ynchausti. On Ynchausti, see note 4. The letter mentioned by the *lehendakari* turned out to be key for his aspirations to leave Europe and travel to America, since it was his first direct contact with the New York delegation, the only one that could give him effective help under the circumstances. It also served to give some reassurance to the Basque leadership in exile. Manu de la Sota communicated the news to London, saying, among other things, "We've had news from father, sixteen handwritten sheets containing enormously interesting material. It's a magnificent document that made an enormous impression on me ... He gives instructions for all of us that I will copy carefully to send to you. Meanwhile, here is a paragraph that I don't want to delay, since it will be useful for Irujo to know it ... "I wrote in a letter, about the arrival of which I'm also not sure—I expect that it will not have arrived—that until the administrative council is safe, Irujo and Ramón Aldasoro should direct the affairs of our family and of that council, consulting with the New York delegation when necessary. I repeat this desire, since

FEBRUARY 1941
TUESDAY 4. ST. ANDREW CORSINI. 35-330

I gave a commission to the Dominican minister, who had asked me to do so.[46] Afterward, we took a long walk until it was time to eat. We had lunch at the Restaurant Kareinski, where they fed us very scantily. We retired to the hotel by chance—since on other days we take a walk or visit friends—and just at that moment the minister, Dr. Despradel, called to invite me to accompany him to pay a business call on the American chargé d'affaires, who would have some information regarding travel. We did this and then agreed to be his guests for dinner at the Kranzler Restaurant. I went to the Panamanian legation, where we finished up various matters with the minister, since he is leaving tomorrow for two weeks in Switzerland. We are still waiting for the visa. We had a very good dinner at the Kranzler, and home and to sleep at 10:30. First I read Cicero's *Republic*.[47] Tomorrow the *Laws*.

FEBRUARY 1941
WEDNESDAY 5. ST. AGATHA. 36-329

Today is Saint Agatha's feast day. A day of memories.[48] I accompanied the consul to the station, since he is going to Hamburg for two days.

---

it seems that my poor companions in Marseilles are finding it difficult to leave. I also repeat my fundamental idea: Union, union, and union. In addition, sacrifice.'" Letter from Manu de la Sota to Ángel Gondra, March 18, 1941. GE-250-3. For more information on Agirre's letter to Ynchausti, see "Extracto de una carta de José Antonio Aguirre a Manuel Ynchausti, GE-250-3," published in Iñaki Goiogana, Xabier Irujo, and Josu Legarreta, *Un nuevo 31: Ideología y estrategia del Gobierno de Euzkadi durante la Segunda Guerra Mundial a través de la correspondencia de José Antonio Agirre y Manuel Irujo* (Bilbao: Sabino Arana, 2007), 320–22; and the article by Manuel de la Sota, "La carta que José Antonio de Aguirre escribió desde Berlín," *Euzkadi* (Santiago de Chile), no. 2 (July 1943), 1 and 4. This article corresponds to document no. 29 transcribed in this book.

46 The commission was probably the letter mentioned in the preceding note, which reached Ynchausti by way of the Dominican diplomatic pouch from Berlin to Washington, where the Dominican ambassador was Andrés Pastoriza, who finally delivered the missive to the *lehendakari*'s Filipino friend.

47 Marcus Tullius Cicero (106 BC–43 BC) was a Roman politician, philosopher, writer, and orator. He is considered one of the greatest Latin rhetoricians and prose stylists. In politics, he was distinguished for his stalwart defense of Rome's traditional republican system against Caesar's dictatorship.

48 Possibly a reference to the *lehendakari*'s experiences on February 5, 1939. On that day, José Antonio Agirre, together with the president of the Generalitat (Catalan

I returned home, where I wrote to Dr. Araujo and then read a bit. Dr. Despradel had invited me, and I arrived at his house at twelve-thirty. Kind as always, he opened a good Pomard wine in my honor. He then offered me a good cigar. It's been a long time since I've been able to enjoy them other than as gifts. But God comes to my aid. He had me accompany him for a walk, on which we were jointed by the Panamanian minister, who is leaving for Switzerland tonight. We conversed about current affairs, and he invited me to dinner again. He values and esteems me a great deal. He's an excellent friend. At ten-thirty, I retired to the hotel, which is fortunately close by. The clear night made a "visit" possible, which is unpleasant in the middle of the street. They force you to go to the shelter, and without knowing the language, the time drags. I arrived without incident.

FEBRUARY 1941
THURSDAY 6. ST. AMAND. 37-328

In the morning, I stayed home until noon. I read Cicero. Problems repeat themselves. Solutions are similar. It had been a while since I was able to get back to these readings from antiquity that have always attracted me so much. There's a reason that they're called classics. I ate lunch alone at a modest restaurant (1.75 marks) near the hotel. I went back to the hotel to kill time in my solitude, since having been invited by the Dominican minister to chat with him at his house, I had to wait until four, because he was at a diplomatic luncheon. I arrived at his gate at exactly the same moment as his car pulled up. We spent a pleasant afternoon remembering many things. At his invitation, I kept him company for dinner. He lives alone. He has his family in Switzerland. I retired at around eleven with a book titled *La Alemania de Hitler* [Hitler's Germany], containing all the achievements of National Socialism.[49] It's well-documented and interesting; I started to read it. It confirmed the ideas I've always had.

---

government), Lluís Companys, Manuel Irujo, and other Basque and Catalan leaders, crossed the Spanish-French border at the Lli Pass, fleeing Franco's troops and going definitively into exile.

49   The book to which the *lehendakari* refers is Cesare Santoro, *La Alemania de Hitler vista por un extranjero* (Berlin: Internationaler Verlag, 1939).

FEBRUARY 1941
FRIDAY 7. ST. ROMUALD. 38-327

I stayed home reading *La Alemania de Hitler*, which I started yesterday. It's a very well-done propaganda book by Cesare Santoro. It's translated into Spanish. I'm pleased to say that my information was exact concerning all aspects of such a transcendental and profound revolution. The book covers as far as August 1939, that is, until the start of the war. It's the most complete account I've read so far. At one, I went to the 1.75-mark restaurant, and since it's a fish day, they served me one that was not very Christian. Around two I left to meet the Dominican minister on the main street, the Kurfürnstendam; he's in the habit of taking a walk every day after lunch. Once we had met, we went to the Dominican legation, where we continued our conversations, and having been invited to dinner there, I stayed until 10:30, when I retired. I'm still reading Cicero and the Hitler book. A contradictory doctrine at a distance of almost two thousand years. Ah, the wisdom of antiquity!

FEBRUARY 1941
SATURDAY 8. ST. JOHN OF MATHA. 39-326

After I had gone to bed, the consul arrived from Hamburg; he did so at one in the morning, since the train had arrived late. We're still waiting for the visas. The Greek consul has very coldly informed us that he will advise us as soon as it arrives. He predicts a ninety-percent chance of a favorable result. We took a little walk before eating lunch at a Hungarian restaurant, where the employees spoke Hungarian and yet there were neither any Hungarian dishes nor any wine from that country. Nothing strange in these times of war. After lunch, we went in search of Minister Despradel, who is friendly to our company. We found him taking his ordinary walk. We then went to his house, where he invited us to a cup of good real coffee, which is one of the things that it's impossible to find. We had a very nice afternoon, and since the consul had been invited by a Chilean colleague, I was again invited by Mr. Despradel to dine at the restaurant. But the house cook, who had prepared a classic Dominican dish, begged the minister that we stay at home. That's what we did. Childhood episodes that make us temporarily forget other profound and transcendental things.

FEBRUARY 1941
SUNDAY 9. ST. APOLLONIA. 40-325

In the morning, I went to the church. A lot of people, as on the previous days. I sat in the first pews. I took a seat I shouldn't have, since they're designated for the people whose names are on the pews. I had to move. Very refined music and composed behavior. When I left, it was raining quite a bit. The crust of snow combines with the water to make a dirty and unpleasant stain. Before lunch, we took a walk, despite the bad weather. We had lunch at the Kranzler Restaurant. A single course. Potato soup with a sausage. We had a second serving, since the waiter told us that it was permitted. After lunch, a walk with our good friend the Dominican minister. He invited us to have coffee at his house and later to have dinner at the Tousculum Restaurant.[50] A first-class restaurant in the Parisian style. A magnificent dinner, fitting for a diplomat. We retired at eleven after spending a good while there. How much time is lost waiting for visas! I read the book about Hitler's Germany.

FEBRUARY 1941
MONDAY 10. ST. SCHOLASTICA. 41-324

[*In the upper margin*: Today is Juan Mª's saint's day.[51] I remember.]

In the morning we went for a walk and continued living like tourists. Tomorrow we hope to visit the Greek consulate to find out whether there is news. We're waiting for various answers, to letters sent to America among others. How long this wait is!

Dr. Villalaz and Dr. Zérrega are in Switzerland. The latter will arrive on Wednesday or Thursday. We'll see whether things move faster once he arrives. God for His part will do what is best. We ate lunch at the 1.75-mark restaurant. It's necessary to adapt to all weathers. Yesterday at the Tousculum among the bourgeoisie and the diplomats who spend like nowhere else. Today among modest employees and soldiers. Yesterday's dinner cost the minister 150 marks, including 20 for the pianist who sits right at the door and plays the diplomats' national anthems as they

---

50 The restaurant's name was Tusculum, and it was located at Kurfürstendamm 68. Around the corner was the high-class brothel Salón Kitty, full of hidden microphones and with SS secret agents in the basement.

51 Juan Mari, the third child of the Agirre-Lekube family, was born on February 10, 1908. The second, Ignacio, had died when he was only eight years old.

come in. More than three thousand French francs in total. Today we paid four and a half marks total. And we ate well. Afterward a walk and a visit to Dr. Despradel's house. We had a modest dinner and arrived home at 10:30. I read Martí, the great Cuban patriot.[52]

FEBRUARY 1941
TUESDAY 11. ST. ADOLPHUS. 42-323

This morning I went to the Greek consulate. The consul, who was very kind, told me that he is expecting an answer within the next two days or so, that I should telephone him on Thursday, and that if there's no news, he will telephone Athens. In sum, that it's necessary to wait again. We had an interesting conversation about the moment of pressure that seems to be approaching. I ate lunch alone at the 1.75-mark restaurant. The consul had an invitation from his Chilean colleague. I met Dr. Despradel on my usual walk. We went to his house. We listened to the radio. Pressures on the Balkans, Spain, etc. My consul arrived. We had a cup of coffee. This life of waiting atrophies activities of all kinds. At six, the Dominican minister's family arrived from Switzerland. His wife and a ten-year-old daughter. They were very friendly and offered to invite us to a meal at their house. We retired. We had a mediocre dinner at a restaurant serving local food. Home at 10:30. It was a night with a dangerous moon.[53]

FEBRUARY 1941
WEDNESDAY 12. ST. EULALIA. 43-322

It's twenty-one years today since *aita* died.[54] I remembered him in my prayers.

We left the house late. The counsel wanted us to visit a Chinese restaurant, out of curiosity. We found a large group of young Chinese students or officials (it's difficult to tell their age). They ate the rice with their classic chopsticks. The food was very bad, bad enough not to go back again.

---

52 José Julián Martí Pérez (1853–1895) was a politician, journalist, philosopher, and poet, the most internationally prominent of the Cuban independence leaders.
53 Dangerous because of the advantage the moonlight could give to British aviators in their nighttime incursions to bomb targets in Berlin.
54 Teodoro Agirre Barrenetxea-Arando, was born in Bergara in 1872 and died in Getxo in 1920. He was a lawyer by profession.

Portraits of Sum Yan Sen and Chan Kai-sek.[55] We left to look for Dr. Despradel. We took a walk. We went to his house. We had our usual coffee. He's truly kind, the minister. At five we went to the Opera in his car to hear *La Traviata*. A good production. The soprano was magnificent. The baritone not so much. The tenor mediocre. The orchestra was very good, somewhat reduced in size. A large audience. Sold out. I enjoyed hearing the opera very much. Dinner near the opera. Home at ten.

FEBRUARY 1941
THURSDAY 13. ST. POLYEUCTUS. 44-321

In the morning Enrique, the Dominican minister's chauffeur, picked up our passports. He was unable to make the departure arrangements because his car broke down. He'll do it tomorrow. The consul was busy. He was invited to a lunch to celebrate his Chilean colleague's saint's day. I had lunch alone at the 1.75-mark restaurant. Then I went for a walk with Dr. Despradel, who invited me to have coffee and a good Armagnac at his house. The consul arrived at five. The Venezuelan minister had just given notice of his arrival from Switzerland. We left and went for a good walk. We had dinner at the Russian restaurant on the Kurfürstensdan. Orchestra and popular songs. They did a good job. They sang a certain number of popular compositions, including "The Volga Boatmen." These songs reminded me of other songs and other choruses. Exiles who sing of their distant homeland have universal accents that are understood in all languages. We retired when the music and singing stopped. Home at 10:45.

FEBRUARY 1941
FRIDAY 14. ST. VALENTINE. 45-320

Dr. Despradel's chauffeur, who is more his secretary, picked up our passports this morning to obtain our German exit papers. An hour later he brought us our meal "tickets" and our passports duly stamped for our time in Berlin. For the exit permit, it's necessary to fill out an application. We did so and signed the papers after meeting all the requirements. We

---

55   Sun Yat-sen (1866–1925) was a Chinese statesman and politician. He is considered the father of modern China. For his part, Chiang Kai-shek (Jiang Jieshi) (1887–1975) was a soldier and statesman who succeeded Sun Yat-sen as leader of the Chinese Nationalist Party (*Kuomintang*). After being defeated by the Communists in 1949, he took refuge in Taiwan.

ate lunch at the Italian restaurant on the Kurfürstendam. It was good this time, in payback for other times they fed us poorly and expensively. We met Dr. Despradel at the door of the Venezuelan chancellery. He was on his way to a meeting with Dr. Zérrega. We returned to the hotel, where we remained until 5:30. A walk along Unter der Linden, and we had dinner at the Kranzler on that street. The consul wasn't feeling well today because of his intestinal complaint. The obligatory fish dish (Tuesdays and Fridays) suited him. We went home at ten. I read Cicero, the second book of the *Republic*.

FEBRUARY 1941
SATURDAY 15. ST. FAUSTINUS. 46-319

Dr. Despradel's chauffeur-secretary came to the hotel room. He gave me the passport. For the exit permit, which will be signed on Tuesday or Wednesday, from what he says, a simple document is needed from the hotel affirming that I will be there for four weeks. This is the period that has been requested for the exit permit. He told me that everything is in order and that the permit will be signed. May it be so. Afterward, I accompanied the consul to the Yugoslav and Hungarian legations. In the former, the employees don't know how to get up out of their chairs. They put us in a room full of badly-dressed people. They neither attended to their visitors nor seemed to be interested in them. Finally, the consul cut in line, with my encouragement. Difficulties. Finally, the visa. Better in Hungary, polite, quick. I'm still waiting for my Greek visa. We had lunch and met up with Dr. Despradel. He let us know that we'll eat with the Venezuelan minister tomorrow. We then took a long walk. We had dinner at a beer garden, and home at nine p.m. We wrote notes for the Venezuelan minister. I read Cicero.

FEBRUARY 1941
SUNDAY 16. ST. JULIENNE. 47-318

Many people in the church, as on previous feast days. The religious songs are serious and have pleasant melodies. The people sing very well. After fulfilling our religious duties, we went for a walk until we met Dr. Despradel. We then had lunch at the Hotel Poristol as guests of the Venezuelan minister. Very good, and with the ministers' hospitality. We had a pleasant and interesting conversation. The minister was coming from Switzerland and Italy. We exchanged impressions about Alfonso

XIII's abdication in favor of his son Don Juan.[56] We went out for a walk and then went to the Dominican minister's house, where he forced us to stay and have dinner with him. His attentions are extreme. His sympathy for us is great. We listened to various radio stations. That way we are able to learn some things. At ten we retired to the hotel. I read Cicero, his treatise *On the Laws*. Ancient problems applicable to today. The classical principle of natural law against utilitarianism. Reason and law against force. Then to sleep, since we already know enough about that topic.

FEBRUARY 1941
MONDAY 17. ST. THEODORE. 48-317

We left the hotel and went to the Panamanian legation to speak to the minister, who called yesterday from Switzerland without finding us. Afterward, we had a good and economical lunch at the Hungarian restaurant. Later, we visited the Dominican minister, whom we left in order to go back to the Panamanian legation in search of two certificates issued in my favor for the American and Swedish consuls. The Dominican and Venezuelan ministers will visit the American chargé d'affaires tomorrow to talk to him about a visa matter. Tomorrow I plan to visit the American consul to obtain a visa for that country. Then the Swedish one with the same request. I'm expecting the exit visa tomorrow or the next day. We had dinner at the 1.75-mark restaurant. Home at 9:30. To read *On the Laws* and to sleep. Today a dozen Russian aviators arrived at the boarding house.

FEBRUARY 1941
TUESDAY 18. ST. SIMEON. 49-316

At ten-thirty a.m. we were already at the American consulate. In order to obtain a visa, they subjected me to an extremely intense interrogation that lasted until one in the afternoon, between questions, duly filled-out forms, fingerprints, and other ceremonies. I say 'ceremonies' because at the end they even asked me to swear that what I was saying was true. That had its humorous side for a Panamanian like myself. Finally, at the end of these operations—they measured my height and even my weight—they granted me the visa. We exhaled when we left. Then—after

---

56 Alfonso XIII renounced his dynastic rights to the Spanish crown in favor of his son Juan de Borbón on January 15, 1941, and died shortly afterward, on February 28.

lunch—we visited the Swedish consulate. They were very kind. With the Finnish visa, they will immediately give me the Swedish one. The police have informed us that the German exit permit can now be picked up. In the afternoon we met with the Venezuelan and Dominican ministers. They had visited the American minister to talk about visas and other matters. After dinner, home at 9:30. I wrote and read. Tomorrow the consul is leaving for Greece. No news at all about my Hellenic visa.

FEBRUARY 1941
WEDNESDAY 19. ST. BONIFACE. 50-315

This morning we were at the Finnish legation. The legation secretary received us politely. He informed us about the ships that leave from Petsamo. Every six weeks for North America. Every week for Rio de Janeiro and Buenos Aires. For the visa, a telegram to Helsignfords.[57] In sum, that two ministers will have to intervene. We informed the Dominican minister accordingly. We got a hair cut. They charged me three marks (thirty-six francs) for a simple cut and shampoo. This is what happens to a poor man who lives like a rich one, or rather appears as if he does. The consul had to leave at six for Greece. We packed his suitcases. I accompanied him to the station. My Greek visa is sleeping. How easy it is to write that! The rest remains inside. I'm alone again. My good Dominican minister obliged me to have dinner with him and his wife, who considers Álvarez a strange creature.[58] Her blessed ignorance and my balancing act did the rest. We listened to the radio. Home at ten. Reading Martí today. How problems repeat themselves, and how they have to keep on repeating themselves![59]

---

57   Helsingfors, the Swedish name for the city of Helsinki.
58   José Andrés Álvarez Lastra, the false identity given to José Antonio Agirre by Consul Guardia Jaén. In *De Guernica*, Agirre wrote, "We combined the names with the aim of having the initials match those of José Antonio de Aguirre y Lecube and also having them be well-known Panamanian surnames. In this way the Panamanian citizen José Andrés Álvarez Lastra entered the world, a doctor of laws and the owner of estates in the province of Chiriquí." Aguirre, *De Guernica*, 117.
59   The *lehendakari*, in this entry as in others later on, notes the parallels that he sees between the processes by which various countries acquired independence and the development of the Basque national question. See, for example, his comments on his reading of a book about Enriquillo (an indigenous rebel leader against Spanish rule on Hispaniola in the early sixteenth century), on Luis Estévez y Romero's *Desde el Zanjón hasta Baire, datos para la historia política de Cuba* (From the Zanjón to Baire: Notes for the political history of Cuba), and on a film about Krüger and the Boer War in the entries corresponding to April 16 and 20 and May 6, 1941.

FEBRUARY 1941
THURSDAY 20. ST. ELEUTHERIUS. 51-314

This morning the Dominican minister's secretary arrived and told me that the German exit permit is not complete without something from the Interior Ministry, since my current permit is to leave Germany and reenter Belgium, and the authorities who issued it also have to issue an exit permit, that is, the German authorities, in Belgium. That it would be a matter of two days. God grant it, and may it be for the best. So the hours and the days pass. Today, for example, I spent alone. The daily visit to my good friend Mr. Despradel was already enough of a bother. He insists, but I don't want to tire him. I had a cheap little meal. Then I walked for about two hours through the streets of Berlin, looking in the store windows. Finally, I went into a movie theater. A film about the Irish revolution against England. It's not a unique case. Here they clap for Ireland, there for others. What is just is to clap for all who suffer, who today are more than those who are fortunate in this world. In sum, things take time. Some of the prison scenes and the prisoners' spirit moved me. How much ...! I ate dinner alone. Home. It's eight, and Cicero is waiting.

FEBRUARY 1941
FRIDAY 21. ST. EUGENE. 52-313

I read a lot during the morning. Today was also scheduled for solitude. Dr. Despradel had a diplomatic lunch. I don't want to bother the others. The weather wasn't good like yesterday. After lunch—now it's the turn of the cheap places—I resorted—as so many times before—to the movies. A very interesting documentary about the life of the indigenous people of the East Indies. Another well-done one about the German navy. Afterward, I returned to the hotel—it was four in the afternoon—and did not leave until seven. Dinner for 1.75, and God grant that it lasts! Back home at eight-thirty. Today it was the turn of *La Alemania de Hitler*. In the social area, a great work has been achieved. In many details, it seems like a copy of what my compatriots wanted and one day will do. Multigenerational family ties, family salary, etc. As of yet, it falls short of what my compatriots had and have prepared. How those who judge Hitler's work from a bourgeois perspective are mistaken! But we will speak abundantly of this if God gives me health and visas, which are almost enough to make one lose one's health, and of course, one's patience.

FEBRUARY 1941
SATURDAY 22. ST. ISABELLE. 53-312

When I got up this morning, the street was again covered with snow. I was sorry to see it, since my shoes are now worn out, and the dampness comes through. That's how I got my previous cold. I can't buy shoes without ration stamps—which we foreigners don't have—and I don't want to bother the ministers, who have to ask permission from the Foreign Ministry or a similar department. I'll walk in my worn-out shoes with holes. It's been many months trotting around, like I've never walked in my life. I ate lunch alone and afterward tried to meet up with Dr. Despradel. I called at his house. He was at his third diplomatic lunch. I went back to the boarding house. At four I went to a movie theater to kill time until it was time for dinner. I tried to go to the church earlier, but I found it closed. Like in our country! After dinner I called the minister. He obliged me to go to his house immediately. Conversation, radio, commentary that lasted until twelve, the latest time I've gone home. After three days alone and without news, there was a lot to talk about. Immediately to sleep.

FEBRUARY 1941
SUNDAY 23. ST. POPE DAMIEN. 54-311

I went to church early in order to be able to take communion. Many of the worshippers did so with me. The mass must have been for some women's association, to judge by the large number of women and handful of men who were in the church. I returned to the boarding house, where I had breakfast and read a bit. At eleven, I went out in search of the Dominican minister, who was awaiting me to take a walk and then have lunch at his house. While we were eating, we heard that the Panamanian minister had returned. We spoke with him by telephone. We arranged to meet at six. After lunch, we took a walk, and at six we arrived at the Panamanian legation. The minister told us his impressions and various anecdotes about inventions in the style of Jules Verne. We were there for a good while. He invited me to visit him at the legation tomorrow at eleven. The Dominican minister dragged me forcibly to his house for dinner. We then had a pleasant conversation. At eleven, I retired to the hotel. Today I want to sleep and am doing so without reading.

FEBRUARY 1941
MONDAY 24. ST. MATTHIAS. 55-310

In the morning, I contacted Dr. Villalaz to tell him that I could not go to his office, since I was waiting for Dr. Despradel's secretary with news of his visit to the police. Neither one actually happened, since the secretary was sick. Dr. Villalaz invited me to his house at seven for dinner. I ate lunch alone. Afterward, I met the Dominican minister on my usual walk. I separated from him, since he had an appointment with the Venezuelan minister. I continued my walk alone through the streets of Berlin. After two hours, I ended up in a movie theater that looked like it belonged to a preschool. A small space and a tiny screen. Then to the hotel. At seven I went to the Panamanian minister's house. We had a very good dinner, just the two of us. He treated me as an honored guest. Afterward, in his office and with a glass of cognac, we chatted until 10:30. Dr. Zérrega wrote an interesting letter to Dr. Araujo on the 22nd.[60] So the Dominican minister informed me. I was in my room at a quarter to eleven. To read a bit and to sleep.

FEBRUARY 1941
TUESDAY 25. ST. WALPURGA. 56-309

This morning the Dominican minister's secretary brought me the ration stamps and the news that the four-week extension has been granted, until March 20. I no longer have to worry about the final deadline of February 28 that was set by my Belgian permit. I still need an answer about the exit permit, which will still take a few more days. God will do the rest. I ate lunch alone at a 1.50-mark restaurant. Certainly very good. After lunch, I met the Dominican and Panamanian ministers. We were then joined by the Guatemalan minister, to whom they introduced me. We walked for about an hour. Afterward, I accompanied Dr. Despradel to the tailor's. A large store. He tried on a dress suit and a tuxedo in the latest style. They measured the size of the crosses and decorations in order to add the necessary attachments. I contemplated these sumptuary operations with my battered shoes, on which I trimmed the ragged edges

---

60 The letter, from the Venezuelan minister to his consul in Antwerp, was probably about how to reunite the Agirre-Zabala family and so enable them to leave Europe together. In the same way, the visit to Alberto Zerega and Rómulo Araujo's letter, mentioned in the entries for January 12 and 22, 1941, have to be understood in connection with the same topic of family reunification.

around the toes with scissors before leaving the house this morning. That's the least of my problems. I had dinner at the Dominican legation. Radio, conversation, and home at 10:30. Tomorrow it's time to receive ashes and remember for a little while what we are. Dust like my shoes.

FEBRUARY 1941
WEDNESDAY 26. *ASH WEDNESDAY*. 57-308

I arrived at the church before eight in the morning in order to receive ashes. I found the doors hermetically sealed. The same thing happened to two women who came for the same purpose. Ash Wednesday, and the church closed! The reduction in worship is taken to this extreme.[61] They then informed me that they will distribute ashes on Sunday. I returned to the boarding house, had breakfast, and read *L'Europe tragique* by Gonzague de Reynold. I'm reading it for the second time, since it's a very profound and interesting study about Europe and the world today. I've finished the Hitler book, as well as the Martí one. I'm still reading Cicero and Plutarch. I will go back to reading Pascal. As Mauriac says, his rigid, extremely severe doctrine is of and for today.[62]

I ate lunch alone at the 1.50-mark restaurant. Then I went for a walk with the Dominican and Panamanian ministers. Dr. Despradel's secretary went to the former's house[63] to ask him for a letter to speed up the issuance of the exit permit. I had dinner at Dr. Despradel's house, and we listened to the radio and conversed. His friendship is generous. My solitude has so much to be grateful for to him! I was home at eleven. I

---

61 The reduction in worship was probably due to the fact that many priests had been called up.
62 Blaise Pascal (1623–1662) was a French mathematician, physicist, and philosopher. For his part, François Mauriac (1885–1970) is considered one of the most important Catholic writers of the twentieth century. In 1952, he was awarded the Nobel Prize in Literature. During the Spanish Civil War, he publicly identified with the Basque people. In addition to signing manifestos, such as the appeal to French generosity to aid the refugees published on February 5, 1937, and the statement known as *Por el Pueblo Vasco* (For the Basque people), he published newspaper articles in which he maintained that the Basques had done nothing other than defend democracy, were not allies of Moscow, and had not taken part in the various massacres committed during the war. Likewise, in January 1939, in another article titled "La victoire des basques" (The victory of the Basques), he affirmed that they had won the battle for public opinion. François Mauriac, "La victoire des basques," *Paris Soir*, reprinted in full in *Euzko Deya* (Paris), no. 142 (January 8, 1939), 1.
63 This must be a mistake; the reference should be to the Panamanian minister.

read a bit, and to sleep. What can Araujo be doing? I don't think about anything else. May God be with everyone.

FEBRUARY 1941
THURSDAY 27. ST. LEANDER. 58-307

In the morning I stayed in my room meditating on many things. My thoughts revolve around the same topic. The people close to me in particular and the people close to me in general. I ate lunch alone at the usual restaurant. Afterward, I went out for a walk. I met the Panamanian minister, and I took a three-quarter-hour walk with him. The Dominican minister had a diplomatic lunch today. Afterward, I continued walking for two hours. My poor shoes! At four-thirty I went to the movies. I got through the time until seven, when I had agreed with my minister to go to his legation in order to go out to dinner. He had kindly invited me. Before we went out, he showed me what he had written for the Foreign Ministry in support of the granting of the requested permit. We had dinner at the beer garden near my boarding house. Certainly a pleasant conversation, which lasted until around eleven. I accompanied the minister to his house and returned to my boarding house very happy with the day. I'm still remembering Araujo. What can this friend be doing, or what can he have done? We're expecting the consul at any moment. To sleep.

FEBRUARY 1941
FRIDAY 28. ST. ROMAIN. 59-306

During the morning I read *L'Europe tragique* by Gonzague de Reynold. Although I don't agree with some of his affirmations, which seem exaggerated to me, the general lines of what he says have a lot of foundation. It's a profound and serious study. His ideas about the French Revolution, the individualist [*illegible*], the nineteenth century, socialism, American power and crisis, the totalitarian regimes as reaction, etc., are extremely interesting. I ate lunch alone at the 1.50-mark restaurant. I met the ministers on my walk along the Kurfürstendam and went to the Dominican legation with that country's minister. They had an invitation to see a war movie today. I left him at twenty to five. Previously, I said hello to Dr. Zérrega, who confirmed to me his letters to Araujo, etc. I thanked him for it very much. Then I went to a movie theater—to pass the time—and had dinner at the 1.75-mark restaurant. After a while,

I arrived home, where I went to bed alone with my thoughts, today on this last day of the expired and renewed permit. May God be with me and with those close to me.

NOTES

[*In the upper margin*: Note received by the Venezuelan minister: Translated into German.]

July 12, Note no. 306

"Please tell the consul in Antwerp Araujo to issue visas to María Aqueche, Margarita, Santiago, Ignacio, Carmen Zabala, and her husband. Gil Bornes. Venezuelan Minister of State."

Letter of August 5 announcing that this official dispatch was sent.[64]

NOTES

NOTES

NOTES

---

64 The dates of July 12 and August 5 mentioned in the note must pertain to 1940 and not, as it might appear, to the years covered by the diary. The *lehendakari* says as much himself in his book *De Guernica*: "Fortunately, my documents had been gradually becoming more complete, and I already had in my power the definitive Panamanian passport in the name of Dr. José Andrés Álvarez Lastra. The only problem was that the date of this passport was after the German entry into Belgium. There was no other way to do it, since the provisional passport with which they gave me the Belgian identification card was dated in June 1940. "[...] The Venezuelan consul, Dr. Araujo, had received a telegram from his minister, Mr. Gil Bornes, in which he ordered him to give visas to both my wife and myself." Aguirre, *De Guernica*, 139. In addition, the July and August dates can hardly correspond to Agirre's experiences during those months in 1941, since in July of that year the Agirre-Zabala family was in Sweden, and in August they were on the high seas on their way to Rio de Janeiro. The date of 1940 is further confirmed by the fact that Venezuelan Foreign Minister Esteban Gil Borges (not Bornes, as the *lehendakari* calls him) was replaced on May 5, 1941, and was consequently not in a position to order visas in the summer of that year.

MARCH 1941
SATURDAY 1. ST. ALBINUS. 60-305

Today is Angelito's saint's day.⁶⁵ I remember. May God help them to be men after all that they have had to experience from a very young age. If they are able to meditate on it, it will serve them well in life. Meanwhile, I am still waiting for permits and news. How many hours have gone by, how many days! There are bitter moments. It will all pass, if it is from God. I read Gonzague de Reynold's ideas about the Russian Revolution. His points of view would be more exact if he had studied Stalin's constitution of 1935.⁶⁶ The book is from 1934. I ate lunch alone. I took a walk with the Panamanian minister. I retired to the boarding house. Moments afterward, the Dominican minister called me. I went to his house. I had dinner there. We went out and immediately returned with the Panamanian minister. We listened to the radio, or rather, we wanted to listen to it. There was so much noise. Today I learned of the death of Alfonso XIII. May God hold him in His glory. I said a prayer for his soul. Home at 10:30. I read all of Il Duce's speech in Italian. There were also photographs . . .

---

65 The *lehendakari*'s younger brother. He was born on February 29, 1920, a few days after his father's death. He died in 1979 in the same place where he was born, Getxo.

66 On the constitution promulgated on December 5, 1936—not in 1935—the *lehendakari* wrote in *De Guernica*, "Man is the greatest enemy of oppression, whether considered as political or social oppression. His rational instinct demands freedom. His faculties of intelligence insist on space for their initiative. Hence it is that all those who follow with interest and without hatred the evolutionary process of the USSR—among whom I count myself—must see with pleasure that man is triumphing there as well. The Stalinist constitution is a notable advance. The measures that reality is imposing on the USSR are another step forward. The recognition of property and inheritance, the progress of religious liberty, and even Stakhanovism are triumphs of man against the materialist and molecular conception to which unfiltered Marxist doctrine leads." Aguirre, *De Guernica*, 288. This positive opinion of the 1936 Soviet constitution had long existed among Basque nationalists. On July 16, 1936, shortly after the draft text was made public, the PNV's official publication, *Euzkadi*, published an article on the topic in its "Labor social" (Social labor) section, saying, among other things, "With the new constitutional system, the dictatorship of the Communist Party will still persist for a while, and it may be that the democratic wave that is now noticeable will not bear much fruit in a country with so long a history of servitude, but what is certain and positive is that in all this we note a fundamental change in the ideas that are being introduced into Russian life." "Sobre la nueva Constitución soviética," *Euzkadi* (Bilbao), no. 7,349 (July 16, 1936), 6.

MARCH 1941
SUNDAY 2. ST. SIMPLICE. 61-304

I went to church with the intention of receiving ashes. Neither ashes on Wednesday nor ashes today. I don't understand these things. I'll find it all out, with God's help. I took a walk before lunch with the Dominican minister. Since today was his birthday, his wife had very kindly suggested that he invite me. I had a very good lunch at the Dominican legation, which is my second home. We then took a walk with the Panamanian minister, and we agreed to meet at his legation at 6:30. Back home, we heard interesting things from a German gentleman who is a friend of the Despradel family. At six-thirty, we arrived at the Panamanian legation. We had a very good dinner there. Then a radio session. The noise made the broadcast impossible. We went out to take a walk. We went to a beer garden. Home at eleven. Today I saw from a distance someone who shares my name and whom I had not seen for a long time.[67] I knew that he was in Berlin. I read a bit before bed, and I am still waiting . . .

MARCH 1941
MONDAY 3. ST. CUNIGUNDE. 62-303

I spent all morning reading Gonzague de Reynold's study of national socialism in his *Europe tragique*. I'm reading it twice. After reading Santoro's book, which is extremely recent and examines the real events of this most recent period, I think that I'm not mistaken in affirming that Monsieur Gonzague de Reynold's fears will grow in relevance. Yesterday I read his critique of Italian fascism. I made the same observation. Time clarifies things. How much the enthusiasms of the *bien-pensants* have changed by now! I went out and ate lunch alone. Today was another day of solitude, since it coincided with a diplomatic banquet. After lunch, I retired to my room and continued reading and meditating. My imagination crossed borders and remembered my loved ones. At four-thirty I set out in search of today's movie theater. It's three hours that I get through. The weather is variable. The cold has disappeared. I

---

67 In the entry for March 14, 1941, the *lehendakari* again mentions this acquaintance, saying that they had not only the same first name, but also the same surname. Finally, in *De Guernica*, again without naming him but saying that they shared the same name, Agirre adds that he was on the staff of the Spanish embassy in Berlin. Aguirre, *De Guernica*, 204.

had dinner alone, took a short walk, and was back in my room at 8:30. And I'm still waiting ... How simple all this is ...

MARCH 1941
TUESDAY 4. ST. CASIMIR. 63-302

In the morning I went to the Greek consulate to let them know that I no longer need the visa. The Greek consul had asked my opinion. The consul wasn't there. I left the message and a greeting. I ate lunch alone. I went for a walk with the two usual ministers. I briefly greeted the Venezuelan one. Araujo had written to him on the 25th. So he hadn't left on the 24th. Better. But how difficult it is for them to write! The Panamanian minister invited me for coffee at his house. He told me about the visit of the Austrian priest sent by the nuncio. Poor Catholics![68] Afterward, I accompanied the Dominican minister to the tailor again. We went to pick up his daughter. How many things I remember ... She came out of the school with the other girls; we went home. There we listened to the radio and conversed. Consul Guardia still hasn't arrived. Tomorrow it will be two weeks since he left. The Panamanian minister is nervous. I'm even more so, since they're planning to go immediately to Belgium and Holland and bring the Widow Guerra and her two children.[69] Considering how much I like this widow! In sum, we have to wait ... Dinner, today a fish day and pretty bad. To read and to sleep. The Jews in Poland are treated like animals.

MARCH 1941
WEDNESDAY 5. ST. ADRIEN. 64-301

In the morning, I continued reading *L'Europe tragique*, the chapters on theocentrism and anthropocentrism. An interesting examination of this philosophical problem, too heavily laden with erudite quotations. It's the mania of professors for whom the lecture hall dominates over the

---

68 In the entry corresponding to March 4, 1941, in his book *De Guernica*, the *lehendakari* notes that the Austrian priest visited the Panamanian minister to request visas for the most prominent leaders of the Catholic party, Catholic organizations, and some members of the clergy, because the Nazi regime had begun to imprison them in concentration camps. Aguirre, *De Guernica*, 200–201.
69 The Widow Guerra was the false identity adopted by Mari Zabala Aketxe, José Antonio Agirre's wife. Mari Zabala was born in Portugalete on November 13, 1906, and died in Donibane Lohizune (Saint-Jean-de-Luz) on October 6, 1987.

experience of the masses and of the real people. His ideas, which are distinctly Catholic, and his orientation are completely pleasing to me. The great leaders of renewal have written without quotations. They think for themselves, not by way of others. Sublimity of the Gospel! I had lunch in my usual solitude. Then I went for a walk with the ministers at the usual time. The Panamanian one seems very worried about Consul Guardia's lateness in returning. The situation in the Balkans is not secure. Today in this sector, tomorrow in Spain. What we still have yet to see going forward! The Dominican minister went to the Venezuelan legation. I waited in the street for an hour. He came back. Araujo wrote. He says nothing about the Venezuelan lady.[70] We must wait, and may God be with everyone. I had dinner at the Dominican legation. Radio, commentary. Home at eleven. I'm reading the *Diario de Bucaramanga* [Bucaramanga diary] about Simón Bolívar.[71] I'm thinking a lot about Leturia's work on diplomatic relations with Pius VII, which I see cited in Monsignor Navarro's study of the Liberator's religious ideas; he's a great figure, slandered in the past, rehabilitated today.[72]

MARCH 1941
THURSDAY 6. ST. COLETTE. 65-300

For the American accounts.

Personal—	1,231
General expenses—	2,319
	= 3,550
	40,000 fr.
	75,000 fr.
	= 115,000

I arrived at the church at around seven, when it was still dark. An hour early, in view of the failure on Ash Wednesday. The doors were shut, but

---

70 The reference is to his wife, Mari Zabala, who was hiding under a Venezuelan passport.
71 The book to which the *lehendakari* refers is probably *Diario de Bucaramanga: Estudio crítico y reproducción literalísima del manuscrito de L. Luis Perú de Lacroix*, edited by Nicolás E. Navarro and published in Caracas in 1935 by Tipografía Americana.
72 Pedro Leturia Mendia (1891–1955) was a Jesuit and a Basque historian; his works include *La acción diplomática de Bolívar ante Pío VII (1820–1823), a la luz del Archivo Vaticano* (Madrid: Administración de Razón y Fe, 1925).

I continued my investigation and found a side door through which the few worshippers entered who heard mass and took communion today. In this way, this birthday that I will spend without my loved ones, sad and alone, began with my religious duties.[73] I think about others who suffer more and about God who directs all things. I read all morning. I had lunch alone. I went for a walk with the ministers. I invited the Venezuelan, Dominican, and Panamanian ministers to have dinner with me. They accepted. That will make my solitude on this day less painful. I spent the afternoon at the Dominican legation. We had dinner at the Restaurant Tousculum. Very good. Entertaining conversation. The ministers argued. I enjoyed myself, until eleven, when we retired. I thought about my loved ones. God wanted this separation. God will reunite us.

MARCH 1941
FRIDAY 7. ST. THOM. AQUIN. 66-299

A telegram came from Consul Guardia in Belgrade announcing his arrival in Berlin on Saturday. Providence directs all things. They will go to Antwerp and bring my loved ones. Unexpectedly and a day ahead of time, Consul Guardia turned up this morning. The minister with the permit to travel to Holland has reserved the berths on Sunday's train. God grant that they have done things properly in Belgium. While out for a walk this morning, accompanying the minister on some errands, I saw Miquelarena.[74] He passed very near me and did not see me. He has aged a great deal. That unfortunate article of his! Falsehoods and stupidities. From a source like that—Ibarnegaray—nothing else could come.[75] Everything will be sorted out when the time comes, but

---

73 Agirre was born in 1904, so he was turning thirty-seven.
74 Jacinto Miquelarena Regueiro (1891–1962) became well-known as a journalist on the board of the nationalist sports daily *Excelsior* of Bilbao. When that newspaper closed in October 1931, he moved to the right-wing Spanish daily *ABC* as a sports editor. When the *lehendakari* crossed paths with him in Berlin, Miquelarena was a correspondent for that Madrid paper in Germany. He collected and published some of his reports from the Reich capital in Jacinto Miquelarena, *Un corresponsal en la guerra* (Madrid: Espasa-Calpe, 1942).
75 The account that Agirre gives in *De Guernica* of his experiences on March 7 includes some interesting information that completes his notes here. In the book, he writes about Miquelarena and his article: "Miquelarena is Basque and was a director of one of our dailies in Bilbao. Now he is at the service of the Falange. And to show what kind of a person he is: a year and a half ago he wrote a shameful article in *La Nación* of Buenos Aires in which he narrated an apocryphal conversation I had with the French cabinet minister Monsieur Ibarnegaray, who is

without killing. I went for a walk with the ministers. Guardia arrived. He is traveling to Hamburg until Sunday. I spent the afternoon at the Dominican legation and had dinner there. After dinner we went out for walk—the Panamanian minister had invited us—and after having a beer, we went home before nine. I read French newspapers published in Greece that Guardia brought. To sleep satisfied.

MARCH 1941
SATURDAY 8. ST. JOHN OF GOD. 67-298

This morning the telephone rang at eight a.m. It was Vaca, the Colombian. At ten, he visited me at the boarding house. He brought urgent messages for Guardia, from Araujo among others. What can it be? I asked him discreetly. He said that Araujo is arriving tomorrow. Alone? I think so. He didn't tell me anything else. He will telephone Guardia in Hamburg at five p.m. I had lunch with the Panamanian minister at his house. I told him these things that had happened. Then I spent the afternoon at the Dominican legation. I informed the minister about these things. I am confused until Guardia arrives tomorrow. May God help me. One more blow: what does it matter? But we must wait . . .

I went for a walk with the Dominican minister for a while. Tomorrow night Dr. Villalaz and Guardia are going to Holland and Belgium. They want to bring the Venezuelan lady. But this news from Araujo? We will know tomorrow. I was detained by my great friend Dr. Despradel, who detains me by force almost every day to have dinner with him in

---

another Basque of the same category as Miquelarena." Aguirre, *De Guernica,* 201. Among other things, in the article published in Buenos Aires, Miquelarena, quoting Ybarnegaray, wrote: "I have met José Antonio de Aguirre; he came one day to ask me for the support of the French Basques. During the meeting, he did nothing but insult Spain and grow pale with anger when I called those of his group Spanish Basques. He did not put forward a single argument, not a single idea. Now the Spanish Basque refugees in France are still seeking to maintain the sacred fire of that anger and that rancor. Among them are some priests with an elementary education, endowed with a special boorishness, against whom we have to warn the French, since their maneuvers are intolerable." Jacinto Miquelarena, "M. Jean Ibarnegaray habla del problema vasco-español," *La Nación* (July 22, 1939). he reply came in a statement by the Basque delegate in Argentina, Ramón María Aldasoro, published in the same paper the following day. "El concepto de los emigrados vascos que están en Francia: Declaración de un ex consejero del gobierno que funcionó en Euzkadi," *La Nación* (July 23, 1939).

order to listen to the radio and distract ourselves by commenting on the news of the day. I arrived at the boarding house at eleven, worried but confident. I've made it through so much already!

MARCH 1941
SUNDAY 9. ST. FRANCES. 68-297

I went to high mass. They sang very well. A mixed choir. Polyphonic music, simple, for four voices, but with a great deal of contrast and sonority. When I returned to the boarding house, I found Consul Guardia, who had just returned from Hamburg. He was with Mr. Vaca. Nothing in particular. The same indecision as yesterday, since this gentleman did not clarify anything definitively. Conjecture, indecision, and lack of communication are the sign of the times. I went for a walk with the Dominican minister before lunch and after lunch. The consul and I were invited to lunch at his legation. The Panamanian minister joined our walk. He and Consul Guardia left tonight for Holland. The Consul will go as far as Belgium. Will the minister arrange things from Holland? That's his intention. I had dinner at the Dominican legation and left to see the minister and the consul off to the train at nine. I returned to the legation, and we listened to the radio. Once more to wait, and the decision is God's. At eleven, I went home and read, finishing the historical-critical study of the Bucaramanga diary.

MARCH 1941
MONDAY 10. ST. BLANCHARD. 69-296

This morning I continued reading *L'Europe tragique*. I've almost finished it. On this second reading, my opinion has not changed. It's very well-oriented, but there's a prejudice in the direction of monarchy and of that still-undefined "right," which leaves the proposed solutions somewhat indistinct. It's always easy to criticize; what's hard and difficult is to present constructive and realistic paths. The work as a whole is a profound and serious study. I ate lunch alone. I took a walk with my good friend the Dominican minister. Afterward, he invited me to take a ride in his recently-acquired automobile. It's a splendid car. That's the only thing I can say, since I don't understand a word about these things. I laughed in the car reflecting about my bourgeois appearance—so the pedestrians will have thought—and my shoes with a hole in each one. It's good to experience everything in life. I then stayed on at his house. Obligatory dinner. His attentions are extreme. We discussed Dr. Villalaz's and Consul Guardia's trip. What can Araujo have done? To live and to hope. An optimistic synthesis of an existence that only I am able to interpret. Home at eleven, to read and to sleep.

MARCH 1941
TUESDAY 11. ST. VINDICIANUS. 70-295

During the morning, I read and meditated. I spend many hours meditating. I've always liked to meditate on things a great deal before acting. Now, besides being an ordinary necessity, it's a resource. And much more so today, since it was to be a day of solitude, given that Dr. Despradel was invited to a diplomatic lunch. I had lunch alone and read *Il popolo d'Italia* from cover to cover. These Italian newspapers that write in "opera" amuse me a great deal. I went for a short walk and took refuge in my room. I started to read, then I wrote, thinking about tomorrow, and later on, being tired—continual thinking is tiring—I lay down and even fell asleep and dreamed. I read some more, and at around 7:30 I went back to the same restaurant near my house, where I had dinner and read *Le Pays réele,* Degrelle's mouthpiece, also from cover to cover.[76] It also amused me, like the Italian newspaper. Home at quarter to ten. I'm still thinking about Dr. Villalaz's and Consul Guardia's trip. May God help them and help us so that our affairs get sorted out.

MARCH 1941
WEDNESDAY 12. ST. GREGORY 1. 71-294

I've finished Gonzague de Reynold's book again. The final conclusions should get down to the practical level a bit more, extending the commentary further. But his thesis is, for me as a Catholic, indisputable. The road that leads to it is perhaps a bit different. I still believe in the people and have a great deal of distrust of certain self-selected "elites," even if selection may always be necessary for good government. But without exclusivity, or tyranny.

I ate lunch alone, as usual. After a wait of about three-quarters of an hour, good old Dr. Despradel appeared. He was coming from the Venezuelan legation. Dr. Zérrega requested a conference with Madrid in

---

76   Léon Degrelle (1906–1994) was the leader of the Belgian Rexist (fascist) party. His newspaper was named *Le Pays Réel.*

order to speak with Araujo and ask him what he has done with regard to his commissions. We will know the answer tomorrow. Afterward, I spent the afternoon at the Dominican legation, and as usual, I ate dinner there. Home at eleven. At around one, sirens and bombardments galore. At three I retired to my room, since they had made us go down to the—mediocre—shelter in the basement. The people were calm. The bombardments weren't nearby. I read Cicero. "Peace amid powder."

MARCH 1941
THURSDAY 13. ST. EUPHRASIE. 72-293

When they served me breakfast, the maid told me that the rest of the guests were in the shelter until six. I went to bed at three and heard nothing afterward. Consequently, I slept well. I read for the rest of the morning. I had lunch in my usual solitude. Since the ministers had the lunch for the Spanish-American representatives today, I remained alone, taking a long walk that lasted an hour and a half. I didn't see anything where I was walking, but they say that yesterday's bombing caused a great deal of damage and casualties. I didn't walk in the areas they indicated. In this as in praise, a large grain of salt. In the afternoon, after my stroll, I continued reading in my room. At 7:30 I went out to have dinner at the usual restaurant. I arrived at the hotel at a quarter to nine. I read a note giving me two messages from Dr. Despradel. I went to his house. There's no news. Dr. Villalaz has returned, but he hasn't said anything. Nor Dr. Zérrega either. So the days and the weeks pass. We listened to the radio and conversed. To the hotel at eleven, a little ... tired.

MARCH 1941
FRIDAY 14. ST. MATILDA. 73-292

The ministers were invited to the funeral of Alfonso XIII. Moved by curiosity—this is the truth—I went with them. Among the "large audience of townspeople," as Consul Guardia likes to say, I witnessed the arrival and departure of the diplomatic corps, headed by the nuncio. I made it into the church and attended the entire mass, a gathering of pagans, as these ceremonies usually are with so many indifferent dignitaries in attendance. Other than the official attendees, very few people. Not even sixty. I prayed for the soul of the deceased, the successor of those who stripped my homeland of its freedom. I encountered only one acquaintance, who shares my surname. Falangists of both sexes in uniform and red beret—five of one and six of the other—were lined up in front of the coffin; another four were in traditional dress and even with sideburns. On the bus, I heard a conversation between two of the Falangists that was a whole poem about "faith" in the future. What a comedy! It will all collapse, and soon. I saw my friends the ministers. I took a walk with them. I had dinner with Dr. Despradel. Afterward, radio, and home at eleven. When I went to bed, I was still thinking about the bastardized red beret.

MARCH 1941
SATURDAY 15. ST. LONGINUS. 74-291

During the morning, I read. We still have no news. Neither from Araujo—the only one who is in Madrid—nor from Guardia, nor from America, nor from the police. That's how I like things. How much I will be able to write someday! What can Araujo have done? I don't know. What can Guardia have found in Belgium? I don't know that either. In America, they will have received my news that was sent in a trustworthy and secure way more than a month ago. I'm still ignorant about that. And in this way, in waiting made up of minutes that last forever, days and days pass. I ate lunch alone, as usual. I amused myself reading *Il popolo d'Italia*. I went for a walk with my friend the minister. Then we went to the Panamanian legation. Dr. Villalaz is leaving for Switzerland tomorrow. In the end, he wrote a note verbale for the Foreign Ministry by way of the police. I thanked him for it. Also two others for the Swedish and Finnish legations in order to obtain the corresponding visas. I then spent a long time at the boarding house—the minister had an invitation to the Iranian legation. I ate dinner alone, and after dinner, I went to the minister's house to converse and listen to the radio. I will never forget his hospitality. Home around eleven. To read and to sleep.

MARCH 1941
SUNDAY 16. ST. HERIBERT. 75-290

I went to high mass, because the seriousness and solemnity with which they celebrate it enchanted me. I also remember my opinions about parish worship, which is so abandoned in many places. Afterward, I went for a walk with the Dominican minister, and inevitably, I had lunch at the legation, at both his invitation and that of his excellent wife. After lunch, another walk. Then to the legation to listen to the radio. We went out for another walk before dinner, until 7:30, when we returned. After the meal, the radio again. Commentary about Roosevelt's speech. This is serious.[77] I went home with a book by the turncoat Manuel Aznar titled *Historia militar de la guerra de España* [Military history of the Spanish war].[78] One day I will read other histories of that war in Euzkadi where many other things will surely be said that will leave Aznar very surprised. To write about certain things requires seriousness. Aznar still has a few flashes of memory of his compatriots. But that Guernika [Gernika] burning as a consequence of the Asturians' dynamite! That's a shameless thing and one that has its humorous side.

MARCH 1941
MONDAY 17. ST. PATRICK. 76-289

During the morning, I continued reading Aznar's book on the military history of the Spanish war. It has large errors, equivocations, and on occasions very bad faith. None of this can surprise us. I ate alone at the usual restaurant. Afterward, when I went to look for the Dominican minister, they informed me that he was invited to the Mexican legation. On his return, he telephoned me and invited me to dinner at his house. I went, since he needed to tell me that his chauffeur Enrique had told him that the police have received Dr. Villalaz's letter, giving assurances that my exit permit will be issued. God grant it. He also told me that the Venezuelan minister has received an answer from Araujo to his inquiry about the matter of the Widow Guerra. He answered saying that the

---

77 Probably a speech by Franklin Delano Roosevelt having to do with the Lend-Lease Act, signed by the U.S. president on March 11, 1941. This law, initially passed in order to help the United Kingdom, made it possible to get around the obstacle posed by previous legislation that required all foreign powers to pay cash for all purchases of military hardware in the United States. Instead, the new law authorized the president to assist any nation the defense of which he considered vital to the United States and to accept in return for the goods supplied any type of payment he found satisfactory. The law was applied until the Japanese surrender (September 2, 1945) and served to help all the Allies, not only to assist the United Kingdom's military effort.

78 Manuel Aznar Zubigaray (1894–1975) was a diplomat, politician, and journalist. In his youth, he was an active contributor to the Basque nationalist press, later transferring his activity to the Madrid press. During the Spanish Civil War, he opted for Franco. The book the *lehendakari* mentions is *Historia militar de la Guerra de España (1936–1939)* (Madrid: Idea, 1940).

family is well. A fine answer! I hope to know the facts soon, since time is passing ... waiting and hoping. We listened to the radio, and home at eleven, to continue reading and asking God to continue His goodness.

MARCH 1941
TUESDAY 18. ST. CYRIL. 77-288

I read during the morning and went out to have lunch at the usual restaurant, alone as always. I've continued reading Aznar's book. When someone writes without freedom, many things get said that are neither thought nor believed. His adulation for the figure of Franco is too obvious. He seems to be the sun set beside the darkness. Time will tell. I took a walk with the Dominican minister. Araujo's letters, which are in Hamburg, have still not been received. It's now more than ten days since he said that the Panamanian vice consul was traveling to that city. It seems that he has not made it to the office. It must be the normal thing that the business of this consulate is everywhere except at the consulate. "This country of mine" has quite a humorous side. But I will never forget it. I discussed all these things with my friend the minister, who appeared indignant. I had dinner at his legation, and after listening to the radio, I went home at eleven. I read some more before bed. Will we know anything more tomorrow?

MARCH 1941
WEDNESDAY 19. ST. JOSEPH. 78-287

A day without mass, despite it being a feast day for me. I spent the morning reading. The minister informed me that he had some news for me. That he had an invitation to the Argentine embassy and would get in touch with me after lunch. I went out for lunch alone, as usual. Afterward, I retired to my room again and continued reading a study demonstrating that Christopher Columbus's remains are in Santo Domingo. The biased commentaries and the polemics made me see that men concern themselves with everything. And I was trying to entertain myself, since I was a bit disquieted about the news. At 5:30, the minister called me. At six, I was at his house. He gave me a note from María that vexed me very much. If I still don't have the permit! What have they told her? What does the note mean? Is it a refusal of the trip? I am disturbed and angry. This lack of communication is disquiet, imprecision, and slow martyrdom. I had dinner at the legation. We listened to the radio, and I retired at eleven. I read, but I was not calm. God will clarify all things. To sleep.

MARCH 1941
THURSDAY 20. ST. CUTHBERT. 79-286

This morning I received word from the police asking me to appear in person. It's about the permit, which according to the Dominican minister's chauffeur has already been granted. That is, the German exit permit. This morning the Venezuelan minister requested an audience at the German Foreign Ministry in order to take an interest in the permit for the Widow Guerra of Brussels. God determines the paths and even the dates. My disquiet of yesterday is gradually disappearing. I hope that all this will be concluded so as to pay another visit to the Argentine ambassador and see whether he has received news from that country regarding the families who are in Belgium. The Venezuelan minister has been given an appointment for eleven in the morning tomorrow morning, pardon the redundancy. I had lunch alone, and then I was at the hotel reading until 5:30, since the minister had another lunch. And the third one tomorrow. As soon as he got home, he called me. I had dinner at the legation, as usual, and after listening to the radio, home at eleven. I'm still reading and making marginal notes in Aznar's book. It will be something for my friend the minister to remember me by.

MARCH 1941
FRIDAY 21. ST. BENEDICT. 80-285

A day of unpleasantness and worry. The Dominican minister's chauffeur informed me that the exit permit has been granted for any border except the ones with Sweden and Russia. Troop movements, some issue related to Russia, in sum that no one is leaving there, literally "even with permission from the Führer." He ingenuously told me that the police told him that ships are leaving for Lisbon and for Barcelona. "It has its humorous side." They're also offering the Swiss border, from what he told me. The order is definitive, due to current military reasons [*Crossed out*: orders]. And in Belgium. What will they do? We have to change the direction of our efforts to obtain a visa. Will they grant a Swiss one, which is extremely difficult? They don't answer from America: what is going on? How many things are piling up! Every detail is a difficulty. I'm familiar with terrible cases. How many honorable pariahs the world shelters! And I can't even write. In the end, I arrived at the minister's house at 5:30. His good will is magnificent, and may God be with everyone. I had dinner at the legation. We discussed things. If it were even possible to make a telephone call to Belgium! Not even the ministers can do it. Nor can telegrams be sent. After listening to the radio, I retired at eleven. I read until three in the morning. I had to read ...

MARCH 1941
SATURDAY 22. ST. LEA. 81-284

I continued reading all morning. Reading, especially meditating on my reading, leads me to the consideration of problems and to certain comparisons with our case that distract me, diverting my attention, which is otherwise too much absorbed with intense worries. I am preparing a plan to develop with the minister. After eating lunch alone, I met my good minster Dr. Despradel on our usual walk; may God repay him for his charity toward me! We discussed the news of the day and prepared the program to implement. Certainly, Dr. Zérrega is planning to leave for Spain on the 27th. He's going to say goodbye to the Venezuelan minister in that country. They say that he will return within a week. Surely not. We went to the legation. The minister went out to pay some visits. I read Marius André's book on Bolívar and democracy. An estimable study, but with strong anti-democratic prejudices, natural in Maurras's school.[79] I had dinner at the legation and retired at eleven. I'm still reading ...

MARCH 1941
SUNDAY 23. ST. VICTORIEN. 82-283

Having fulfilled my religious duties, this morning I took a Sunday-morning walk with Dr. Despradel. On holidays, I eat not only dinner but also lunch at the minister's house. His wife, who is familiar with all my vicissitudes, is extremely kind to me. She is a generous and entirely pleasant woman. After lunch, we went for a walk, and we decided in principle to apply for a Swiss visa once my permit has been granted. We hope to receive news from Belgium in the meantime. The absence of

---

[79] Charles Maurras (1868–1952) was a politician and writer, the chief founder of Action Française. Marius André was one of Maurras's secretaries. The book mentioned in the diary is *Bolívar et la démocratie* (Paris: Excelsior, 1924).

communication is always horrible! We returned home and listened to the radio. We had dinner. As we were saying goodbye (it was eleven, as usual), the alarm siren went off. I stayed, since in the street they oblige you to enter the closest shelter, and it's unpleasant among people who don't know you, in this case "not in the slightest." It was four in the morning, and they still hadn't sounded the all-clear. Nevertheless, the bombardment and the raid had stopped. I decided to leave, even though the alarm continued. I arrived home in silence and went to bed. It was a quarter after four.

MARCH 1941
MONDAY 24. ST. GABRIEL. 83-282

Today was really poor Encarna's saint's day, even though it was usually celebrated tomorrow.[80] I remembered her in my prayers. May she help us all from up there.

Today was a very satisfying day. I received a note from María that accompanied a letter from Consul Guardia to the Dominican minister. The note completely clarifies the previous one and leaves me calm. The previous one was dry, harsh, strange. This one says everything. Will they grant me the requested permit for Switzerland today? God knows. Will they grant the permit in Belgium, given the Swedish case? These are the doubts and uncertainties of this situation. But my faith does not weaken. It seems that a world is calling and that God wants us to do many things and carry out our responsibility by bringing them to a conclusion. I've discussed with the minister what's best to do. He's willing to do anything. I had dinner at the legation, and after listening to the radio, I retired at 10:30. I read the interesting life of Máximo Gómez, liberator of Cuba.[81] There's nothing new. To sleep.

---

80 Encarnación Agirre Lekube (1911–1940), José Antonio's sister, died as a consequence of injuries suffered during a bombardment in De Panne/La Panne when she was trying to flee the invading German troops together with a group of Basques, including the *lehendakari*. See note 125.
81 Máximo Gómez Báez (1836–1905) was a Dominican soldier who fought in the Cuban War of Independence.

MARCH 1941
TUESDAY 25. ANNUNCIATION. 84-281

This morning I finished the biography of Máximo Gómez and began some studies of San Martín. This obligatory waiting allows me to recall things I read in the past and meditate on deeds, things, and men.

I had lunch alone at the usual restaurant (1.75 or 2 marks, depending on the menu). In this way, I keep my expenses to the unavoidable. The days are passing, and my wallet is getting thinner.

When the minister returned from the Chilean legation (where he was invited to lunch), he telephoned me and invited me to his house, as usual. When I arrived, he told me that his chauffeur Enrique had agreed with the police to ask again for an exit permit by way of Sweden (from there by way of Finland there are ships for America). While they answer, the exit by way of Switzerland, which he says they will grant at once, remains pending. I don't think that an exit by way of Sweden will be possible, since it seems that the troops continue moving in that direction. We will know one of these days. The minister is leaving for Switzerland on Thursday. He will return on Monday. By then, there will be something, and his trip will be used to obtain the Swiss visa, which is very difficult. And so we keep on pulling. The Uruguayan chargé had dinner with us. I talked about Spain as much as I "liked." It has its humorous side. Home at 10:30. To read and to sleep.

MARCH 1941
WEDNESDAY 26. ST. LUDGER. 85-280

This morning I finished the study of San Martín. I started a new one by Mitre on the same topic.[82] I had lunch alone, and since the minister was busy, I took bus no. 1 to Unter der Linden, where I witnessed all the preparations for the welcome planned for Matsuoka for this afternoon.[83] It's the Anti-Comintern Pact, aimed right at Russia.[84] Since it was

---

82 Bartolomé Mitre (1821–1906) was an Argentine politician, soldier, and writer who served as president of the Argentine Republic between 1862 and 1868. The book to which the *lehendakari* refers is *Historia de San Martín y de la emancipación sudamericana* (Buenos Aires: La Nación, 1938).
83 Yosuke Matsuoka (1880–1946) was Japan's foreign minister between 1940 and 1941 and was a supporter of the alliance between Germany and Japan. He signed the Tripartite Pact with the two countries in 1940.
84 The Anti-Comintern Pact was signed by Germany and Japan on November 25,

three, and the welcome seemed to be planned for six, I left and looked for the minister. I saw thousands of meters of cloth used for flags and thousands of people and assault formations of all kinds. These Germans are like no one else when it comes to these displays.

The minister is leaving for Switzerland tomorrow. He has left things very well-arranged beforehand, and he will finish them in Switzerland. Since he has the will, it will get done. He returns on Monday. The German Foreign Ministry has indicated that there is nothing in Brussels (embassy) with regard to Mrs. Guerra. They mixed up the embassy with the police, which is where one applies for permits. But this too will be sorted out. Faith in God. Since the minister was busy with the preparations for the trip, I preferred to leave him alone. I said goodbye to his excellent wife and headed for the restaurant, once again inaugurating several days of absolute solitude. Home at ten and to read.

MARCH 1941
THURSDAY 27. ST. JOHN OF DAM. 86-279

I began Salvador de Madariaga's interesting book titled *España* [Spain].[85] Written in 1929, it's somewhat or very out-of-date. I'm sure that Mr. Madariaga's good judgment and great intellectual gifts would make the same evaluation today. Those praises for the Generation of 98! Unamuno and Ortega y Gasset[86] have left their apologists in a fine fix! They are

---

1936, with the aim of opposing the Communist International (Comintern) and, in particular, the Soviet Union. The members of the pact committed, in the event of a Soviet attack on one of the signatories, to engage in mutual consultations with the aim of protecting the interests of the pact's members, and they agreed not to sign any political treaties with the Communist power. Italy joined the pact in 1937, and Spain in March 1939.

85   Salvador de Madariaga Rojo (1886–1978) was a Spanish diplomat and writer. The book mentioned is *España: Ensayo de Historia Contemporánea* (Madrid: Bolaños y Aguilar, 1934).

86   Miguel de Unamuno y Jugo (1864–1936) and José Ortega y Gasset (1883–1955) were two writers and philosophers who powerfully influenced the Spanish cultural and political life of their generation.

The *lehendakari*'s comment possibly refers to the positions taken during the Spanish Civil War by the two thinkers. In the case of Unamuno, a native of Bilbao, even if it is true that he made statements favorable to the rebellion, it is also the case that he declared his opposition to the military leaders at the celebration of the Festival of the Race on October 12, 1936, to the point that he was removed from his post as rector of the University of Salamanca and put under house arrest. When he died, on

totally unfamiliar with certain problems, like those of Unamuno's compatriots. But time will teach. I ate lunch alone. Afterward, I almost instinctively directed my walk toward the avenues that feed into Unter der Linden in case I could see something. And in effect, shortly after passing the Monument to Victory, I saw the Japanese minister Matsuoka pass by, preceded and following by a large entourage. General Oshima was with him.[87] I went as far as the new chancellery, where a large audience was waiting for Hitler and the Japanese minister to come out after their meeting. It lasted two-and-a-half hours. I stood firmly in place, in intense cold, to wait for the moment. Everyone was waiting. Finally, Hitler, Matsuoka, Ribbentrop, and Oshima came out.[88] I was around fifty meters [165 feet] away. I witnessed with my own eyes the famous appearance on the Chancellery balcony. I had in my hand some Nazi and Japanese pennants that some members of the SS had "courteously" distributed to us. I enjoyed myself very much. Dinner alone and home at 9:30.

MARCH 1941
FRIDAY 28. ST. SIXTUS. 87-278

This morning I finished Salvador de Madariaga's book on Spain. It has very good observations. The defect of the clerical obsession. How many errors in the governance of the state have been committed as a consequence of this prejudice! He doesn't recognize the importance of certain problems. Well, it's true that the book was written more than ten years ago. How much I could write! In sum, we have to wait; everything will come. I ate lunch alone, following the schedule of the days of solitude that await me. Afterward, a while at the hotel. I started to read Vicente Gay's *Las constituciones políticas* [Political constitutions].[89] My

---

the other hand, he was acclaimed as a Falangist hero. For his part, Ortega declared himself in favor of the Republic at the beginning of the war, but he soon abandoned this position, going into voluntary exile and moving toward Falangist positions.

87 Hiroshi Oshima (1886–1975) was Japan's ambassador to Germany during World War II.

88 Joachim von Ribbentrop (1893–1946) was a Nazi politician. Before becoming foreign minister, the post he occupied at the time the diary was written, he had been Germany's ambassador to the United Kingdom (1936–38), charged by Hitler with obtaining a rapprochement between the two countries, inducing the British to break with France, and ensuring a German-British alliance.

89 Vicente Gay y Forner (1876–1949) was a professor of economy and public finances at the University of Valladolid and the Central University of Madrid. The book

old professor won't remember that in an exam I defended the theory of nationalities against his opinion. My opinion is still contrary to the theme of force—dictatorship—that is the topic of the book. At five I went to the movies. I saw a propaganda film about youth organizations. I had dinner at the same restaurant. They have an estimable orchestra in the evenings. I enjoyed myself. Today my neighbor was a deep-voiced bass who, like the famous shoemaker of Bergara, accompanied the orchestra's melody with his low notes. The shoemaker took the bass part to the whistling of the boys who crowded around his window. And meanwhile, waiting, waiting. Home and to sleep at 10:30.

MARCH 1941
SATURDAY 29. ST. EUSTACE. 88-277

During the morning I continued reading Gay's book. Like all honest studies, it has many worthwhile things and demonstrates the professor's concern and preparation. But in the desire to be new, they go back to what is oldest, to satrapism. Man is neither that bad nor that good. He is man. And as such, it is necessary to direct and govern him. Neither the optimism of the encyclopedists nor the pessimism of dictators. Simply Christianity. But real, effective, not simulated. I continue in my solitude. After the time that has passed, it's irritating. Faith and hope are capable of more. I like the restaurant because it's cheap and because few people go there. There is one exception, today, Saturday. A multitude of couples invades the room. The thing is, there's a dance above, on the second floor. The same things that there are everywhere, now that I observe here a desire to keep up appearances that does not correspond to reality. They smoke everything, men and women, and they drink everything, but "extras." A people that deserve a better destiny. Not only the behavior, but the way of thinking—which is worse—is confused! What speech could be more humorous than the one given in the middle of the room by a woman collecting for the Winter Relief![90]

---

mentioned by the *lehendakari* is *Las constituciones políticas* (Madrid: Compañía Ibero-Americana de Publicaciones, 1930).

90 In order to improve the regime's image and convince the public that everything possible was being done to promote the solidarity of the more fortunate with the poor, on September 13, 1933, the implementation of a short-term aid program was announced, and baptized with the name of the Winter Relief Program of the German People. As happened with other emergency measures during the Third Reich, Winter Relief became a permanent feature of the sociopolitical landscape. The program was put on a firmer foundation on November 5, 1934, by a collection

Not even one by the "Salvation Army"! I entertain myself with these innocent displays. Home at 10:30. To read a bit and to sleep, thinking about a thousand things.

MARCH 1941
SUNDAY 30. ST. VERON. 89-276

Today I went without mass. I spent a strange night—with dreams—something that is not usual for me. Having woken up in the middle of the night, I had a hard time getting back to sleep. I've given instructions for them to call me at a prudent hour in the morning. Today they didn't call me. End result that between being up half the night and sleeping late, I missed the time for mass. I went to the church in the afternoon. God will have pardoned this involuntary infraction of the commandment. Everything had to come together for it to happen. I envy those who wake up when they want to. I can't. I sleep too well. Maybe it's also the case that they have less on their minds than I do. Today, between being up half the night and the tiredness I've been carrying for a long time, I could have slept all day. In the church in the afternoon, there were two soldiers, four or five other people, and myself. Afterward, I entertained myself listening to a band play while next to some "live wires." I situated myself behind the flugelhorns in order to remember my schooldays. They played worse than I did. They skipped a lot of notes. Entertaining myself like a child until five, when I went to the movies. An interesting film about the polar region. The dialogue was in Swedish. Dinner at 7:30, and the clock struck 10:30 while I was listening to the restaurant orchestra. Home thinking that uneasy solitude is the worst.

MARCH 1941
MONDAY 31. ST. BENJAMIN. 90-275

I spent the morning reading Gay. I didn't modify my earlier judgment of his work. He believes in force as a solution. Force builds nothing permanent. Certainly, he tries to hedge on occasion, but the foundation

---

law that allowed the interior minister and the Nazi Party treasurer to suspend all charitable agencies and foundations that might compete with it. Winter Relief was yet another Nazi organization that was financed by collections and benefited from the labor, more or less voluntary, of ordinary Germans. At the same time, these collections and work campaigns did not cease to be a new tax that burdened the finances of the Third Reich's citizens. R. J. Evans, *El III Reich*, 478–81.

is already laid. It's a false foundation. I ate lunch alone at the usual restaurant. Today I spent the day thinking about my loved ones. What can they have done in Belgium? What news will the Dominican minister bring me from Switzerland if he returns tomorrow, as he said when he left? How time passes! After lunch, I set out to walk, and between streets and plazas, I walked for three and a half hours. I needed to breathe. They're taking down the banners along Unter der Linden. Is it a sign of something? At six-thirty, the hotel. At seven, the Russian restaurant. To hear the music of exiles played and sung. It reminds me so much of my own music! I listened to them with deep emotion. A nice couple, a German officer and his fiancée, looked at me with surprise upon seeing my emotion at the music. The thing is that their Russian songs are so similar to many of our melodies! I passed the time until ten, when I retired to my room. I visited the tomb of the unknown soldier. There were wreaths from the Führer, from Matsuoka, from Oshima, etc. I prayed an Our Father. Will I have news tomorrow? How true it is that one's fatherland is no more than an extension of one's family. My two earthly loves.

NOTES

Ask for Gros Rotwein in Hacon.[91]

—Letter to Jesús accompanying the one from Araujo.

—Letter to the Widow Guerra about her situation.

—Telegram to Araujo sending passport with instructions to apply for permit.

—Send legation papers Dr. Villalaz and at the same time that they write and send note verbale to Finland.

Here ends the month of March, 1941. How much more I could write if the limits of this notebook and other, greater limits did not prevent me! May God, Who penetrates the depths of souls, help those who have no other desire when passing through this life than to love those close to them dearly and seek their greater happiness by all licit means. May He also help us in the struggle that is underway, and however great the reverses may be, may our faith and our confidence be greater. May what has been sowed in sacrifice be followed by a well-earned harvest. A Christian and therefore optimistic presentiment tells me that it will be.

---

91 The meaning of the phrase is *ask for a large red wine in ?*. It might be a phrase copied by Agirre to use in restaurants when he was without a German-speaking companion, since the *lehendakari* did not know German.

2nd TRIMESTER

NOTES

—His Excellency the Dominican minister, Roberto Despradel—Wieland Strasse 25/26—Tel. 91-55-24.

—His Excellency Dr. Villalaz, the Panamanian minister. Tel. 91.02.76

—His Excellency Dr. Zérrega, the Venezuelan minister, Hotel Adlon, Berlin. 91-72-27 (Legation)

—His Excellency Dr. Olivera, ambassador of the Argentine Republic—Berlin.

Victoria Boarding House—Tel. 91-05-11.

APRIL 1941
TUESDAY 1. ST. HUGH. 91-274

[*In the upper margin*: See notes.][92]

—Dr. Paul, at Salvador de León 71. (Olaz) Box 1129—Tel 92.620.

—Carlos Alfonso Guardia Jaén, Box 1175—Caracas.

—Piñango at Llaguno 2-1—Constan.

—Rodolfo Arrigorriaga—Buenos Aires.

—Antonio Constantino Arrigorriaga—New York.

—Inst.—12 East 36th Street. New York.

—Man. 60 East 54th Street. Hotel Elysee—New York.

—González Roa (Mexican consul), 175 Boulevard de la Magdalena—Marseilles.

---

92 This note and the identical one in the entry for April 2, 1941 refer to the fact that the entries pertaining to these days are found in the spaces reserved for notes following the pages for the days corresponding to the month of April of that year.

—Trini, Rue du General Humbert n° 2. Paris XIV—Ponte Vaures.

—Eduard. 87 Rue Saint Hubert. Tel. 950.51. Berchem (Antwerp)

—Ecleston Square 14—Chicago. (Liz)

—Consulate General of Panama, Ferdinand Strasse 56. Hamburg.

APRIL 1941
WEDNESDAY 2. ST. FRANCIS OF PAOLA. 92-273

[*In the upper margin*: See notes.]

—Tomás—Hotel Majestic (Mexico)

—Teres—Place Jean Jaurés 14—2nd floor, H. Pyrines—Tarbes.

—Marie Thérèse, 133-9.

—José Sebastián da Silva Freitas. 25 Rua do Amparo, 2nd floor. (Banco Lisboa y Açores) Lisbon.

—Harrazpi—Atalaya, Biarritz.

—Monsieur Emanuel de Berthier de Sauvigny. P. n° 1832—Ofslag. va. Deustshland.

—73 Avenue d'Mexique—3. 4.

—Mrs. Guardia Jaén, Box 1075—Panama.

—15 Rue Bourla, Antwerp (Venezuelan consulate).

—Lei Mikolei—Moorweiden 34—Hamburg. Tel. 44-51-64.

—Ziegler Hof Boarding House 4-16-93/4. Ecke Duforstrasse—Seehofstrasse.

His Excellency Minister Despradel, Villalaz. Zurich.

APRIL 1941
THURSDAY 3. ST. RICHARD. 93-272

—Baron Albert van den Branden de Reeth—10 areve des Fumuli Boits Forts. Brussels.

—Gamboa, Joaquín. Sarmiento 424—Buenos Aires

This morning I read. Around eleven-thirty, I went to the house of an ear specialist, and he removed a blockage that had formed in my left ear. It's a good thing that all the evil humors of these times have been reduced to that. The minister insisted that I have lunch with him. I did so. We took a walk together. All the Western Hemisphere ministers are worried about the seizure of German ships. Their task here is to present notes of protest in response to the boarding by German naval personnel.[93] We spent the afternoon at the legation. We continued discussing yesterday's letter. An interesting conversation with the German professor. I had dinner at the legation. Dr. Villalaz still has not arrived from Switzerland. We listened to the radio. At eleven, I retired and read and waited.

APRIL 1941
FRIDAY 4. ST. ISIDORE. 94-271

In the morning, I did calculations and worked out numbers for various projects for future application, much of it about what has already been studied so many times with such enthusiasm. To unite the old and the new. Continue the story by adapting it. That's the secret that will lead to a good result. Out of this will come a complete organizational program with hierarchies and functions. Applicable to any case that may present itself and a solution to all problems. The effort and the ambition are not small, but faith can do more. Everything will come to pass in good time. After eating lunch alone, I took a walk with my good friend the Dominican minister. We discussed the taking of Benghazi by Axis troops.[94] Another episode in this war, a war decisive for civilization. Later, we arrived at the legation. We spent the afternoon and went for another walk. We had dinner at the legation. We listened to the radio with its different opinions. The war is entering an acute phase. The minister had been with the Venezuelan chancellor. They're still waiting for the permit from Brussels. They take it to be certain. May it be so. I have no other way to express myself than that. Home, to wait and hope and to sleep.

---

93 Agirre provides additional information in *De Guernica*, ascribing the following commentary to the Dominican minister: "All of us Western Hemisphere ministers are running around like crazy, composing the notes that we have to deliver to the foreign minister, protesting against the sabotage that German naval personnel are carrying out with their ships anchored in our ports." Aguirre, *De Guernica*, 208.

94 Benghazi was taken by German troops on April 4, 1941, as part of Gen. Erwin Rommel's offensive against the British in Cyrenaica.

APRIL 1941
SATURDAY 5. ST. VINCENT. 95-270

I continued making plans all morning. The ideas that have been tossed around so many times are in this way becoming more concrete, for the time when God so disposes. The world moves quickly and in surprising ways. What seems impossible today is a reality tomorrow. What never fails is the ground won each day with an effort that is also daily. This is what the pessimists always forget. But in life, either one has faith and therefore works, or it's better not to live. I had lunch alone and then went for a walk with the minister. Afterward, we spent the rest of the afternoon at the legation. There was no mail from Belgium. Things are very much delayed. If desiring things could achieve them, how many things would I have achieved! Before dinner, we took another walk. We've also had no news of the Panamanian minister. Apparently, he's happy in Switzerland. On the other hand, the Venezuelan minister's arrival is announced for Monday. He's coming from Madrid. He'll bring news. After eating dinner and listening to the radio, I went home at eleven. Holy Week begins tomorrow. I'll have time to meditate.

APRIL 1941
SUNDAY 6. PALM SUNDAY. 96-269

The church was packed with worshipers. The mass began with the procession with palms. The choir performed polyphonic compositions taken from the liturgy of the day. The Hossana was very well sung.[95] It's too bad that I can't understand these simple preachers, who seem to me to preach very well! I follow them by imagining for myself what they are saying. Before lunch, I took a walk with the Dominican minister, whom I looked for in our well-known place, which is always the same—Kurfürstendam Strasse. I had lunch as a guest at the legation. They served us a magnificent platter of chicken, which I had not been able to taste for a long time. I remembered my daily meals at the 1.75-mark restaurant! But when one has ministers for friends . . . We went for another walk after lunch. We spent the afternoon at the legation listening to the news. The taking of Adis Abeba, etc. Our comments

---

95 *Hosanna* is a word of Hebrew origin, according to the Spanish Royal Academy. It is used as an exclamation of praise and jubilation in the Psalms and in Jewish and Christian liturgies, and it is also the name of a hymn sung on Palm Sunday, as the *lehendakari* indicates.

were in accord. Yugoslavia, Greece . . . then others.[96] In the end, we went for a walk before dinner, ate, and continued listening to the radio. Home at eleven. I began to read "our" Unamuno.

APRIL 1941
MONDAY 7. ST. SATURNINUS. 97-268

I'm still reading *En torno al casticismo* [On purism] by Miguel de Unamuno. Brilliant things as in almost all his productions. But how much chaos there is in his head! How many episodes—some from my own experience—does this original and deracinated personage remind me of when he forgets very proper purisms that he was only able to deal with by denigrating them unjustly! A contradictory figure, he has displayed this stamp so characteristic of him even to his grave! May he in heaven understand how pure and profound is the cause of those who defend what he sang as a boy in the language of his parents!

I had lunch alone and went for a walk with the minister today, the 7th. Three months since I arrived in Germany. How long these months have been! Only God and I can appreciate it. He giving me faith without limits, and I enduring and hoping. But in the end, everything will be sorted out. And probably at the right time and opportunely.

I had dinner at the legation, and we listened to the radio. The great Battle of the Mediterranean is beginning. At eleven, I retired and continued reading.

APRIL 1941
TUESDAY 8. ST. PERPÉTUE. 98-267

I continued reading Unamuno and finished António Ferro's book on Salazar, the Portuguese dictator.[97] Salazar is an interesting figure who has always attracted me due to his honesty and firm character. It's possible not to share his ideas, but it's easy to understand that certain procedures of government may be necessary in some tumultuous countries. What is

---

96 On April 6, 1941, the Germans launched Operation Marita, in which they occupied Yugoslavia and Greece within a few days. Simultaneously, as part of British military operations in Ethiopia, that country's capital, Addis Ababa, was liberated on the same day, April 6.

97 The book by António Ferro to which Agirre refers is *Oliveira Salazar: El hombre y su obra* (Madrid: Edic. FAX, 1935). On Ferro, see note 205.

unjust is the attempt to apply them everywhere. I've heard even Salazar's own adversaries speak well of him. That's something in his favor. Today I was invited to have lunch and dinner at the legation. The minister's extraordinary friendliness confuses and embarrasses me. He does not want to accept my excuses. We get along well, and he takes charge of my situation and even of my shoes, which had reached the point of causing scandal and compassion. They've been repaired, and I'm somewhat presentable again. Tomorrow the Swiss visa will be requested, in view of the fact that the Swedish border is apparently still not open. May God push these applications forward a bit! Nothing from Belgium ... for now. Home at eleven. I continued reading.

APRIL 1941
WEDNESDAY 9. ST. WALTRUDE. 99-266

I spent the morning reading. When I went for a walk with the Dominican minister after lunch, he told me that his chauffeur had been to the Swiss legation. That they don't issue visas there but at the consulate. That for this purpose a note from the Panamanian minister is required. Since he is in Switzerland and took seals and stamped paper with him, and since he isn't returning until the 15th, I have no alternative but to wait again. And many will be thinking, 'Why don't you leave?' How easy the question, how desperate the answer! I now keep silent in my soul my thanks for what we have done. In recent days, these repressed evil humors, which are never reflected in the exterior, have accumulated in my mouth. Because it's necessary to suffer with a smile. Today, for this reason, I have a quite intense toothache. My mouth was left half treated, and only God knows when I will be able to finish the treatment. In sum, my good minister detained me for dinner, and we listened to bad news on the radio. Home at eleven. Today I want to go to bed right away, since tomorrow is Holy Thursday. There's no lack of topics for meditation.

APRIL 1941
THURSDAY 10. MAUNDY THURSDAY. 100-265

I attended the solemn Holy Thursday services: mass, procession, communion, adoration before the monument. Everything very simple. The worship is affected by the situation. If only it were no more than that! I obtained from the minister's library a book of the Gospels and the Holy Scriptures. This has been my reading today, which will continue tomorrow. In the absence of a missal, it's a good substitute. I returned to the hotel, where I remained until noon. I ate lunch alone. I then went for a walk with the minister, discussing last night's bombing raid. Since I had already gone to bed, I stayed there without going down to the shelter. This afternoon, we went to the most badly hit area by car. The opera theater and a bank (a business one) were destroyed, along with some other damage to houses, including the library of one of the universities. The raid lasted around two-and-a-half hours. I had dinner at the legation, listening to the radio. I left at eleven. My reading for today is the book of Genesis and the Gospel of Matthew. Afterward, to sleep.

APRIL 1941
FRIDAY 11. GOOD FRIDAY. 101-264

I attended the services for the day. Solemn and simple. Many people. Today was a day off, and the great emptiness of the streets was noticeable in the morning. The "Agios o Theos" was very well sung by a good choir.[98] How many memories of my past days! The minister was waiting for me to take a walk before lunch, as we do on holidays. Invited to his house, I tried to observe the fast within the limitations of the circumstances. We took a walk in the afternoon, to the chapel where the staff of the Spanish embassy and the "wives" of the Western Hemisphere embassies and legations hear mass. It reminded me of that time when the Andalusian soldier told me with his regional accent, "That's for the gentry," or for the gentry's wives, I would add. Without prejudice, naturally, to taking up arms in the name of "that." In the end, today is Good Friday. I read and meditated on the Gospel of Luke and the books of Exodus and Leviticus. I had dinner at the legation. Home at eleven.

APRIL 1941
SATURDAY 12. HOLY SATURDAY. 102-263

Today is Don Constan's saint's day. I remember and lament that my ambition to be together or in communication on this day has not been fulfilled. I went to the church. There were no services. I meditated on the Gospel of Luke for an hour. I asked on account of his saint's day that God grant blessings of all kinds both to him and to the whole

---

98 *Hagios o Theós* ("Holy is God"), a refrain repeated in the *Popule meus! Quid feci tibi?* ("My people! What have I done to you?"), one of the pieces sung during the second part, the adoration of the cross, of the liturgy of the Passion on Good Friday.

family. I returned to the hotel, reading and meditating on Ecclesiastes and King David's proverbs. I had lunch alone and went out for a walk with the minister, who arrived with the secretary of the Cuban embassy, who knows Álvarez and nothing more. We talked about the war and the future of the world. The topic offers plenty of material. We returned home and listened to the radio. We went out for a walk, and I had dinner at the legation. This obligation is now a ritual. Like the radio. How much I have to thank my good friend Despradel for! Home at eleven. To bring these days to a close, I read and meditated on the Gospel of John. Also the Acts of the Apostles. How grand and simple the Gospel is! Every day, a greater treasure of application is found. A public and private norm, for individuals and for peoples.

APRIL 1941
SUNDAY 13. EASTER. 103-262

Easter Sunday. Day of the Fatherland [Basque national day]! I tried to celebrate it in the solitude of one who has been cast out from his own. In the morning, having fulfilled my religious duties, my thoughts were in communion with the thousands who in different places will be thinking and hoping as I am. As I remembered all of them, they will have remembered me. Especially in Belgium, from where I still have not received news. When I went for a walk with the minister before lunch, he informed me that the Venezuelan minister has arrived. That he was with Araujo in Madrid and has things to tell me. Naturally, I am interested in hearing him. Today we spent the afternoon glued to the radio. What news! Tobruk, Bardia . . .[99] The world is large, and God directs all things. I had dinner at the legation. We continued listening to the radio. Home at eleven. I read the Acts of the Apostles. Will this Easter week be a week of resurrection for me? I commended the solution to God. For this reason, I am calm.

---

99 The furthest points reached by Axis troops in their North African offensive. Bardia fell into German hands on April 15, 1941, but Tobruk resisted.

APRIL 1941
MONDAY 14. ST. JUSTIN. 104-261

Today is a holiday. I went to mass this morning. Afterward, I went out for a walk and met the good Dominican minister. I had lunch at his house. Obligatory on holidays. After lunch, he went out to converse with the Venezuelan minister. He returned three and a half hours later. He brought news from Madrid. What we all know and other things that he interprets in his manner. It's evident that he talked to ill-informed people and South American diplomatic circles. He said, for example, that they assured him that in Catalonia they're all monarchists. It has its humorous side, there in particular. But that the whole world is against Franco. The same as always. Araujo sent many greetings for me. That the family is well. His news is old, since Consul Guardia's letter is more recent. We'll see whether there is anything positive tomorrow. Tomorrow, we think, Minister Villalaz will arrive. My Swiss visa is being held up because his seal and his stamped paper are lacking. Small details, but how important and transcendental! I had dinner at the legation, and home at eleven somewhat worried.

APRIL 1941
TUESDAY 15. ST. PADARN. 105-260

I continued reading Unamuno. His whole study of purism, which overlaps a great deal with *majismo* [an eighteenth-century Spanish fashion popularizing the style of the lower classes], is interesting as an example of the acorn not falling far from the tree, or what is the same thing, "unfortunate are those who live near these purists, since they will not have a day of peace until they bring down the curtain." I had lunch alone. The minister, who was busy, telephoned me as soon as he was free. We spent the afternoon at the legation and then went for a walk. I needed it. This life of waiting and the rest of it is enervating. It exhausts, tires, depresses. How easy it is to say, "Wait." Only faith can do more. We are still without news, and I'm here waiting for the arrival of Dr. Villalaz, who will be here the day after tomorrow, it seems. And back to the beginning again. Application, signatures, etc. And meanwhile, isolated from everyone. In the end, I had dinner at the legation, I arrived home at eleven, I finished the book of Numbers, and for consolation I read the extravagant Unamuno. But I wait and hope always in God.

APRIL 1941
WEDNESDAY 16. ST. BENEDICT LABRE. 106-259

I spent the morning reading part of Deuteronomy, and I finished the historical novel about the Dominican indigenous hero Enriquillo.[100] Very interesting, especially for the accomplished study of the first days of the Spanish colonial regime. Those first days have been applied without interruption across time and with peoples of all kinds. And everything will end as it did there.

After eating lunch alone, I took a walk with the Dominican minister, who informed me that the Panamanian minister would arrive tomorrow. Then we listened to some not-very-good news on the radio. War is like that. Then we went out for a walk after dinner. Another lap around "our Kurfürstendam retreat," as we call the small area in which our life passes. And one day and another... But I can't complain. We'll see whether Dr. Villalaz wants to give matters a definitive push tomorrow. After eating dinner and listening to the radio, home at eleven. To read and to sleep.

APRIL 1941
THURSDAY 17. ST. ANICETUS. 107-258

I started reading Pedro Gorgolini's book *El Fascismo* [Fascism].[101] It corresponds to the heroic, anti-Bolshevik, and very Italian epoch. Between then and now, what twists and turns! Precisely today I learned about the rumors that are going around in the Western Hemisphere about a Soviet entry into the Tripartite Pact. Next, they will sign the Anti-Comintern Pact. That way the affair will be more complete. May God hold us in His hands and enlighten our reason. The Panamanian minister has arrived. My good Dominican minister visited him this morning. Reticent about my matter. Where I say, he says, I said... But is it possible at this stage? How much one suffers with these indecisions, and especially when promises are taken back! Everything half-done, without decisiveness. The poor man and the one who has fallen are worthy of compassion for someone who only considers today. But there is a tomorrow that God is preparing. Then there will be plenty of

---

100 Enriquillo (?–1535) was a Dominican indigenous chief known for leading the Bahoruco insurrection, which sought to put an end to the exploitation and extermination of the indigenous people of Santo Domingo.

101 The book by Pedro Gorgolini to which the *lehendakari* refers is *Comienzos del fascismo italiano* (Madrid: Compañía Ibero-Americana de Publicaciones, 1923).

friends. And so it will be now also, because God wills it. The Dominican minister is very angry. He will work.

APRIL 1941
FRIDAY 18. ST. URSMAR. 108-257

This morning I went out to visit the Panamanian minister. He was out. I had lunch alone after stopping at various kiosks. There were no cigarettes. I got my revenge by smoking the Dominican minister's box of pipe tobacco. The wrath of a smoker is terrible ...

After lunch, I met the Panamanian and Dominican ministers on my walk. I arranged to stop in at the Panamanian minister's house at eight. I spent the afternoon at the Dominican legation, where I had dinner. At eight, Dr. Villalaz received me. We exchanged impressions, and yesterday's pessimistic reference is switched today for an optimistic one. Will it be the last turn of the wheel? Today he proposed to me a plan that is undoubtedly the best. We'll see whether it is carried out, even though it has been proposed with the best of wills. In sum, God has the last word. Home at ten-thirty. Yesterday we had a bombing raid. It wasn't much, but it produces a lot of panic among the population.

APRIL 1941
SATURDAY 19. ST. LEONIE. 109-256

During the morning, I read I Kings. I also finished *El Fascismo* by Gorgolini. Overall, a weak effort, even if Mussolini's prologue says that it's the best thing written since 1921. Better studies have been published since, even if the behavior deserves the harshest characterizations. I had lunch alone and went for a walk with my friend the Dominican minister. Dr. Villalaz has left for Holland. In the afternoon, we visited a hotel situated on the outskirts of Berlin (about forty kilometers [twenty-five miles]), on a picturesque lake, surrounded by trees. It's the refuge sought out by the diplomats alarmed by the nocturnal English visits. I saw the place thinking that for me and my loved ones, there would be no room there. But God will grant other things. We drove at 120 [kilometers] per hour along the magnificent two-lane roads of this land that deserves a better fate. I'm still without news from Belgium. What can be happening? After eating dinner with the minister and listening to the radio, I retired at eleven.

APRIL 1941
SUNDAY 20. ST. AGNES. 110-255

Aintzane's saint's day.[102] How much I remember! Here they're celebrating Hitler's[103] saint's day. Posters, flags. There are hearts full of black crepe that think, "What fault is it of children who can't even celebrate their saint's day with their father? And what fault is it of their fathers who defend the freedom of their people with honor?" The multiplication of so much misfortune will determine God's finger straight to reparation. The task has already begun. At the church, I prayed for my loved ones that we may all be like little ones, as the saying goes. I imagine that I have them at my side, drawing pictures and telling *ipuñak*.[104] *Amatxu* will have reminded them of their absent *aita*.[105] The minister was busy; I ate lunch alone remembering and following what my loved ones will do today. It rained quite a bit. I read Estévez y Romero's book *Desde el Zanjón hasta Baire* [From the Zanjón to Baire] all afternoon. It's the Cuban journey between freedom and revolution. As happens to others. Everything is the same. The result will also be the same.[106] I ate dinner alone and retired at 8:30. I continued reading and comparing.

APRIL 1941
MONDAY 21. ST. ANSELM. 111-254

This morning the Old Testament book of Chronicles occupied my attention. I then continued reading Estévez's book. Everything repeats itself; Hispanic bad faith has always been similar. Promises, programs, then nothing. It's natural that the peoples take the legal road, because they can't leave themselves open to any argument that can be used against them, but the end will be the same in both cases. After having lunch alone, I met the Dominican minister, who informed me that the

---

102 The oldest child of Mari Zabala and José Antonio Agirre, Aintzane was born in Getxo in 1935.
103 The German dictator was born in 1889, so this was his fifty-second birthday.
104 *Ipuñak* means "stories" in Euskara. In modern standard Basque it is spelled *ipuinak*.
105 *Amatxu* is an endearing form of *ama* "mother," while *aita* means "father."
106 Luis Estévez y Romero, *Desde el Zanjón hasta Baire, datos para la historia política de Cuba* (Havana: Tip. la Propaganda Literaria, 1899). When Agirre says that Estévez y Romero's book is "the Cuban journey between freedom and revolution," he means to compare this work and the Cuban process of independence with Euzkadi's situation and his own book *Entre la libertad y la revolución, 1930–1935: La verdad de un lustro en el País Vasco* (Bilbao: Tall. Graf. E. Verdes Achirica, 1935).

Venezuelan minister has again spoken to the Foreign Ministry about the matter of the Widow Guerra and her two children, which is so delayed. They promised him activity. We'll see, and we'll hope. I had dinner at the legation with the minister and a Romanian couple who had just arrived from Bucharest. Very interesting. With the conversation, we left off listening to the radio. At eleven, I retired and continued reading.

APRIL 1941
TUESDAY 22. ST. ADALBERT. 112-253

In the morning, I read, as usual. Afterward, I ate lunch alone, as I usually do every day. I went for a walk with the minister. He showed me a telegram that the Venezuelan minister had given him to show me. It was from the Venezuelan foreign minister taking an interest in Mrs. Guerra and her children and requesting that efforts be made for their urgent departure. It made me very happy. Our friends are working. God grant that everything be fulfilled. We spent the afternoon at the legation, where I had dinner. In the evening, listening to the Berlin Spanish radio broadcast, we found out about the constitution of the Basque National Council in Manuel's city.[107] This separatist "shamelessness" has its humorous side. Affairs of the English, if it's true. Poor Spain!

---

107 Manuel Irujo, considering that the *lehendakari*'s whereabouts were unknown and the rest of the councilors excerpt for Aldasoro were in German-controlled territory, believed that it was necessary to create a body that would substitute for the Basque government. This body was named the Euzkadi National Council (*Consejo Nacional de Euzkadi*) and was constituted in London in July 1940, but the news was not immediately made public due to British pressure, since the British believed that Spain might interpret it as a motive for British hostility toward the Spanish regime. In the summer of 1940, the United Kingdom was at its lowest point in its war against the Axis, France had fallen, Italy had entered the war, and it appeared that Spain was going to take part in the conflict on the side of the totalitarian powers. The manifesto creating the Euzkadi National Council said, among other things, "By our own decision, we hasten to gather up the government's flag, for the purpose of giving continuity to its work and organic unity to Euzkadi [...] No one should see in us more than transitory depositaries of the government's powers, until they can be entrusted to a more direct representation than ours [...]. "Our program is the same as that government's [...] As Basques, we aspire to achieve the national freedom of Euzkadi and its recognition by the peoples of the earth. As men, we unite our effort to that of the democracies [...]. As a representative of the Basque nation, we propose to aid the citizenry of our country [...]. We swear before God and before our people, scattered throughout the world, to be faithful to these postulates." Manifesto of the Euzkadi National Council, London, July 1940, GE-250-3.

Tomorrow I expect the Panamanian minister. God grant that the proposed solution does not fail. And so we live one day and another day... At eleven, I arrived home and continued reading.

APRIL 1941
WEDNESDAY 23. ST. GEORGE. 113-252

In the morning, I read. I began to read *Cinco ensayos* [Five essays] by José Enrique Rodó: grand style and solid ideas, even if I might not accept various of his propositions and themes.[108] His study "Ariel" is noteworthy. I also practiced my languages a bit; they've been somewhat abandoned in this time of inactivity. Alone at the restaurant, I ate lunch as usual. When I went out to take my usual walk, I met the Panamanian minister, who had arrived a day early. We met up with Dr. Despradel and took our usual walk. News from Holland, news on upcoming events in Spain, etc. I will visit the minister tomorrow at ten. It's about my case. May God hold us in His hands, and may we be able to arrange my departure for Switzerland. We're still here. I had dinner at the legation, and after listening to the radio—and what news!—I went home at eleven. I continued reading.

APRIL 1941
THURSDAY 24. ST. VALERIE. 114-251

At ten in the morning I was already at the Panamanian legation for my appointment with the minister. We talked about my departure. Despite the existence of some unfavorable circumstances or probably self-interested concurrences, the minister wants to obtain my departure for the first part of next week. His good will is evident, but decisiveness, character, continuity of effort are lacking in so serious a matter. I have only reasons for gratitude, since everything he does in my regard is voluntary and disinterested. My situation presses pleading and human sympathy almost to point of becoming demands. These ideas reflect the conversation we had; may God will that it turn into concrete action in the coming days. Permit from the police, Swiss visa. I will wait there, preparing things to welcome my loved ones and continue the itinerary.

---

108 José Enrique Rodó (1872–1917) was a Uruguayan writer, playwright, and essayist. The book of his that the *lehendakari* was reading was *Cinco ensayos: Montalvo, Ariel, Bolívar, Rubén Darío, Liberalismo y Jacobismo* (Madrid: Edit. América).

The Dominican minister wanted blinding speed. He wants to take me with him to Switzerland on Monday.

The rest of the schedule as on previous days.

APRIL 1941
FRIDAY 25. ST. MARK. 115-250

I read and studied all morning. Rodó's Spanish is marvelous. His education is exquisite. Despite our ideological difference, I think that I would have been a good friend of his. There's nothing clumsy in him; everything is of a high spiritual elegance. I'm rereading "Ariel." His essay on Bolívar is very good. The polemic on "the crucifix in the hospitals" that he titles "Liberalism and Jacobinism" has all the magnificence that can be asked of a human spirit that does not enjoy the enormous good fortune of faith. I ate lunch, and I went for a walk with the Panamanian and Dominican ministers. The Panamanian one today revealed to me the secret behind all the delays. He's sent a cable to the president of Panama, Dr. Arias, requesting authorization to act freely.[109] And I've been in Germany three and a half months! A terrible struggle in which it is necessary to combine tenacity and energy in order to obtain the objective, and discretion and delicacy in order not to wound susceptibilities or arouse misgivings. God understands me and helps me. Faith comes from Him. In the end, I hope that I have entered onto firm ground. The rest of the day as usual.

APRIL 1941
SATURDAY 26. ST. ANACLETUS. 116-249

Early this morning, the Panamanian minister appeared in my room. He told me that Consul Guardia had arrived in Hamburg and had told him over the telephone that it is impossible for now to obtain the permit for Mrs. Guerra and her children. He invited me to go to Hamburg. I accepted. One more thing. It doesn't surprise me. Things get half done. A great [*Crossed out*: frivolity] lightheartedness prevails

---

109 Arnulfo Arias Madrid (1901–1988) was a nationalist Panamanian politician. His political program took shape in the so-called Panamanian Doctrine, which rejected foreign intervention and called for reforming and modernizing efforts. He was elected president of the republic three times, holding that position in 1940–41, 1948–51, and 1968. Each time, he was deposed by a coup d'état.

in the actions. They're not attacked in depth. My soul has become used to blows of all kinds, and I always remind myself of those who suffer or have suffered more. So we will see what news Guardia brings from Belgium. President Arias still has not answered. Will the telegram have been dispatched in Berlin? That doubt isn't mine, it's the Dominican minister's. I don't believe it, I can't believe it. Dr. Despradel is leaving for Switzerland on Monday. He wanted to take me with him. But it can't be. I hope that Dr. Villalaz will do things well this time. I spoke with the Venezuelan minister. He has filed a complaint with the ministry. We'll see what comes of it. After three and a half months! In the end, I had lunch alone, I spent the afternoon at the legation as usual, I ate dinner there, and home at eleven.

APRIL 1941
SUNDAY 27. ST. ANASTASIUS. 117-248

Mass as usual. Today a Dominican friar preached in his habit. I mention this because all traces of habits or cassocks disappeared from the streets some time ago. Except for a few rare nuns. An apologetic sermon from the sound of it; I imagined the arguments from certain words. I had lunch at the Dominican minister's house. The secretary of the Cuban legation and his wife were also invited. A friendly and cultured couple who observed the grave Dr. Álvarez with attention and respect. We then went for a walk with the Panamanian minister. This minister told us that Petsamo is open starting this week, and consequently, the Swedish border is also. We again turned our gaze in that direction. Tomorrow I'm accompanying the Panamanian minister to Hamburg. We'll meet Guardia there and make a plan. May God grant us definitive success. We suppose that Mrs. Guerra's permit will also come through. The Dominican minister is leaving for Switzerland tomorrow. We said goodbye with much emotion. I don't know whether I will see him again here. How grateful I am to him and his wife! May God grant them the good fortune I desire for them. The rest as always.

APRIL 1941
MONDAY 28. ST. VITALIS. 118-247

I got up at six a.m. The Panamanian minister and I left for Hamburg on the 7:30 train. We had breakfast on the train. We arrived in Hamburg at 11:15. Guardia was waiting for us. The minister went to see to his affairs. Guardia told me in detail everything he could about the friends in Belgium. I received two letters from Juan and Xabier.[110] Many of the stories pained me. I expected it all, nothing took me by surprise. But how one feels these things and this situation inside! With God's help, everything will be sorted out. He knows well that I have done everything that was within my power. Guardia will stay on here and will come with me to Sweden or Switzerland. Then he will seek out Mrs. Guerra. The minister is still waiting for the cable from President Arias. We were expecting it today, and it hasn't arrived. What can be happening? Everything is disquieting when one is waiting and waiting. Tomorrow I'll go to the travel agency with the minister. After getting information, we'll see whether it's possible to reserve passages. We returned at 3:15. In Berlin at seven. I had dinner with the Panamanian minister at the legation. We walked for a while, and home at ten with my thoughts and those of the others weighing me down. Gracia has died.[111] I prayed for him (may he rest in peace). He was a good and honorable man. God will have received him.

APRIL 1941
TUESDAY 29. ST. PETER MARTYR. 119-246

This morning I went to the legation, where I had an appointment with Minister Villalaz. We went to the American travel agency. They told us that there is a direct ship from Sweden to New York that will certainly leave at the beginning of June. We can book passage on the 6th. In the face of a flanking move by the minister, I indicated to him that it was better for him to make a strong push for my visas instead of leaving it to the agency, which the employee said could obtain them. If difficulties arise and I am alone, days and days will be lost. And meanwhile the telegram from President Arias has not arrived. And the one that was sent from here was in cypher, but what cypher! May God hold us in His hands. I spent a day of deep unease. We sent word to Guardia to

---

110 Agirre refers to his brother Juan Mari and to Francisco Javier Landaburu.
111 Juan Gracia Colás (1888–1941), a Basque socialist leader, was part of the Bizkaia Defense Committee (*Junta de Defensa de Bizkaia*) during the Spanish Civil War and occupied the post of social welfare minister when the Basque government was formed. In June 1940, with no mechanical means of transportation by which to flee Paris, he tried to escape the French capital on foot, heading toward southern France. Outpaced by the occupying troops, he had to retrace his steps and return to the city on the Seine, where he died on April 1, 1941.

come to Berlin. As if he had guessed it, my friend Guardia suddenly appeared. The minister, Guardia, and I had dinner together. Tomorrow the minister will accompany me to the police to see about arranging the visa for Sweden. At 10:30, we retired.

APRIL 1941
WEDNESDAY 30. ST. CATHERINE OF S. 120-245

April came to a close with great good fortune. This morning the minister, Guardia, and I went to the police. Objective: request my exit visa for Sweden. After a brief explication and telling us that for Sweden the answer was no, the police chief consulted his superiors, and they answered affirmatively. I now have the German exit visa! Since tomorrow is a holiday, we will request the Swedish entry visa at the requisite consulate the day after tomorrow. It's necessary to hurry. The cypher . . .! We left satisfied. We visited the Venezuelan minister, who informed us that he has composed an energetic note and that he visited the official responsible for these matters at the German ministry. He hopes that Mrs. Guerra's case will be resolved quickly. Since it seems that there is a ship from Sweden on June 6, it's necessary to hurry to see whether we can make that ship for New York. God helps a little bit every day. Since today was a noteworthy day, I invited the minister and Guardia to have dinner at the Krauzler. We spent a good while there, until 10:30, when we went home.

NOTES

[*In the upper margin*: APRIL 1941

Tuesday 1—]

Because I was distracted, I filled the pages corresponding to April 1, 2, and part of 3 with addresses. They're substituted here, except for the one for the 3rd.

I was reading this morning, having already lost hope that the Dominican minister would return today, when a telephone call announced his arrival and an invitation to have lunch in his company. I arrived, we exchanged impressions. Kind as always, he explained his plan to me. Dr. Villalaz arrives tomorrow. We determined to find out what will be best. Have the two of you requested a visa for me in Switzerland? I asked. No, they answered. What can we do? This will mean new delays, because if the request is made here, they will consult Bern, and God only knows how long this back-and-forth will take. Since his good will is beyond doubt and his friendship is generous, there's nothing I can say. We went for a walk, and I spent the afternoon at the legation. I had dinner in his company, and we listened to the radio, discussing the events in Yugoslavia and the taking of Asmara.[112] I had a good day. Home at eleven.

NOTES

[*In the upper margin*: APRIL 1941
Wednesday—2.]

Today was a good day. I spent the morning reading Gay. His prejudice is premeditated. He accumulates quotations—facile erudition, it's enough to copy—and criticizes democracy, but he says nothing about the regime of freedom. He stops there. When it comes time to move on from criticism to a solution, he says even less. The same as always. Agreed on the reform of the democratic system, but between freedom and tyranny, which one do these ivory-tower critics choose? I had lunch alone. I took a walk with the Dominican minister. We went to the legation. At four a letter arrived from Washington. They received mine! It was delivered to Inchausti! They know about all my affairs! Praise be to God! Finally, I'm calm, because the reins are in good hands. The letter from the Dominican minister in Washington was short, clear, and expressive.[113] He carried out the commission and will help with everything. One unknown has been cleared up. God will clear up the rest. I had dinner at the legation. We celebrated the news with Burgundy wine. We listened to the radio. Good news. To sleep satisfied at 11:30.

---

112 The *lehendakari* is referring to the coup d'état that took place in Belgrade on March 27, 1941, carried out by the army and supported by the United Kingdom, against the government that, due to German pressure, had signed the Tripartite Pact on the 25th of the same month. At the same time, he also makes reference to the British capture of the Eritrean capital, Asmara, on April 1.
113 At the time and until September 1941, the Dominican minister in the United States was Andrés Pastoriza.

MAY 1941
THURSDAY 1. STS. PHIL. AND JAMES. 121-244

Today is a holiday, Labor Day. And in effect, everything is closed despite the war. The events and parades of normal times have been cancelled. I was sorry for it, since to judge by the photographs, they were still sights worth seeing. We took a walk along Unter der Linden. We had lunch at one of the restaurants in that area and then walked as far as the War Museum. There we saw the famous plaque from Sarajevo that memorialized Princip, the student who provided the pretext that sparked the previous war by killing the Austrian archduke in 1914.[114] This plaque has been brought and put on exhibit by the Germans. We contacted the minister. He told us that he would come to meet us in his car. He took us for a ride to the Kurfürstendam in his car. We had dinner at a classic restaurant as Guardia's guests. We went home at ten. Yesterday there was a bombing raid, although not a very significant one. Tomorrow to see about the Swedish visa. May it be God's will that they grant it quickly. So May begins, the month that I hope will be the definitive one.

MAY 1941
FRIDAY 2. ST. ATHANASIUS. 122-243

This morning, accompanied by Consul Guardia, I went to the Swedish consulate. The consul received us. In response to our visa request, he replied that in order to grant a visa, it's necessary to demonstrate that the passages have already been obtained, by means of a notification that the Swedish navigation company has to send to the Swedish authorities. They gave me some papers that have to be filled out. They promised to telephone if necessary. Consequently, we called Dr. Despradel in Switzerland and dictated a telegram to Inchausti, asking him to send it by way of the Dominican minister in Washington. He promised to do it right away today. In the telegram, I asked him to pay for and reserve the passages in Gothenburg in order to be able to obtain the visa here with this formality. But my God, how much back-and-forth! I'm afraid that the passages will be sold out, according to what they told us at the

---

114 Gavrilo Princip (1894–1918), a member of the organization *Ujedinjenje ili Smrt* (Unification or Death), also known as the Black Hand (*Crna Ruka*), which called for the incorporation of Bosnia-Herzegovina, then under Austro-Hungarian imperial administration, into Serbia, assassinated the heir to the Austro-Hungarian throne, Franz Ferdinand, and his wife, Sophia Chotek, in Sarajevo on June 28, 1914.

travel agency. Everything will depend on the lucky actions that may be taken. Guardia is leaving for Hamburg tomorrow. He's written a very well-conceived letter to Mr. Abreu about Mrs. Guerra's case.[115] In the end, after dinner we went for a walk with Minister Villalaz, and at 9:30 we were already at home. I read and wrote.

M A Y 1941
SATURDAY 3. FEAST OF THE HOLY CROSS. 123-242

Mari's saint's day. I remember, thinking about what will be best for her and the others. Guardia left for Hamburg today to do it. His activity with regard to my case has been very good. Thanks to his decisiveness, the permit was obtained. He pushed the minister. I was left alone again, even if the good Dr. Villalaz, who is very attentive, invited me to have coffee with him in the afternoon. After an hour in his company, back to solitude. The minister informed me that something important is going to happen next Monday. The source is reliable; he's in the *alderdi del buru*.[116] Russia? Spain? And I'm thinking about my own concerns; if it's the former, our travel to Sweden will be in danger. The latter is already known, but it seems that the time has come. All the attempted solutions having collapsed, a profound constitutive period is again opening on the peninsula, during which my compatriots will have something to say. May God guide their minds so that intelligence governs the solutions. I ate lunch and dinner alone. I went home at nine and wrote down as many details of my case and those of my loved ones as came to mind for Dr. Villalaz to take to Switzerland so that he and Dr. Despradel can telegraph, confer, and arrange everything.

---

115 Pedro Abreu was the Venezuelan consul in Antwerp. It is appropriate to note that there is convincing evidence that he worked for the German secret services from at least June 1941, and so shortly after these contacts with the *lehendakari*. His reports for the Germans were not limited to his time as a diplomat in Europe, and he continued spying for the Third Reich after his return to Venezuela in June 1942. J. C. Jiménez de Aberasturi, in *De la derrota*, 271–72.

116 *Alderdi del buru* means "the leader's party" in Euskara and refers in this case to the Nazi Party.

MAY 1941
SUNDAY 4. ST. MONICA. 124-241

After hearing mass, I spent the morning at home, until one, when I visited the Panamanian minister in order to determine the time at which I was to see him in the afternoon. I then ate lunch alone, and afterward I retired to the hotel, where I spent the time until 6:30 preparing all the letters and copies of telegrams that the minister will take to Switzerland and that have to do with my embarkation for Sweden. Opportunely, since a telegram was received today from Washington giving Inchausti's address. Thank God! The telegram sent from Switzerland reached its intended destination. At 6:30, I was at the legation, where there also arrived an old employee of the Spanish embassy named Méndez who serves as a letter-carrier. The conversation was about "Spain and its regions," as Monzón would say, and the answers to our questions could have made the whole world laugh.[117] People and things paraded past with the appropriate characterizations, without forgetting the treasures seized even by the one who was sitting there listening to such a strange tale. Home at ten, thinking about how history is made.

MAY 1941
MONDAY 5. ST. PIUS V. 125-240

By ten a.m. I was in Dr. Villalaz's office. We went out to mail several letters, among them one from Guardia for Dr. Abreu. In the letter, he tells him about having requested the passages and includes various instructions concerning Mrs. Guerra's case. I handed in a personal letter for the Dominican minister with a detailed account of my current situation and the communications he should send to America until the Swedish passages are assured. The Panamanian minister is personally carrying this letter and a copy of the telegram to the Panamanian consul in Gothenburg. I hope that they will act rapidly, posting the dispatches and holding the meetings. Since it seems that the ship for New York leaves on the 20th, there is no time to waste.

---

117 Telesforo Monzón Ortiz de Urruela (1904–1981), a Basque nationalist leader who took charge of the interior department when the Basque government was formed. Once France was occupied by the Germans, he managed to embark on the *Alsina* and reach Mexico, where he continued his political work at the head of the Basque government's delegation in that country.

I ate lunch alone. The minister left for Zurich at 4:30. I have been left absolutely alone once more. I took refuge in a movie theater until dinnertime. Home at ten. I read Rodó's study of Montalvo.

MAY 1941
TUESDAY 6. ST. JOHN BEFORE THE LATIN GATE. 126-239

This morning I was visited in my hotel room by a friend of Guardia's who thought that he was in Berlin. He's a Chilean who is studying philosophy and legal history in Berlin in hopes of becoming a professor in his country. A serious and cultured man. Over the course of more than two hours, we went through a century and a half of philosophy until reaching our own day. At the end, he asked me whether I had studied at the Sorbonne. In sum, it seems that I didn't make a complete fool of myself. I spent an entertaining morning, and I obtained important clarifications about the magnificent "academic freedom" that is enjoyed here. I had lunch alone and went for a walk alone with my thoughts. Then to the movies, my resource for the long hours of the afternoon. It was the story of the South African president Krüger and the Boer War.[118] English tyranny and its horrors. When will these unworthy oppressions end, those of the South, those of the North, and those in between! Because on the other side they will show the same themes with different protagonists. And the weak, the oppressed are always the ones suffering. I had dinner and was home at nine. I read.

MAY 1941
WEDNESDAY 7. ST. STANISLAUS. 127-238

The anniversary of *aita*'s saint's day. I remember and ask him to help us all from heaven. Today would have been his sixty-eighth birthday.

In the morning, I headed to the Dominican legation. I did not find the lady who takes care of affairs in the minister's absence. They told me that she would not be there during the afternoon either. I left

---

118 Probably the German propaganda film *Ohm Krüger*, made by Hans Steinhoff in 1941 with Emil Jannings playing Paul Krüger.

The Boer Wars, for their part, saw the British Empire fighting the Afrikaner colonists of the Transvaal Republic and the Orange Free State. The first war took place between 1880 and 1881, and the second between 1899 and 1902. The film that the *lehendakari* saw referred to this second conflict.

telephoning the minister in Switzerland until tomorrow. Will news have come from America regarding the passages? This solitude and lack of communication are always painful. Not a word from Belgium. Will Guardia's letter arrive in time? After lunch, I walked for a while. It rained quite a bit. To the movies to pass a few hours. I ate dinner alone across from the boarding house. Beer has begun to be rationed. I retired at nine and started reading Plutarch again. Today was the turn of the life of Alexander the Great. The itinerary followed seems relevant today, even the picturesque description of the "naphtha liquor" or liquid that spreads as it burns. Then, they didn't know its applications; today, blood is shed to possess it. But geography sets its own laws ... Today makes four months that I've been in Germany.

MAY 1941
THURSDAY 8. ST. DESIDERATUS. 128-237

Anniversary of the trip to Belgium. A year already!
In the morning, I headed for the Dominican legation, where they gave me a telegram from Washington informing me that the money needed to cover the passages and the expenses had been sent to Nordisk Resenbyrå. How much gratitude I owe to the kindness of my friend Inchausti! Just at that moment, providentially, Minister Despradel called from Zurich. I was able to tell him the news and ask him to send a new cable asking whether the reservation of the passages has been confirmed, in addition to the payment. I also asked him to see to it that Minister Villalaz dispatched the telegram I wrote for him to the Panamanian consul in Gothenburg, which Despradel tells me he hasn't even shown him. What lack of a sense of reality! And what reality! Minister Despradel will do it all. He is a great friend. After eating lunch alone, I went for a walk and to the movies. Later, I read the life of Pompey in Plutarch. I ate dinner, and at nine I continued reading Plutarch. Pharsalia and its antecedents are an exact summary of the current struggle. Pompey did not know how to wait. Ah! knowing how to wait ... The alarm sounded at one. Without incident.

MAY 1941
FRIDAY 9. ST. GREGORY OF NAZ. 129-236

I continued studying grammar and also reading Plutarch. It was Julius Caesar's turn. Before lunch, taking advantage of the good weather, I went for a half-hour walk. After lunch, I continued walking and did so for three hours straight. I went through working-class neighborhoods where one sees the faces and clothes of needy people in wartime. At six, I arrived in my room, where I was very glad to sit down. I must have walked around twelve kilometers [seven miles]. It reminded me of other walks approximately a year ago.[119] Better not to remember them. Back to the restaurant at 7:30. Obligatory fish dinner. Twice a week, Tuesdays and Fridays. Back home at nine to continue reading Plutarch. Anthony came on stage, that magnificent figure full of grandeur and of brutal vices who along with Cleopatra has filled so many pages of literature and music. Still without news from Belgium. God will provide. Tomorrow I will ask whether there's been any answer from New York about reserving the passages.

MAY 1941
SATURDAY 10. ST. ANTONINUS. 130-235

In the morning, I studied and read. I took a short walk before lunch. I had lunch alone, as is now my custom. Afterward, I went to a movie theater. A very interesting Swedish film about whaling. It's the second time I've seen it, but what matters is to pass the time. Then I took another walk, and summoned by the bells of the church I go to, I went in. People were confessing. Due to the language difficulty, it's been a while since I've confessed. I made up my mind, and between Italian, Latin, and Spanish, or rather in an Italo-Hispanic Latin, I made myself understood. The confessor, apparently little versed in these languages, answered in German. I don't think he understood much of what I said. I understood nothing of what he said. But God understood both of us, which is what matters. After eating dinner alone, I retired at nine and meditated on the American campaign. I'm building castles in the air, and I still don't have the Swedish visa. And still nothing from Belgium. But God is above us all, and everything will come.

---

119 The *lehendakari* is referring to his attempts, together with his family and several dozen Basques living in Belgium, to reach the French border and flee the German invasion, as recounted in his mentioned book, *De Guernica*.

MAY 1941
SUNDAY 11. ST. MAMERTUS. 131-234

I arrived at the church early this morning. It must have been about eight. The doors hermetically sealed. After going back to the boarding house, I returned at nine. The doors were still closed. After a while, some worshippers began to arrive. They gathered at the door. I waited with them. At a quarter to ten, the sacristan arrived. They asked him to open the church. But since five minutes to ten seems to be set as the opening time, it was necessary to wait in an unpleasant temperature and even with snowflakes falling. This spirit of adherence to regulations is not compatible with common human sympathy. Finally, we entered the church. They distributed communion. Quite a few worshippers took communion. I returned to the boarding house to have breakfast and then heard mass at eleven-thirty. I still don't understand the liturgical and service schedule of these good Germans. Several times now I've found the doors closed at reasonable hours. How much it reminds me of our neck of the woods ... ! I spent the day alone. The movies in the afternoon to distract my mind from the same thoughts and the same irremediable worries. And time passes and the tickets are running out ... Patience and faith once again.

MAY 1941
MONDAY 12. ST. NEREUS. 132-233

They telephoned me very early from the Dominican legation to inform me that a telegram had arrived from Washington in which Minister Pastoriza indicated that all the instructions sent in our cables from Switzerland had been carried out. I went to the legation and had the good luck that they connected me with Switzerland in five minutes (naturally in the name of the legation and only with Switzerland), and so I was able to talk to Dr. Despradel. I informed him in full, and he agreed to send a telegram to the Swedish company asking whether the passages have been reserved. The minister will arrive in Berlin Thursday. We'll see whether things get sorted out and move in such a way that we or I can leave before May 25. The rest will be done from Gothenburg. I continue in the greatest solitude. I'm finishing the Psalms and have started in on Proverbs. Little by little, and using it as a topic for meditation. Eternal language, eternal doctrine, and eternal application. I also continued reading Demosthenes in Plutarch.

MAY 1941
TUESDAY 13. ST. SERVAIS. 133-232

This morning, the Venezuelan minister called me. He invited me to lunch. When I arrived at the Bristol, he told me that Mrs. Guerra is arriving tomorrow. And he showed me a letter from Consul Abreu. I hurried to make the hotel preparations, went to the station to be familiar with the routes, informed myself about the train schedule. By that time it was eight; I had dinner and was home at nine. I give thanks to God. Today Psalm 107 came up, and I read there, as something signaled by Providence, "Praise Yahweh, for He is good, for His mercy endures forever. Let the redeemed of Yahweh say so, those whom He has redeemed from the power of the enemy. And those whom He has gathered from the lands of the east and of the west, from the north and from the sea. They wandered lost in the desert, in a trackless solitude, finding no inhabited city. Hungry and thirsty, their soul fainted within them. But having cried out to Yahweh in their anguish, He freed them from their afflictions. And He led them by a straight path, that they might come to an inhabited city." Yesterday I remembered them all when saying Psalm 102, "He will have regarded the prayer of the solitary and will not have cast aside their plea. To hear the groaning of the prisoners, to release those sentenced to death." Day by day, the designs of the Most High will be fulfilled. It is enough to have faith and act.

MAY 1941
WEDNESDAY 14. ST. BONIFACE. 134-231

I got up at six-thirty. I was at the Friederichenstrasse station by 7:30. A long wait, because the train from Brussels arrived with about an hour's delay. It was after nine. Mrs. Guerra and her children arrived. I waited for them alone, with an emotion that I need not describe. We took a taxi to the Hotel Majestic, where we installed ourselves. Good fortune does not arrive singly. They notified me from the Dominican legation that a telegram had just arrived from Washington saying that Nordisk Resenbyrå had informed them that they had sent the necessary and awaited telegram to the Swedish legation in Berlin. Tomorrow I will speak with the Venezuelan minister to see about concluding this affair immediately. Minister Despradel will arrive tomorrow. What I would like is that we would leave on Sunday, acting quickly and having obtained American and Swedish visas for Mrs. Guerra and the Swedish one for me. May God help us as He has up to now. The account that the lady gave me of the situation of our relatives fills me with pain. As does the situation of so many friends. God well knows what my intentions have been and are. I move forward with faith to put them into action. But how many wounds and sorrows along the way . . . !

MAY 1941
THURSDAY 15. ST. DYMPHNA. 135-230

This morning I notified the Venezuelan minister that Mrs. Guerra had arrived very well, together with her children. That I have installed myself with them at the Hotel Majestic, which is discreet, in a good location, and comfortable without being luxurious. Yesterday I called the minster without being able to find him. We made an appointment for eleven. I left the Hotel Adlon. Mrs. Guerra, after finding out whether the American consulate is open for business in the afternoon, was supposed to visit the Venezuelan minister at 2:30 p.m. She did so. She kept calm, even though the chancellor of the legation, who is "also" from Mérida in Venezuela, ended up with something of a frown on his unsociable face. He wanted news from home, but Mrs. Guerra "left" Venezuela at the age of four. There was neither news nor a greater motive for local curiosity, just the frown. The legation notified the American consulate, they said. I accompanied the lady to that consulate after the legation. It wasn't here, despite what they said at the Venezuelan legation. The American consul was pleasant, polite, magnificent. He finally granted the visa. There remained the questionnaire, fingerprints, etc., conducted by an embittered "old maid" who cut no corners in asking her questions. The lady was brave. Tomorrow they will turn over the rest of the papers when the photos are handed in. Then we took a walk through Berlin.

MAY 1941
FRIDAY 16. ST. UBALD. 136-229

I was at the Hotel Adlon by 10:30 and found the Venezuelan minister waiting for me. We agreed that I would accompany Mrs. Guerra to the Swedish consulate. The minister will speak with the Swedish minister if we advise him that there are difficulties. It's already a variation from yesterday's plan, a step down. In the end, to the consulate alone. We waited an hour and filled out the forms; they received us at one. The consulate has the notification and a deposit in dollars verified by Nordisk Resebyrå. In sum, some confusion, since the information from America was that the passages were paid. Why did Nordisk send the money at the disposition of the Berlin legation? They agreed to clarify the matter by telegraphing Stockholm and Nordisk. The photos weren't ready at four, but rather tomorrow at ten. Nevertheless, the American consulate issued all the documentation, which can be picked up tomorrow once the photos are delivered and attached. I waited in the street for an hour and a half, entertaining the children, who are tired and perplexed by so much running up and down. In the afternoon, after lunch, the Dominican minister had coffee with us. Informed of everything, he will act. I had dinner at his house, and the lady at the hotel with the children.

MAY 1941
SATURDAY 17. ST. PASCHAL BAYLON. 137-228

In the morning I accompanied Mrs. Guerra to pick up the photographs for the American documents. Then I went to the Hotel Adlon, where I conversed with the Venezuelan and Dominican ministers. We hoped for an answer today from the Swedish legation, with whose minister Dr. Zérrega spoke. We went to the Swedish legation. Mrs. Guerra first had to stop at the American consulate again so that they could take the children's fingerprints. At the Swedish legation, they told us that they were expecting word from Stockholm by five p.m. That we should call at five-thirty. Invited by the Dominican minister, we had lunch at his house. As kind and generous as always. The minister went out after receiving a call from Dr. Zérrega. They agreed to visit the Swedish minister on Monday to see about obtaining the visa even if we don't have paid passages, but rather potential ones. The move was opportune, since speaking with the Swedish legation at five-thirty, they confirmed to me that the ship is probably full and its departure uncertain in view of still-incomplete arrangements. New difficulties. We had dinner at the hotel.

MAY 1941
SUNDAY 18. ST. VENANT. 138-227

In the morning I accompanied Mrs. Guerra to the church, together with the two children, who could not be left alone at the hotel. The little boy was unable to be quiet even for an instant after the first half hour. The mass lasted more than an hour with the sermon, and this was more than his two-and-a-half-year-old brain had room for. The girl was very formal. We had lunch at the hotel with the Dominican minister as our guest. Afterward, we went for a walk with this great friend. Then to his house so that the children could play with his daughter's toys (she is away in Switzerland today), and the adults could converse and then have dinner in his company. We retired to the hotel at nine. During the day, the Dominican minister was twice called by his Venezuelan colleague, who was worried about the affair of the Swedish visa. Tomorrow they will both visit the Swedish minister to see about getting this matter definitively sorted out. May God permit it. It is to be hoped that this final step that has been so long in gestation will be brought to a fortunate completion.

MAY 1941
MONDAY 19. ST. PETER CEL. 139-226

[*In the upper margin*: Teodoro's saint's day.[120] May he continue being a good man, and everything else will come in addition. So I hope.]

In the morning, after breakfast, Mrs. Guerra kindly sorted out my suitcases. I don't know how, but there where everything was stuffed and full, she found sufficient space to put in some of the children's clothes. A woman's hands! After lunch, I visited the Dominican minister. I took a walk with him so as not to interrupt our usual stroll. During the walk, he informed me that the Swedish minister has given them an appointment for tomorrow. He will attend the meeting with Dr. Zérrega. This is the final step for departing and taking flight. After so much time, will God have so disposed? Tomorrow is *ama*'s saint's day. Is it childish to suppose that it's a coincidence, that the prayers that she and our loved ones raise up to the Most High will obtain it? Faith can do so much! Afterward, around four-thirty, we took the children to the zoo. We all enjoyed ourselves. We went about as if we owned the place. If children have guardian angels, I must be a member of their society, to judge by the special protection that surrounds me. Dinner at eight. I went back to the legation. The radio. Hess's flight.[121] Then home.

---

120 Teodoro Agirre Lekube (1917–1974) was the *lehendakari*'s brother.
121 Rudolf Hess (1894–1987) was the Führer's lieutenant and a minister without portfolio. On May 10, 1941, he flew from Augsburg to Scotland, with the intention, he said, of trying to negotiate peace with the United Kingdom.

MAY 1941
TUESDAY 20. ST. BERNARDINE. 140-225

Amama's saint's day.[122] Our prayers and those of the children mingle, asking that God give her the best days of her life, enjoying them in the peace won by sacrifice and amid the love of all of us who owe her a firm and severe education and have seen her pass through life amid so much misfortune and so much sorrow. Today the Dominican and Panamanian ministers visited the Swedish minister. They returned with a favorable impression. The Swedish minister promised to dispatch a telegram requesting authorization to give us the visas. In the afternoon I took Mrs. Guerra and the children to visit Unter der Linden and the old monumental district. Upon returning, we had dinner at the hotel. At nine, we received a note from the Dominican minister and word by telephone from the Swedish embassy. The visas! But we had first finished praying the rosary. Tomorrow we have to pick up this final step, so much hoped-for and so fortunately obtained by our friends the ministers. A good end to our *ama*'s saint's day. May God continue helping us, even though we do not sufficiently deserve it. We rested well satisfied.

MAY 1941
WEDNESDAY 21. ST. VALENCE. 141-224

In the morning, we were expecting a call from the Swedish legation, and when it didn't come, I called myself. They gave me an appointment for five p.m. We had lunch at the beer garden across from my old boarding house. At five, I was at the Swedish consulate. They made me wait until six to give me the visa, which had to be signed in Tiergarden, that is, at the legation, quite a distance from the consulate. I was accompanied by a legation usher, who as a good "sportsman" rejected taxis (admittedly not very abundant), because he wanted to get some exercise, despite the heat. Result: I started sweating halfway there. Finally, the legation, and later the signing of the visa. Thank God, we finished all the procedures. We're planning the journey for Friday. Guardia arrived from Hamburg. He had dinner with us. His arrival brought the work he began to a close with his providential presence. We were satisfied.

---

122 *Amama* means "grandmother" in Euskara and refers here to Bernardina Lekube Aranburu (1876–1950), a native of Mutriku.

MAY 1941
THURSDAY 22. ASCENSION. 142-223

We've been so absorbed in visas, papers, bureaucratic procedures of all kinds, and questionnaires, that we hadn't even realized that today was the Ascension. When I set down today's notes this evening, I saw the name of the feast in the heading. May God pardon us. This life is among the best fitted to bring about this kind of forgetfulness. This morning I continued the diligences to obtain the ticket, change money, etc. They proposed traveling to the German border, that is, to the coast, by car, and I accepted, since it's comfortable and not expensive. The rest of the ticket by ship and train is via Gothenburg to Stockholm. In the afternoon, we took the large suitcases to the customs office and sent them directly to Gothenburg, where we will collect them. We had lunch as the Dominican minister's guests, and we invited him and Guardia to have dinner at the hotel to say goodbye. We enjoyed our time together. I prepared all kinds of letters for various people.[123]

MAY 1941
FRIDAY 23. ST. GUIBERT. 143-222

Finally, we left Berlin. We made the trip from Berlin to Sasnitz, the last port in Germany, in a car provided by Enrique, Minister Despradel's chauffeur. We had lunch in the preceding town, and at 3:30 we were at the German customs post. We had sent our suitcases to Gothenburg (Sweden) from Berlin. The suitcases we had left after this odyssey full of loss and spoliation. We had only small bags with us. At the border, polite behavior toward us "Latin American" foreigners. When we got on the Swedish ship, we exhaled. Finally free! But our emotion was so great that we didn't even realize it. A four-hour crossing to Trelleborg (Sweden), where we arrived at eight p.m. We got on the train that was to take us to Gothenburg, where we arrived at three in the morning. The train allows travelers to rest at the same station until eight the next morning. On the train, we said the rosary in thanksgiving. We've been through so much that it's still difficult to react fully. But faith and I don't know what fulfilled presentiment have achieved everything that seemed difficult to human strength alone.

---

123 These were three letters. One addressed to Francisco Javier Landaburu, one to Doroteo Ziaurritz, and finally a letter for the prisoners. Transcriptions of the three missives are included in this volume as appendixes 2, 3, and 4.

MAY 1941
SATURDAY 24. ST. DONATIAN. 144-221

We left the train at eight a.m. The suitcases sent yesterday from Berlin were already at the station customs office. We collected them and installed ourselves at the Kung Karl hotel. In the old style, it doesn't have the comfort of modern ones, but it's enough for us. We had breakfast, and I headed to the Dominican consulate with a recommendation from Minister Despradel. The consul was away until Monday, when I will return to greet him. I went to Nordisk Rosebyrä to see about the passages. I changed money, confirmed the passages, and turned over our passports for the extension, since the first ship will leave in mid-June, and our visa is until the 4th. Very attentive at the agency. We had lunch at the hotel. In mid-afternoon, we went for a walk through the town. The weather was better. The city is handsome. The port an important one. The children enchanted and braver than the adults. Blessed innocence! We visited the Catholic church to find out about the masses tomorrow. After dinner at a nearby restaurant, we retired to the hotel at eight-thirty.

MAY 1941
SUNDAY 25. ST. GREG. VII. 145-220

This morning we went to the church, the only Catholic one in Gothenburg. Sung mass, celebrated liturgically. Few worshippers, very serious and devout. The fruit of Gustavus Adolfus's battles in this country.[124] I had to go out into the street with Joseba during the sermon, since he couldn't keep quiet in church. During the second part of the mass, he was more formal. Aintzane was very serious. After taking a walk, we had lunch in Swedish style, watching our wallet in case of what may come. After this meal, we took a long walk through the magnificent park on the outskirts of Gothenburg, even if the rainy and damp weather took the shine off our stroll. We ate dinner at 6:30 in order to put the children to bed at eight. Before going to sleep, they said their prayers, and I told them the obligatory *ipuña*. Despite all these formalities, there was a maternal intervention with several cracks of the whip in view of Joseba's naughtiness, not letting Aintzane sleep. Then peace, and while everyone was sleeping, I continued reading and writing.

---

124 Gustavus II Adolfus (1594–1632) was king of Sweden between 1611 and 1632.

MAY 1941
MONDAY 26. ST. PHIL. N. 146-219

In the morning, I visited the Nordisk Resebyrå offices to get an answer about the visas. It's necessary to fill out various forms with the information and other personal details again. We signed the forms as a married couple, since private cabins are difficult to get on the ship. As a group of four, the possibilities are greater, from what they tell us. The difference in surnames was noted, but I don't think that this will pose an obstacle in the end. They understood it at the agency and will explain it as us having gotten married after our passports were issued. But no matter what, we're anxious to get to America! Our passports have gone to Stockholm to obtain the visa extensions. It will take another week. In these times, the difficulties multiply. We ate a cheap little lunch and dinner. Today Joseba had to kneel as a punishment. He's a devil. Mari and the little one have colds, but everyone has a good appetite, having come from a country with rationing.

MAY 1941
TUESDAY 27. ST. BEDE. 147-218

On the hotel concierge's recommendation, we went to the botanical garden, where the children had space to run around and there are services of all kinds, even a restaurant with orchestra. We had lunch there; it was very good although a little expensive. Tomorrow we'll go after eating lunch someplace else that's more economical. Life in Sweden is extraordinarily expensive. Before leaving for the botanical garden, we received a reply from Inchausti and his wife to the cable in which we announced our arrival. They kindly asked us to tell them our financial needs. We will resist as much as we can before bothering such excellent friends, but we need to make some expenditures in order to be able to present ourselves with basic decency. God presses, but He does not drown, and in cases like ours, he sends true lifelines. We had dinner in a very modest but good restaurant. Home at eight-thirty. After the obligatory *ipuña*, the children went to sleep. I'm happy that they have maintained their Euskara very well.

MAY 1941
WEDNESDAY 28. ST. GERMAIN. 148-217

This morning we went to a large department store to buy a bucket and some shovels for the children. After lunch, we went back to the botanical garden, where they've set up a small area with sand for the children. That's where the bucket and the shovels were put to use. The heat was suffocating today, especially considering the Nordic climate of these latitudes. No less than 32º [90º F] on the thermometer. We entertained ourselves at the park until 6:30, when we headed for the restaurant near the hotel where we had dinner. At 8:15, we were already in our room. Today Joseba, who is incorrigibly naughty, had to be punished again. In this way, he will come to heel little by little. With our time in the park today, we skipped the lesson on letters and numbers that I give the children, all in Euskara. *Amatxu* teaches them the catechism. We still haven't received a reply to the letters sent to Berlin. The Louvain ones will take somewhat longer.

MAY 1941
THURSDAY 29. ST. MAXIMIN. 149-216

In the morning, we took the streetcar to head to the park on the outskirts for the purpose of spending the day breathing fresh air. We had lunch there, and the children were able to play as they liked. In this life of obligatory waiting, it's necessary to invent something every day to entertain the little ones, who luckily don't understand other, more serious worries. Despite the days that have passed, our spirits are still affected by an unease that only arrival in America will be able to dispel. The work to be done and the memory of our loved ones will be motives for unease there as well, but once we have gotten away from fiction, simply being able to breathe as authentic persons will give our action the necessary energy. Our passports are in Stockholm, the departure of the ship has still not been fixed with certainty, even if the 15th has been announced as a possible date, the dangers of an extension of the war, etc., are always reason for worry. But God will facilitate things, as He has done up to now. Today, for example, we received a telegram from Berlin announcing that the bundle with Mari's overcoat, lost along the road on our trip out of Germany, had been found. We were very happy, since we don't have much to lose.

MAY 1941
FRIDAY 30. ST. FERDINAND. 150-215

Today also we headed for the park on the outskirts, a magnificent place where the children are getting some color, which they were in need of. We had a quite good lunch there and stayed until 6:30 p.m. We had dinner at a restaurant near the hotel where they know us by now and feed us well. We spent a little more than we had planned; lunch and dinner came to more than ten crowns for the four of us. Of course, this would make us laugh in peacetime, but now . . . When we arrived at the hotel, they informed us that a Nordisk employee had been there because he had something to tell me. Unease invaded us once again. We read it in Swedish, but we understood from one of the reports in the newspapers that a Gothenburg steamer has been torpedoed. Might the agency's news have to do with our voyage? Will there be difficulties? Is it about our visas? In the end, we'll know tomorrow, and to sleep with faith, keeping in mind that there are no obstacles to a firm will.

MAY 1941
SATURDAY 31. ST. ANGELA. 151-214

Today, the last day of May, we went to the church, remembering the anniversary of that unlucky May 31 last year. We prayed for Cesáreo, who died that day. We remembered Encarna's injuries and all those who suffered on that sorrowful night.[125] After some shopping, we had lunch on the terrace of a restaurant located next to and above one of the department stores. We then headed to the park on the outskirts, where the children played in one of the park's fields with lots of fresh air. The weather is splendid, strangely for this time of year. We had dinner in the park and returned at 8:30, after hearing a speech and songs by members of the Salvation Army in full swing. Listened to with respect,

---

125 On May 31, 1940, the group of Basques that included Agirre and his family were in the Belgian coastal town of De Panne/La Panne, cut off by German troops who were shelling the British as they withdrew through the town. In these circumstances, Cesáreo Asporosa Aristondo (1899–1940) went out accompanied by three women to look for a boat in which to flee to Great Britain, but he was hit and mortally wounded by a shell. He was a member of the Antwerp Basque Trade Delegation created during the war to provision Euzkadi. Encarna Agirre Lekube was also wounded on the same day when a shell hit the house where the group of Basques had taken refuge. Encarna died some days later in a hospital. Aguirre, *De Guernica*, 103–6.

they certainly deserve consideration for their good faith and as the people in this land who uphold a spirituality that is so necessary. A comical note was not lacking: three women played guitar and flugelhorn in the band. In the morning, I was at the agency. Our disquiet of yesterday was put to rest. The news was a telegram from National City Bank, that is, from Inchausti, asking about our departure date and whether there were difficulties. The agency answered well. I sent Inchausti, our good friend, another one.

NOTES

In this way, the month of May ended. Greater clarity, always relatively speaking, may in the future succeed the concision and security of the notes composed in Germany. We will surely make the trip to America around June 20, as our ship has to wait for the arrival in Swedish waters of the previous one, which seems to be arriving in an American port right now. That is, between unloading and loading plus the return trip, it may well take around twenty days. The controls are rigorous. Even here, in a free land (at least *de jure*), German and English permits are required in order to embark. As of today, we have the German one, and we hope to have the English one shortly. Then we will suffer new interventions at sea. With all these formalities, travel certainly becomes unpleasant. But for us, there is no alternative but to give thanks to God, Who seems to have pointed us out with His finger. Otherwise it's difficult to understand our case.

JUNE 1941
SUNDAY 1. PENTECOST. 152-213

Mari got up early today to go to eight o'clock mass. On account of the feast day and because it's become necessary to divide our attendance at church into two shifts given the little one's behavior, since he doesn't understand long religious ceremonies. So I stayed home taking care of them in the morning and attended the second mass, which is at eleven. We then spent the day at the botanical garden, enjoying a very pleasant temperature; the children played on the artificial beach. After eating dinner at the Saturno restaurant, which we are attached to as a consequence of its economical prices (dinner for four cost us six crowns), we retired to the hotel at 8:30.

A great deal of movement is evident during these Pentecost holidays. The villagers come to town, and the inhabitants of Gothenburg go out to the country. The elevated standard of living and the polite behavior of all social strata are noteworthy. A model to imitate. We still haven't received letters from anyone. We write to the family every three days.

JUNE 1941
MONDAY 2. ST. POTIN. 153-212

Today the second day of Pentecost is celebrated in Sweden with an absolute stoppage of work. The bells have rung continuously, both from the several different Protestant churches and from the one Catholic one. We attended the high mass at this church, of course, and I went for a walk with Joseba during the sermon. We spent the day at an amusement park for children that was open because of the holiday. There we forgot all our sufferings for a good while. I went on the merry-go-round with the children and then on the electric cars and the roller coasters. Today we lived through the children. They've continued their lives, which we cannot and should not infect with our worries. Would that everyone was able to take care of his children the way that God has willed that I was able to today! During these holidays, I have asked the Lord that His Spirit may descend on all men of good will who are fighting for the freedom of the Basque fatherland, uniting them in one faith, one heart, and one coming reality.

JUNE 1941
TUESDAY 3. ST. CLOTILDE. 154-211

We made today a country day. In the morning, we went to the market. There Mari bought some cold cuts and fruit with which she put together the day's menu. This diet did not go unnoticed by the little ones, since Joseba especially, who asked twice for an afternoon snack, indicated his vote against such novelties. We got fresh air and sunshine. We were expecting a letter from Berlin and some kind of telegram from New York today. They haven't arrived. We'll hope for tomorrow, since these Pentecost holidays are celebrated very extensively in these countries, and no one works. During these days, we've been able to observe native types, even in their picturesque national dress. The Swedish people are physically of great beauty; their life is tranquil, and their ordinary way of life denotes abundance. The dry politeness of their behavior and the lack of drama or expressiveness in their manners suggest a certain coldness, but the overall impression is of strong, consistent manners that attracts sympathy. We're thinking a great deal about all our loved ones without exception, remembering especially the ones in Louvain. We're anxiously awaiting news of them.

JUNE 1941
WEDNESDAY 4. ST. OPTATUS. 155-210

This morning I visited the agency to find out whether there had been any news from America or about our visas in Stockholm. They didn't know anything yet. On the other hand, they did know that our departure will be delayed another few days, certainly into the first week of July. This news came as a blow to us, not only because it extends our uncertainty, in view of the international situation and in view of our personal one, but also on account of our financial situation, which is always delicate, given that we are dependent on our friends' generosity. In these circumstances, in view of the extraordinary cost of living in Sweden, another two weeks are a serious problem. In the end, nothing is irremediable while we have our lives and our honor. The delay in our departure is due to the fact that the ship whose return to Swedish waters will mark the departure of ours has reached New York safely, but its return voyage to Sweden depends on when the loading of its cargo is finished. Given the crowding in that port, it's been ordered to wait.

We spent the day at the botanical garden. The children arrived at the hotel so dirty that you couldn't recognize them. Water was put to work. We still have no letters.

JUNE 1941
THURSDAY 5. ST. BONIFACE. 156-209

This morning we received a cable from our great friend Inchausti. He covered our financial needs and urged us to use as much as we need. Our gratitude for his generosity can be imagined. God grant that one day we'll be able to repay him for so much sacrifice and so much kindness. With this money we were able to acquire some things, shoes and the indispensable improvement in our clothing situation in order to be able to present ourselves decently in America. Everything is expensive, and our crowns go quickly. We left the less indispensable items for the end.

Only God knows what we've lost by this time, but His help is more visible every day. We had lunch at the restaurant of a large department store, and after another tour through the streets and shops, we arrived at the hotel, where Joseba had to be shut up in the children's room. Once the situation and our authority had been reestablished, we went out to eat dinner at a nearby restaurant and retired to the hotel again at 8:30. We still have no news from Berlin or Louvain and no communication with the world, since we don't understand Swedish.

JUNE 1941
FRIDAY 6. ST. NORBERT. 157-208

Early on we met a young employee of Nordisk Resebyrä who speaks French very well. His wife, who is Norwegian, also speaks it perfectly. Today she accompanied Mari on a shopping trip to buy some things. I went with Aintzane and Joseba to pick up the money Inchausti sent and then to the port, where the little questioners were given as many explanations as were requisite. We invited the Perssons to have lunch at the botanical garden restaurant in order to thank them in some way for their graciousness and friendliness.[126] In the afternoon, accompanied by Mr. Persson, we had the good fortune to attend an athletic and military gathering at the stadium. It was the king's birthday, and the armed forces, schools, and other organizations, including religious ones, celebrated the day with a joint parade. The celebration was presided over by Prince Wilhelm, the king's second son, who delivered from the platform a speech of which we did not understand a word. Magnificent gymnastic exercises by the boys and girls from the schools, refined choirs, and a military parade. A well-executed and very entertaining program. We had a good day, and the little ones were enchanted.

JUNE 1941
SATURDAY 7. ST. ROBERT. 158-207

In the morning, we did some shopping, and after lunch, we spent the afternoon at the botanical garden. Since the children have come down with a bit of a cold, we retired to the hotel at 5:30 and did not go out

---

126 Persson was an employee of the Nordisk Resebyrä travel agency. In *De Guernica*, in which the *lehendakari* describes him as sent by Providence, his surname is transformed into Petterson.

again. The streets were very lively today, since it was Saturday. The brusque transition from liveliness to an absolute, more than provincial quiet is noteworthy in this large city (it has around 300,000 inhabitants). There's a pleasant contrast between a city with all the conveniences of modern life and the simplicity of what is almost a *campagnard* life, especially once work stops. A deeply-rooted democratic sentiment can be observed, in harmony with the elevated standard of living of the working classes. The war has imposed restrictions and an increase in prices. Certainly, it is to be believed, according to what they tell us, that life in Sweden in peacetime had to be pleasant. If we have money and visas, we plan to go to Stockholm to deepen our observations of an interesting small people.

JUNE 1941
SUNDAY 8. ST. MEDARDUS. 159-206

Yesterday I failed to note that I received a letter from my excellent friend Mr. Despradel. He informed me that Enrique has now sent the bundle that was lost along the road and fortunately found. From what Don Constan indicated to us from Chile, we were expecting some news at the Chilean embassy in Berlin about that nation's passports issued to our relatives to facilitate their travel to the Americas. Nothing is known about this in Berlin. I don't think that it will be easy to sort this matter out. Just remembering our difficulties . . . We'll do as much as we can for the ones in Louvain.[127] Mari again went to mass early today. I stayed home in the role of inspector of our young pair, who are giving more trouble every day. I went to mass later. We had lunch at the botanical garden, where we stayed until 4:30. Aintzane has a sore throat and complains somewhat. Joseba has a cough, but his cold is going away. We took three photographs, plus one ruined by Joseba in the two seconds

---

127 The arrangements about which Constantino Zabala informed his son-in-law did in fact exist, as did the promises received by the Chilean Basques who met with that country's authorities to obtain the emigration of the majority of their fellow countrymen in danger in countries under Nazi occupation. Along these lines, the efforts made by Eduardo Díaz de Mendibil, at the time in exile in Chile and during his years as minister of the Spanish Republic a close collaborator of the president of the Euzkadi National Council, Irujo, bore fruit, even if only on paper, since due to the circumstances of the war, nothing came of them. In a letter of January 19, 1941, Díaz de Mendibil told Irujo, "We have recently obtained the entry into the country of all the *lendakari*'s family, which as you know is in Louvain; we made this arrangement at the request of Don Constantino Zabala." Letter from Eduardo Díaz de Mendibil to Manuel Irujo, Santiago de Chile, February 19, 1941, GE-251-1.

in which the camera fell into his power, which was enough for him to push the button. We've acquired a modest camera, thinking that these photographs will always be interesting.

JUNE 1941
MONDAY 9. ST. FELICIAN. 160-205

Some days ago now, the coastal town of Båstad was suggested to us as a good place to wait for our embarkation, since we could spend time in the sun and it's more economical. We accepted the suggestion, and today after lunch we took the train that brought us to this beach. Installed in a picturesque hotel where the first thing we encountered was a council meeting of Protestant clergy, we have a pleasant impression of the place and above all, a great feeling of satisfaction at being able to save at least a third of what we were spending in Gothenburg. Our documents cause surprise in all the hotels at which we arrive. This widow and this doctor who have no proof that they're married, trailing two small children . . . etc., etc., make the managers frown, when the obligatory questions don't arrive: if you're married, how come you don't have the same surname? . . . In sum, to fill in once again the holes in our deficient documentary situation and to wait anxiously for the embarkation that will free us from so many things, among them the disagreeable one of appearing to be what we aren't.

JUNE 1941
TUESDAY 10. ST. MARGUERITE. 161-204

Today is Margari's saint's day.[128] We remembered her several times during the day, as did the children. May God keep her in good health is what we asked.

This morning our summer optimism was quenched by a cold shower. The manager approached us to tell us that there was a mistake in the price that the Gothenburg agency fixed for our stay here and that we've paid, since it refers only to the rooms, meals not included. So much for our good spirits. The Gothenburg agency called with apologies and excuses. In sum, having been satisfied with this hotel, which we had been contemplating in admiration for its comfort and economy, making

---

128 Margari Zabala Aketxe (1908–1979), the *lehendakari*'s wife's sister.

advantageous calculations of the savings that we were obtaining from this fortunate stay, today as a result of this mistake we have to pay double, spending our last savings. It never rains but it pours. However, we haven't for this reason stopped getting out in the sun, which has been shining splendidly. They don't charge for that, fortunately, and its owner doesn't make mistakes.

JUNE 1941
WEDNESDAY 11. ST. BARNABAS. 162-203

Today when we woke up, it was pouring. The rain continued all day, preventing our outing. After so many benefits received, we can't complain, especially if, as we're told, the country people needed this rain for the growth of their crops. At the hotel, they turned on the heat. It being June, it was necessary to remember how far north we are in order to understand it. We received our passports from Gothenburg with visas nicely issued in Stockholm and good until July 16. We hope to already be on our way to New York by then. Yesterday one of the clergy participating in the Church of Sweden synod approached us. He spoke Spanish from having lived in Chile. We had an interesting conversation as fellow residents of the Western Hemisphere. We play our role very well by now. Almost, almost as if we were convinced. The mentioned synod fathers are more afraid of Hitler than of us. I gathered interesting information.

JUNE 1941
THURSDAY 12. *CORPUS CHRISTI*. 163-202

We remembered our country's great religious festivals today. Here there's not a single Catholic church even within a circle of three hours by train from this town. Our prayers stood in for the liturgical aspect of the festival. It continued to rain, and we were only able to take a walk during the morning, taking advantage of a break in the clouds. In the afternoon, at home. The radio entertained us. Fortunately, we can find out the news of the world directly these days. The evils suffered by those closest to us, and by those others who have some role to play in the efforts that our people are making and must make on behalf of their freedom, are constantly in our thoughts. The lack of communication is very hard. For this reason, we are very anxious to know the exact departure date of the ship that will free us. God, Who has smoothed our path thus far, will do the rest. Aintzane and Joseba have constitutions of iron. It's good to be grateful for this benefit, when it's a matter of children who are still so young.

JUNE 1941
FRIDAY 13. ST. ANTHONY OF P. 164-201

Today we received a letter from Enrique, the Dominican minister's secretary. The loss of the bundle with the travel rugs and Mari's overcoat has cost us 226 marks for the reward that has to be given to the person who found the items and turned them in to the police. In sum, another drain on the wallet ... And on and on ... This morning we were at the beach. We were struck to see an elderly man in his eighties, with a long white beard, plunge bravely into the water for a swim in a temperature of barely twelve degrees [54º F]. In the afternoon, we took a long walk along the seashore, which is edged with pine trees that are very reminiscent of those landscapes around Biarritz or near Txatxarramendi. We still haven't received news from Louvain, and we still don't know our ship's exact departure date. We can imagine what the anxiety of those in America must be, knowing what ours is. At the same time, the news about the spread of the war is not such as to calm one's nerves. As always, may God be with everyone.

JUNE 1941
SATURDAY 14. ST. BASIL. 165-200

Ten years ago, the Assembly of the Municipalities of Euzkadi regarding the Statute of Autonomy was held in Estella.[129] Looking back, the step our people took toward its freedom is clear to see. To somewhat impressionable minds, this affirmation will appear foolish. To those who take a long view and have a little familiarity with how freedom is won, the reverse. Beyond our people's heroic suffering, the days of happiness can be clearly perceived. Today, the problem has been delineated; tomorrow, we will enter the stage of bringing things into being. Spirits that have been prepared and tempered in study, experience, and struggle will arise. In ten years, our people has lived as it did not for centuries of its sad

---

129 On June 14, 1931, an assembly of municipal representatives was held in Estella-Lizarra to approve the draft Basque statute of autonomy developed by Eusko Ikaskuntza-Sociedad de Estudios Vascos (Society of Basque Studies).

history. Another ten will complete the work of redemption, freedom, and realization of its political and social plan.

The very mediocre weather prevented us from going to the beach. In the afternoon, we walked a good deal. Today we received the first letter from Louvain. It was from Juan Mari. With what happiness we read it! Mari answered right away today in order to keep up the contact.

JUNE 1941
SUNDAY 15. ST. MODESTE. 166-199

[*In the upper margin*: 18 Extras

3—Postage stamps]

It was raining when the sun came up this morning, and as the day went on, the rain became heavier. We spent the whole morning at the hotel. After lunch, we took a walk along the seashore. The weather was tending to improve. We ate dinner at the hotel's new pavilion over the water. It's quite reminiscent of Txatxarramendi. We retired with the children, and I went to listen to the London radio. The manager came to the radio room and wanted to hear Moscow in Swedish. She told me that the news about German-Germanic[130] relations is disturbing. They, the Swedes, are very afraid of Russia. They're afraid of getting caught up in a Russian-German conflict. I received all this news as if was just another bit of information, and nevertheless, it made me think about the thousand difficulties that will arise for our voyage. A Swedish diplomat who is living at the hotel expressed the same thoughts to Mari. Until we're on the ship, we won't rest. But everything will come about if God has so disposed.

JUNE 1941
MONDAY 16. S^E LUTGARDIS. 167-198

In the morning we made our preparations to return to Gothenburg. We haven't had good luck with the weather in Båstad. Nor where our wallets are concerned, as mentioned. Aintzane and Joseba are very happy because the Swedish diplomat who lives at the hotel gave them a good-sized rubber fish to play with in the water. We thanked him when we said goodbye. After lunch, we took the train. In Sweden as

---

130 A clear mistake. The reference should be to German-Soviet relations.

well, the war is evident even in transportation connections. Slow speeds are added on to the reduction in service. It took us four hours to go the same distance we covered in two-and-a-half hours on the way here. The little ones got somewhat tired. At the Gothenburg hotel, they gave us the same rooms we had during our previous stay. Very little activity is evident in hotels and restaurants due to the crisis produced by the war. During our trip, we saw a long German transport train. It's the price Sweden pays in exchange for its somewhat precarious neutrality.[131] They informed us that a telegram had arrived from New York.

JUNE 1941
TUESDAY 17. ST. ADOLF. 168-197

I headed for Nordisk after having received the mentioned telegram. It was from our friend Inchausti. In it, he asked me to send him our news by cable, not using the telephone, via Sweden, Berlin, and New York. To send a radiogram when the ship is two or three days from concluding its voyage. Mr. Persson wasn't at the agency. I said that I would return tomorrow. I'm preparing an answer for our friend Inchausti. It won't please him, since we still don't know the exact departure of the ship, which won't leave until the one that's in New York returns. His solicitude on our behalf is admirable. How much we owe him! Since the time of our stay here may be extended, we're starting to tighten our purse strings even further. We took a walk after lunch and retired to the hotel at eight. We listened to the London radio, a French broadcast. Before now, we hadn't used this unmatched way of getting the news directly at the hotel. Our obsession is our ship's departure. Since we've already practiced patience quite a bit, this delay finds us somewhat experienced in the matter.

JUNE 1941
WEDNESDAY 18. ST. MARCELLIAN. 169-196

Today is the anniversary of Encarna's death. We remembered her in our prayers, and we remembered those tragic moments in which the poor woman had to suffer so much due to the lack of the most minimal assistance, surely resulting in her death later on, a year ago today. May she help us all from heaven. A year has gone by, and how many things

---

131 See note 135 below.

have happened in the course of it![132] Today we received a piece of bad news. The Germans and the English can't agree on the point at which the inspection of the *Renmaren*, the ship on whose arrival in Gothenburg from New York the departure of ours depends, should take place. The delay of our departure is getting worse, and the uncertainty of the international situation (tensions in the Americas, Russian-German tensions) makes it problematic. I sent off a long telegram to Inchausti, who has been supposing that our departure would be on the 20th, to judge by another new telegram received today. I explained the situation clearly and told him that I'm preparing to travel by way of Russia and Japan if ocean traffic is suspended. Visas again. Will we obtain them? We're going back to unpleasant times.

JUNE 1941
THURSDAY 19. ST. JULIANA. 170-195

This morning, I was at the agency again. The news continues to be disturbing. My plan of traveling by way of Russia is viable if conflict doesn't break out between Germany and Russia. Viable, also, if visas are obtained. Our situation is delicate, since at the same time, German-American tensions are getting worse. At the agency, they've put our names forward for a Swedish ship that will be making, or rather is planning on making, a Gothenburg-Panama-China voyage. In that case, we would go as far as Panama. All this after our Calvary until arriving in Sweden, after already obtaining the German and English departure permits here, after changing the departure of our ship three times. In the end, God Who brought us here will guide our steps. The situation is so confused and complicated that it's impossible to risk anything. We spent the day in low spirits. We're waiting for an answer from America, where we can imagine the pain our cable will have caused them. Today we took the children to the botanical garden, where they played happily while Mari and I sunbathed and exhausted the same topic in a thousand variations.

---

132 See notes 80 and 125.

JUNE 1941
FRIDAY 20. *SACRED HEART*. 171-194

Today we received a letter from Margari. It made us very happy to receive news from Louvain. Mari answered right away today, sending not very pleasant news. With the international situation as it is these days, especially in view of the imminence of a break in German-Russian relations, our situation is very delicate. If this conflict breaks out, our travel by way of the East will be impossible, and departure by sea from here may possibly be blocked, if the Baltic and the straits that separate it from the Atlantic are declared a war zone. In sum, that these days seem serious to us and are serious in reality. I'm waiting for Inchausti's answer in order to make a quick decision, even if, in this as in everything, man proposes and God disposes. And in this disposition of the Most High all my hope resides and my faith rests. Today we took the children to the big park. I played soccer with Joseba, and in the evening I told them the usual *ipuña*. They have no reason to suffer.

JUNE 1941
SATURDAY 21. ST. ALOYSIUS DE G. 172-193

They contacted me from the agency. A telegram had arrived there from New York. I ran to visit Mr. Persson. Right as I was entering his office, a messenger brought a new telegram for me from our friend Inchausti. This excellent friend does not worry about costs. In the telegram, he said that they are starting to work on the arrangements requested in my most recent dispatch and recommended air travel to reach a location that would get me closer to America. The telegram to the agency clarified this confusing section. They're proposing travel by air to England. This news, added to the very bad news that's already circulating here in Sweden, filled us with apprehension. I composed a telegram asking that the efforts to arrange travel by the Eastern route continue. We think that traveling to England (it seems that there are planes on irregular schedules and for which it's necessary to have permits that are very difficult to obtain) has to be left as the last alternative. That has been attended to; America requires more attention. In sum, doubts and evil moments once again. We're very anxious.

JUNE 1941
SUNDAY 22. ST. PAULINUS. 173-192

Mr. Persson telephoned me this morning: The war between Germany and Russia has begun! [*Between the lines*: he told me, and] Instinctively, my spirit suffered two shocks, one of joy: Hitler is lost; the other of regret: my God, by what route will we be able to leave? Will maritime communication, suspended today, be definitively closed? Will Sweden become entangled in the war, and will we see the Germans and the *Komandantur* here again? All these anguished doubts are blows to our spirits. Nevertheless, I feel an interior calm that gives me a presentiment that there will be a solution for my individual case (which is not that individual), if I'm not confusing it with my sense of gratitude at seeing the triumph of freedom, which I have not doubted for a moment, assured. In the end, as always, God will dispose what is best. We spent the day at the big park after fulfilling our religious duties in the morning. We got some good sun amid the ordinary people, who snatched up the newspapers, listened to the radio in religious silence, and reflected their emotions and fears on their faces. It wasn't an occasion for anything less. But they were still at home . . .

JUNE 1941
MONDAY 23. ST. MARIE D'OIGN. 174-191

Mr. Persson had given me an appointment for this morning. I was punctual. Mr. Persson had not yet sent the telegram to Inchausti, since he had the feeling that something might happen overnight from Saturday to Sunday (every dictator's favorite moment), as was in fact the case. Today, in awareness of the new complication for the world, for Hitler, and for us, I composed a new dispatch without mentioning the voyage by way of the East, now naturally blocked. I asked him to send instructions to the American ambassador in Stockholm, leaving the crossing to England for the last moment and as a last solution. My desire to arrive in America has deep repercussions in my spirit. It seems that it's there that the great task is to be carried out just at this moment, the task of uniting all our compatriots behind a single impulse and a single ideal. With this solid base, the rest will be easier, including my presence in London. We were invited by Mr. Persson to his house. We continue playing our role very well. Mr. Persson continues to believe that there will be a ship and that Sweden will remain neutral. God grant it, because otherwise ...

JUNE 1941
TUESDAY 24. ST. JOHN THE BAPT. 175-190

Today is a holiday with absolutely no work in Sweden. Counting yesterday and Sunday, they take a classic long weekend, made up of three days of general vacation corresponding to the long weekend at the beginning of August in English-speaking countries. We spent the day at the big park, full of families of modest means who were enjoying the splendid sunshine. The loudspeakers amplifying the radio belonging to one of the park restaurants summoned the people to silence, and they listened religiously to the news. The German propaganda, which has been very intense here, is promoting the anti-Communist slogan again. It's a little late for that. It's a failed argument by now. The people here are essentially anti-Communist and anti-Nazi. But they all understand that the German propaganda line is governed by circumstances, since it lost sincerity and truth during a year of contacts with the Soviets.[133] When freedom triumphs, all dictatorial tyrannies will fall, whatever their color and whatever their location.

JUNE 1941
WEDNESDAY 25. ST. WILLIAM. 176-189

First thing in the morning, the hotel concierge informed me that they would call me from Washington at six p.m. I went to Nordisk, and they gave me two telegrams from our friend Inchausti. Another was addressed to the agency. He announced his telephone call, or rather, that of the Dominican minister in Washington. In the other telegram, he worried about our financial situation. I spoke with him and with the minister at six. They subjected me to an interrogation, which I answered. They expect and hope that the ship will leave. They asked me whether it will leave within two weeks. Whether the airline to London is commercial. I answered that the ship will perhaps leave some day, if Sweden is

---

133 The *lehendakari* is referring to the August 1939 German-Soviet pact in which the two countries, adversaries until that moment, reached a mutual non-aggression agreement, as well as dividing up Poland and the Baltic states between them.

neutral. The airline to London is private, and it's difficult to obtain a place, since it's official in nature. Efforts are necessary on both sides, one set with instructions for the American minister, another with the English minister. He promised me that they would do it. I listened to the radio in the evening. A dispatch from Stockholm said that Sweden is letting German troops pass through the north from Norway. What repercussion will all this have? Will we end up blocked again? We're living under a very dark cloud. God is above all.

JUNE 1941
THURSDAY 26. STS. JOHN AND PAUL. 177-188

Today was Joseba's third birthday. May God give him His grace and make him a sincere believer and a good man. One day he will understand what his parents suffered because of their belief in and love of God and their homeland. He was born in exile and accompanies us as a passive instrument. When as time passes he comes to know the adventures that he also participated in as a child, he will understand how hard the road of honor and truth is in life, but also that it is the only worthy and right one. May he never forget it. We celebrated his saint's day at the children's amusement park, where we had a special lunch. Then we went on the merry-go-round and the electric cars. Aintzane and Joseba were enchanted. Joseba asked whether that was America. I told him that it was America-*txiki*, because *aundi* required the ship.[134] Of course, at the agency this morning they informed us that within three weeks we will probably be able to leave for Rio de Janeiro!!!! Where are we going to end up?!? And only God knows what will happen in three weeks. But since He is the steersman, I continue to have confidence . . .

JUNE 1941
FRIDAY 27. ST. CRESCENS. 178-187

Despite the pleasant news they gave us at the agency yesterday, we're still worried about the international situation and Sweden's situation in particular. The people here are very upset about the Parliament's agreement to grant passage to the German troops headed to Finland.[135]

---

134 In Euskara, *txiki* means "little," and (*h*)*aundi* means "big." In modern standard Basque the latter is spelled *handi*.
135 The parliamentary agreement and the public debate mentioned by the *lehendakari*

It's a little late for these displays of bravery as well. Earlier, much earlier was the time to demonstrate Scandinavian solidarity. Now, encircled by the Germans, what are they going to do? We spent the afternoon at the big park playing with the children and like children. When we step away from this condition, the memories that are always present begin to arrive, memories of our relatives in difficult situations, of our friends who are suffering, of our heroic prisoners, of all those who are destined for tears in this world, which thanks be to God is in the process of being reordered. All the problems and all the individuals who are working for our cause live in my spirit in all their fullness. I think about them and feel that we understand one another. For this reason, I await the day when I will be able to embrace them all, across the many kilometers, a distance that will decrease as the day of triumph draws closer.

JUNE 1941
SATURDAY 28. ST. LEON. 179-186

After the intense heat of previous days, today it began to rain. Nevertheless, we were able to take a short walk before lunch, going to the port by way of the magnificent metal bridge that crosses it and overlooks it. That walk of ours must have been a reflection of our deep preoccupation and our longing for ships. After lunch, and seemingly driven by a similar impulse, we took a boat ride along the Gothenburg canals and around the port. The rain caused an untimely postponement of the outing that had been promised to the little ones for Joseba's saint's day and that we were unable to go on at the time. Despite the damp, the excursion was pleasant. On returning to the hotel, I received a new telegram from our friend Inchausti, in which he informed me that the English embassy

---

resulted from a German request for the transit of the Engelbrecht division from Norway to Finland in order to enable this military unit to participate in the invasion of the USSR. The request led to a political crisis in the Swedish cabinet and a threat of abdication by King Gustav V. Finally, Sweden agreed to the German soldiers' passage, on the grounds that the formal petition had been made not by the Reich but by Finland, which made it more in line with existing Swedish policy, and due to the exceptional circumstances. According to the historian Manuel Ros Agudo, the policy of neutrality Sweden followed during the war was an opportunistic one, maneuvering with concessions or restrictions according to the fortunes of war. In his opinion, "Throughout the conflict, Sweden was guided by a policy based on the strict defense of its national interests, the most important of which was to avoid being caught up in the war," Manuel Ros Agudo, *La guerra secreta de Franco (1939–1945)* (Barcelona: Crítica, 2002), 5–10.

has now issued its instructions, including for a plane flight if there are no ships. The Americans will act, he adds, automatically if necessary. How much gratitude we owe to such a good friend! God grant that there be a ship, and if not, that all of this be carried out.

JUNE 1941
SUNDAY 29. STS. PETER AND PAUL. 180-185

After fulfilling our religious duties, we went for a walk before lunch. Today, Saint Peter's feast day, we remembered the Bergara festival that we attended for so many years as children. They will have remembered us there also. All the ties will be restored when the time comes. The weather was iffy, and we decided to go to the botanical garden near our hotel. There we ran into the Perssons. He confirmed me in my hope that we will be able to embark soon. He invited me to visit him at his office tomorrow to find out whether any news came in during today's holiday about the Swedish ship's awaited departure from Brazil, the arrival of which, along with the prior arrival of the one from New York, will determine our ship's departure for Rio de Janeiro. There's another couple with three children who will sail with us if this hope becomes reality within a few weeks. More waiting; there's no other choice. If the impatience of our friends in America is reflected in their continual telegrams, ours is deeply graven in our souls.

JUNE 1941
MONDAY 30. COMM. ST. PAUL. 181-184

I arrived at Mr. Persson's office in the morning. Aintzane and Joseba accompanied me, since Mari went shopping today with Madame Persson. The people at the agency confirmed to me that they are optimistic about the ship's departure. They asked me for the most absolute secrecy. It's possible that things will turn out favorably, but there's a mystery in this whole affair that's somewhat disquieting. Despite the fact that they assure us that we will depart on the first ship, we understand that there are many people who are, if not in the same situation, in a similar one. For this reason, I reiterated in the new telegram that I sent to Inchausti that he should immediately send me news of whatever instructions the American and English ministers may have or receive. With this security, I will go to Stockholm to gather that support that is so necessary and on which a final decision may depend. Anxiety is what characterizes us. Events follow one another, and nothing can be foreseen from one day to the next. So June comes to an end, a month that instead of being decisive has been marked with shadows of disquiet and doubt.

NOTES

I said last month that greater clarity might in the future succeed the obscurity of the notes composed in Germany. The adjective of "relative" [*Crossed out*: with which I accompanied] [*Added above the line*: that I added to] that affirmation was accurate and prudent. After we had passed with the aid of the Most High through a thousand difficulties and obstacles that could hardly have been greater, after we had believed ourselves already on the other side of the abyss, recent events have thrown the coldest possible water on our hopes, and in the most abundant possible quantities. Our spirits are not cast down by this, but there are bitter moments, considering the time that is passing, the individuals who might commit a dangerous indiscretion (some of them have crossed the border heading over there),[136] and the international problems themselves, which may become even more complicated. But Providence, which chose our route and has taken care of us during our journey, will also arrange the effective way for us to be able to continue onward now. We will never be able to forget that one of its emissaries is named Inchausti.

---

136 The *lehendakari* is probably referring to the possible indiscretions that could have been committed by the relatives of the Agirre-Zabala family who had decided to leave Belgium and return to the Basque Country.

NOTES

Majestic Hotel—Berlin. Tel. <u>97-76-51.</u>

We left the Gothenburg Hotel.

—Two suitcases for Mari.

—Two for J. A.

—One hat box.

—One fur coat.

—My heavy blue overcoat.

—Grey hat.

3rd TRIMESTER

NOTES

NATIONAL CITY BANK.
RUA DO RÍO BRANCO 83.
RÍO DE JANEIRO

JULY 1941
TUESDAY 1. THE PRECIOUS BLOOD. 182-183

The weather was unsettled today. We went out with the children before lunch in order to buy a trinket for Aintzane for her good behavior. Joseba has not yet reached this level of merit. The two little ones are in magnificent health, thank God. With this life that's unsuitable for their ages, it's a wonder that they hold up without any complaints and without demanding anything, especially in the restaurants, with their food and customs that are so different. We live tied to them. They can't be left alone anywhere, due to their ages, and also due to I don't know what child's instinct that makes them understand the situation much better than we believe. Aintzane's discretion is an extraordinary thing. May we give thanks to God for everything, and may He will that this month of July be the definitive one. We're quite worried about the children, subjected to an unsuitable life and one that undoes their education. I always think about those who have lost their children . . . ! Today we spent the afternoon at the botanical garden . . . At eight, as usual, we were already in our hotel room.

JULY 1941
WEDNESDAY 2. VISITATION. 183-182

In the morning, we did some shopping for cold food with which Mari put together the menu for our day in the countryside, in the forest of the big park. It was a very beautiful day, which we took full advantage of. At seven, we had dinner near the hotel, and at 8:15, we were already glued to the radio, listening to the day's news. Thanks to this means, we find out about the way events are moving. Yesterday I neglected to note that we received a postcard from Juan Mari. The news that our mothers are calmer and feeling much better filled us with satisfaction. We've been very worried about them. This life of shocks and unpleasantness in a foreign land, with so many uncertainties and difficulties, could have caused them great harm, especially with our presence there, which was such a torture to them. The letter was answered right away yesterday. Today I received a very kind letter from Minister Despradel. The news of Guardia's dismissal as consul in Antwerp saddened me. It's petty politics that these Western Hemisphere republics practice! Especially when personal matters are mixed in!

JULY 1941
THURSDAY 3. ST. ANATOLIUS. 184-181

After a visit to the church and a short walk, we ate on the terrace of a downtown restaurant. Good food, and very economical. We then took the children to the botanical garden, which I left at four for a meeting with Mr. Persson. He wasn't in the office, they told me. Later, back at the hotel, I received a call from the said gentleman, who told me, among other things, that it seems that the ship whose return from South America we are awaiting has now left. The news is so welcome—since our ship's departure depends on this one's arrival—that after so many bad experiences, we're reserving our happiness until we know that it's already off the Swedish coast. At the hotel, I heard a report in French on Stalin's speech. A magnificent program. He talks like Roosevelt now, or like the pope. Justice and freedom for men and for peoples. War on bloody imperialism. Certainly, he's on the side of reason now, but up to now? The postwar period will liquidate tyrannies of all kinds, white and red.

JULY 1941
FRIDAY 4. ST. ODO. 185-180

Today we faced a day shrouded in fog and damp. The heat of the previous days was succeeded by rain, which fell in abundance. We went out strictly in order to have lunch at a nearby restaurant. Taking advantage of a brief break in the rain, we did some shopping. Then back to the hotel. I went to the agency, where they gave me a new telegram from Inchausti. He informed me of the restrictions on sending funds due to American government regulations. We will hold out however we can until we sail. Inchausti's generosity and concern are beyond all praise. Life here is extremely expensive. And it goes up day by day. Today we received a card from Juan Mari and a letter from Margari. The news pleased us. Guardia has arrived and has delivered my letter to Juan Mari. They liked it and indicate that they are in agreement with its content and my advice for the future. The letters for Dorota, Xabier, and the prisoners have also arrived and are on their way to their destinations.[137] It will bring them some consolation ...

JULY 1941
SATURDAY 5. ST. ANTH. MARIA ZACC. 186-179

We left the hotel late, and after lunch and a short walk, the botanical garden was again the chosen location for crossing today off the calendar. With taking care of the children, we can't think about anything. Even reading and other work gets pushed aside. During the day, because it's necessary to keep an eye on them; at night, due to the light. We've received slightly more optimistic news about our departure. The ships' movements are subject to an impenetrable confidentiality. Nevertheless, it seems that the ship that we are awaiting is already at sea. There must be some secret in the affair, to judge by the mystery that surrounds it. But it seems that the voyage has now begun. If it arrives without incident, we'll leave, probably headed for Rio de Janeiro. Only God knows what we still have to see and renounce. But He is still at the tiller, and meanwhile we're going along well ...

---

137 Doroteo Ziaurritz Aginaga (1883–1951), who served as president of the PNV's Euzkadi Buru Batzarra from 1936 until his death, and Francisco Javier de Landaburu, a parliamentary representative and the *lehendakari*'s collaborator. Transcriptions of these letters are found in appendixes 2, 3, and 4.

JULY 1941
SUNDAY 6. ST. TRANQUILLINUS. 187-178

After fulfilling our religious duties and paying the bill for two weeks at the hotel, making a considerable dent in our wallet, we went to the horse races. We've never seen more democratic horse races. The stands held a picturesque mixture of the locality's elegant residents (very few) and sailors with tattooed arms, from the wealthy industrialist's daughter to the young lady who takes care of the children at the botanical garden and is a friend of Aintzane and Joseba. Our hotel's concierge, on whose advice we had gone to the races, was there. In the middle of the trials, King Gustav of Sweden made his appearance.[138] He's very old now and passed two meters [6.5 feet] from us. He received a lot of applause. We found his extraordinary simplicity noteworthy. It was the sight of a democratic king in the midst of his democratic people, who are made equal in a very estimable standard of living. The children enjoyed themselves very much with all of this, and so did we.

JULY 1941
MONDAY 7. STS. CYR. AND METH. 188-177

In the morning, Mari went shopping with Madame Persson. I took the two little ones for a walk across the large metal bridge that overlooks the port. We looked at the ships, and I had to supply the requisite answers to the hail of questions with which Aintzane and Joseba attacked me. Naturally, they had to do with the ship, its interior arrangement, and the voyage to America, on hold because they are giving the smokestack a good coat of paint and cleaning the staterooms. With this explanation, they were satisfied. We spent the rest of the afternoon at the botanical garden. I left for a moment to go to Nordisk to send a telegram to Inchausti thanking him for the new remittance of funds and indicating our hope of embarking this month. Certainly, while I was at Nordisk, the news arrived that the ship we are awaiting has reached New York and will leave there before the 10th. It's possible that it's already at sea, in the same way that it sailed about two weeks to get from Rio de Janeiro to New York without them telling us.

---

138 Gustav V (1858–1950) reigned in Sweden from 1907 to 1950.

JULY 1941
TUESDAY 8. ST. ELIZABETH OF P. 189-176

Today was our eighth wedding anniversary. We gave thanks to God for all the favors He has granted us, which are many. We remembered the singular coincidence that starting on this date eight years ago, we traveled through these Scandinavian lands for our honeymoon. Back then, we would never have suspected this forced repetition. We invited the Perssons to celebrate our anniversary with us, and we did so with a very good dinner at a good restaurant in the amusement park. We spent the time very pleasantly. Only Joseba complained a bit about his stomach, which contributed to Mari not enjoying herself appropriately. We discussed the American occupation of Iceland and its repercussions.[139] The war is acquiring the full extension necessary to make it possible to start to glimpse its end. I see it as still far away, but the outcome is certain. Once more, freedom will triumph, and with her, those who knew how to suffer.

JULY 1941
WEDNESDAY 9. ST. LEONARD. 190-175

Today was even hotter than yesterday. The thermometer read 31° [88° F] in the shade. It doesn't seem believable in countries as cold as this one. We went to the botanical garden with the children; it's a pleasant place, more so today because of the great heat. We had lunch, that is, we tided our stomachs over, with an *amaiketako* [mid-morning snack], following the general Swedish custom. Compared to our people, these people eat like birds. They tell us that it's because of the war, but I don't think that they get very excessive in peacetime either. Perhaps they overdo it on the side of restraint, although not as much as my compatriots do on the side of excess. At four, I visited Mr. Persson. Dealing with visas again!

---

139 In view of the German occupation of Denmark, to which Iceland belonged, in April 1940, and the blockade imposed on Norway by the United Kingdom, the island acquired significant strategic importance in the North Atlantic, as a consequence of which it was occupied by the British Admiralty on May 10, 1940. *De facto* liberated from Denmark, and in view of the uncertainty of a British victory in the war, the legation that Iceland had opened in New York proposed that the United States protect the island on the basis of the Monroe Doctrine. British Prime Minister Winston Churchill did not resist the Icelandic proposal, since he saw the U.S. occupation as another step toward getting the United States involved in the war. The American troops arrived in Iceland on July 7, 1941.

The prolongation of our stay here requires filling out sheets of forms for everyone again. I remember Manu Sota when he used to say that it was necessary to create the society of those who don't have papers. I replied with the condition that in order to enter that society, it not be necessary to fill out any papers. In sum, we're still filling out papers and waiting for the liberating ship, which seems to be at sea. May God protect it and speed it forward!

JULY 1941
THURSDAY 10. ST. FELICITY. 191-174

The suffocating heat continued today. We ate lunch at the botanical garden, fleeing the swelter. It got up to 33º [91º F] in the shade. At four, I visited Mr. Persson. He had announced a long-distance call to Minister Despradel in Switzerland. The minister is in Berlin. I requested a call for Berlin for tomorrow. As I feared, we have to do a little pulling on what strings we have. The ship's probable departure for Rio de Janeiro (the other one is already on its way back to New York) has begun to be public knowledge, despite the secrecy. People are starting to make requests, and each of them has his influence and his friends. Mr. Persson warned me that despite our passages being assured, we shouldn't relax. First the visa for Brazil, and we're now at visa number I-don't-know-how-many, then the nudge to the English and American ministers, in addition to the prolongation of the Swedish residency visa. In sum, the paperwork continues and between telegrams and long-distance calls, a good number of crowns will disappear tomorrow.

JULY 1941
FRIDAY 11. ST. GODELIEVE. 192-173

This morning while Mari went shopping, I stayed with Joseba and Aintzane. Today we had a geography lesson describing the Gothenburg-New York-Buenos Aires-Euzkadi itinerary, which is the one we're planning to follow if God does not determine otherwise. Today was a day of exceptional application and seriousness. Then with Mari and Madame Persson, who kindly accompanied us, we went to the police station for the purpose of affixing our signatures as God commands. My head, which is occupied with other things, did its typical fine job yesterday. I signed Mari's form, and Mari signed mine. In sum, today it was necessary to undo what had been badly done. We lost a day for the extension of our Swedish residency visas. At Nordisk in the afternoon, they informed me that there are two Swedish ships on their way back to Gothenburg, and that two others will depart from this port once they arrive. The news is encouraging, and our impatience is growing. Today I spoke by telephone with Minister Despradel. A good friend as always, he agreed to work on our visa for Brazil, in case we end up in those latitudes. It was extraordinarily hot. More than 40º [104º F] in the sun. Preparation for the tropics!

JULY 1941
SATURDAY 12. ST. JOHN GAULBERT. 193-172

This morning I was at Nordisk again to ask the British legation in Stockholm whether there was any information there on my behalf, as they tell us from Washington. Neither the minister nor his secretary was there. They agreed to find out for Monday. In view of the probable departure of the ship or ships, the requests are frightening and influential. We can't relax. Let's wait for Monday to put our friends and acquaintances to work. Today, Mari and the two little ones went with Mrs. Persson to swim in a magnificent public pool in this magnificent country. I went later. I was a spectator while they went in the water. The heat was suffocating. Tomorrow I'll follow their example. Aintzane was very brave. Joseba very cowardly. He complains a bit these days. He must be a little indisposed. But he's still so naughty! He's promised to be brave at the pool tomorrow. Magnificent hygienic and public institutions that this people have!

JULY 1941
SUNDAY 13. ST. ANACLETUS. 194-171

Mari and I split up today also, going to church at different times. Afterward, we went to the pool, where we passed the time very enjoyably until four. I went in the water with the children, amid a crowd of little ones who were escaping from the day's suffocating heat by staying in the water until nightfall. At four, the Perssons had invited us over; they offered us coffee and pastries. We spent the rest of the afternoon with them, retiring at 7:30 to eat dinner. It's still hot. The faces of these good Swedes, accustomed to very low temperatures, reveal by their red flush that they are not entirely content. Today in Ligberg Park we saw the cannon or artillery man who is in the habit of being shot forty meters from the mouth of a large-caliber cannon, although one made of cardboard. The noise of the blast impressed Joseba, and the threat of being put in the cannon himself even more so.

JULY 1941
MONDAY 14. ST. BONAVENTURE. 195-170

At Nordisk this morning they gave me good news. Our names have been included on the short list of around ten people for the ship to Rio de Janeiro expected to leave at the end of the month. I went joyfully to the pool, where Mari was waiting for me with the little ones. We spent almost the whole day at the pool, which has a limited but sufficient restaurant service. Upon our return to the hotel, a contrary obstacle appeared before us. Mr. Persson had just called to tell us that children are not allowed on the service for South America. The previous voyage must have been a bad one for some children who were traveling, since two sailors had to take constant care of the sick little patients. Since they won't be taking a doctor or nurse on this voyage either, they've decided to bar children. And so again I find myself facing a setback. [*Crossed out*: Tomorrow] I've been given an appointment for tomorrow. We'll see what the final decision is. And as always, to hope.

JULY 1941
TUESDAY 15. ST. HENRY. 196-169

At the agency in the morning, they confirmed to me the prohibition on children for the South American line. I think that there must also be other reasons involved that aren't expressed, economic ones among them, since on these vessels passage is much cheaper than on the ship that will go to New York. And I say that it will go, because that's the latest news and it's a very firm probability that we will leave in the middle of next month. That's what Nordisk's director assured me. In the end, more waiting, and that it will be the last time, because all these ships will leave if the ones that have already left New York arrive. In view of this new delay, we've accepted Mr. Persson's proposal to spend a few days at a boarding house located on the shores of one of the lakes between Stockholm and Gothenburg. In effect, now that we've arrived at the place, which is called Västra Bodarna, it's [*Crossed out*: in effect] magnificent, located on the shores of a precious lake edged with pine trees all around. It's also very economical.

JULY 1941
WEDNESDAY 16. O. L. OF M. C. 197-168

Yesterday, I forgot my pen in Gothenburg. Today, I take it up again. Västra Bodarna is the town where we have arrived. Four houses and as many boarding houses on the shores of one of the countless lakes along the route from Gothenburg to Stockholm. We made the trip and installed ourselves like true workers on vacation. The journey was in third class, and the boarding house reminds me a great deal of the big old houses inhabited by our refugees in France. The food is good, the comfort is very limited, since there's no running water, but the nature is splendid. In addition, our expenses are cut by more than half, and we're taking a summer holiday, something that we had not been expecting amid so much calamity. Today, since it was the feast day of Mari's patron saint, we celebrated it by inviting the Perssons to have dinner with us. We ate in Alingsas, a town located a few kilometers from our hamlet. We had a good time. In the morning, we swam in the lake with the children.

JULY 1941
THURSDAY 17. ST. ALEXIS. 198-167

We made good use of the day on the lakeshore. We went swimming. The children were very brave. Joseba goes in the water alone; he doesn't want help from anyone. *Ni bakarrik*, he says.[140] Aintzane will have learned to swim within a few days. She likes it and is in good health. The little ones sleep very well with the change of air and the exercise. Amid so much worry, Providence takes care to give us these satisfactions. I always think about those who are suffering more. We're living right in the middle of nature, surrounded by very extensive pine forests. The lake must be about a square kilometer. There's fishing. At the invitation of a picturesque fellow guest at our boarding house, Mr. Persson, the inviter, and I went out fishing. It fell to me to make a fool of myself. I

---

140 *Ni bakarrik* means "I alone" ("just me") in Euskara.

didn't catch a single thing. The others caught four, of a species similar to mullet. We still have no news from Louvain, and this worries us. Despite the distraction of these days, Mari and I are living with our thoughts very far away. The ships are still at sea, it seems.

JULY 1941
FRIDAY 18. ST. CAMILLUS. 199-166

Today I went to Gothenburg to run errands, among other things to bring our clean laundry that hadn't been returned to us. Despite the supply of clothes obtained with our purchases, we still have to economize quite a bit in their use. It's good to get to know everything in life. They loaded me up with commissions of all kinds. They doubted my qualifications in this regard, and I was even more doubtful, but I came through with flying colors. Since we're around fifty kilometers [thirty miles] from Gothenburg, it's an easy trip; the train doesn't take more than an hour. I returned in midafternoon for dinner, since in this Swedish meal regime, they serve us what we would call dinner at four. At ten in the morning a breakfast that is more of a full meal, at one coffee with some pastries, at four a full dinner, and at seven-thirty tea with some sandwiches. We're all very happy. Only the lack of news (no letters had arrived in Gothenburg) has us concerned.

JULY 1941
SATURDAY 19. ST. VINCENT DE P. 200-165

The weather, which started the day rather doubtful, gradually improved as the day went on. One of the small beaches along the lake serves wonderfully for the children to play and for all of us to go in the water. Almost alone in this spot, enjoying good sun and clean water from snowmelt, we can do no less than thank God, Who takes care even of these details, according to the principle that He tempers the wind to the shorn lamb. At the same time, our hotelkeepers' friendliness toward us is noteworthy. Good people, these Swedish peasants, serious and polite. Today I received a letter from my good friend the minister, Dr. Despradel. The restrictive measures imposed by the Americans on Sweden and Switzerland, the only countries excepted up to now, make it difficult to receive dollars in cash. This difficulty would be an obstacle for me, since I had agreed with the minister on a way to help my family.

They're hoping that the restriction will be lifted. We'll be able to help them from the Americas. Our families are our greatest worry. And by analogy, all the others who are suffering.

JULY 1941
SUNDAY 20. ST. JEROME. 201-164

The day dawned amid fog and rain. We were unable to fulfill our religious duties, since there are no Catholic churches outside of Gothenburg. We supplied this defect with our prayers. We stayed at the boarding house for the whole morning. After the meal at four p.m., quite a few of us guests went on an interesting excursion. It's a cultural institution in which young teachers of both sexes take short summer courses in all those practical disciplines and trades they need to know, especially in rural milieus, in order to teach them properly, perfecting their students' knowledge. Agriculture, trades like carpentry, tool use, etc. for men; home economics, cooking, etc., in addition to agricultural knowledge for women. We observed the folkdance session. The male and female teachers learn the folkdances, dancing and singing, in order to teach them in the schools afterward. A magnificent institution.

JULY 1941
MONDAY 21. NATIONAL DAY. 202-163

This morning Mr. Persson, who received a call from his director two days ago, went to Gothenburg. He agreed to advise us of anything new. In effect, he called at four, transmitting not very pleasant news. Delay and doubt again. The ship for New York won't leave until September 5. A month and a half yet, and only God knows the complications that might come about during this time. The radio announced new American measures against the Nazis. Elsewhere, the activity in Spain and Portugal. Franco's decisive pro-Nazi speech, no less decisive because unexpected by me.[141] In sum, all this is greatly concerning for us amid a life of imposed physical calm. Only the children fully enjoy it, which is their good fortune and strengthens them. We spent the day at the

---

141 Franco's speech to the National Council of the Falange on July 17, 1941, in which, noting "the anxiety of these moments in which along with the fate of Europe, that of our nation is at issue," he attacked the Allies and affirmed, "The war has been badly framed, and the Allies have lost it." Quoted in Jiménez de Aberasturi, *De la derrota*, 769.

little beach at the lake, going in the water and sunbathing. Our spirits don't match the corporal benefits received. But everything will come and will work out. God is still the steersman.

JULY 1941
TUESDAY 22. ST. MARY MAGD. 203-162

In the morning, Mr. Persson called and told me that the ship for New York won't leave until at least September 5. That the New York ship on whose arrival this departure depends won't leave before August 10. That he will speak to me tomorrow if, as he expects, they give him a few days off. The news was not comforting. The delay is due to I don't know what order by the Swedish government having to do with the loading of the New York ship. The traffic is subject to constant and dangerous indecisions and delays. Madame Persson and Mari went to Alingsäs today to buy things for the children. I stayed behind as inspector of the small "troupe," with whom I went out in the boarding house's small boat. Mr. and Mrs. Persson's daughter, Aintzane, and Joseba were my companions. We rowed as far as the small beach and then walked along the lake. They were enchanted, and I envied them, since it's well said that nothing will be obtained except by those who are like little children.

JULY 1941
WEDNESDAY 23. ST. APOLLINARIS. 204-161

Despite the indecisiveness of the day, we went to the little beach that delights us. Taking advantage of a period of sun, we went in the water. Later, we endured a good cloudburst in order to again enjoy some not very bright sun. Joseba, to make life difficult, threw himself into the water with all his clothes on after having gotten dressed. He'll do it again, despite the fright. In the afternoon, we waited at the station for Mr. Persson to arrive. The news he brought discouraged us. The ship for New York won't take that route, but rather the South American one. That the departure date is not fixed, because there are a thousand difficulties, between outfitters, exporters, English, Germans, etc. That there will be a ship, but that it's necessary to wait. In view of this, I decided to make an effort and called the Dominican minister in Washington. Luckily, they put the call through for me in three hours. I charged him and Inchausti with urgent efforts to obtain places on the ship that will leave for Rio de Janeiro on the 30th and on which they aren't allowing children to leave. The efforts may be decisive for the permission.

JULY 1941
THURSDAY 24. ST. CHRISTINE. 205-160

After breakfast, I headed to the telegraph office to send a long telegram to our friend Inchausti explaining everything that is happening and confirming yesterday's long-distance call with Minister Pastoriza. In the telegram, I explained how we put off our departure in view of the certainty that there would be a ship for New York in August. Otherwise, despite the length of the voyage, we would have definitively chosen the Rio de Janeiro route. The prohibition on children would perhaps have been resolved with effective efforts. Now it turns out that there's no ship for New York, and the ones that may leave after the one that's going to depart for Rio de Janeiro on the 30th will do so in September at the earliest. In these circumstances, convinced that the prohibition on children was a pretext like any other and that the condition of the voyage to New York has not been fulfilled, I've decided to beg my friends to make decisive efforts to get me permission to travel on the ship on the 30th, searching for any solution available. The passages are sold out. It's only taking eight or ten passengers. The arrangements are very difficult.

JULY 1941
FRIDAY 25. ST. JAMES THE GREAT. 206-159

We spent the day waiting impatiently for an answer from New York. I've spent more than 350 Swedish kroner between the telegram and the long-distance phone call to Washington and New York yesterday and the day before yesterday. But if I obtain passage, it will be more economical than an extended stay in Sweden. They advised us that even though eight gentlemen have been given the passages, requests are continuing, and the influence battle is beginning to make itself seriously felt. I decided to go to Stockholm [*Crossed out*: by] immediately tonight, and in effect, we're now on our way to the Swedish capital. Mr. Persson, an excellent person and another of those who have known how to understand and esteem me, is accompanying me. Our heads are full of audacious plans. Up to now, I've lived in silence, because it was suitable to do so and things were going along normally. Today we decided to employ the method of speed and clarity in certain milieus. It's necessary to win the battle. Mari and I are making a novena to Saint Ignatius. I'm calling on his aid, as I've done so many times. I have confidence.

JULY 1941
SATURDAY 26. ST. ANNE. 207-158

We arrived in Stockholm, the magnificent Baltic capital, which was full of sunshine to receive us. We lodged at the Hotel Regina, whose director, a very nice old bachelor, is a very good friend of Mr. Persson. We immediately headed to the central headquarters of the Swedish Social Democratic Party. We wanted to get to see the prime minister. The party secretary received us. I opened myself up to him and introduced myself. He received me with extraordinary warmth and sympathy, heaping undeserved praise on me. He wanted to speak with the interior minister. He wasn't in. Saturday's a bad day in this summer season. He informed the prime minister's office. Prime Minister Jansson, who belongs to the party, wasn't in.[142] He was finally located at his summer cottage. He took up the case sympathetically. He promised to do as much as he could upon his return on Monday. For us, the hours are days, the days are months. The ship is leaving not on the 30th but on the 31st, Saint Ignatius's feast day. My optimism is growing, but the news that we received at the Nordisk office in Stockholm filled us with fear. The fight is a formidable one. My competitors are Jews. Also unfortunate people.

JULY 1941
SUNDAY 27. ST. PANTALEON. 208-157

We left Stockholm yesterday evening, arriving in Västra Bordarna this morning at 7:15. We returned partly satisfied and partly fearful. The ship on the 31st, or rather its eight available places, are the object of a terrible struggle among influences of all kinds. But they let us know that authorization has still not been received at the Brazilian legation to issue visas to the eight Jewish passengers who have the places reserved. I informed Inchausti of the news, requesting preference for "Latin

---

142 Per Albin Hansson (1886–1946) was the leader of the Swedish Social Democratic Party. He was prime minister between 1932 and 1946, except for a period of three months in 1936. During World War II, he led a national coalition government in which the Communists were not represented.

Americans." Poor Jews or poor me! I requested a Brazilian visa. We went to the legation. Reticence, delays. I informed Dr. Despradel in Berlin. They agreed to speak with the Panamanian and Venezuelan ministers. They cannot consent, he told me, that we Latin Americans should come after any non-Latin Americans, even Jews. They went to speak to the Brazilian ambassador in Berlin. We Latin Americans have a *per se* right to a visa according to instructions from Brazil. Why are they posing difficulties? Ah, influence. My friends are working all over. It's necessary to win the battle. I'm going back to Stockholm.

JULY 1941
MONDAY 28. STS. NAZ. AND CELS. 209-156

A great day today. I arrived in Stockholm at 7:30 in the morning. Yesterday afternoon we brought our families to Gothenburg; then I caught the train with Mr. Persson. The first visit was for the Nordisk director, whose behavior did not seem clear. He knows my identity, and I won him completely to my cause. But he can't do anything without instructions from some Swedish ministerial authority. The passages have been given out, and it's not honorable to deprive anyone of what they've acquired. The secretary of the social democratic party informed us that we could call the prime minister, who was already well informed. We called. He spoke with Mr. Persson in Swedish. The prime minister said that we should tell the director of the company in his name that it's his wish that I go. We communicated this magnificent intervention to the director. He said that this indication is sufficient, but that if the passengers have Brazilian visas, it will be difficult to deprive them of their rights. The prime minister's intervention has revoked the prohibition on children. We visited the Brazilian legation. The minister had received four telegrams from the Berlin ministers on my behalf. He received me. Álvarez and Mrs. Guerra will have their visas in Gothenburg tomorrow. Visit to the British legation. Magnificent. Visit to the German embassy. Very good.

JULY 1941
TUESDAY 29. ST. MARTHA. 210-155

We arrived in Gothenburg this morning after having triumphed in our efforts. We'll leave, God willing, on the 31st, the feast day of Saint

Ignatius, our patron. Yesterday, after visiting the German and English legations in order to obtain acceptance of the changes to the list in the event of obtaining passage, we went back to the Brazilian legation again. It was a picturesque meeting, chaired by the minister and with the high-ranking officials and Mr. Persson in attendance. The Jews' influential connections were visible on all sides, but mine were beginning to make themselves felt. Four Latin American ministers in Berlin, the Brazilian ambassador in Washington, the Swedish minister in Washington influenced the Brazilian minister and the company. The former gave us the visas, which we received today in Gothenburg. The company, in view of the prime minister's indication, racked its brains for the way to give us the passages. It demanded immediate payment with risk of complete loss of the passage. In sum, almost all the Jews withdrew, since they wouldn't risk their money without the Brazilian visas. Those still haven't arrived. My friends, I think, have done yeoman work. I've conquered in the fight. The merit belongs to everyone except myself. And God's help. We're preparing our things for the trip. Tired but happy.

JULY 1941
WEDNESDAY 30. STS. ABDON AND S. 211-154

A day of preparations. They informed us that the ship will leave at eight a.m. tomorrow, instead of at noon. We had to quickly make sure we had all kinds of shopping done. From the first-aid kit—since the ship won't have a doctor on board—to the light suits that they call tropical. The little ones thought it was all a form of entertainment. Poor Mari worked today for all of us. I remained calm, thinking that the ship's pilot is that Basque whose feast day is celebrated tomorrow, and that along with Xavier, a better Basque than he was, they're my two friends and protectors.[143] We arrived at the hotel exhausted. We had ordered a good dinner, since Mr. and Mrs. Persson were our guests. They more than deserve it. Both of them. I've written many letters to Louvain, to Dorota, to Xabier, for Jesús, Eli, Santi, Gonzalo, Picabea, Lasarte,

---

143 Saints Ignatius of Loyola and Francis Xavier. The former was a native of Azpeitia and the founder of the Society of Jesus, and the latter was Navarrese and one of Saint Ignatius's first companions. Iñigo de Loyola was wounded at the siege of Pamplona in 1521 when he was fighting with the Castilians against the Navarrese, who were trying to reclaim Upper Navarre. Among those fighting on the Navarrese side were several brothers of Francis Xavier, whose family had to go into exile after the annexation of Upper Navarre to the crown of Castile in 1512.

Jauregui, etc.[144] I'm carrying all these friends with me. We will all meet again. I recommend unity. It will come to pass, and we will triumph. We went to bed very late on the eve of our departure.

JULY 1941
THURSDAY 31. ST. IGNATIUS OF L. 212-153

[*In the upper margin*: Today we completed the novena to Saint Ignatius. We commended our voyage and its successful conclusion to his care. We were not able to celebrate the feast day religiously in the way we would have wished and would have done if we had left at noon.]

We were already up by six-thirty. We were supposed to be on board the *Vasaholm*,[145] which is the name of the ship, at eight. It has a displacement of 6,700 tons, and only eight of us passengers are traveling on it. Two Polish Jewish engineers and a Latvian couple, also Jewish. All people of distinction and against whom I had to fight a few days ago. We left at eight-thirty. We headed for the outer port of Gothenburg to meet two other ships—magnificent oil tankers—with which we will travel in convoy for three days. A Swedish destroyer accompanied us to the edge of Swedish territorial waters. Then we went on alone. A peaceful day, excellent treatment on board, the children having a truly wonderful time. Oh! novelty and ignorance! Mari was a pile of nerves. I was calm and sure that everything would go well. Mr. Persson cried as he said goodbye to us on the dock. At night, we have the lights on, and strong spotlights

---

144 Doroteo Ziaurritz Aginaga, president of the PNV's Euzkadi Buru Batzarra; Francisco Javier Landaburu, parliamentary representative for Araba and a close collaborator of the *lehendakari*; Jesús María Leizaola, counselor for justice and culture; Eliodoro de la Torre, counselor for treasury matters; Santiago Aznar, counselor for industry; Gonzalo Nardiz, counselor for agriculture; Rafael Picavea, delegate in Paris; José María Lasarte, parliamentary representative and head of the information and propaganda services; and Julio Jauregui, parliamentary representative and the official in charge of emigration for the Basque government. Of the mentioned letters, we have found only one, sent by the *lehendakari* to relatives of his living in Louvain. It appears here as appendix 7.
145 The M/S *Vasaholm*, which belonged to the Svenska Amerika Mexiko Linien (SAML) company, was built at the Göteverken shipyard in Gothenburg and delivered to the outfitters in January 1930. During its existence before being scrapped in Istanbul in 1973, it belonged to various owners and sailed under different names, *Victoria*, *Stavros*, and *Priamo*. It measured 119 meters (390 feet) in length, 16 meters (52 feet) in width, and 7.16 meters (23 feet) in depth and recorded 4,259 tons gross weight, 2,487 tons net weight, and 7,345 tons deadweight.

illuminate the flags. It's an impressive sight. A German seaplane flew within twenty meters [65 feet] of our smokestack. The dance begins.

NOTES

The month of July came to an end at sea. As I write, the low, constant noise of the ship's engines as it proceeds at moderate speed amid great precautions, the lights and spotlights set up to illuminate the enormous Swedish flags painted on the decks, the noise of the engines of the German seaplane that passed a little while ago, buzzing the ship's masts, and I don't know what mysterious effect caused by contemplating three ships, one behind the other, seeming to step lightly and on tiptoe like people who don't want to wake up their neighbors, all create the impression that our voyage has a great deal of audaciousness and more than a little of adventure about it. But the same faith as always says that it's necessary to keep moving forward, disdaining the obstacles and trusting in the One Who promised blessings to those who suffer persecution for the sake of justice. Onward, then.

AUGUST 1941
213-152 ST. PETER IN CHAINS— FRIDAY 1.

Mari made an appearance around six. I sent her to go back to sleep. Mari is concerned only about the two little ones. She neither sleeps nor rests; thank God that she's from a seafaring family and never gets seasick. She has a quite good cabin with Aintzane and Joseba. Mine is next to the captain's cabin. Small, but very sufficient and above all, clean. The food on board is good, and the officers behave very politely.

Around noon, a strong storm began, increasing in intensity hour by hour until nine, when there started to be some improvement. Mr. Letón, Mari, Joseba, and I stayed on our feet. None of the others appeared in the dining room. Aintzane, who was a little seasick, fell asleep, and we didn't want to wake her. Joseba turned into a tough guy, defying the waves that came over the deck and enjoying it when the spray made it up to the bridge. But today and the night ahead are dangerous. We passed two mines 100 and 150 meters [330 and 490 feet] from us.

AUGUST 1941
SATURDAY 2. ST. ALPHONSUS. 214-151

The sea was calmer than yesterday. The route that begins in Kristiansand, passes the Skagerrat, and continues as far as the latitude of Stavanger does not fail to have its dangers.[146] We've passed two hundred meters [650 feet] from two floating mines that displayed their threatening tentacles. The night especially produces a strong impression. Truly, there's nothing to be done except to leave it all in God's hands. I keep myself absolutely calm through the presentiment that has accompanied me during the entire course and antecedents of a fourteen-month adventure. Women are more impressionable. Mari has the great good fortune of never getting seasick. Aintzane has been very brave. Joseba has become a seadog. Today we met up at sea with the fourth Swedish steamer that is traveling in convoy with us. Due to its slow speed, it left two days ahead. We're continuing on our way toward the Faroe Islands.

AUGUST 1941
SUNDAY 3. INV. ST. STEPHEN. 215-150

First Sunday at sea. Our prayers supplied the inability to fulfill the commandment that our circumstances imposed. A print of Saint Ignatius, reproducing Sánchez Coello's masterwork, presides over the cabin where Mari and the children are. We have commended the care and guardianship of our voyage to him, and he will do all the rest. The night was dangerous. We crossed the front lines between the forces in combat. Two English airplanes flew around our convoy. They did it at low altitude, about twenty meters [65 feet] above the sea. The temperature has gone down. It's cold enough to order the heat to be turned on. We're sailing toward the Faroe Islands, where we have to submit to an English inspection. So we're between Norway and Iceland. We've again passed three mines along the way. The children are brave. Today we invented a thousand ways to pass the time. The two oil tankers passed us, since they're supposed to go through the English inspection tomorrow morning. We're scheduled for midday tomorrow. It rained at the start of the evening.

---

146 Kristiansand and Stavanger are two Norwegian towns, the former located at the point of confluence of the Skagerrak and Kattegat Straits, which unite the Baltic and North Seas, and the latter on the North Sea coast.

AUGUST 1941
MONDAY 4. ST. DOMINIC. 216-149

We approached the Faroe Islands. We arrived there around eleven-thirty. Guided by a Norwegian tugboat, we sat at anchor for an hour and a half. The Faroe Islands were covered in mist atop their small peaks, which fall straight down to the sea. It's cold, very cold, and the view, worthy of Nordic legends, makes a strong impression, due to the inhospitableness of the landscape and due to the stamp of mystery added by the fact that the islands are one of the bases of the war at sea. English inspection. An officer arrived with two sailors. They searched the ship. Asked for our documents. Everything seriously and politely. We were permitted to leave. It's like a license that is granted in order to enter the world of freedom. And there's even a gate in the form of the narrow strait between two of the islands through which the ship had to pass in order to begin its Atlantic route. We did so amid a strong storm. The waves covered the deck and reached the bridge.

AUGUST 1941
TUESDAY 5. OUR LADY OF THE SNOWS. 217-148

Yesterday's cold and fog was followed by sunshine today. The sea is still choppy, but the storm with its strong winds and high waves has lessened considerably. Joseba and Aintzane watched from the bridge yesterday how the waves broke over the deck and sprayed us up on the bridge. The sight filled them with enthusiasm. We can give thanks to God, Who grants us the gift of good health. Mari is the one who suffers on their behalf, worried about the dangers. I believe that the chief danger has now passed. For me, it was the mines, especially at night and on dark nights. Mines have no intelligence. The commanders of submarines and airplanes have eyes with which to see our ships' enormous colors, and they have orders to obey. More than a hundred miles from the Faroe Islands, we encountered the first English patrol ship. It hailed our convoy and was answered using signal flags. We ate dinner at six. We took a walk on the deck afterward. Then we listened to the radio, and at eleven we retired.

AUGUST 1941
WEDNESDAY 6. TRANSFIG. OF THE LORD. 218-147

When we got up, they told us that at around six in the morning, we had crossed paths with some British patrol ships. They let us sleep, notwithstanding how interesting these encounters are. A ship of around 2,500 tons, named *Canadia*, is traveling in the convoy. Its progress is very slow, since it does less than nine miles an hour. Today and yesterday, due to a problem with its engines, its speed has been reduced to six miles. The convoy moves slowly, about five miles an hour. At this pace, we won't get to Rio de Janeiro this year. But the appropriate orders have not been received to leave the *Canadia* and continue our voyage with the two grand oil tankers—16,000 and 12,000 tons—that make up the rest of the convoy. That way we'll sail at twelve knots per hour. We're more than 350 miles from the Faroe Islands and have passed Iceland 120 miles away. After dinner, an English airplane flew over us, descended to greet us, and continued on its way. We continued without incident.

AUGUST 1941
THURSDAY 7. ST. CAJETAN. 219-146

Today we left the *Canadia* behind, thereby increasing the convoy's speed. We're sailing at twelve miles an hour. Around midday tomorrow we'll cross the border of the area declared as a war zone by the Germans. The calm produced by this fact is evident on board. It's true that the anxiety of these days and the consequent nervousness has not even left time to think about the dangers, even if this statement may seem paradoxical. Today, after what we've been through, it's frightening to consider where we've sailed, amid fields of mines, many of them scarcely visible, and exposed to a disagreeable surprise, especially at night. The lifeboats in position, the lifejackets within reach—they made special ones for Joseba and Aintzane—the worry on the faces of the captain and the officers: in sum, thanks be to God that everything has come through safe, but [*Crossed out*: that] it's all been very serious and grounds for worry, despite the tranquility of spirit that I have sincerely maintained. We continued the voyage in good health. English airplanes flew over.

AUGUST 1941
FRIDAY 8. ST. JUSTIN. 220-125

We sailed through fog. Yesterday the ship's foghorn sounded constantly for this reason. It's more impressive in the middle of the Atlantic than when leaving port or as a ritual greeting. Under these circumstances, it seemed like a summons that could wake up sleeping submarines. We've sailed more than two hundred miles through fog. Today the weather was better, although it rained quite a bit. The cold is decreasing as we move south. We're at the latitude of England. Early this morning, at one a.m., the convoy will separate, as we follow the southern route and the two oil tankers head for Venezuela. They aren't carrying passengers. There's an absolute prohibition, due to the danger of their cargo. Our life continues normally. Calm is gaining dominance over our spirits. At nine in the morning a big breakfast, at one lunch, at six the main meal. The rest of the time we pass as well as we can. The children are very brave. Today as night fell, the sea was rough. On Sunday we're planning to send the first telegrams to the Americas. We're thinking about everyone.

AUGUST 1941
SATURDAY 9. ST. ROMANUS. 221-144

Last night was very rough. A strong storm accompanied by hurricane-force winds tossed the ship violently around like a toy. At one in the morning, when the waves were coming over the deck and reaching the bridge, I wanted to witness the farewell of the two oil tankers, our travel companions during recent days. The two tankers, which are faster than we are—they do fourteen miles and were built two years ago—passed us with all their lights on. The sight was worth seeing, especially because of the sober frame added by the raging sea. From that point on, we've continued alone. During the day, we entertained the children however we could. In Gothenburg, I bought some fishing rods in order to maintain their dream that we were going to fish at sea. Today, with two tinned sardines, we staged the "miracle" of catching fish. Joseba was enchanted to see that a fish appeared hanging from his hook. So we entertain them and entertain ourselves on so long and monotonous a crossing.

AUGUST 1941
SUNDAY 10. ST. LAWRENCE. 222-143

Today the sea appeared calmer, and the sun was shining. On our second Sunday at sea, we celebrated the captain's birthday; he's a well-mannered person and fits the type of one of our captains accustomed to the sea, serene, always friendly. In Gothenburg before leaving, we bought some toys for Joseba and Aintzane without their knowledge, telling them that ship's captains usually keep presents in their cabins for children who behave well during the trip. Today, since it was the captain's saint's day, he gave Joseba a wooden horse and Aintzane a little car, also of wood, with a doll. The children's emotion and promises of good behavior were extraordinary. In the afternoon, a large dinner offered by the captain. Drinks on a large scale, cocktails, champagne, liqueurs, and whisky. These Swedes drink more than we do. I used to think I held up well in such tests, but I was absolutely defeated. Txantxote, the guy from Bergara, was the one who should have been called. We celebrated the day very well.

AUGUST 1941
MONDAY 11. ST. GAUGERICUS. 223-142

Very dense fog accompanied by suffocating heat made today very unpleasant. The humidity is very high and so penetrating that all our clothes are damp. At nightfall, the sea appeared as smooth as a pool of oil, and everything seems to indicate that we will have a very hot day tomorrow. We spent today at the latitude of our country. We remembered it, promising that we would return. Our thoughts accompanied all those we've left behind in these European lands, scattered and suffering. We left behind various letters in Gothenburg to be put in the mail little by little. By the time they receive certain news of our departure, we'll have been at sea for quite a few days. In this way, we'll spare our mothers and relatives from the worry of the first days. We remember them constantly, reaching out with our thoughts to all who wait and hope as they suffer. Tomorrow we'll pass around three hundred miles from the Azores, at the latitude of New York and Lisbon. The ships' officers wear white starting today. The heat is approaching.

AUGUST 1941
TUESDAY 12. ST. CLARE. 224-141

A very hot day today. The captain had the great idea of ordering the construction of a small pool on the deck, using a square wooden framework covered with waterproof canvas. The foresight is praiseworthy, especially in view of the approaching tropics. All of us passengers and officers took a dip. It goes without saying that our two little ones enjoyed it. It was impossible to get them out of the water. We hope to defeat the heat in this way. Today we sent the first telegrams to the Americas since our departure from Sweden. One to our good friend Inchausti and one to Father in Buenos Aires.[147] We suppose that they'll be happy to receive them. They'll have started to receive our letters in Louvain at the same time, definitively announcing our departure. With our affections in both hemispheres, we're the exact representation of the catastrophe to which the enemies of freedom have brought the world.

AUGUST 1941
WEDNESDAY 13. ST. HIPPOLYTUS. 225-140

It's still hot, although the wind made the atmosphere more refreshing today. They set up awnings over the command bridges and the machinery. The crew works half-naked, and the officers have started to wear white shorts. I've done the same, since despite being a "Latin American" from the tropics, I can't endure the heat. Our little ones are brave, in the water almost all day and with big appetites. Mari has slept wonderfully for the last two days, catching up on the sleep she lost during the days of worry. Thanks be to God, she is in excellent health. We're happy, only worried—and how!—about our relatives in Belgium and about so many friends, among whom we can't forget Tere and Juan and their comrades Telesforo, Basterretxea, etc., etc.[148] All are doing excellently today in

---

147 Mari Zabala's father, Constantino Zabala.
148 Basque refugees who embarked on the steamer *Alsina*. The first two are Teresa Agirre Lekube, the *lehendakari*'s sister, and her husband, Juan Madariaga; the other two are Telesforo de Monzón (see note 117) and Francisco Basterrechea. Francisco Basterrechea y Zaldibar (1887–1975) was a lawyer and a prominent Basque nationalist. During the Spanish Republic, he was a parliamentary representative and a member of the Constitutional Court (*Tribunal de Garantías Constitucionales*). During the Spanish Civil War, as the *lehendakari*'s special representative, he took on missions related to arms purchases and prisoner exchanges. During World War II, he managed to get to Argentina, where he became the Basque government's

Casablanca after having suffered a true Calvary. Right at the end of the day, we received a communication from New York informing us that Father did not receive our cable, because he could not be found at the address given. We were very sorry to hear it.

AUGUST 1941
THURSDAY 14. ST. EUSEBIUS. 226-139

Today we passed around a hundred miles from the Canary Islands. The sun beat down, but the sea breeze made the temperature pleasant. We were constantly in the water in the pool. Mari didn't go in the water this afternoon, because she didn't feel very well. The past days of sleeplessness have left their mark. The waves on the open sea are very rough. She'll be fully recovered tomorrow after sleeping properly, as she is doing now. The children are still very brave. Joseba gets on my shoulders, and in that way we swim the three meters [10 feet] of length that the pool has. He thinks he's a phenomenon with this great deed. We continued our voyage entirely normally, without encountering anyone along our route. The ocean is vast, and anyone who wants to dominate it must be even greater. With great difficulty, we heard the Roosevelt-Churchill

---

delegate in 1946, following Ramón María Aldasoro's return to Europe. With regard to the *Alsina*, it is worth noting that it transported one of the last groups of refugees to reach the Western Hemisphere. After overcoming numerous difficulties, it left the port of Marseilles on January 15, 1941, arriving in Dakar on the 27th. After spending almost six months in the Senegalese capital waiting for navigation permits (Navicert and others), it had to retrace its route back to Casablanca, for which it left on June 3 and where it arrived on the 15th. On the day after the ship's arrival in Casablanca, using various subterfuges, the French authorities took practically all the passengers to two concentration camps, where they held them for about two weeks, until the beginning of July. Thanks to the efforts of the Basque and Spanish authorities and in large part to the Argentine immigration decrees (the first of which was approved on January 20, 1940, and the second on July 18) and to that country's pressure on Vichy France (to the point of threatening to bar French citizens from entering Argentina), the passengers were embarked on the steamer *Quanza* on November 4, 1940, headed for Mexico, where they arrived in the port of Veracruz on the 18th. On November 29, the *Quanza* reached the port of Santa Clara, Cuba, where the passengers were again interned in what was called the Ciscornia camp. The *Alsina*'s last passengers (those known as "Alsinoids") left for Argentina on board the Río de la Plata on March 12, 1942, arriving on April 15, not without first suffering a new fright in the form of a German submarine that intercepted them when they were sailing at the latitude of the Brazilian coast.

agreement. Its eight points are enormously interesting.[149] Freedom is opening its doors. We still haven't received a reply from New York.

AUGUST 1941
FRIDAY 15. ASSUMPTION. 227-138

Today we remembered the feast day of Our Lady of Begoña. We completed her novena and commended the care of our voyage to her also, remembering the faith of our seamen preserved for eternity in the sanctuary's ex-votos. Our voyage continued normally, solitary amid the immensity of the ocean. These days we're crossing the region of the trade winds, today at the latitude of Cuba, about 20°. Tomorrow we'll pass close to the Cape Verde Islands, and in four or five days we'll cross the equator. Today we prohibited the little ones from going in the water. They've done nothing but get in and out of the pool. The waves are very

---

149 The *lehendakari* is referring to the meeting between U.S. President Franklin D. Roosevelt (1882–1945) and British Prime Minister Winston Churchill (1874–1965) at Placentia Bay in Newfoundland. As a result of the meeting, a declaration, known as the Atlantic Charter, was published, setting out eight points: According to the Charter, the signatories (1) were not seeking to annex any territory in the war; (2) did not desire any territorial changes that were not based on the wishes of the peoples involved; (3) respected the right of all peoples to choose their form of government, restoring the sovereignty and rights of self-government of those peoples from whom they may have been taken away; (4) committed to promoting the access of all states to raw materials and trade, on the basis of equality of opportunity; (5) committed to collaborate to the highest degree for the purpose of ensuring improved labor conditions, economic development, and social security; (6) after the defeat of Nazi tyranny, hoped to see the reestablishment of a peace in which nations could live in peace and security within their borders; (7) a peace that would ensure navigation in all seas; and (8) established that, in order to achieve collective security based on the renunciation of force, aggressors should be disarmed. On his arrival in Latin America, the *lehendakari* declared to the Montevideo daily newspaper *El Tiempo* about the Atlantic Charter, "The eight points of the Atlantic Charter are a fortunate herald of better days, making the national freedom of peoples compatible with a system of extensive federations and agreements that is a prelude on the doctrinal and aspirational level to the full Federation of European Peoples. If an authority with effective force is necessary in domestic affairs, a hand that can bring morality to the disturbing environment and remedy the injustice inflicted is becoming perceptible with the same force on the international level. "I am one of those men of good will who believe in the nearness of a happier hour once violence has been defeated." Julio V. Iturbide, "Abrirá definitivamente los ojos del mundo el cataclismo actual," *El Tiempo*, reprinted in full in *Euzko Deya* (Buenos Aires), no. 89 (October 25, 1941), 9–10. See the transcription of Iturbide's account in appendix 15.

rough, and we're afraid that with the tropical heat on top of this, they'll suffer an accident that would be very unpleasant in this situation. Mari was better than yesterday, but still somewhat indisposed. The sea was very choppy because of the wind that was blowing. We still haven't received a reply from New York. We listened to comforting commentaries on the Roosevelt-Churchill agreement on the radio. Everything will move forward.

AUGUST 1941
SATURDAY 16. ST. JOACHIM. 228-137

Today we passed the latitude of Santo Domingo and approached Dakar, the name of which is starting to be in the news again these days due to London's natural concerns regarding Vichy's inconceivable attitude. There was nothing that couldn't be expected from the French "realists," ultimately collaborationists. The anti-Bolshevik "crusade" gives them their great argument. Like those of the other "crusade." The bell has tolled for all these heroic crusades. We're continuing our tranquil life on board. With time, the passengers have come to trust one another more. With trust come questions, and with questions come comical situations for us again. They ask us about Latin America, about our business affairs—our travel companions are Jews—about our families. We're pretty used to playing our role by now, and we know more about Latin America than Batista, but the truth is that we would like to get there already in order to be able to speak without masks and veils, which are always unpleasant. How much we have to learn in life!

AUGUST 1941
SUNDAY 17. ST. HYACINTH. 229-136

Third Sunday at sea. Our voyage is proceeding tranquilly, without encountering a single ship along our route. During the night, undoubtedly attracted by our ship's lights, several flying fish jumped out of the sea onto our deck. The captain ordered them collected in order to make a present of them to Joseba, who is the ship's main attraction. Joseba was enchanted. In the pool, he caught a flying fish five times today. He was enchanted to see it hanging from his hook, without caring whether it was the dead one from the previous night. Aintzane accompanies her brother in these entertainments. Innocence is a great thing in all matters, even in order to sail in peace amid the greatest dangers. Today the sea was quite rough, since we're crossing the windy region of the tropics. We made a gift of champagne to the captain, returning his hospitality on his saint's day. That day we appeared at table properly dressed. Today we did so in shirtsleeves. Circumstances oblige.

AUGUST 1941
MONDAY 18. ST. HELEN. 230-135

We continued approaching the equator. The atmosphere is warm, but the wind that has been blowing strongly the last few days makes us forget that we're sailing in the tropics. We're now at 12°, the latitude of the Venezuelan coast. We remembered so many friends who have taken refuge in that country, and especially Constan and Vicen.[150] When we passed through the latitude of Mexico, we talked a lot about Tomás, who will be waiting for us, according to what he wrote to Louvain.[151] Our monotonous and orderly life takes place generally around the pool, where the children in particular are beginning to demonstrate their prowess, having lost their fear of the water. The voyage is tiring due to its length. Our ship doesn't get above twelve knots, and there's always some weather-related reason that slows our progress. Fortunately, it sails smoothly. All of us passengers are "acclimatized" by now.

AUGUST 1941
TUESDAY 19. ST. DONATUS. 231-134

Last night we sent a new telegram to Don Constan, this time care of Joaquín de Gamboa, whose information they gave me in Belgium. We're waiting anxiously for a reply.

Today we continued our voyage toward the equator amid strong wind and rain. We were all expecting suffocating heat. The officers and we passengers are wearing shorts. Instead of the tropical sun, we've found clammy temperatures and fog and even drizzle, like outside Atxuri. But we shouldn't make too hasty a judgment, since we haven't arrived at 0° yet. We were very happy to receive late in the day a telegram from Father replying to the one we sent yesterday. He congratulated us and informed us that he won't be able to come to Rio de Janeiro. We were sorry that we won't be able to give him a hug upon our arrival on Western

---

150 Constantino and Vicente Zabala Aketxe were brothers of Mari Zabala.
151 Tomás Agirre Lekube. See note 9.

Hemisphere soil and because it means that his documents (and those of the others) aren't very good. In the end, we'll see when we get there.

AUGUST 1941
WEDNESDAY 20. ST. BERNARD. 232-133

As I write these lines, we're approaching the equator. We'll cross it tomorrow morning. Following tradition, there will be a celebration on board for the uninitiated, that is, those who have never crossed the equator before. Only three of us in the entire contingent are exempt from the rite. And I say "us" because I pass for a veteran of these battles. The comedy extends even to these details, and the seriousness with which it is necessary to play our roles breaks down when we are alone and give way to laughter. But how unpleasant this prolonged situation is, and how eager we are to get to a place where they call us by our names! The most humorous part of the whole thing is that we have to play the role of protectors and spiritual counselors of our travel companions, Jews whose life is an odyssey. They listen to us because we're neutral, respected, and rich Latin Americans. If they only knew that we could beat their fund of stories! But how much we learn by listening to someone else's sorrow!

AUGUST 1941
THURSDAY 21. ST. JOAN FRAN. 233-132

At noon today we crossed the equator. A solemn ceremony, mandatory in the seafaring world, was held to mark the occasion. Neptune and his entourage made an appearance on the deck, taking their places next to the pool. He greeted the captain, who received him in his dress uniform. With great pomp and sonority, they called up one by one each of the passengers and crew who were crossing the equator for the first time. A speech by Neptune, costumed in an original manner and provided with a large beard. Afterward, an individual examination of the initiates, seated on a bench and on the edge of the pool. Auscultation by the doctor with unusual instruments, requiring the patient to ingest various spoonfuls of not very pleasant liquids, and after a shave with paste, the ducking. So for women and men. They exempted the children, who were terrified for a time by the makeup of Neptune's companions and the rigor of the policies that threw their *ama* into the pool headfirst. The festivities were very pleasant.

AUGUST 1941
FRIDAY 22. STS. TIM. AND C. 234-131

All the passengers having been provided with a certificate issued in Neptune's name, with signatures and seals, by reason of which they will be respected by authorities of all kinds in a similar situation, they continued discussing yesterday's festivities, which were celebrated at the main meal with extra offerings of wine and liqueur. The children breathed easier upon learning that Neptune and his clique had made a definitive departure by submarine. The strongest sailor, wearing a top hat and frock coat and made up in blackface, was in charge of dunking the poor initiates several times headfirst into the pool, throwing them violently into the water with their feet in the air. It was against the black man with the top hat that Aintzane and Joseba directed their shouts and wails of protest. For a time, we forgot other memories.

For the first time since the Faeroes, we saw three ships today, one Norwegian in English service, one English, and one American. Certainly, we had our crossing of the equator with the most pleasant temperature of the trip, with a fresh breeze like in Mutriku.

AUGUST 1941
SATURDAY 23. ST. PHIL. BENIZI. 235-130

All day today we sailed in sight of the immense Brazilian coast, not twenty miles away. We crossed paths with two oil tankers, both Panamanian-flagged, as a consequence of which, in addition to the captain's call informing me of the ships' appearance, I had a session of Latin American economics after dinner, from oil and shipping to cotton. The travelers, Polish Jews, have still not said that is who they are. Our discretion, which on this occasion is charity, omits all varieties of questions along these lines. They are polite, relatively cultured, and above all, we have the impression that they are good people. The Landau brothers especially, who are engineers, give the impression of being socially elevated individuals, due to their technical knowledge and their manners. But they very clearly manifest characteristics of their race in their liveliness and their interest in economic matters. They are persecuted and victims of a brutal injustice. For this reason, I look on them with respect and sympathy.

AUGUST 1941
SUNDAY 24. ST. BARTHOLOMEW. 236-129

Fourth Sunday at sea. Since we've been sailing near the Brazilian coast, we are well informed. We're constantly listening to Brazilian broadcasters, and at eleven-thirty at night (three in the morning in London) the BBC broadcast for Latin America. Today we were able to hear the almost complete translation of Churchill's speech and some pertinent commentary on it. The program of the Atlantic Conference is magnificent, and even if strong doubts persist in our minds as a result of the unfulfilled promises from twenty years ago, I nevertheless think that it's serious this time, due to the lessons learned. I believe that all those who are suffering can congratulate themselves because of it. The fight for the restoration of freedom among all peoples will be long and hard, but the outcome is foreordained. Tyranny will disappear once more, in Germany as in Russia, in Italy as in Spain and the peoples Spain subjugates. God will protect Euzkadi.

AUGUST 1941
MONDAY 25. ST. LOUIS. 237-128

Right at the end of the day yesterday, we sent two telegrams, one to Buenos Aires and one to New York, announcing our arrival for the 27th. We're waiting to receive an answer, since we suspect from Inchausti's silence that he didn't receive the previous telegram. Our Israelite travel companions are anxious about our arrival in Brazil, since they don't have transit visas for that country, only Argentine visas. The Gallarts' American visas expire on the 30th. If they can't disembark in Brazil, and their Yankee visas aren't extended, their situation may be serious, since they're thinking of returning to Sweden. Every Jewish case is a tragedy. We console the others. It has its humorous side, but that's how it is. Tomorrow we will be heading straight for Rio de Janeiro, where we hope to arrive the day after tomorrow at midday. A group of dolphins leaped alongside the ship, fleeing afterward. Amid all these small things, I meditate and meditate on what can and should be done in the Americas. And with God's help, it will be done.

AUGUST 1941
TUESDAY 26. ST. ZEPHYRINUS. 238-127

Finally, we have reached the end of our voyage. Today we received a cable from our great friend Inchausti, in which he told us that he had received the one we sent him on the 12th and that there was no answer because no line of communication with our ship, the *Vasaholm*, could be found. Attentive as always, he asked us for our information in Rio de Janeiro. We hope to arrive in that capital tomorrow, if God helps us as He has done up to now. We have had a very good voyage, taking into account the enormous dangers through which we have passed, dangers that grow larger in our minds as times passes. Since it was the last day on board, the Captain hosted us for a splendid dinner. We thanked him for his attentions, and he wished us all good fortune in the future. Today I threw into the sea poor Cesáreo's slippers (may he rest in peace), which had traveled with me for more than a year. They were no longer presentable.

AUGUST 1941
WEDNESDAY 27. ST. CAESARIUS. 239-126

By seven a.m., Rio de Janeiro was in sight. Around nine, we entered the mouth of the natural port. A splendid landscape, marvelous nature, a handsome city. Then came the formalities, health inspectors, state police, port police, customs. Everything done politely. Our poor Jewish companions will surely lose their American visas. They can't arrive in time. They won't give them Brazilian visas. The Argentine ones expire. A tragedy. And we continue consoling them. On a bad day, certainly. Mari received two letters from her father that made a strong impression. It was the first blow upon our arrival in the Americas. He didn't give her good news. God will arrange everything, but for the moment I don't know who is worse off, the Jews or us. Telegrams and letters from Inchausti. Always generous, he offered us his hospitality. We will probably accept it. The black gang of workers invaded the boat. They made a strong impression on Aintzane and Joseba. They had never seen so many black people, and such ugly ones. They thought that the Americas were something else, judging by *aita*'s *ipuñas*. But in half an hour they were getting used to it.

AUGUST 1941
THURSDAY 28. ST. AUGUSTINE. 240-125

Our first visit upon leaving the hotel this morning was to Saint Ignatius's Church, where the Jesuits also have a large school. There we thanked our saint for his protection. From the heights of the spirit we descended to those of the dollar, visiting the City Bank branch in Rio de Janeiro. Our friend Inchausti had made suitable arrangements, and we lack for nothing. It's sad to live on alms, but it's pleasant to have true friends. He called me from New York today. He wants us to enter there under our true names. I don't know whether that will be possible. At all events, it's decided that we will travel to New York. Inchausti recommended that I still maintain absolute silence. So we'll continue the comedy for now. We spoke with Father. A clear connection with Buenos Aires. We were able to say the main things. He was enchanted, and so were we. Providence continues helping us. In Rio de Janeiro we met Mr. Stevenson, our great friend, who is consul here and was previously consul in Bilbao.[152]

AUGUST 1941
FRIDAY 29. BEHEADING OF ST. J. THE BAPT. 241-124

This morning Mari received a large bouquet of flowers sent by Mr. Stevenson, our good friend the British consul. He's invited us to his house tomorrow. He wants to honor us and help us. On Monday we'll visit the American ambassador to discuss our papers, documents, and visas with a view to our travel to New York. Certainly, Inchausti called me from New York again today. This great friend wants me to enter the United States as a professor at Columbia University, no less. This is too big an idea to be able to be carried out, given the prestige it would mean and the facilities it would provide for traveling throughout the rest of America, following my compatriots' plans for unity and preparation of the instrument of victory for Euzkadi. Inchausti says that it can be done. May God help him and help us as He has done up to now.[153] Rio de Janeiro is magnificent, but our spirits fly further afield, dream, and hope.

---

152 See note 28.
153 On the weekly page published by the Euzko Ikasle Batza (EIB) student association in the journal *Euzkadi*, the caption of an aerial photograph of Columbia University said, "Columbia University, in New York, is considered the largest in the world in terms of the number of buildings that make it up and the number of students in its classrooms. Forty thousand students from all nations appear on its enrollment

AUGUST 1941
SATURDAY 30. ST. ROSE OF LIMA. 242-123

In the morning we went out to buy a bouquet of flowers to send to Mrs. Stevenson, to whose house we had been invited this evening. The heat increased, and it easily does us in as soon as we're out and about for more than an hour. For this reason, we preferred to return to the hotel. Consul Stevenson called me on the telephone to remind me about the invitation and announce a surprise for the evening. Soon after we arrived at his house at 7:30, we witnessed the arrival of Mr. Jones, who held the post of British vice consul in the *txoko* [Bilbao]. His wife accompanied him. He had arrived from Lisbon a week ago. He was posted to Rio de Janeiro. It's a small world. We talked about many interesting things. He gave me news that I hadn't heard. He confirmed that our people are in good spirits. Tomorrow or Monday Mr. Stevenson will visit the American consul. We spent a pleasant evening among friends.

AUGUST 1941
SUNDAY 31. ST. RAYMOND. 243-122

[*In the upper margin:* Manu's saint's day. We remembered him and Miren, whose saint's day I think was yesterday.][154]

After yesterday's invitation and the long post-dinner conversation in which only some of our episodes and adventures over the last year and more were celebrated—others remain in reserve—we dedicated the day today to ourselves, starting with fulfilling our religious duties. After lunch, we rented an open car in which we ascended the mountain that overlooks Rio de Janeiro and on the peak of which a colossal statue of Christ makes a majestic appearance. It's a charming excursion and a unique landscape. At the peak, we prayed that His Providence may continue helping us as it has up to today, since our difficulties have still not come to end, and others may appear. But everything will move forward. The heat was even worse today. I sweat a great deal, despite

---

rolls. The university was founded in 1754 and currently has an endowment of 700 million dollars." External Relations Section, Euzko Ikasle-Batza, "Los estudiantes y la guerra," *Euzkadi* (April 25, 1935), 5.

154 Manu Zabala Aketxe and his wife Miren Bikuña.

being "a native of the tropics." But this is minor compared to what we have already gone through and what others—alas!—must be going through. I remember them always.

NOTES

The month of August, unforgettable for so many reasons, comes to an end. Almost all of it was spent at sea. Now, having recovered the serenity that a few days' rest provides, we can appreciate the adventure we survived in crossing a sea full of dangers. But in the end, God willed that everything would go well. No one other than Inchausti and Father knows about our arrival here in the Americas. Starting today—if the letter has arrived—Aldasoro will know about it. My instructions have been strict in this regard. Silence for now, in order to avoid any indiscretion that might turn out to be dangerous. Once we've arrived in New York, things will change. I'm impatient to be in communication with our compatriots in the Americas again. I have a head full of plans and a heart full of enthusiasm. All the obstacles will be gotten past, as they have been up to today. We will conquer. I'm nagged by the thought of the people in Louvain and of all who are suffering. May God be with them.

SEPTEMBER 1941
MONDAY 1. ST. GILES. 244-121

In the morning, Consul Stevenson called me. He said that the American embassy is celebrating a holiday and that he will let me know tomorrow the result of his discussion with the Americans, which he naturally postponed.[155] I spent the day at the hotel today. In the afternoon, Mari went out shopping with the children. We've hired a servant girl to look after the children, especially when we have to leave them alone at the hotel due to some commitment, like the other day. She's Portuguese, a good woman who arrived eight months ago from a Portuguese village. Joseba, who is beginning to realize that there are different languages, explained to her today that *bandeira* ["flag" in Portuguese] means *ikurriña* ["flag" in Euskara] "in Spanish." And he was so pleased with himself. Mari and I went out today for the first time after so many months to see a newsreel.

---

155 The holiday was Labor Day, celebrated on the first Monday in September in the United States.

SEPTEMBER 1941
TUESDAY 2. ST. STEPHEN OF H. 245-120

Mr. Stevenson called me again on the telephone to tell me that I could go to the American embassy. I was received by the embassy secretary, who was already informed about me. Even though Inchausti told me that I should see the ambassador, I hastened to say that it was sufficient that he be informed, since in effect, as always happens, he is "very busy." Even if he wasn't, I replied, I don't think that it's necessary that I see him, but rather that he be familiar with my case. They won't do anything without instructions from Washington. We live in a democratic world that is still subject to the ritual forms of the nineteenth century. Von Ribbentrop has a different system for his friends. But in the end, the visit was cordial, and I was invited for a cocktail. Our documents and visas are in order, but my friends in New York want me to make a grand entrance, and I don't know how these changes can be made. To me, it seems more natural to enter as Álvarez and leave as Agirre, but my good friends in New York want to do me too much honor, as always. Tomorrow I'm visiting Mr. Stevenson again.

SEPTEMBER 1941
WEDNESDAY 3. ST. REMACLUS. 246-119

Mr. Stevenson sent me the list of our compatriots living in Casablanca. How many dear names! It's the first time I've seen the list. And it was printed on the front page of *Euzko Deya* of Buenos Aires on May 30, 1941.[156] *Euzko Deya* is still alive! My happiness was immense after more than a year of complete ignorance. My presentiments will be fulfilled one by one. I visited the British consulate. Mr. Stevenson was sick. I wanted to thank him for sending the clipping from *Euzko Deya*, talk to him about my visit to the American embassy, and invite him and his wife to a meal, reciprocating their invitation from Saturday. Another day. I also visited the bank to request a new supply of funds. Our expenses are extraordinary. There's four of us. My greatest defense is staying in good hotels here, especially since external display is considered so important. And meanwhile the days pass, and the money disappears.

---

156 *Euzko Deya* was a newspaper published in Buenos Aires by the Basque government's delegation in Argentina. In its first incarnation, it appeared between 1939 and 1975 and was directed by the Basque government's successive delegates in that southern country, Ramón María Aldasoro, Francisco Basterrechea, and Pedro Basaldua.

I still haven't received news from Inchausti, and that disturbs me. We thought that once we arrived in the Americas, our difficulties would come to an end, but that's not the case. This will also have to be brought to a close, like the war.

SEPTEMBER 1941
THURSDAY 4. ST. ROSALIA. 247-118

This morning we were planning to go to the Venezuelan consulate to renew Mari's passport, which expired on the 21st, that is, at sea. We supposed that there would be no difficulties. We supposed … But a long-distance phone call from our friend Inchausti in New York diverted our efforts in a different direction. There are difficulties for sending money. I visited Consul Stevenson at his house. He was sick and in bed with a severe cold. We found a formula for them to give me money here and deposit it in the United States under the name he gave me. And we still have difficulties on all sides. Small ones, not overarching ones, but difficulties in the end, which are always dangerous in these circumstances. We received a letter from Father in Buenos Aires. He's still very worried and recounted another litany of lamentations. He informed me that I won't find my path strewn with roses. I'm well aware of that and am arriving forearmed. But the one who persists to the end wins the prize. Some people confuse optimism about a cause's final victory with the successes, failures, or passing achievements of a single day. It's not so.

SEPTEMBER 1941
FRIDAY 5. ST. BERTIN. 248-117

This morning Inchausti called me again from New York to tell me that he had received the cable I sent him yesterday with Stevenson's formula for sorting out the economic problem. It looked good to him. He then told me about his visit to Columbia University this morning. In the end, his sleepless hours and his tenacity can't easily be compared to anything else. In a time so full of grief, God has set exemplary friends along our path. The solution that Inchausti is proposing and that he hopes to obtain next week is a splendid one. It can give the prestige needed at this stage of our struggle for freedom. This stage, I say, since the struggle that began in 1936, or rather in 1931 with our political appearance as a people representing the majority of Basque opinion, is now entering a decisive phase. May God be willing to help us as He has done up to today, and may He enlighten us along our path.

We spent the afternoon at the botanical garden with the children, admiring the splendid variety of tropical plants.

SEPTEMBER 1941
SATURDAY 6. ST. ONESIPHORUS. 249-116

After the recent days of intense heat, the weather for the last two days has been considerably more temperate. Today there was enough rain that the children couldn't leave the hotel.

We find ourselves right in the middle of the holidays celebrating Brazilian independence. There's parade after parade, of school children, university students, athletic associations, etc., but the bad weather puts a damper on everything. Tomorrow, the exact day of the anniversary, there will be a large parade. Delegations have arrived from Argentina, Uruguay, Paraguay, etc. Part of the parade will pass in front of our hotel. A great current of renewal exists in this country.[157] The monumentality of this capital is increasing day by day. There's no doubt that the future of the great continent that is Brazil is looking splendid, if there's the necessary skill among its leadership. How many topics of meditation and future study these Western Hemisphere countries suggest! But our spirits are still preoccupied. There will be time later on to concern ourselves with everything.

SEPTEMBER 1941
SUNDAY 7. ST. REGINA. 250-115

This morning we witnessed a magnificent parade by the Brazilian armed forces. I would never have suspected such a display of organization and force. Truly, these countries have taken the matter of Western Hemisphere defense seriously, or else it also serves as a pretext to create

---

157 In 1941 Brazil was governed by Getúlio Vargas, who came to power in 1930. In 1937, after orchestrating a coup on his own behalf, he established the so-called New State (*Estado Novo*), a dictatorship with elements of fascism (known as "integralism" in Brazil) and populism. Between 1937 and 1945, the duration of the Estado Novo, Vargas gave continuity to the restructuring and professionalization of the state, tending increasingly toward state intervention in the economy and toward economic nationalism, and strongly promoting industrialization.

and maintain loyal armed forces for the more certain preservation of the personal power to which they are so attached in these South American latitudes. But the parade was a model of order, of force, of modernity, and even of art. In the afternoon, Mari and I attended the horse races. At prices truly within ordinary people's reach, we left terrified by the degree of passion, shouts, and arguments that the event aroused among the Brazilians. They gamble if there's anything to gamble. Men, women, and even children. Our little ones were at the botanical garden. Certainly, they behaved in exemplary fashion at mass today. I haven't gotten past my shock at seeing Joseba quiet.

SEPTEMBER 1941
MONDAY 8. *BIRTH OF BLESSED V. M.* 251-114

Since it was the Virgin's feast day, we went to church this morning. Afterward to the Venezuelan consulate. The consul wasn't in. We returned at four. He received us. He's a gentleman who looks like he doesn't have many friends. He's from Mérida, the same town that María the Venezuelan is from. It was pure chance. The same as in Berlin with the chancellor of the legation. The unpleasant questions and situations began. Mari maintained her composure, but I shared her suffering. Truly improper. The consul was not very friendly. He found it strange that this passport had been issued in Antwerp. He had a point, along with everything else. He'll discuss the case with the ambassador tomorrow. And here we are, once again entangled in the need for new introductions and explanations, all of them unpleasant. Because it's necessary to enter as Álvarez everywhere, and there are a lot of people named Álvarez in the world. Tomorrow I want to see the Venezuelan and Dominican ministers. Will I be able to? I want to put a clean end to this matter. Who will these ministers be, and how will they think? Here's another reason for doubt and worry, and we've arrived in the Americas.

SEPTEMBER 1941
TUESDAY 9. ST. GORGONIUS. 252-113

Yesterday late in the day I visited Consul Stevenson to ask his opinion on the plan I was thinking about implementing. He thought it was a good one. He was still in bed. I headed to the Dominican legation this morning. In order to get in to see the minister, I claimed that I was coming from Berlin and brought a commission from Dr. Despradel for his colleague in Rio de Janeiro. I was received at ten a.m. Álvarez began his speech, and once he had examined the minister's face and reactions, Álvarez turned into Agirre. The minister stood up, shook my hand, and heaped attentions on me.[158] Providence again. We talked about Mari's case. He recommended that I not visit the Venezuelan ambassador. He's married to a Brazilian woman who has ties to Axis people. The Dominican minister picked up the telephone and spoke directly with the Venezuelan ambassador. He asked him for the renewal as a favor to him, recommended from Berlin. The ambassador will study the case. Fifteen minutes later, he answered favorably. At four in the afternoon, we picked up the renewed passport. The Dominicans once again …

SEPTEMBER 1941
WEDNESDAY 10. ST. NICHOLAS OF TOL. 253-112

Last night we attended the gala performance of *The Barber of Seville* with performers from the Metropolitan Opera in New York, including Tito Schipa and the baritone Borgioli.[159] The former is very old now, the latter magnificent in voice and artistic presence. It's been a long time since I've been able to enjoy this pleasure that's so much to my taste. We enjoyed ourselves very much listening to a *Barber* that it will be difficult to equal. This morning I was at the bank to collect the damned money that I always need. I received three letters from Inchausti all at once today. One of them had been censored by the British. They were dated August 12, August 29, and September 1. The mail is slow even in the Western Hemisphere. Freedom, freedom! In the letters, he gave me very interesting news. I was very pleased by Manu Sota's exemplary behavior. He's continuing his efforts to obtain the position at Columbia University. I'm impatient on behalf of the people in the Americas and on behalf of the tragic situation of the people in Europe.

---

158 At this time, the Dominican ambassador in Brazil was Sánchez Lustrino.
159 Tito Schipa (1888–1965) and Dino Borgioli (1891–1960) were considered the best *tenore di grazia* and one of the best lyric tenors, respectively.

SEPTEMBER 1941
THURSDAY 11. ST. EMILIAN. 254-111

This morning I again visited the secretary of the American embassy. In view of Inchausti's letters, I insisted on seeing the ambassador. He's received instructions from Washington. In effect, the ambassador gave me an appointment for eleven-thirty tomorrow morning. One of the missions of secretaries is usually to prevent visits to their superiors, as is natural, but this time the opposition was defeated, since according to what Inchausti tells me, the ambassador has already been appropriately informed. We'll see what happens tomorrow. The weather is bad; it drizzles incessantly like in the *txoko*. Despite the weather, the children went out with their Portuguese babysitter. She's a very good woman whom the children already love a great deal. Their dialogues are quite humorous, especially when Joseba speaks to her in Euskara. In view of the good performance the other day, today we went to hear *Traviata* with Schipa and Borgioli. We were in the seats for penniless "intellectuals." The performance wasn't like that of *Barber*. The baritone Borgioli in particular, perhaps affected by the humidity, wasn't the Figaro of the other day.

SEPTEMBER 1941
FRIDAY 12. *HOLY NAME OF THE BLESSED V. M.* 255-110

[*In the upper margin*: Tomás's saint's day. We remembered him. We hope to visit him one day in Mexico.]

At eleven-thirty the secretary of the American embassy came down to the waiting room to conduct me to the ambassador.[160] Even the protocol changed. The effect of the instructions was evident. The ambassador received me with great friendliness. He's an individual of a little over fifty, with an extraordinary simplicity and pleasantness. I set out our case; he asked me for details of our adventures. All with great interest, full of affection. He recommended that I wait for a definitive solution from Washington. He doesn't think that I should enter the country with my current documents, since difficulties could come up later. He said that very distinguished individuals were taking an interest in me and

---

160 The U.S. ambassador to Brazil from 1937 to 1944 was Jefferson Caffery (1886–1974), who had previously occupied the same diplomatic post in El Salvador, Colombia, and Cuba.

that my permanent entry permit is a sure thing. The bureaucracy always takes time. We spoke about politics in general. Absolutely in agreement, as well as about the role of the Basques in the Western Hemisphere, a problem that he was familiar with and valued. I left very satisfied. We received a letter from Father saying that if he had known there would be these delays, he would have counseled us to go to Buenos Aires. At least Mari and the children. We'll see.

SEPTEMBER 1941
SATURDAY 13. ST. AMATUS. 256-109

In the morning, after writing to Inchausti, I went out with Joseba so that Mari and Aintzane could do some shopping in peace. Joseba was enchanted, since when he takes my hand he likes to say *guk gizonak aurretik eta amatxu eta Aintzane atzetik*.[161] A fierce defender of hierarchy after his fashion and of the rights of masculinity. In the afternoon I wrote to Juan M^a.[162] In this interim situation that prevents me from taking any action in favor of our people, strange as it may seem, I didn't know what to tell him, and for that reason, I put off writing to him until today. But it was getting to be a long time to keep putting it off. They will be surprised to learn that I'm still here. The case of the people in Louvain worries me deeply. God grant that their situation can be definitively sorted out. A territory under blockade, a poor economic situation, dangers, front lines, exile with no end coming soon. In sum, this worry does not permit me to be calm. I also wrote to Father, who always writes me by return mail. It's his necessary consolation.

SEPTEMBER 1941
SUNDAY 14. EXALT. HOLY CROSS. 257-108

It was terribly hot in church, since the heat produced by the crowd was added onto the natural heat of these latitudes. For this reason, Mari and I took turns going to church at different times. Since the weather was bad (it rained all day), I took the children to see Disney's animated film *Fantasia*.[163] They said it was for children. I was mistaken, not because

---

161 "We men in front, and mother and Aintzane behind."
162 See appendix 11.
163 The Walt Disney production *Fantasia* (1940) was made up of eleven sketches directed by James Algar, Samuel Armstrong, Fort Beebe, Norman Ferguson, Jim Handley, T. Hee, Wilfred Jackson, Hamilton Luske, Bill Roberts, Paul Saterfield, and Ben Sharpsteen.

of the moral aspect, which was absolutely clean, but rather because of its technique in describing Mussorgsky's[164] beautiful and difficult music. Not just children but also a great many adults are incapable of understanding this curious graphical and musical interpretation of a true fantasy of its author. I don't understand how they're promoting it and recommending it for children. Scarcely any of his famous animals and characters appears in it. Inchausti called me again today. He informed me that he'll have a definitive answer about my case on Wednesday. If this situation is prolonged, we'll have to await the solution in Buenos Aires. Here . . .

SEPTEMBER 1941
MONDAY 15. OUR LADY OF 7 SORROWS. 258-107

Today I made another visit to the Dominican minister, with whom I talked about many things for more than two hours. He's very friendly and is deeply interested in things. I wanted to thank him again for his intervention in the fortunate solution of the renewal of Mari's passport. Staying here is becoming more tedious for me every day. The Dominican minister thought that I had left. He's a very good friend of Raimundo Fernández Cuesta, Franco's ambassador sent into semi-exile by Serrano Suñer.[165] I'm afraid that he might have said something to him about

---

164 Modest Petrovich Mussorgsky (1839–1881) was a prominent Russian composer.
165 Raimundo Fernández Cuesta y Melero (1897–1992) was imprisoned by forces aligned with the Republic during the Spanish Civil War and exchanged for a Socialist former minister. Indalecio Prieto, although he was opposed to the exchange on the grounds that he considered it disproportionately favorable to the Nationalists, met with Fernández Cuesta on several occasions and requested that after his liberation, he oppose "the policy that the rebels are putting into practice with the extermination of workers and peasants and the preponderance of the clergy." The Socialist parliamentary representative for Bilbao thought that this "old shirt" [*camisa vieja*] could be a seed "of discord and oppose pristine Falangist ideology to the mystifications of Franco's supporters." Once Fernández Cuesta was in rebel territory, Franco named him general secretary of the Falange in December 1937 in order to neutralize the discontent of longtime Falangist activists dissatisfied by their scant representation in the FET and JONS leadership. Nevertheless, Fernández Cuesta did not oppose the dictator and followed his line. In the cabinet reshuffle of August 1939, the greatest beneficiary among the factions and individuals supporting the Spanish regime was the group represented by Ramón Serrano Suñer (1901–2003), a "new shirt" [*camisa nueva*] but the dictator's brother-in-law and interior minister, who also had sufficient influence to install his loyalists in key positions in the single party. With this balance of forces, and viewing Fernández

my presence in or passage through Rio de Janeiro. Naturally in all good faith and believing me absent. I noted some surprise in the minister and a strange explanation that gave me to understand something of the sort. At the same time, he also thinks that it would be better for me to be in Argentina and so on ... In the end, it has to be suspicions of mine that neither the welcome the minister has given me or his gentlemanliness deserve. But in any event, between the fact that they're whispering something in Argentina and the fact that it's not an entirely holy place here, it's going to be necessary to make a decision.

SEPTEMBER 1941
TUESDAY 16. ST. CORNELIUS. 259-106

The weather continues to be changeable. It's raining, and for the natives, it's intensely cold. It's quite humorous to see how the newspapers inform the public of the "cold front" that is currently crossing the center of Brazil, coming from the south. The temperature is 17° [63° F], above zero naturally. The press consoles its readers by telling them that the forecasters are predicting good weather and good temperatures soon. While my anxiety is growing in this forced wait, I'm doing what I can to counteract it by reading. Mari, who has suffered quite a bit, is accompanying me. I've been acquiring since Gothenburg and have continued to acquire here a good part of the French war literature that aims to explain the causes of the French disaster. Maritain's book is good. The ones by Maurois, Jules Romains, and others are anecdotal and don't get to the heart of the matter in my judgment.[166] With this reading I've gotten myself somewhat up to date on current concerns.

Cuesta as an adversary, despite the loss of faith in him by the "old shirts," Serrano dispatched him first to Brazil as ambassador and then to Italy. José Luis Rodríguez Jiménez, *Historia de Falange Española de las JONS* (Madrid: Alianza Editorial, 2000), 319–20 and 335. Herbert Routledge Southworth, *Antifalange: Estudio crítico de "Falange en la guerra de España: la Unificación y Hedilla" de Maximiano García Venero* (Paris: Ruedo Ibérico, 1967), 181.

166 André Maurois (1885–1967) was a novelist, essayist, literary critic, and historian of French literature. His works include *Les origines de la guerre de 1939* (Paris: Gallimard, 1939), *The Battle of France* (London: Right Book Club, 1940), and *Why France Fell* (London: Bodley Head, 1940).Jules Romains (1885–1972) was a French novelist, playwright, poet, and essayist. He wrote *Sept mystères du destin de l'Europa* (New York: Éditions de la Maison Française, 1940) and *Message aux Français*(New York: Éditions de la Maison Française, 1941). For his part, Jacques Maritain (1882–1973) was a French Catholic philosopher

SEPTEMBER 1941
WEDNESDAY 17 ST. LAMBERT. 260-105

Today it continued raining. In the morning, we took a good walk with the children. In the afternoon, they went out with their babysitter and Mari, and I stayed at the hotel in case they called from New York. Our friend Inchausti will surely call tomorrow. We've received a letter from Father in which he rejoices that we're thinking about the possibility of traveling to Buenos Aires. With the letter that he'll receive tomorrow, in which I charge him and Aldasoro with arranging our visas, he'll have seen that these possibilities are increasing. I'm reading a lot these days. The most profound of the French writers' works is the one by Father Ducatillon.[167] He goes to the heart of the question, is solid in his judgments, and poses in a universal and accurate way the burning question of the struggle and ideological revolution of these days. I'm also reading Berdyaev, whom I've studied and admired for many years.[168] Today it was Count Keyserling's turn.[169] I've already read the books by General Rojo and Álvarez del Vayo.[170] The latter is interesting, although

---

deeply concerned with the relationship between Christianity and culture and open to the great events and problems that agitated the society and the Church of his time. During the Spanish Civil War, he repudiated and condemned the ideas of crusade and holy war, as well as the rebellion's legitimacy. In addition, he praised the Basques' heroic struggle, conducted "according to the rules of international law, with a constant desire for justice, even if they may have made mistakes due to their particularist psychology." Javier Tusell and Genoveva García, *El catolicismo mundial y la guerra de España* (Madrid: Biblioteca de Autores Cristianos, 1993), 106–7, and Gregorio Arrien and Iñaki Goiogana, *El primer exilio de los vascos: Cataluña 1936–1939* (Barcelona: Fundació Trias Fargas; Fundación Sabino Arana, 2002), 85–86.

167 Joseph Vicent Ducattillon was a French member of a religious order who went into exile in the United States during World War II. The book to which the *lehendakari* refers is *La guerre, cette révolution: Le sort de la civilisation chrétienne* (New York: Éditions de la Maison Française, 1941).

168 Nikolai Aleksandrovitch Berdyaev (1874–1948) was an exiled Russian philosopher who founded a philosophy of the person that influenced Emmanuel Mounier and personalism.

169 Hermann Count Keyserling (1880–1946) was a German philosopher.

170 Julio Álvarez del Vayo Olloqui (1885–1975) had been minister of state alongside Juan Negrín. The book mentioned by the *lehendakari* is *La guerra empezó en España (lucha por la libertad)* (Mexico City: Séneca, 1940). Vicente Rojo Lluch (1894–1966) was the most distinguished Spanish Republican general during the 1936 conflict. After the war, he went into exile in Argentina, where he published *¡Alerta los pueblos! Estudio político-militar del período final de la guerra española* (Buenos Aires: Aniceto López, 1939).

biased. I've also read Aunós's work with his hundred years (1808–1936) of Spanish history.[171] How much error and bias!

SEPTEMBER 1941
THURSDAY 18. ST. STEPHANIE. 261-104

I spent the morning and the afternoon in my hotel room waiting for a call from my friend Inchausti. He didn't call. There must surely be more difficulties than he thought. Nothing surprises me any more. Tomorrow I'm expecting a letter from Father in Buenos Aires and possibly a telegram, since I charged him and Ramón with urgent arrangements for our visas to enter Argentina and instructions to that republic's ambassador in Rio so that he will receive me. And so it goes, another visit and another explanation and . . . other difficulties? Everything is possible in this democratic world full of slowness and phantasmal fears and that despite everything is called to triumph for the good of the world. But how much rot will have to be scraped away in order to enter onto the right road! I considered the trip to New York to be necessary in the first instance on account of our fatherland's affairs, but since definitive solutions are taking a long time and things are getting too warm for me in this country, we're going to see whether it's God's will that we come to the land of the tango. It'll be for a reason.

SEPTEMBER 1941
FRIDAY 19. ST. JANUARIUS. 262-103

I'm still waiting for an answer or call from New York and a letter or telegram from Buenos Aires. They haven't arrived. There are surely delays or difficulties. To practice patience again! I'm reading Keiserling these days. His judgment of Spain is a calque of everything I've read in Unamuno and in Ortega y Gasset. I'm not finding much originality. I've started Stefan Zweig's book on Brazil.[172] A clear, profoundly psychological, and accurate study. Today we had dinner at Consul Stevenson's house, since he wanted to lavish his hospitality on us once again. We had an

---

171 Eduardo Aunós Pérez (1894–1967). The book mentioned is *Itinerario histórico de la España contemporánea (1808–1936)* (Barcelona: Bosch, 1940).
172 Stefan Zweig (1881–1942) was an Austrian writer and pacifist. As a consequence of the Nazi rise to power, he left Austria for exile, ultimately ending up in Brazil. There he wrote *Brasilien, Ein Land der Zukunft* (1941), in which he discussed the country's history, economy, and culture.

interesting conversation about his impressions of Russia during his stay in that country in 1939. One learns something every day. Stevenson is a good friend who is helping us a great deal. We went home worried about the delay in the resolution of our affairs, but this is nothing compared to those who are suffering more. The desire to sort out many pending and delicate issues as soon as possible, the Louvain case and the case of those who remain in jail and in Europe, sharpens and quickens that desire and increases our impatience.

SEPTEMBER 1941
SATURDAY 20. ST. EUSTACE. 263-102

Today is Tere's saint's day.[173] The news we have about them is very confused. May God help them to bear the suffering that has fallen to their lot, like so many and such dear compatriots. Certainly, since we know that Alcalá Zamora is in a concentration camp in the Sahara, we're afraid that Telesforo might be there.[174] What horror and what ignominy for France, which calls itself Christian, but which is, like all groups that monopolize that august name, Christian without charity. Saint Paul's [*Crossed out: Nihil sum*] *Nemo sum* resounds more sternly than ever.[175] We received a letter from Father in Buenos Aires. He received ours requesting the visas. He and Ramón are working on it. He says in the letter that they sent me a telegram yesterday, Friday, confirming that they were granted, a telegram that did not arrive. We're expecting another letter tomorrow in which he can explain what's happening. They're also talking about entering by the wide gate in Buenos Aires. That's all very well, but meanwhile, time is passing. The difficulty is understandable, since the passports are issued under false names... but how bureaucratically things work in these countries!

---

173 Teresa Agirre, the *lehendakari*'s sister.
174 Niceto Alcalá Zamora y Torres (1877–1949) was a conservative politician and a supporter of the Spanish Republic. He served as president of the Second Spanish Republic between 1931 and 1936.
175 *Nihil sum* means "I am nothing" in Latin, and *nemo sum* means "I am no one." The phrase and its significance are taken from Saint Paul's First Letter to the Corinthians (I Cor. 13:2): *Et si habuero prophetiam et noverim mysteria omnia et omnem scientiam, et si habuero omnem fidem, ita ut montes transferam, caritatem autem non habuero, nihil sum.* In the King James Version: "And though I have the gift of prophecy, and understand all mysteries, and all knowledge; and though I have all faith, so that I could remove mountains, and have not charity, I am nothing."

SEPTEMBER 1941
SUNDAY 21. ST. MATTHEW. 264-101

Mari and I took turns going to church at different times. I returned to the hotel with the hope of having a letter or telegram. Nothing arrived, either from New York or from Buenos Aires. This silence indicates at least that things are not proceeding with the desired speed. If this interpretation is not optimistic. It seems that I am classified among those dangerous men who keep chancelleries busy. I would like to be mistaken with respect to Argentina, which has done so much for us and for which we have so much esteem. But that idea is already making the rounds—and often with all the good faith in the world—that the people are good ... but the leaders ... Even if the leaders have left behind everything, everything for the people. And even if they're ready to continue leaving it behind. But attesting to that is history's task. Meanwhile, to smile and wait. God gives strength for everything, pointing out the path of duty, which is a difficult path. Good old Inchausti, my great friend, called me. He's spending a fortune on long-distance calls. He hopes that the matter will be resolved this week. I explained to him my fears about my prolonged stay in this city and my probable trip to Buenos Aires. He understood. He will continue his efforts.

SEPTEMBER 1941
MONDAY 22. ST. THOM. OF V. 265-100

We didn't receive any letters from Buenos Aires today either. In view of this, I sent a telegram this morning expressing our surprise. I'm anxious about the loss of time, because in addition to spending a lot of money in this hotel life, I'm delaying contact with my compatriots, very necessary contact given that not everything that has gotten back to me is irreproachable, and without iron unity, we'll obtain nothing. I'm delaying the possible solution, or at least the channeling of efforts toward a solution, of the terrible problems of our relatives and compatriots who are suffering in Belgium, in France, in Euzkadi, in Spanish prisons, and even in Africa. Like everything else, this delay stems from the good faith and excellent will of my compatriots who want to honor me—and from the bureaucracy that prevents it; I can't blame anyone for anything, rather the reverse. But that doesn't change the fact that my spirit is more impatient every day. I think that when things happen like this, it's because it's God's will. I have a presentiment that I will arrive at the opportune time.

SEPTEMBER 1941
TUESDAY 23. ST. LINUS. 266-99

We still have no news from Buenos Aires, increasing our anxiety. It seems that unforeseen difficulties have arisen. Since Father's last letter, written on Thursday, in which he announced a telegram with what he expected to be the satisfactory result of his efforts, we've received neither the announced telegram nor an explanatory letter. We haven't been able to get beyond this state of uneasiness and anxiety always produced by the lack of news and the absence of exact knowledge of the real situation. Is it that the favorable atmosphere in Argentina has changed? How little our relatives in Louvain and our friends in Europe can imagine about our situation! Today we invited the Stevensons, reciprocating their repeated gestures of friendship. We talked about our situation. They expressed surprise, since they were unable to understand the reasons for the supposed difficulties. Although in these times, anything is possible. We talked about many other things. At the restaurant where we ate dinner, a trio of exiles was playing, one Czech, one Russian, and one Austrian. They played very well, and the Slavic music had an accent in their hands that spoke to us very much.

SEPTEMBER 1941
WEDNESDAY 24. OUR LADY OF MERCY. 267-98

Today we finally received a letter from Father, dated the 20th. Surprised by the delay (letters never take more than two days from Buenos Aires), we made a thousand conjectures over the course of the day. In the letter, he said that the matter won't be resolved until Thursday. He promised us a telegram on Monday from Montevideo, where he's going with Ramón to obtain our Uruguayan visas. We haven't received that telegram either. Our uncertain and confused judgment gained some understanding when in the afternoon we read the news in the newspapers about an aborted Nazi or Nazi-sympathizing plot in Argentina.[176] The delay of

---

176 The references to a Nazi plot in Argentina mentioned by the *lehendakari* may reflect the news that must have appeared in the Brazilian newspapers around that time regarding the first four reports published in September by the Special Investigative Commission

the mail, the lack of letters and telegrams, the possible delay of the trip to Montevideo, etc., are now explained if, as it seems, the subversive movement was as significant as the press indicates. Certainly, our request arrived at a bad time. But it is to be hoped that this new attempt by the tyrannical coalition, upon being repressed, will improve the situation of its victims who have been washed up on this continent's shores. What we still have to see!

---

on Anti-Argentine Activities (*Comisión Especial Investigadora de las Actividades Antiargentinas*), established by the Chamber of Deputies on June 20, 1941, to shed light on Nazi activities in the country. In its first report, the commission described the National Socialist Party's organization in Argentina and its activities under the cloak of the Federation of German Charitable and Cultural Circles (*Federación de Círculos Alemanes de Beneficencia y Cultura*). In its second report, it demonstrated the collection of funds for illegal purposes by the German Chamber of Commerce in Argentina, as well as detailing German investments in Argentina. The third document produced by the investigative commission, for its part, described the Nazi propaganda activity carried out by the Transocean agency in the country and its dependence on orders from Germany and showed that Buenos Aires served as a distribution center for Nazi propaganda throughout South America. Finally, the fourth document analyzed Argentina's German school system and its similar subordination to directives from the Reich. The special commission produced two other reports as well, but they were published in 1942. In addition, the commission drew up a draft declaration stating that the German ambassador had exceeded the functions of his office and abused his diplomatic privileges. The declaration also recommended the dissolution of the principal Argentine Nazi organizations and the expulsion of their leaders from the country. Although the declaration was approved on September 30, 1941, with seventy-eight votes in favor and one against, President Ramón S. Castillo ignored the parliamentary resolution. At the same time that some of the news that the Basque president could have read in the Rio de Janeiro press might have referred to the special commission's reports, it might also have been related to several scandals that occurred in connection with the Nazi activities investigated. One example was the flight of the press attaché of the German embassy in Argentina from Buenos Aires to Rio de Janeiro in late August, when the commission summoned him to testify about his alleged espionage activities in Argentina. Silvano Santander, *Técnica de una traición: Juan D. Perón y Eva Duarte agentes del nazismo en la Argentina* (Montevideo: Talleres Gráficos Tricromía, 1953), 45–48. "Historia general de las Relaciones Exteriores de la República Argentina," http://www.cema.edu.ar/ceieg/arg-rree/9/9-028.htm. Carlota Jackisch, "El nacionalsocialismo en la Argentina," *Revista Libertas* (Buenos Aires), no. 8 (May 1988), www.esaede.edu.ar.

SEPTEMBER 1941
THURSDAY 25. ST. FIRMINUS. 268-97

First thing in the morning—before eight—we received a cable from Inchausti. This tireless fighter and friend has obtained my appointment as a professor at Columbia University. Tomorrow he's going to Washington to obtain from the state department the indispensable requisites for my permanent residency permit in America. In the contest that's established between North and South, the North is in the lead. I'm satisfied, since this appointment will put me in an advantageous situation for my necessary work and travel on behalf of our cause. My compatriots will judge it this way as well. We then received a letter from Father. He said that there are difficulties, but that they will be successfully overcome. He informed us that Ramón de Aldasoro was leaving for Montevideo to meet with that country's president and obtain my entry, it seems, under my true name. In effect, a telegram from Ramón in Montevideo announced that today, Thursday, he hoped to call me on the telephone sometime after noon to give me "excellent" (he says) news. I waited all day, and no news came. These matters are like that, but how many annoyances there are! And how great the enthusiasm of these friends is!

SEPTEMBER 1941
FRIDAY 26. ST. JUSTINE. 269-96

This morning they informed me that I would receive a long-distance call from Aldasoro at seven p.m. Inchausti called me at midday. He spoke to me from Washington. He said that everything was arranged, that the state department had sent an urgent telegram to Rio de Janeiro with the relevant instructions. I went to the embassy. They haven't received anything, they'll let me know as soon as they arrive. Inchausti wants us to take the first ship or plane to New York. Classes at the university begin on October 1. But how can I make my appearance there without a little rest for my head and also a little preparation? Ramón Aldasoro called me at seven. I should go urgently to Montevideo, where they're waiting for me to sort out serious matters concerning our cause and our compatriots. I will be received with all honors and will have an audience with the president of the Republic. I consider this trip necessary above all in order to establish contact with my compatriots in these lands. And the trip to New York? And the professorship? Today was a day of indecision for me, because everything is necessary, and my greatest desire would be to be able to do the right thing. They all deserve it, more than I do.

SEPTEMBER 1941
SATURDAY 27. STS. COSMAS AND DAMIAN. 270-95

Today they called me from the American embassy. The instructions have arrived, and everything is in order. I went. They introduced me to the consul, a truly pleasant person. He took all the true information and noted the false information in order to have it correspondingly annulled. But a problem immediately presented itself: how to leave Brazil with one name after having entered with another. I mentioned my possible trip to Montevideo and the welcome they've told me to expect from the authorities. They judged at the embassy that my trip to Montevideo is a solution. That's where there's an authority that will turn a blind eye, as Stevenson put it. Here in Brazil, arranging something like that would be difficult and dangerous. My friend Inchausti trembles whenever I talk about leaving for the south. I well understand what his arguments to the Americans were, but here the situation is different from what they imagine it to be there. Ramón today answered the telegram I sent him yesterday, saying that he's writing. Good, since the long-distance telephone call was a disaster of a connection to hear him. Can it be God's will that I will be able to meet my obligations to everyone, informing myself properly about everything? I believe and hope so.

SEPTEMBER 1941
SUNDAY 28. ST. WENCESLAUS. 271-94

Having fulfilled our religious duties, we took a walk in the morning, giving a day's rest to our heads, preoccupied for several months now with visas and bureaucracy of all kinds. How much time lost for fruitful action in favor of our case and of all those who are suffering on account of it! All plans, all dreams suffer delays. May it be God's will that in the coming week we again start to move forward with firm and definitive steps. We're all nervous, those in New York, those in Argentina, and us here. We don't want to think about how our families in Louvain and our compatriots in France will be doing. And I can't complain. This afternoon we went up to the Pão de Açúcar, the marvelous rocky mountain that presides over the entrance to Rio de Janeiro. It falls straight down to the sea and offers the most marvelous views from its peak. The cableway that goes up to the peak is an audacious construction. The children were very brave, almost more than the adults. We spent a good while breathing fresh, pure air.

SEPTEMBER 1941
MONDAY 29. ST. MICHAEL. 272-93

[*In the upper margin*: May Saint Michael, our Mikel Deuna, help us on our path and in the struggle that has been launched for the redemption of our fatherland. I asked him for this today.]

Today is the feast day of Saint Michael, the patron of Euzkadi. In the morning we were issued permanent American visas and an affidavit that serves as a passport to enter the United States. A great success by our good friend Inchausti. The operation took all morning. Of course, I haven't yet received the announced letter from Ramón. I'm expecting it tomorrow. With this delay, our decision to travel to Uruguay and the choice of route have been put off for a day. We'll surely travel by sea (Rio Janeiro to Rio Grande do Sul) for four days to reach a location around two hundred kilometers [125 miles] from the Uruguayan border, where our friends will be waiting for us. Tomorrow, with a letter or without one, it will be necessary to decide on the trip and obtain the tickets. At the very end of the afternoon, Don Enrique de Abaroa announced his visit; he's a Basque patriot who has been living for years in Argentina, where he has a high profile.[177] He brought us greetings from Father and from Ramón. He gave us a lot of news; we spent a very pleasant period of time with him and were invited to have dinner with him tomorrow. We'll continue our conversation with the first herald we've met along our road.

SEPTEMBER 1941
TUESDAY 30. ST. JEROME. 273-92

We still have no news, and we're not calm. We can't imagine what the reason can be for the delay of the letter Ramón announced. In view of all this, I took the plunge of reserving passage on the steamer *Itapé*, which

---

177 Enrique Abaroa Rodríguez was a native of Mundaka and was employed by the Massey-Harris tractor manufacturers as general manager in charge of the South American region, the reason for the contacts and the knowledge of the Basque reality in Latin America he possessed.

sails the Rio Janeiro-Rio Grande do Sul route for a Brazilian coastal shipping company. Rio Grande do Sul is located a few hours from the Uruguayan border. Having decided on the trip, I wrote two letters, one to Ramón and one to Inchausti, explaining our situation with details of all kinds and with absolute clarity. Our compatriot Abaroa will carry them, but he promised me to first speak by telephone right away tomorrow with Aldasoro or with Don Constan. That way everyone will know the details of our trip. Abaroa invited us to dinner at the Casino de Urca, so renowned in this capital. We had a very pleasant time hearing from his mouth the narration of so much news that was new to us. We said goodbye until Montevideo.

NOTES

As September comes to an end, it's now one month and four days that we've been stuck in Rio de Janeiro. It's all been necessary in order to finally obtain proper documents, and this time documents of great value, since they have our own names and are American. The admirable tenacity and enthusiasm of Inchausti have borne fruit, and the success is a credit to him and does him honor. At the same time, from the time Aldasoro was subsequently informed of my arrival, he has put all his eagerness and generosity into obtaining free passage through the countries of the South for me. Faced with these proofs of affection, it's appropriate to bless God, Who has placed in the hearts of our compatriots a deep sense of loyalty and of estimable human virtues. There must exist defects among us, unfortunately, and even more than one deplorable attitude, but I've had the good fortune to hear from our friend and compatriot Mr. Abaroa that

NOTES

the behavior of the Basques in the Western Hemisphere (Mr. Abaroa has traveled through fifteen countries on this continent) is in general and almost in its totality excellent, and they maintain a deserved and well-earned prestige everywhere. There will be small miseries, generally produced by our excessive spirit of criticism and by the natural irritation caused by emigration, which sows so many illusions, but the instrument, the foundation is healthy, and on that foundation the edifice will be built of which we dream with increasing longing. To that edifice and to its perfection we must dedicate our efforts, in order to be even a little worthy of those who have given their lives for the fatherland and who are suffering in the jails and prisons. Our fatherland's freedom will come, and with it the freedom of all those who are suffering. We've all had parts of our souls torn to pieces. This should make us understand the necessity of sacrifice and of carrying out our duties. We exist in the Western Hemisphere. We will exist as free people in Euzkadi, with God's help.

4th TRIMESTER

NOTES

OCTOBER 1941
WEDNESDAY 1. ST. REMIGIUS. 274-91

The month of October has begun, and we're still without news. In view of this, I sent a telegram to Montevideo, where Aldasoro and Father are, or at least the latter is. I've also picked up and paid for the passages to Rio Grande do Sul. So they now know that we're leaving and for where.

Early in the afternoon I received Father's answer. He said that Ramón sent me an airmail letter yesterday with instructions. We're hoping that it arrives tomorrow. Today I suppose that Abaroa will also have communicated with them. In this way, setting out to move forward once again, we add another link to this interminable chain of events that we urgently desire [*Crossed out*: that] to see come to an end. Our thoughts this afternoon were in Louvain. Their situation worries us deeply. And we're irritated by this dance that necessarily delays the possible and desired resolution of their affairs. We've thought about those in France and those in Euzkadi. I hope that the thousands of Western Hemisphere Basques will understand this tragic reality. They are coming to understand it. One day we won't need to call them; they'll come on their own.

OCTOBER 1941
THURSDAY 2. GUARDIAN ANGELS. 275-90

Today Ramón's letter arrived. Clear, magnificent, and generous, like all his letters. Immoderate in its affection for me and its valuation of me. They aim to honor me too much. He tells me that I will be received by official personages. In sum, they invoke reasons of prestige for all of that. When it's a matter of the common cause, I don't set up obstacles, either in the name of humility or in the name of anything else. Let the means and the end be honorable and licit, and let those who want to laugh, laugh. I've never cared about what others say, especially those on the other side, when conscience, a reflection of God, dictates the right path, and our fatherland, Euzkadi, asks for and needs it. So let my friends do what seems right to them. I'm following the path. We embark tomorrow. Today I said goodbye to the American ambassador, Mr. Jefferson. He was extremely friendly. Yesterday I said goodbye to the Dominican minister, a good friend as always and extremely affectionate. Today I wanted to greet the Chilean consul here, who is the writer Gabriela Mistral. I wanted to thank her for her dedication to the Basque children. She was absent. I'll write her.[178] It seems that God is now getting us out of this mire.

OCTOBER 1941
FRIDAY 3. ST. GERARD. 276-89

In the morning we took care of all the preparations for the trip. I left some of our suitcases at the British consulate yesterday. We left at one with the rest of our luggage to embark on the steamer *Itapé*, where I am writing this. This ship, which sails the Rio de Janeiro-Porto Alegre route, that is, toward the south of this immense country, displaces 8,000 to 10,000 tons and carries around four hundred passengers. Since the price of passage is modest, the people are simple and without pretensions. This pleases us.

We left an hour late. The good Portuguese woman María, who has looked after the children during our stay in Rio de Janeiro, came down to the dock say goodbye to us. She was crying, the poor woman. The children were enchanted with her and have been sorry for the separation. We're sailing through a lot of fog. The foghorn is sounding constantly, keeping the passengers awake. Tomorrow we'll arrive in Santos, and on Monday we expect to be in Rio Grande, where our friends are waiting for us.

---

178 Gabriela Mistral, the pen name of Lucila Godoy Alcayaga (1889–1957), was a diplomat, professor, and writer. She was the first Latin American to win the Nobel Prize in Literature. The dedication mentioned by the *lehendakari* was her donation of the royalties from her book *Desolación y ternura* (Desolation and tenderness) to the Basque children evacuated as a consequence of the 1936 war.

OCTOBER 1941
SATURDAY 4. ST. FRANCIS OF ASSISI. 277-88

Feast day of the great saint of charity, the human Christ, as they called him. In these days of egoism and of adulteration of the essentials of Christianity, his invocation and intercession are more necessary than ever.

Due to the requirements of the cargo-loading operations, our steamer will remain in this port of Santos, where we arrived at six a.m. today, until tomorrow, Sunday, at the same time. We have a free day. We took advantage of it to visit the capital of the future, São Paulo. It's an hour and a half by road from Santos, along a picturesque and well-maintained route. São Paulo is an impressive, feverish, dynamic town. Its growth is fabulous. In 1920 it had 500,000 inhabitants. Today it has over a million and a half. You can see the city growing. It's said that a house is built every hour. It's impressive for what it will be, and it leaves a tragic doubt in the observer's spirit about what its spiritual orientation will be in the future. There's an air of too much of the material. We returned at six. The ship was still being loaded. We've lost twelve hours.

OCTOBER 1941
SUNDAY 5. ST. PLACID. 278-87

Another Sunday at sea. Yesterday I stayed until very late watching the picturesque cargo operations, with the no less picturesque note of color lent by the variegated mix of races among the longshoremen. We set off this morning at six a.m. With this delay, we won't arrive in Rio Grande until Tuesday. I've sent a telegram to Aldasoro advising him of that, since I would regret it if they made a trip to the border in vain. The telegraph operator sent it quickly. In Santos, new travelers embarked, among them a group of very brave and nice little nuns who, it seems, are going to found some mission or school. Today they were even listening to a jazz band made up of three black men, who were pretty bad. In proportion as we get closer to Uruguay—where we will change our skins like snakes—our impatience is growing, as we are always thinking about those in Europe who hoped that things would go more quickly. But as always, man proposes . . .

OCTOBER 1941
MONDAY 6. ST. BRUNO. 279-86

The night was rough. This ship doesn't have the stability of the *Vasaholme*. The service is also deficient. The staff aren't very friendly. The food is frankly bad, and served in a hurry like in old station restaurants. In Rio de Janeiro, we were surprised by the cheapness of this trip (around forty dollars for the four of us in first class), and now we have the explanation. The children aren't as happy as they were on the Swedish steamer. They can't eat a lot of the dishes. In the end ... tomorrow we expect to arrive on dry land. Since our friends will have received by now all the communications that we sent, we're expecting them, if not at the port of disembarkation, at least at the Brazilian-Uruguayan border. We're dreaming of embracing them all and putting an end to this comedy, which is horribly lugubrious.

Today they asked for the passengers' passports. When I went to the office a little while ago, an officer got an unpleasant look on his face as he looked at my passport. This bachelor and this widow ... In the end, I believe that this will be the last time ...

OCTOBER 1941
TUESDAY 7. OUR LADY OF THE HOLY ROSARY. 280-85

At eight-thirty a.m. we arrived in Rio Grande, where our compatriot Uriarte from Montevideo and an Uruguayan parliamentary representative, Mr. Iturbide, were awaiting us, along with the Uruguayan consul in Rio Grande.[179] We went to the hotel, where they had reserved rooms for us. It's the first time in such a long time that we find ourselves among our own people. Aldasoro and Father are waiting for us at the Uruguayan border. The connections are bad, since the train doesn't run every day. Because of the steamer's delay, we missed today's train. There won't be another one we can take until Thursday. Another two-day wait in Rio Grande. We would never have thought it. The consul invited us to lunch at his house and hosted us in grand style. We already have Uruguayan

---

179 Juan Domingo Uriarte, Dionisio Garmendia, Ricardo Guisasola, Juan Uraga, Mario Pablo Uribarri, Aitor Hormaeche, and Pedro Arteche formed the organizing committee for the welcoming ceremonies prepared for the *lehendakari*. "Arteche nunca fracasa," *Euzko Deya* (Buenos Aires), no. 89 (October 25, 1941), 11. For his part, Julio V. Iturbide was a journalist and a parliamentary representative for Uruguay's Colorado Party.

visas in our passports. They heaped attentions on us, surrounding us with an undeserved importance. Mari retired early with the children, and I was invited again to have dinner with all these friends. After so many obstacles, it seems that the paths to heaven are being opened.

OCTOBER 1941
WEDNESDAY 8. ST. BRIDGET. 281-84

We had a good rest after the fatigues of the voyage and the emotion of yesterday. Endless conversations, with questions of all kinds that have to be satisfied all at once—in sum, the desire to get to know everything—led us to set today aside for an interview with Representative Iturbide. I'm not all satisfied with the result of the effort, even if it filled pages and pages. Tomorrow I have to go over his typed transcript, and afterward I'll submit it to Aldasoro's judgment of its appropriateness at this time, which I'm not in a position to discern. I kept my answers regarding the different problems on a very general level. It's not for this reason, but rather because of the disorder and imperfection in my exposition, that I think that the effort leaves much to be desired and that it's necessary to rectify it, or better, complete it.[180]

We had dinner as the guests of a Tolosan compatriot named Mugika, who has been living in this town for years. The man was overcome by emotion. These are proofs of affection that it is impossible to forget.

OCTOBER 1941
THURSDAY 9. ST. DENIS. 282-83

At six a.m., we took the train to the border. A typical and sparsely inhabited landscape. We arrived at the border. On the last leg of the route on the Brazilian side, a compatriot arrived, Father Irizar.[181] We recognized him by the *ikurriña* he wore on his lapel. They took me by the arm and brought me across to the other side with no more preambles or inspections or stamps. A true bold strike. These good Uruguayans didn't want to tolerate even a minute of delay. We met Father, Aldasoro,

---

[180] The interview with Iturbide that the *lehendakari* mentions gave rise to an article published by the Colorado representative in the daily newspaper *El Tiempo*. The exposition of Agirre's ideas found in the article led *Euzko Deya* to reproduce it in full: "Abrirá definitivamente los ojos del mundo el cataclismo actual," *Euzko Deya* (Buenos Aires), no. 89 (October 25, 1941), 9–10. See appendix 15 for a transcription.

[181] Javier Irizar, parish priest in Melo, Uruguay.

etc. Emotion, weeping, enthusiasm. We continued on our way. First, I shaved off my mustache, my inseparable companion on so many adventures. I did it in the hotel in Río Branco, the first town in Uruguay. Everyone, consuls, border authorities, etc., extremely friendly. In Treinta y Tres—that's what the town is called—many people, flowers, speeches. In Montevideo, many compatriots, a microphone, firm handshakes. I arrived at the hotel in a sweat. A delegation of prominent Uruguayans was waiting for me. Speeches. To sleep exhausted.

OCTOBER 1941
FRIDAY 10. ST. GEREON. 283-82

The overwhelming, exhausting work began. Visits, compatriots arriving from Buenos Aires. Telegrams from Basques all over the world. What a consolation! If those in prison could see it! The parliamentary representatives' visits began. Interview with the journalists. Reporters came from Buenos Aires. We visited the foreign minister.[182] A magnificent welcome and a meaty conversation. My compatriots are extremely well respected. The homage belongs to them and to all who are suffering. The minister, a experienced man who has spent a lot of time in Europe, heaped attentions on me and invited me to dinner on Monday. Telegrams arrived from Buenos Aires, from our organizations imperatively urging my presence there. From Chile also. We haven't decided anything yet, since the homages in Montevideo are exceptional, and the ship for New York leaves on the 17th. Barrena made an appearance, Zabala, the Extraterritorial Committee, our good friend Abaroa, etc., etc.[183] Kuntxillos, arrived, Artxanko, in sum, it seems like we're in Euzkadi.[184] There's no room for so many impressions in these brief pages.

---

182 In October 1941 the Uruguayan foreign minister was Alberto Guani.
183 At the time, the PNV's extraterritorial committee in Uruguay was made up of Ricardo Guisasola, president; Luis Aizpuru, vice president; Tomás Yoldi, secretary; Dionisio Garmendia, assistant secretary; Juan Domingo Uriarte, treasurer; Eugenio Arin, assistant treasurer; and Adrián Otegui, Juan Arin, José Tomás Mujica, and Pedro Arin, voting members. This nationalist leadership derived its authority from an election held in 1934; another one would not be held until 1943.
184 Santiago Cunchillos Manterola (1882–1953) and Pablo Archanco Zubiri (1892–1962), both from Navarre, were charged in 1938, along with Isaac López Mendizabal and under the direction of Ramón María Aldasoro, with a propaganda mission in favor of the Basque government in Argentina, a mission that was converted into the Basque government's delegation in Buenos Aires in response to the end of the 1936 war and the start of World War II.

OCTOBER 1941
SATURDAY 11. ST. GUMMARUS. 284-81

Visit to the newspapers. Mass welcomes at their editorial offices. The reports on my journey fill pages. I would never have believed such a thing. I'm stunned. I'm afraid that my improvised statements and speeches won't get the appropriate interpretation. The change has been so abrupt! But they're good people; they're all happy, almost crazy with happiness. Everything seems magnificent to them. People of all ideological leanings are visiting me, from the Catholics to the socialists. They tell me that there will be a dinner at the Jockey Club on Monday where the cream of the intellectual segment of Montevideo society will gather. The speeches will be broadcast on the radio. I accept everything that our committee imposes on me. My duty is to obey and to go from one side to the other and back again like a ball. Interviews one after another. I don't have a minute free. The party's representatives are magnificent in their discipline, the *gudaris*, disabled veterans, Catalan centers, Galician centers, Spanish centers. Prominent Uruguayans of all persuasions. Newspapers of all ideological leanings without exception.

OCTOBER 1941
SUNDAY 12. ST. WILFRID. 285-80

In the morning, I went to take communion, in order to give thanks to God for so much help and to ask that His well-aimed finger continue guiding our cause. At eleven, a solemn mass of thanksgiving with the attendance of all the Basques and Uruguayan friends. Afterward, to lay wreaths at the monuments to Artigas, the creator of Uruguay, and to Zabala—our compatriot, the founder of Montevideo.[185] We went through the streets with *txistu* and *espatadantzaris* [Basque flute and sword-dancers]. The public watched us with extraordinary sympathy. As if we were in Euzkadi. In the afternoon, invited to the stadium by the Uruguayan Soccer Federation. River Plate and National were playing. I had to make the opening kick. Wanting to make a good appearance, I ended up mediocre, with the ball going a bit to the near right, since my kick-off went to the edge. In any event, it made it. A great deal of

---

185 José Gervasio Artigas (1764–1850) was the hero of Uruguayan independence. Bruno Mauricio de Zabala (1682–1736) was the founder of Montevideo. The latter was a native of Durango.

sympathy. How things change. I was scarcely able to speak with Aldasoro and with Isaac Mendizabal.[186] I didn't have time.

OCTOBER 1941
MONDAY 13. ST. EDWARD. 286-79

The foreign minister advised us that the lunch will be tomorrow. I received many visits without interruption. We agreed on travel to Buenos Aires, where I will take the steamer for New York on Saturday. It's necessary to request Argentina visas. They'll give the appropriate orders from Buenos Aires. Still visas!

Two important daily newspapers, *El Tiempo* and *El Día*, invited me to champagne.[187] I was visited by the director of the Catholic daily, who was with Franco and today is with us.[188] That's how things are changing, and I do everything to please everyone. A magnificent banquet at the Jokey Club. University professors, Supreme Court justices, the general who heads the military academy, lawyers, etc. The former ambassador to Argentina, Mr. Larreta, spoke. They heaped praise on our people and embarrassed me. He said that we "are their liberation." He was referring to the democrats of the whole world. Our problem is being universalized. My speech left everyone happy, they say. It's better like that.[189] To sleep a few hours.

---

186 Isaac López Mendizabal (1879–1977), who held doctorates in philosophy and in law, was an editor and writer. Before the war, he carried out significant promotional work in favor of Euskara and of Basque culture, work that he continued in exile, first in Iparralde and later in Argentina, where he arrived on a propaganda mission on behalf of the Basque government. In Buenos Aires, he and Andrés Irujo founded the Editorial Vasca Ekin publishing house, one of the most important Basque cultural institutions in exile.
187 Both *El Tiempo* and *El Día* were affiliated with the Colorado Party, the party in power in Uruguay at the time.
188 Tomás G. Brena, the director of the daily *El Bien Público*.
189 *Euzko Deya* in Buenos Aires reported about the banquet at the Jockey Club: "On the initiative of a professor of constitutional law at the Uruguayan University, Dr. Héctor Payssé Reyes, Dr. José Antonio Aguirre and Dr. Ramón María Aldasoro were offered an intimate dinner, to which distinguished figures from Uruguayan military, financial, university, social, and political circles were invited. [. . .] "The guests of honor were lauded over dessert, in a brilliant speech, by Dr. Eduardo Rodríguez Larreta, the co-director of the important Montevideo daily newspaper *El País*." The *lehendakari* and Aldasoro also gave speeches, which were broadcast on the radio like the others. "En honor del Presidente Aguirre se realizó una demostración en el Jockey Club de Montevideo," *Euzko Deya* (Buenos Aires), no. 89 (October 25, 1941), 15.

OCTOBER 1941
TUESDAY 14. ST. DONATIAN. 287-78

[*In the upper margin*: Today we had lunch at the foreign minister's house. Our wives attended. Aldasoro and two parliamentary representatives, one of them Catholic, were our fellow diners.][190]

After receiving countless visits, including those of the treasury minister, Mr. Mendibil, and of a candidate in the upcoming presidential elections, Mr. Blanco,[191] I was received by the archbishop of Montevideo, with whom I had an extremely pleasant interview of around two hours.[192] We spoke about the false position of many Catholics at the present hour. The archbishop is a serene man and one of very healthy and well-oriented ideas. He enjoys widespread fame.

In the morning—the newspapers announced the meeting—a Spanish Falangist appeared at the archiepiscopal offices saying that he could not meet with me because I was a murderer. They answered him appropriately. All these slanderers and the regime they represent are in frank [*franco*] decline, paradoxical as it may sound. The Uruguayan Parliament has agreed to receive me in a solemn session. Representative Iturbide, to whom we will never sufficiently repay our debt of gratitude, presented the motion, which was approved overwhelmingly, except for one vote. I visited the president of the chamber, who informed me of the accord.

OCTOBER 1941
WEDNESDAY 15. ST. TERESA. 288-77

In the morning I was received by the president of the republic, General Baldomir.[193] He was full of affection; the interview was pleasant in the extreme. The engineer Urbano Agirre and Dr. Lasarte, our good friends,

---

190 The representatives mentioned by the *lehendakari* were Dardo Regules, a member of the Catholic parliamentary minority, and Alberto Chouy Terra, of the ruling party.
191 It is possible that this is an error and the *lehendakari*, instead of meeting with "a candidate in the upcoming presidential elections, Mr. Blanco," actually met with Luis Alberto de Herrera, the candidate of the Blanco or National Party in the seven elections held between 1922 and 1950 for the post of president of the Oriental Republic of Uruguay.
192 Antonio María Barbieri (1882–1979) served as archbishop of Montevideo between 1940 and 1976.
193 Gen. Alfredo Baldomir (1884–1948) was president of the Oriental Republic of Uruguay between 1938 and 1942.

had arrived from Buenos Aires.[194] They attended the interview with the president, along with Aldasoro. The visits continued. In the afternoon, I scarcely had half an hour to withdraw and think a little about what I would say in the chamber. The extraordinary session at seven. I sat in the seats among the representatives. All the minority parties spoke, from the Catholics to the Communists, from the socialists to the conservatives by way of the Blancos and the Colorados. The apotheosis of Euzkadi was magnificent. I answered moved by emotion. They say that my speech made an impression because its tone was unfamiliar here. The press of all persuasions praised us. From the Parliament to the hotel. To the ship at a run, and amid dear compatriots, I'm now headed to Buenos Aires.

OCTOBER 1941
THURSDAY 16. ST. GERARD M. 289-76

We arrived at seven a.m. Despite the unreasonableness of the hour, many compatriots were on the docks, *ezpatadantzaris*, factory girls with flowers for Joseba and Aintzane. Representatives of our associations greeted me. Everything very cordial and emotional. We went to the magnificent Hotel Plaza. They obliged me to stay in accommodations more suited for favorable days. I obeyed. The visits began, for me and for Mari. Honors, affection, emotion, and enthusiasm. The journalists' assaults began at the ship. *La Prensa* and *La Nación*, the two great South American papers, were especially determined.[195] The [Latin] American correspondents besieged me. The reception and its importance belong to Euzkadi. In the afternoon, a visit to President Ortiz.[196] He received me first alone.

---

194 Elpidio R. Lasarte (1898–1960) was at the time the president of the Laurak Bat association and vice president of the Committee in Favor of Basque Emigration (*Comité Pro Emigración Vasca*). José Urbano de Agirre Guisasola (1888–1957) was an Argentine engineer and politician. He was president of the Committee in Favor of Basque Emigration to Argentina (*Comité pro-Emigración Vasca a la Argentina*).

195 *La Prensa* and *La Nación*, Buenos Aires daily newspapers of conservative leanings, the former founded by José Clemente Paz in 1869 and the latter by President Bartolomé Mitre in 1870. In the Archivo del Nacionalismo Vasco (the Archive of Basque Nationalism) there are two reports about the Basque president's time in the republics of the Río de la Plata. One was published by the daily newspaper *La Razón* on October 16, and the other by *La Nación* on the 19th. Transcriptions of them can be read in appendixes 12 and 13.

196 Roberto Marcelino Ortiz Lizardi (1886–1942) was president of Argentina between 1938 and 1942. Despite the fact that he came to power by fraud, his political program included a return to democratic principles. He was ultimately unable to carry out this program in full, due to his premature retirement from his post because of the

Then the others came in. He singled me out exceptionally. Affectionate, cordial, a great friend. We had an appointment with Castillo, the vice president, but a thunderous objection from Franco by way of Magaz prevented that interview after we arrived at the government palace.[197] We were all expecting it. There were too many honors. President Ortiz paid no attention.

OCTOBER 1941
FRIDAY 17. ST. HEDWIG. 290-75

Yesterday we had an intimate dinner at the Basque center as guests of the organizing committee. Today there was supposed to be a banquet with two hundred seats offered in my honor by the British Chamber of Commerce and attended by the English and American ambassadors. Strong objections were raised in London. The English got frightened.

---

health problems he suffered and to his consequent replacement as head of state by the conservative Ramón S. Castillo. His term saw the promulgation of the decrees of January 20 and July 18, 1940 that enabled Basque emigration to Argentina during World War II, a period during which legal restrictions generally made emigration to that southern country very difficult.

197 Antonio Magaz y Pers (1863–1953), Marquis of Magaz. According to Hilari Raguer, "he was a figure who, well into the twentieth century, seemed like a ghost from Philip II's Spain, something like a Duke of Alba who, at the head of Philip's Flanders infantry, burst into the Europe of fascism and socialism." As a naval lieutenant, he took part in the battle of Santiago de Cuba against the Americans, a battle that for Spain meant the end of empire and for Magaz meant becoming a prisoner of the Yankees on whom he had until then looked down. Later, he was part of the military directorate of Primo de Rivera's dictatorship, and in 1926 he was named ambassador to the Holy See with the principal mission of "obtaining Vatican support for the repression of Catalanism and Bizcaitarrism." He remained in that post until the dictatorship fell in 1930. Once the Spanish Civil War began, the Burgos junta sent him back to Rome as its unofficial agent, a post from which he was relieved in May 1937 due to an incident with Pope Pius XI, when the pontiff pointed out to him that the Nationalists also committed acts of vandalism and shot priests, and the Spanish representative took the liberty of replying to the pope. Before his diplomatic position in Argentina, he occupied the post of ambassador to Germany. Hilari Raguer, *La pólvora y el incienso: La Iglesia y la Guerra Civil española (1936–1939)* (Barcelona: Ediciones Península, 2001), 126–41. For his part, Ramón S. Castillo (1873–1943) was a conservative Argentine politician, a member of the National Democratic Party. He served as this party's candidate for the vice presidency on the "Concordance" ticket—in alliance with the Radical Civic Union—that triumphed in the fraudulent elections of 1938. He became president in June 1942, when Roberto Marcelino Ortiz resigned for health reasons. He was removed from power by a military coup in 1943.

Disgust in the local British community. But always this cowardice ... Excuses, expressions of support, but this event would have been transcendental on account of its speeches and the presence of the ambassadors. The Duke of Alba still has a great deal of influence, and the English still don't have their act together.[198] An intimate, select lunch was held at the Jockey Club. They introduced me to Foreign Minister Ruiz Guiñazu, to the education minister, to former president Roca, to the American ambassador.[199] I've visited and been cordially received by former presidents Alvear and General Justo.[200] Photos with all those indicated above. Their attentions and affection were great. In the evening, a large Basque celebration at Laurak Bat.[201] Choirs, dances, everything very well done. The people were enchanted. This is moving forward.

OCTOBER 1941
SATURDAY 18. ST. LUKE. 291-74

Yesterday we also attended a cocktail reception at the house of the engineer Urbano de Aguirre, who thanks to his distinguished social position brought together around a hundred people from the most select Buenos Aires society at his house. It was an excellent move and a success that it would not have been possible to carry off a few months ago. The press has unanimously dedicated pages and pages of great praise to us. I'm acting strictly along Basque lines, without other complications or adherences that might cause problems for my compatriots' good [*illegible*] and moral dedication. At midday, a large banquet with around a thousand seats. Galician, Catalan, and Spanish delegations. Warmth, enthusiasm, emotionally moving speeches. A great event, this one today. From there to the dock. An emotional farewell until a few months from now. The

---

198 Jacobo Fitz-James Stuart y Falcó (1878–1953), seventeenth Duke of Alba, was Spain's ambassador to the United Kingdom, a post he occupied until 1945.
199 Julio A. Roca was the vice president of Argentina during the term of Agustín Pedro Justo, from 1932 to 1938.
200 Máximo Marcelo Torcuato de Alvear Pacheco (1868–1942) was the leader of the anti-personalist faction of the Radical Civic Union, that is, the faction opposed to the supporters of Hipólito Yrigoyen, whom his detractors considered a demagogue. He served as president of Argentina between 1922 and 1928. For his part, Agustín Pedro Justo (1876–1943), a military man, diplomat, and politician, was president of Argentina between 1932 and 1938.
201 Laurak Bat, founded on the private initiative of thirteen Basques who gathered informally on March 13, 1887, was at the time the most important Basque organization in Argentina and probably in the entire Western Hemisphere.

passengers on the Uruguay were filled with enthusiasm when the people sang the national anthem on the dock.[202] It sounded strong, manly, magnificent. I think that they heard it in Euzkadi. The ship departed.

OCTOBER 1941
SUNDAY 19. ST. SAVINIEN. 292-73

We arrived in Montevideo in the morning. I was received by the president of Euskal-erria [the Basque center], Mr. Gorriti, and many distinguished compatriots. Mr. Gorriti invited me to chair the luncheon that this association is giving for me. A few days before, the leadership committee, in the hands of Hispanists [*españolistas*], had refused. They've rectified the accord. The said leadership committee received me privately. Excuses, explanations. They're old Carlists. We spoke in Euskara. Some of them wept. We won them over by generosity. A few days ago, many patriots wanted to resign their memberships. I prevented it. They didn't know us. Today they do. The flag of the fatherland of all Basques presided over the banquet. Microphone, speeches. Everything very well done. A magnificent closure, the conquest of this wealthy and prestigious Montevideo association with around a thousand members. I'm crazy with happiness, as the Gospel says that heaven will be happy about a repentant sinner. Having made good use of the hours in Montevideo, I spent the last of them amid Basque fraternity. A large farewell. The ship departed at 3:30 to the sound of *txistu* and drum.

OCTOBER 1941
MONDAY 20. ST. IRENE. 293-72

We're sailing on the steamer *Uruguay*. In first class like VIPs. I gave orders to obtain the more appropriate and more modest tourist class. My friends were indignant, and good old Inchausti blew up and imposed the highest category. There they go. I can only thank them for so much caring among them all. The ship is very good. We have an ample cabin for the four of us, comfortable and clean. All the services are excellent. The food is very good. In the kitchen, there are four Basques. The one with the highest status, from Busturia, has visited me. He promised to send me casseroles of our *makalu, lebatzak*, etc.,[203] in the dining room. He was

---

202 On the steamer *Uruguay* and the company that owned it, Moore-McCormack Lines, see the company's website, www.moore-mccormack.com.
203 In Euskara, "cod" and "hake" respectively.

thinking only of our nutrition, with an affection that was evident on his face. What an excellent people we have! Like the people of Montevideo, like the people of Buenos Aires, like the people everywhere! Ramón Aldasoro has carried out a marvelous labor of construction, patriotism, and self-denial. He and the companions who have helped him deserve well of the fatherland. Our ship is sailing toward Santos.

OCTOBER 1941
TUESDAY 21. ST. HILARION. 294-71

We're still intensely moved by the events in Montevideo and Buenos Aires. Their importance is certainly extraordinary. Time will reveal their true proportions. The patriots are happy, spirited, united, disciplined. National union is setting out on the path of a fortunate reality. All without exception have a sense of the race and its freedom. The problem has been delineated. What remains is to perfect the organization and harvest the fruit, which will come. After everything that has happened, it seems that we're living in a dream. We remember those who are suffering. I wrote to Louvain.[204] The exiles, the prisoners: that's my deepest concern. If they could have seen all these events! Will our prestige accompany them, or on the contrary, can it harm them, since hatred has no limits? Here's another doubt, but my duty and my responsibility are so strong that I can't doubt. Onward.

We arrived in Santos, where we will stop for twenty-four hours. The loading of coffee began. Mari and the children continue to be in excellent health, having recovered from the uproar and agitation of recent days.

OCTOBER 1941
WEDNESDAY 22. ST. ALODIA. 295-70

Last night I had an interview that I judge to be transcendental. I met Don António Ferro, the Portuguese head of press and propaganda and the right-hand man of President Oliveira Salazar. God willed to put him in my path. During my stay in Brazil, Mr. Ferro appeared in the press everyday amid flattery and celebrations of all kinds. Lectures, official receptions. It was the work of the current Portuguese regime in

---

204 The Agirre-Zabala family preserves a letter with this date sent by José Antonio Agirre to "Jean Pertusa" and included in appendix 14. "Jean Pertusa" was a false name for Juan Mari Agirre.

Brazil. I met him on this ship. He observed with fright the welcomes and farewells that were being offered to me. He was startled to read the long accounts in the newspapers. He was interested in meeting me. A long conversation about Portugal, about Salazar, about Euzkadi, about the future of the Iberian Peninsula. He asked me for a long note to present to Salazar. I'd been desiring this contact for a long time. God facilitated it. I believe that it will be of great interest for the future. Ferro is intelligent and cultured. He was unfamiliar with many things. He left impressed.[205]

OCTOBER 1941
THURSDAY 23. ST. SEVERINUS. 296-69

I've made a good friend on board. The Uruguayan ambassador to Brazil. He's going to Rio de Janeiro to take up his diplomatic post. We've spent several good periods of time conversing. A pleasant person, formerly a supporter of Franco in good faith, disillusioned after personal experience of Spain under Franco. Very interesting descriptions and telling observations gathered in that paradise. We arrived in Rio de Janeiro. We saw it with emotion, remembering the adventures of Dr. Álvarez and family. On our arrival in Rio de Janeiro, we were awaited by Mr. Stevenson and his wife and children. Mr. Jones and his wife then arrived. They had lunch as our guests. We had a pleasant time. Mr. Stevenson expressed his enchantment at the news he had read in the press and the news we told

---

205 The Basque president wrote to Manuel Irujo and José Ignacio Lizaso about this meeting: "On the steamer *Uruguay* coming from Buenos Aires, I spoke with António Ferro. . . . He openly confessed to me that they're afraid of the current Spanish regime, but since they were very afraid of the 'reds', Portugal's position in helping Franco had a chronological logic. . . . He sought out the meeting, having been impressed by the columns and photos that *La Nación* and *La Prensa* dedicated to me, an unusual thing, according to him, outside of extraordinary cases. . . . We talked about everything, even the future of the peninsula. Although they prefer not to talk about the confederal problem for now, not only do they understand, but they believe that it's necessary in the future. . . . "I think that an interview with Salazar would be of the highest possible interest. Ferro, despite being a cultured and intelligent man, heard about many things for the first time. He promised me that he would speak to Salazar at length about everything that he had seen and heard. . . . A Portuguese count who was his friend confirmed to me that when he spoke to him the next day, Ferro had been strongly impressed by our meeting." Letter from José Antonio Agirre to Manuel Irujo and José Ignacio Lizaso, New York, December 18, 1941. GE-259-2.

him. I was assaulted by some Brazilian journalists and photographers who came on board for that purpose. At five, we left for Trinidad. There's a strong current, and the ship moves quite a bit.

OCTOBER 1941
FRIDAY 24. ST. RAPHAEL. 297-68

We began the standard life on board. I'm studying English in forced marches. That academic appointment that I have such dreams about is worrying me because of the language. In the end, everything will get done, and I hope that at the beginning they'll be understanding about my absurdities in the language of Shakespeare. The children have a room with toys. For them, this is life. Mari has to take care of them more than before, since I'm now buried in papers and books. I just received a telegram from Inchausti. He proposes that we disembark in Trinidad and arrive in Miami by plane. From there to New York. He sent me the telegram from Washington. Why from there? The proposal surprised me. I answered that we prefer to continue our journey on the steamer, unless more important reasons advise something else. The telegram surprised me. Today the festivities on board began. A cocktail reception offered by the captain. I wrote to everyone. Yesterday we sent two letters to Louvain. I asked Buenos Aires for rapid communication with my fellow members of the government who are today in France.

OCTOBER 1941
SATURDAY 25. ST. CHRYSANTHUS. 298-67

The heat has started again. In a few months, we've known climates of all kinds. The pool was in full operation today. I went in the water with the children. In two days, we'll cross the tropics again. A few days later, we'll reach the temperate zone to enter the cold of New York.

I'm dedicating myself intensely to the study of English and of those disciplines most necessary for my future situation. I wrote various letters. In my mind, I'm maturing plans and plans to achieve the efficacious union of all Basques, a union that is today making a fortunate beginning.

I wrote to Venezuela to find out the real state of affairs in that country, where it appears that good fortune has not accompanied my compatriots.[206]

---

[206] The *lehendakari* is referring to the crisis of the Pesquerías Vascas del Caribe fishing company, the continuator of a similar enterprise also created by the Basque

And consequently the unpleasant incidents have been more frequent than in other countries. Everything will be sorted out. The useful men of good will, as always, will remain. I look to the future with hope and with faith. God will do the rest. Today is October 25! An ill-fated date.[207]

OCTOBER 1941
SUNDAY 26. *CHRIST THE KING*. 299-66

In the morning, we heard mass, said by a pleasant Dominican, picturesque like all these Latin American travel companions of ours. He gets in the pool with the whole world and like the whole world. He dresses as a perfect traveling sportsman and attends the ship's dance every night. I wouldn't be surprised to see him dance one day. He would have won me over then. He's niceness itself and shines with virtue. But even so ... will it be better because it's a franker system? I don't want to enter into this issue, about which I have my own ideas. Hypocrisy is so repugnant ... ! Today they served a luncheon on board. Contemplating this abundance, our thoughts inevitably go to that Europe where our relatives and friends lack so much. It's the constant idea that is always torturing us. And then ... the prisons.

OCTOBER 1941
MONDAY 27. ST. FLORENTIUS. 300-65

Today we crossed the line of the tropics at five-thirty p.m. The heat is very strong. Mari was almost flushed today. Since I sweat a lot, all the ills go out that way. I received a disconcerting telegram from Inchausti

---

government, Pêcheries de la Cote Basque. Both were established for the purpose of giving jobs to some refugees and obtaining income for the Basque executive branch. In view of the impossibility of working in French waters due to the impediments posed by the unions, and after crossing the Atlantic in 1939, Pesquerías Vascas's ships, the *Donibane* and the *Bigarrena*, dedicated themselves to coastal fishing in the Venezuelan Caribbean, but using techniques and equipment that were characteristic of the Cantabrian Sea and clearly ineffective in those waters. At the same time, Venezuelan dietary habits also were not inclined to the consumption of fish, with the result that what small catch there was could not be sold for profitable prices. All this led to the bankruptcy of Pesquerías Vascas and to personal and political conflicts among the nationalist exiles in Venezuela. GE-250-2.

207 A reference to October 25, 1839, the date that the Spanish parliament confirmed the Bergara Convention and the traditional Basque laws and privileges [*los fueros*] with the famous caveat, "without prejudice to the constitutional unity of the Monarchy."

today. He said that Washington prefers that I disembark quietly in Trinidad and go to Miami without saying anything to anyone, like a criminal who has to hide. Poor Inchausti, how much this friend, a model of generosity and nobility, has to suffer! How Manu Sota, always upright, will be raging! I could not accept this humiliation for my Basque fatherland after the homages that our people have received in the South American republics. And that's how I answered, saying that there is a Basque dignity. Then they'll do with me as they wish there. I'm an instrument, a bird of passage, but my fatherland is Euzkadi, and Euzkadi has to be respected, even in the United States.

OCTOBER 1941
TUESDAY 28. ST. SIMON. 301-64

Today was a very painful day for me, since Inchausti and Manu Sota each answered my telegram from yesterday with another telegram. My explosion yesterday must have left them petrified. How much these excellent friends have to suffer! They talk about special circumstances, very serious reasons, irreparable harms, and invoke the good of the Basque cause. What to do? They know the atmosphere better than I do; they're living in it. How can I aspire to give them lessons in patriotism? I answered accepting the solution of getting off in Trinidad and continuing the journey by plane to Miami, but since I think that it's a matter of unworthy American diplomatic cowardice, I told them in the telegram that I'm accepting this solution due to my affection for and trust in my friends.

With all this, I spent an anxious day, one on which the pride of a thousand generations was defying the skyscrapers built yesterday and of cement.

OCTOBER 1941
WEDNESDAY 29. ST. ALFRED. 302-63

I'm still suffering the anxieties of yesterday. Very late in the evening, when I was already in bed, I received a telegram from Inchausti. He said that my acceptance has satisfied Washington in full. Out of bed, with the telegram in hand, I was nervous and asking myself whether ... In the end, my good friends, who are representatives of Euzkadi, have more than enough reasons for me to trust them; they know better than I what I should do. The telegram says that the American consul

in Trinidad will give me explanations, visas, assistance, etc. Irazusta—
our Jon Andoni—will welcome me in Puerto Rico and will come to
Miami with me.[208] Inchausti or Manu will surely be there. Wherever
God wills that I still have to walk. With all this, Don Inda is writing
alluring articles.[209] We Basques are now the fundamental point of the
future. Negrín has sent me from London a dispatch full of affection
and embraces.[210] It's right to think about Euzkadi, but for ourselves.

---

208 Jon Andoni Irazusta Muñoa (1884–1952) was a writer and a Basque nationalist politician. During the Republic, he was twice elected to the Spanish parliament as a PNV representative for Gipuzkoa. Before going into exile, he worked with the nationalist press, and after reaching the Western Hemisphere, he published two novels, *Joañixio* and *Bizia garratza da* (Life is hard), both with Editorial Vasca Ekin in Buenos Aires, the first in 1946 and the second in 1950.

209 Indalecio Prieto Tuero (1883–1962) was a Bilbao socialist politician. During the Spanish Civil War, he first occupied the post of naval and air minister and later that of national defense minister. He left the government in 1938 due to conflict with Prime Minister Juan Negrín and the Communist ministers. He traveled to the Americas as an official envoy of the Spanish Republic to the inauguration of Pedro Agirre Cerda as president of Chile. While he was in Mexico on his way back from this mission, the yacht *Vita* arrived in that country with part of the treasure the government of the Spanish Republic had evacuated abroad for the purpose of supporting the needs of the exiles. Due to exceptional circumstances, the agent named by SERE (*Servicio de Emigración de Republicanos Españoles*, Spanish Republican Emigration Service), the organization created to handle political emigration, was unable to take charge of the property, and the treasure passed into the hands of Prieto, who created another organization, politically opposed to the one that already existed, in order to manage it. This new aid organization for political emigrés was called the Spanish Republican Board of Aid (*Junta de Auxilio a los Republicanos Españoles*, JARE). The article by Indalecio Prieto to which the *lehendakari* refers was published in the Mexican daily newspaper *Excelsior* on October 4, 1941. In this article, the Bilbao socialist leader said, "It is unknown what he [José A. de Agirre] thinks about the problems that present and future reality pose to the Spanish Republic's defenders who are today in exile. The wandering public mind has a tangential familiarity with these problems, although without even glimpsing the more serious and delicate ones, which in my judgment may be the ones originating from the attitude of the Basque and Catalan nationalists. Luis Companys, the president of the Generalitat, fell silent forever when he fell—barefoot, since he wanted to be in contact with the soil of Catalonia—beneath a hail of bullets from the firing squad. José A. de Agirre has only fallen silent temporarily. Who knows whether we will be able to hear from him soon? I have great confidence that he will fully employ his demonstrated prudence, his exquisite tact, that moderation, in sum, with which he consolidated and increased his prestige, in order to dissipate the shadows of irreconcilable positions." Quoted by José Ignacio Lizaso in a letter sent to Agirre. Letter from José Ignacio Lizaso to José Agirre, London, October 24, 1941, GE-259-1.

210 Juan Negrín López (1889–1956) was a renowned physiologist and a Spanish socialist politician. He served as prime minister from 1937 until the end of the

OCTOBER 1941
THURSDAY 30. ST. ERMELINDE. 303-62

We arrived in Trinidad at midday.[211] A tropical landscape with mist. Suffocating heat and humidity. The American consul and vice consul appeared. Polite in their behavior, they gave me the message with instructions from Washington. A month ago, running after the last visa, I would not have believed that we would rouse so much interest and so much fear. What Franco must be working on! They treated me according to the instructions, as a VIP. First at the visa desk, first to leave, no luggage searches, the consulate's car at the seaport. It's the honey after the vinegar. I'll write about this someday. The old-school diplomats whose cosmetics have softened their brains believe that the injury is cured with these band-aids. I'll write about this someday, since I believed that in the United States, they didn't do things in the old style. Uruguay! Argentina! I thought that in those countries, Franco would be something, and it turns out that where he is something is among the American diplomatic caste—not among the people.

OCTOBER 1941
FRIDAY 31. ST. QUENTIN. 304-61

Today began with another vicissitude. After the ceremonious welcomes yesterday, they informed me at the hotel, when I returned from accompanying Mari and the children, who are continuing their journey

---

war, when he was removed from office by the coup d'état led by Col. Segismundo Casado. In exile, he created the Spanish Refugee Emigration Service to assist the Spanish exiles and continue his political work. In June 1940, after France fell to the Germans, he was one of the few Spaniards who succeeded in fleeing, ending up in the United Kingdom.

211 The United States took possession of the Trinidad military base in August 1940, upon signing an agreement with the United Kingdom according to which, in exchange for fifty mothballed destroyers, the Americans received the right to establish bases at this and seven other locations in the Caribbean and Newfoundland. The destroyers were indispensable for the British in summer and fall of 1940 if they were to counter the German submarine threat and the danger of invasion. For their part, the bases ensured American control, among other things, of the shipping routes for oil and bauxite from Venezuela, Surinam, and Trinidad itself. Another of the important sites ceded in the Anglo-American accord was the base at Placentia in Newfoundland, precisely where the Atlantic Charter was signed and a customary gathering point for the convoys that would cross the Atlantic to Iceland during the war years.

on the steamer, that since payment had not been received for the plane tickets tomorrow, my departure was being delayed until it was received. Since I didn't have two hundred dollars to pay it, I sent a telegram to Inchausti—poor Inchausti!—asking him to send it before eleven tomorrow, the departure time. Since they closed the telegraph office at seven, there was no way to obtain the dispatch of the cable saying that they sent it first thing today. Certainly, my social standing dropped a great deal yesterday when they found out that I didn't have dollars to pay for my ticket. I noticed it even in the disdainful air of the bellhop who brought the cable. Shortly before the plane's departure, the matter was sorted out. I just missed getting stuck in Trinidad. At customs and the police, they granted me diplomatic status. Attentions and no search. I boarded the plane. A pleasant trip. I arrived in Puerto Rico after a four-hour flight. Jon Andoni was there.

NOTES

I never would have believed the complications of a journey like this one, the last stage of which began five months ago now. Much emotion yesterday when I found my good old friend Jon Andoni de Irazusta waiting for me at the airfield. Embraces, and to his house. He's the Colombian consul and enjoys a deserved good reputation due to his conduct. He keeps our banner flying high. He'll come with me to Miami, but since he doesn't have a ticket yet, we're leaving the trip until tomorrow or the day after tomorrow. Inchausti called us on the telephone and sent various cables. For Inchausti, there are no obstacles. We're expecting the tickets for Miami at any moment. I sent a cable to Mari announcing my safe arrival in Puerto Rico. October has come to an end, and I'm still traveling. But we're now in friendly territory and receiving the most diplomatic attentions.

NOVEMBER 1941
SATURDAY 1. ALL SAINTS. 305-60

The tickets for Miami having been cancelled yesterday, the American immigration authorities called me today. Extremely courteous, they proposed that I go through the formalities in Puerto Rico instead of in Miami. I agreed, and at once, without further requirements, they handed me my provisional passport issued in good order. Despite the orders from Washington, and precisely because of those orders, they treated me in a truly exceptional way. It's terribly hot in Puerto Rico. I'm sweating through all my pores. I'm dealing with a bad bronchial cold, which this heat isn't helping at all. Jon Andoni and his excellent sister Rosario are going out of their way to make my stay a pleasant one. Plates of potatoes with green beans, cod, tomorrow *lapikoko*, etc.[212] It's nostalgia for the fatherland reflected even in the cuisine. Today an excellent compatriot from Sopuerta, Mendizabal, had dinner with us; he couldn't get over his astonishment.

NOVEMBER 1941
SUNDAY 2. *ALL SOULS*. 306-59

Trinidad and Puerto Rico. Santo Domingo and Haiti nearby. Cuba further away. The stage for so many great deeds by the Latin American liberators. In Trinidad I remembered the great Bolívar, who trod that soil of exile and refuge. Who would have told me that it would fall to my lot to follow this itinerary in similar circumstances?

Yesterday and today we fulfilled our religious duties in the nearby church of the Augustinian Fathers. They're Spaniards and supporters of Franco, the kind who invoke the crusade and the rod. They don't have much standing here. How could they have it? Today we met two other compatriots. One was Captain Beotegi, from Mundaka, a magnificent exemplar of the race, popular in all these seas; the other was Zubillaga, from Donostia [San Sebastián] and some kind of relative of Leizaola's. We didn't want to identify ourselves, but God provoked the meeting, the emotion, the embraces, and as Beotegi said, raising his arms, *didar eiteko gogua daukat*.[213]

NOVEMBER 1941
MONDAY 3. ST. HUBERT. 307-58

The planes were still full. Despite the efforts being made in Miami and New York, they still hadn't given us the two seats requested. Finally the notice arrived. We'll leave tomorrow on the 8:30 am. plane. Today, we had another invitation from our compatriots. Excellent people. They tend to stare at me to make sure whether I'm really the same person. Many times, this prolonged look ends in a gesture . . . moving the head

---

212 *Lapikoko* means "stew."
213 Literally, "I have an urge to shout."

and striking the table. There's no need for any expression of affection more characteristic of us. A profound national sentiment is being created, one that extends to previously indifferent or forgetful regions. All Basques today feel the pride of being Basques, and from this the spirit of proselytism is born. Good old Inchausti continues spending his fortune on long-distance calls and telegrams. He's tracking us step by step. Mari and the *txikis* [little ones] will arrive in New York tomorrow. They've beaten me. We're preparing our departure for tomorrow.

NOVEMBER 1941
TUESDAY 4. ST. CHARLES BORR. 308-57

We left at eight-thirty. We flew to San Pedro de Macoriges in the Dominican Republic.[214] We passed over Ciudad Trujillo. I gratefully remembered so many good friends, Dr. Despradel above all. We landed in Port-au-Prince, the capital of the black republic of Haiti. A precious landscape, but a sensation of backwardness. That strange mixture of the progress indicated by certain installations and the miserable life of the indigenous population. We leapfrogged to Cuba, landed in Antilla, left Havana off to the side, and flying over wetlands and extremely clear water, we arrived in Miami at five p.m., after having eaten lunch on board. In Miami, an individual named Aguirre Etxebarria was in charge of immigration. He had orders from Washington. Facilities on

---

214 Regarding the stopover in San Pedro de Macorís, Jesús Galíndez informed Manuel Irujo, "José Antonio spent five minutes on a plane at the S. Pedro de Macorís airport; he couldn't let me know at the last moment, since he thought he was going direct to Miami, according to what I was told by Beotegi, the captain of the *San Rafael*, who had dinner with him and Irazusta in San Juan, in Puerto Rico." The *San Rafael* and the *Presidente Trujillo* made up practically the entirety of the Dominican merchant fleet, in which some of the officers were Basque exiles. Both ships were sunk by German submarines, the former on May 3, 1942, and the latter on the 21st of the same month. In the *San Rafael* incident, two crew members perished, one of them Alejandro Solaetxe, captain at one time of the *Nabarra*, a fishing boat armed and pressed into military service in the Spanish Civil War, known as a *bou*, and in the attack on the *Presidente Trujillo*, twenty-four sailors died, included the first machinist Txomin Urrutxua, who was part of the crew of the *bou Bizkaya* during the Spanish Civil War. The survivors of the sinking of the *San Rafael*, including Captain Beotegi, were able to reach the Isle of Pines (Cuba) after seven days drifting in two lifeboats. Letters from Jesús Galíndez to Manuel Irujo, Ciudad Trujillo, November 10, 1941, and July 12, 1942. GE-258-2. Bernardo Vega, *Nazismo, fascismo y falangismo en la República Dominicana* (Santo Domingo: Fundación Cultural Dominicana, 1985), 227–41.

all sides. Captain Beotegi's son who works in Miami arrived. Carmen Zalduondo, another immigration employee, greeted us. In sum, patriotic warmth and enthusiasm once again. Jon Andoni and I were very happy. Mari and the children have arrived in New York and are enchanted. Inchausti called.

NOVEMBER 1941
WEDNESDAY 5. ST. ZACHARY. 309-56

Inchausti called me by eight. Yesterday they went on board to welcome Mari, Joseba, and Aintzane. The ones who went were Inchausti with his wife Anabelén, Marino Gamboa with his wife, Manu, and Ramonchu Sota.[215] Everyone very happy. Today Jon Andoni and I left at 10:20 for Philadelphia, where we'll arrive tomorrow at 9:38 a.m. Inchausti and Manu Sota will be waiting for us there. Finally!

Miami is a marvelous locality, full of enchantments with its houses and gardens of all kinds. The landscape that can be seen from the train is monotonous, with an abundance of palm trees, later of pines. The food in the dining car is good. After dinner, we proposed to rest. The trip is passing relatively quickly, remembering so many, many stories with Jon Andoni. Finally, we're reaching the end of the journey, which will finish tomorrow morning, God willing.

NOVEMBER 1941
THURSDAY 6. ST. LEONARD. 310-55

After sleeping on the train, we approached Philadelphia after passing Baltimore. We arrived in Philadelphia at something like 9:30 a.m. We had agreed to get off in this town, around two hours from New York, in order to have a prior meeting there regarding various matters that

---

215 Marino Gamboa was a businessman of Filipino origin who lived in Euzkadi. During the Spanish Civil War, using and relying on his American passport—the Philippines were under U.S. administration—he performed numerous services related to the shipping business for the Basque government and the government of the Spanish Republic. One of these services was the chartering of the yacht *Vita*. See note 209. Marino Gamboa was married to María Ibargaray Artaza, a native of Gorliz. For his part, Ramón de la Sota MacMahon (1915–71) served as secretary of the Basque government's New York delegation until he enlisted in the U.S. Army following the attack on Pearl Harbor. Wounded in combat, he had to leave active service, subsequently acting as an agent of the Basque secret services in Argentina on behalf of the United States.

I should be familiar with before arriving in the big city. Inchausti and Manu Sota were waiting for us at the station. The moment of our meeting was emotional, since that instant concentrated so many memories and anxieties of which our friends have been the depositaries. We immediately headed to the Benjamin Franklin Hotel, where we began to study various matters, explanations of the measures adopted, letters from London, from France, etc. Everything very well done. Great spirit, firm hope. In the afternoon, we left for New York and then for White Plains, where Inchausti is welcoming us in his house until we've rested sufficiently.

NOVEMBER 1941
FRIDAY 7. ST. WILLIBRORD. 311-54

I telephoned various friends, including Gamboa and Valentín de Agirre, to whom we owe attentions.[216] The New York Basques are upset, because they don't know the reasons why I'm not being given the welcome in New York that they had all been preparing with exemplary enthusiasm. The press is asking where I am, asking for details and requesting interviews. I have a sore throat and a rather moderate case of bronchitis. This is serving us as a pretext. The press was given a statement recounting our arrival and my state of health. The state department indicates that it is happy with my attitude. Its determination with regard to my case was radical. They were ready to use all their force to prevent more or less reputable elements from getting involved in the welcoming ceremonies with the aim of taking them over. Various prominent Spaniards were among them.

I spent a tranquil day at Inchausti's house.

NOVEMBER 1941
SATURDAY 8. 4 CROWNED MARTYRS. 312-53

Since nobody knows where I'm living, generally speaking, I can work in peace. Manu Sota brought me a good pile of papers, reports, letters, telegrams. I began my study, especially concerning the London conflict.[217]

---

216 Valentín Agirre Esquibel (1872–1953) emigrated to the Western Hemisphere as a teenager, ultimately establishing himself in New York, where he opened the Jai-Alai hotel, restaurant, and travel agency, which would end up becoming a meeting place for New York Basques and a source of support for Basque emigrants arriving in the United States.

217 The dispute to which the Basque president alludes in his diary arose in 1940 when

I want to be well informed in order to make radical decisions. We can't put on a show like the Spaniards are doing, quarreling and provoking scandal everywhere. At Columbia University, they're preparing some events and meals in my honor. I'm confounded by the importance they're giving me. I would never want to lose my sense of proportion. I'm plugging away at my English so as not to make a poor appearance. Although my cold is now on the way to getting better, the pretext hasn't been a bad thing to get a little space that has allowed me to rest from so many emotions.

NOVEMBER 1941
SUNDAY 9. ST. MATURINUS. 313-52

My compatriots from the New York Basque center wanted to visit me. I told them to come this afternoon. I couldn't keep them away from me any longer. In the morning, we went to church with the Inchausti family. Inchausti, Manu Sota, and I took a walk. My first walk and my first excursion. In the afternoon, Don Valentín de Agirre arrived with his son-in-law.[218] Later, the board of directors of the Basque center. What a pleasing impression!

All our conversation, more than two hours, took place in Euskara. They were all *euzkeldunes* [Basque speakers]. All industrious men, all with good reputations. They were happy. They promised to work with all their strength. Good things will be done in New York. I expect it. The union of the Basques in a single effort, in a single way of thinking for freedom, is continuing its march.

I spent a pleasant day.

---

the Basque government, facing a lack of liquidity, ordered the liquidation of the Continental Transit Shipping Company, created in Great Britain with funds from the Basque executive branch to provision Euzkadi during the Spanish Civil War and headed by Luis Ortuzar Peñeñuri. Manuel Irujo was charged with carrying out the liquidation. Nevertheless, in May 1940, when the *lehendakari*'s whereabouts in Belgium were unknown, Ortuzar, accompanied by a British secret agent, went to Paris, where he received orders from the counselors Jesús María Leizaola and Eliodoro de la Torre to reassert control of the company and its assets and put them at the service of the British. Irujo was not informed of this mandate, which contradicted the previous one, and continued to believe that he was responsible for the company and should be the one administering its assets.

218 Valentín Agirre's son-in-law was Jon Zabal, an Americanization of his original surname Zabalandicoechea.

NOVEMBER 1941
MONDAY 10. ST. ANDREW AVELLINO. 314-51

The press is pressing me. I've set a time for Thursday at a New York hotel. There are many requests for interviews, articles, etc., etc. We'll see what can and should be done. The university is asking questions. They're truly friendly. They're giving me a status that makes me blush but that I should put to use for the good of the fatherland. The valuable friendships that this post should give me and the meetings that will follow will serve to open the way to new sources of support for the Basque national cause. I'm still annoyed by the attitudes of the old-lady diplomats, but it seems that even from this, very estimable advantages will come. The determination to keep me away from anything that might mean a loss of prestige is evident. Perhaps we'll soon be called on to provide important services. Our success in South America has made a big impression.

NOVEMBER 1941
TUESDAY 11. NATIONAL HOLIDAY. 315-50

Today I signed numerous pieces of correspondence in order to answer, even if briefly, so many good friends who are writing to me from all over. I made good use of the day by plugging away at my English, which is still less than seasoned. I'm dedicating more than three hours a day to this study. Once the topics for the Columbia professorship have been determined, I'll start studying them to prepare the classes. Days at the grindstone are awaiting me. Meanwhile, reports and more reports are arriving from our delegations. I don't know when I'll be able to answer all of them, dictate guidelines for all of them. I like to take my time studying matters, and time is short now. Everything will get done with *Jaungoikoa*'s help.[219] Don Valentín de Agirre and his family were invited today. Anecdotes and memories filled dinner and the after-dinner conversation in the salon. Good people, these Basques who emigrated a while back.

---

219 *Jaungoikoa* means "God" in Euskara.

NOVEMBER 1941
WEDNESDAY 12. ST. MARTIN. 316-49

Today we went to New York. We invited the representative of the official commission for refugee aid to lunch; he's leaving for France. He was already there previously and visited Torre and Lasarte. I gave him many commissions for those good friends, informing them of my plans to try to get them out of those territories. Their situation concerns me enormously. The thought of them is on my mind all day.[220] Today I received a letter from Juan Mª. It was another reason for worry. What to do with my family? Still without money to assist them, at so great a distance, almost without communication: it's another reason for great suffering and the solution of which can only be commended to God. I received a telegram from Monzón. The caravan of sorrow is arriving on the 17th.[221] Dear compatriots who have suffered so much. Finally! How they will arrive! And so by suffering the stepping-stones are laid for a fatherland that no one will be able to understand without freedom.

NOVEMBER 1941
THURSDAY 13. ST. STANISLAUS K. 317-48

Today is Mari's saint's day. We celebrated it as guests in Marino de Gamboa's house. I also greeted our friend Maurice Olivier there; he

---

220 The representative was Patrick Murphy Malin (1903–1964), director of the American Branch of the International Migration Service and member of the President's Advisory Committee on Political Refugees created by President Roosevelt. We know something more about his first voyage to Europe, mentioned above, thanks to a report by José Ignacio Lizaso on the meeting between the two on August 6, 1941, in London, when the American delegate was making a stopover in the British capital. The primary topic of discussion was the situation of the refugees and the possibilities for their departure from France, but on this latter point, according to what Lizaso wrote, the difficulties were nearly insuperable, since the French authorities denied the necessary permits to all refugees, whether they were of military age or not. At the same meeting, Malin gave the Basque delegate two reports, one on the situation of the Basque refugees in the two zones into which France was divided, and the other on the situation of the Spanish exiles. The former originated with José Mari Lasarte and Eliodoro de la Torre, and the latter was signed by Josep Maria Trias. From the two reports, it could be deduced that there were around 65,000 refugees in France. Letter from Manu de la Sota to Ángel Gondra, New York, August 4, 1941. GE-250-3. Report on an interview with Patrick Murphy Malin by José Ignacio Lizaso, London, August 6, 1941. GE-238-3.

221 The reference is to the steamer *Alsina*. See notes 148 and 252.

helped us a great deal in Europe.[222] God willed that we spend this day among good friends. Mr. and Mrs. Intxausti were also invited. In the morning, we received the press. Rather, part of the press, since the other part, and precisely the American part, stood out by its absence. Yesterday we committed a gaffe, and they did us a bad turn. Having committed to an interview with the great journalist Madame Tamara, we believed that the report would come out with her byline. It was a standard editorial. The other newspapers were annoyed, it appears. In the end, things that go with the territory. There's no hurry, I told my alarmed friends. They'll seek us out another day, because we have to go to Euzkadi.

NOVEMBER 1941
FRIDAY 14. ST. JOSAPHAT. 318-47

Today was the day appointed for my entrance at the university. By common agreement, the event today won't be a formal one; it will be private and will take place in the office of President Butler, one of the most respected men in America.[223] When my English is fully robust, the formal ceremony will be held. We had lunch with the head of the history department, Professor Hayes, and entered Columbia University's enormous campus with him.[224] We were received by the president, and the interview was most cordial. I took possession of my office at the university, and they're giving me two months (until January) to prepare my classes on the influence of European countries on South American thought. The whole Basque problem comes in here. Today was a very satisfying day. Everything is working out acceptably.

---

222 Maurice Olivier was a businessman who had ties to Marino Gamboa. The assistance to which the *lehendakari* refers was acting as a middleman in capital transfers by the Basque government, difficult for the Basque executive branch to conduct legally since it lacked a legal status recognized abroad.
223 Nicholas Murray Butler (1862–1947) was the president of Columbia University. He had been awarded the Nobel Peace Prize in 1931.
224 The U.S. historian Carlton Joseph Huntley Hayes (1882–1964) had served as chair of the Columbia University history department since 1935. He earned his undergraduate and doctoral degrees at the same university and began teaching modern European history there in 1907. He wrote various historical articles and books, in addition to *Wartime Mission in Spain, 1942–1945* (New York: The Macmillan Company, 1945), in which he recounted his time as U.S. ambassador to Spain between 1942 and 1945. Jiménez de Aberasturi, *De la derrota*, 351.

NOVEMBER 1941
SATURDAY 15. ST. LEOPOLD. 319-46

Today was our day for houses. We have to find a place to stay, since we can't keep bothering our good friends the Intxaustis. If it were up to him, we'd never leave their house. Their generosity is embarrassing. We saw several houses. We like a little one next to the church, especially considering that we'll be living without staff, and all the housework will fall on Mari. This experience won't do us any harm. We should give thanks to God, Who permits us to live in peace and modestly. If all our relatives and compatriots could be in the same situation, our happiness would be complete. Everything will come, little by little. In the afternoon, we went with the Inchausti family to confess at the church of the French-Canadian Fathers. Much reverence, much seriousness, and calm. The children's health is improving a great deal here. The climate is very good. The weather was excellent today.

NOVEMBER 1941
SUNDAY 16. ST. EDMUND. 320-45

In the morning, after fulfilling our religious duties, we waited for Manu Sota to arrive. We took a long walk until midday with him and Inchausti. On these walks, we examine with tranquility many pending issues and others that will arise in the future. We spend Sunday away from the bustle of New York, since this town on the outskirts of the great city is for us what Neguri was in Euzkadi, a place of rest and an especially pleasant place on holidays. The children are admirably well. Joseba especially is getting healthier day by day. His color is magnificent. Aintzane still hasn't entirely gotten back to how well she looked in Paris. She's still carrying the nervous impressions of so many episodes that, without our realizing it, left their traces on her child's psychology. Joseba, for his good fortune, knows nothing of this.

NOVEMBER 1941
MONDAY 17. ST. GREGORY TH. 321-44

I dedicated the whole day to English. I'm making progress, but I should have attained mastery by now. My head is full of worries. The people from the *Alsina* (now the people from the *Quanza*) indicated that they would arrive today. We haven't received any word. On the other hand, the people in Belgium. On yet another hand, the people in prison. My companions and compatriots in France. The organization of the Western Hemisphere. The lamentable London dispute. The economic issue. The future of Euzkadi, which it's necessary to work on day by day. The consultations from the delegations, the instructions they request, the Basque government guidelines needed for the upcoming campaign, etc., etc. Not to mention letters and letters: they drown me in work and cause me to get to bed around two in the morning every day. Today I wanted to forget everything and plug away at my English. But I only partly succeeded.

NOVEMBER 1941
TUESDAY 18. ST. ODO. 322-43

I worked during the morning, since it wasn't going to be possible for me in the afternoon. In the afternoon, accompanied by the two Sotas (Manu and Ramón) and Intxausti, I headed to the university, where the South American group had invited me a few days ago to be a guest of honor at their regular meeting this month. Father Ford, a Catholic priest who is a member of the group and very highly respected at the university, introduced me.[225] I answered with a short speech in Spanish that Ramón Sota translated for the English and Yankees who had come to hear me out of curiosity. Everyone was satisfied. Father Ford said that he was absolutely in agreement with everything. A year or two ago, they wouldn't have let him say that. But everything is changing. The event was very well attended. Numerous students came to greet me.

NOVEMBER 1941
WEDNESDAY 19. ST. ELIZABETH OF H. 323-42

I continued studying all day. I worked on the plan for my lectures, which will be focused on these two topics, "History of the last hundred years of the Iberian Peninsula" and "Influence of European thought on South American political formation." Two interesting topics to enable me to set out, in the former case, our true history, and in the latter, the influence of Basque thought, among others, in South America. With

---

225 George Barry Ford (1885–1978) was the parish priest of Corpus Christi Church, located on 121st Street in New York, near Columbia University, where he served as a spiritual advisor for the Catholic students.

these materials, there will be sufficient topics with which to work on writing useful books. President Butler recommended to me some days ago that I write a book, since he would like to see a work of this kind published. I'll see, if God gives me health and time to deal with so many things that can and should be done in His service and for the salvation of my fatherland in freedom.

NOVEMBER 1941
THURSDAY 20. ST. FELIX OF V. 324-41

Today the visits began again. It was the turn of the English. One of them was sent directly by the embassy's political research services. He deals with Spain. He's seeking the union of Spaniards, as he puts it, because the attitude regarding Franco is changing radically. England now (ah!!!) realizes that Franco is not a friend but an enemy. They want contact with the Basques. We can be major elements for the future. The English left with what they came for. They were familiar with the problem of Euzkadi, but from now on, I believe that they won't easily forget it. It was a pleasant and very important conversation. Certainly, things are moving forward.[226] In the evening, we were invited to Don

---

226 In May and June 1940, the British government created the British Security Coordination Office "to do all that was not being done and could be done by overt means to ensure sufficient aid for Britain and eventually to bring America into the war." The agency was headquartered in New York's Rockefeller Center. Norman Moss, *Nineteen Weeks: America, Britain, and the Fateful Summer of 1940* (Boston: Houghton Mifflin, 2003), 244. Nothing was reported publicly about the meetings mentioned in the diary, obviously, but today we can connect certain items that appeared in the Basque press with these events. Thus, an account of the *lehendakari*'s activities in the Basque newspaper of Buenos Aires said, "The *lendakari* divides his days among Columbia University, where he will soon begin to teach his classes, the delegation, and his personal office. The *lendakari* is very optimistic and happy with the work done recently. He has had some political meetings with certain foreign representatives. Extremely delicate and easily understandable reasons forbid any detailed mention of these extremely important meetings, of great transcendence for our fatherland's future. However, it can be said that Euzkadi's value is recognized internationally and that the reconquest of the rights she has lost cannot be far off, if things go as the *lendakari* hopes. For the moment, he is not saying anything about these meetings, about which this correspondent was able to acquire some vague information. Faced with this correspondent's insistent questions, the *lendakari* answered only, 'The time will come for me to speak publicly and clearly'." The mentioned correspondent was probably Manu de la Sota, and the article was published as "Don José Antonio de

Valentín de Agirre's house, where we had a large dinner with speeches by Don Valentín. Very amusing, and a good table.[227]

NOVEMBER 1941
FRIDAY 21. PRESENT. OF THE BLESSED VIRGIN MARY. 325-40

This morning, I studied and worked. We went to New York on the 1:10 train. I had two interviews. One with the Information Coordination Committee for President Roosevelt, the other with a large Boston newspaper.[228] The former extremely important. It's a private office at the president's service. They visit those individuals whom they think are important so that the president can be informed, and if appropriate, Roosevelt can receive them. The envoy told me that it's probable that I'll be received by the president in two or three weeks. I'm not building

---

Aguirre en Nueva York," *Euzko Deya* (Buenos Aires), no. 99 (January 30, 1942), 6.
227 The article mentioned in the previous note also states, "On November 20, a magnificent banquet was held at the Basque-American Center in honor of the *lendakari*, attended by the most distinguished element of the New York Basque community. The *lendakari* was introduced by the center's president, Mr. Elorriaga. He was followed by Don Valentín de Agirre, the honorary president of the Basque-American Center and the father of Basque boxers and athletes in the Western Hemisphere, who spoke in a truly classic Euskara. Then the *lendakari* spoke. We are not going to narrate his speech, which was full of warmth and enthusiasm and moving in the extreme. It was the last speech of his journey and his first to the Basques of America. He spoke only in Euskara. For many, it was the first time that they had heard the leader of the Basque national cause, and tears of emotion were not lacking. Finally, the secretary of the Basque delegation, Don Ramón de la Sota, spoke in English. The banquet concluded with the singing of "Euzko Abendaren Ereserkija," and after the *lendakari* and his wife signed all the commemorative menus, designed with true artistic taste by the Bermeo patriots Don Pedro de Toja and Don Vidal de Mendizabal, they left for White Plains in the company of Don Manuel de Intxausti, the wife of Don Marino de Gamboa, and the members of the delegation." Ibid.
228 On the advice of the British, who were interested in drawing the Americans ever closer to the war, President Roosevelt created the Office of the Coordinator of Information (COI) with the mission of coordinating the intelligence work carried out by different agencies, chiefly military ones. The man put in charge of launching the new agency was William Joseph Donovan (1883–1959), who also went on to head the Office of Strategic Services (OSS), the organization that succeeded the COI when the United States entered the war. The latter organization developed an intelligence network covering the entire world except for the Western Hemisphere, which was reserved for the activities of the Federal Bureau of Investigation (FBI) and the Office of the Coordinator of Inter-American Affairs, headed by Nelson Rockefeller.

castles in the air, but in the end, it's better for things to go that way. The second interview was with an English journalist from a Yankee newspaper. A bit picturesque. He told us very seriously, making himself out to be well informed, that in Santander especially, there exists a terrible anti-German spirit. Precisely in Santander. After that, I cut short the interview, since I wasn't in the mood to laugh.

NOVEMBER 1941
SATURDAY 22. ST. CECILIA. 326-39

In the morning, I studied and continued taking care of business. I've now sent answers to our delegation in Mexico regarding their inquiries with respect to the attitude to adopt in view of the continuous importunities of the Spanish Republicans. I advised calm, much calm, strong Basque unity, and no compromises.[229] We have to move forward, looking ahead for the good of Euzkadi. From this place of observation, where I hope to become familiar with everything, I'll figure out which path we should take when God indicates the hour of attack. The London *Daily Mail* is asking me for a thousand-word article. It's significant. During our war, they supported Franco. Álvarez del Vayo visited me. He told me interesting things for more than an hour. I let him talk the whole time. The Spaniards are still so divided. We're united, as I've counseled, marching firmly forward.

NOVEMBER 1941
SUNDAY 23. ST. CLEMENT. 327-38

When we enter the church, we attract attention, since it's unusual to see two couples with six little ones. There's no way to leave Joseba at home, and he thinks he's old enough to go to church with everyone else, but then he can't stay still. Like every Sunday, Manu Sota arrived in the morning. The weather, which was very bad, prevented us from going for a walk in the morning. We went in the afternoon. We take advantage of these walks to prepare the week's affairs. I've received a long letter from Aldasoro. He worries too much in the letter about things in the past and about his difficulties. López Mendizabal sent me some material for my classes. These good friends have taken the professorship at Columbia as something that belongs to them all, and rightly so. How good our

---

229 See appendix 16.

people are! I plan on answering them this week. This evening we went to the movies. A very pretty film. Then I worked until three a.m.

NOVEMBER 1941
MONDAY 24. ST. JOHN OF THE CR. 328-37

I worked in the morning. In the afternoon, I went to New York. I received the delegation of English heads of the South American service. They all left satisfied with their letters of introduction to all our delegates.

Later, I was visited by the English representative here who deals primarily with the Iberian Peninsula service. He gave me a telegram in which the British government asked him to visit me and ask me to put an end to some differences in London between Ortuzar and the delegation. I composed a report and addressed all these compatriots along the indicated lines, which matched my own point of view. They offered me the diplomatic pouch for the purpose. If the English government desires our unity, why be arguing about trifles? Unity and unity, I don't tire of repeating it in all contexts. I believe that everything will be sorted out, but how much damage these things do!

NOVEMBER 1941
TUESDAY 25. ST. CATHERINE. 329-36

I received a letter from Telesforo, who is now in Mexico. Full of spirit and of faith in the future. It made a magnificent impression on me. Not only do our compatriots not flag when faced with sacrifice, but rather the reverse. It's a sign that reveals a great future. I've also received a letter from Ramón in Buenos Aires. The news he gives me is excellent. The effect of my journey through those lands is producing its effects. I began an answer with guidelines of all kinds right away today. I'm preparing answers for all the delegations. Inquiries, requests for instructions, for letters, for plans pour in. I don't have time. We need more staff at the delegation, but we don't have money. This too will be sorted out. Meanwhile, I never get six hours' sleep. Studying these matters takes up many hours of the day and the night. And my English . . .

NOVEMBER 1941
WEDNESDAY 26. ST. JOHN BERCHM. 330-35

I continued answering the delegations. A very long letter to Ramón. Another letter, also long, to Telesforo. Instructions to the Mexican delegation to avoid compromises with the Spaniards. To the Catalans in Mexico, an answer to their truly deferential and respectful inquiry, encouraging them to continue along the national path on which they have begun, without premature and unreliable compromises. Calm and calm. This evening, I was invited to a rigorously formal dinner at Professor Hayes's house. Representatives of state from Washington, university presidents, professors, a representative of the archbishop (a unique case), etc., etc. We've gained entry to the best Yankee society; I'm well situated, and they're announcing visits for me even at the very highest levels. God will say what will come, but the whole thing doesn't fail to be symptomatic. I think that the work here is showing signs of being fruitful. They informed me at the dinner that the archbishop of New York will receive me on Monday.

NOVEMBER 1941
THURSDAY 27. ST. ALBERT. 331-34

I spent the whole day working. In the morning, plugging away at my English. In the afternoon, dealing with reports and correspondence of all kinds. Ricardo de Leizaola arrived right at the end of the afternoon.[230] He came to say goodbye, since he's leaving for London. He's taking my commissions for the delegation, with a plan of action in South America in agreement with the English. Now they're seeking us out. The plan is part of the one that was presented in London in 1939 and has been neglected until now. He's taking good recommendations for the information minister. Nothing will be done without submitting it to the evaluation of the delegation, which has always followed the matter. In this way, the unity and discipline of the Basques will be demonstrated. In the evening, I composed the article that the London *Daily Mail* asked me for. I finished it at two-thirty in the morning. I have other things that I've been asked for pending as well.

---

230 Ricardo Leizaola Sánchez was a printer and publisher, as well as the brother of the Basque government's counselor for culture and justice, Jesús María Leizaola.

NOVEMBER 1941
FRIDAY 28. ST. SOSTHENES. 332-33

In the morning, I arrived in New York. I took care of pending business at the delegation. Later, at the invitation of Álvarez del Vayo, lunch at a restaurant on 34th Street. Álvarez de Vayo, who was extremely friendly, wanted us to talk about "Spanish policy," as he put it. I talked about Basque, Peninsular, and European policy. I explained to him clearly that after spending six years amid such terrible struggles, our people cannot look backward but forward. The Basque national personality has been delineated; it has to come out of this universal test triumphant and with its head held high. Vayo, who is understanding and broad-minded, listened attentively. He's supporting Negrín's policy. They're all divided, the Spaniards. For this reason, Basque unity is needed now more than ever.

NOVEMBER 1941
SATURDAY 29. ST. SATURNINUS. 333-32

Since the celebration and banquet I was being given by the New York Basque center were in the evening, I spent the day in New York dealing with the most urgent business. After lunch at Gamboa's house, I continued working at the delegation for a while. We arrived at the Basque center at something like seven. This association is the Basques' old bastion in this large city. Its merit derives from the fact that they have known how to preserve this point of reference and unity amid so many political variations in the Iberian Peninsula and even with a peculiar Americanization that has not managed to denature the essential Basque spirit. When I spoke in Euskara before 150 *euzkeldunes* at the banquet, the most intimate heartstrings of these compatriots were set vibrating. Like in Montevideo. We'll do great work with them. The limited size of the facilities prevented huge numbers from attending the dinner. The center was decorated for a gala with national colors and flags. The national anthem was sung for the first time. It's the influence of the new generation.

NOVEMBER 1941
SUNDAY 30. ST. ANDREW. 334-31

Saint Andrew's feast day. Our thoughts went straight to all those suffering for justice and freedom. From the prison depths there arises this clamor that is spreading in concentric circles through all the locations where there are Basques. This topic occupied all our attention this Sunday, on which, as on previous Sundays, Intxausti, Manu Sota, and I went out walking. Good old Intxausti invites us to his house every Sunday. We spend pleasant moments thinking about our affairs and our friends and relatives. This town, distanced from the noise of the big city, gives us that tranquility necessary to work on planning projects of all kinds. We're also satisfied because with peace the children have recovered their good appetites and good color. They get a lot of fresh air and enjoy playing with other children, which they were much in need of. Tomorrow morning we have an appointment at the residence of the archbishop of New York.

NOTES

Another month passes, and finally, in this one I've arrived on dry land where once I'm settled, I'll be able to start useful work. In the short time I've spent in the Western Hemisphere and more specifically in America, the number of friends visited and the importance of the relationships established have certainly been very great. I can say that we haven't had a failure. Even all the diplomatic maneuvers that annoyed us so much at the time seem to have been well intentioned. English and Americans are visiting us to coordinate our action in South America. Some days, the delegation doesn't seem Basque, but rather American or English. For these reasons, the name "Basque" is heard every day in London and Washington. This is how the causes of freedom are prepared, while President Roosevelt's Coordination Office examines my upcoming visits in order to get down to fundamental topics.

May God grant us the light and the deftness needed.

NOTES

Life in New York is insane. A lot of time is wasted here, because since the distances are so enormous, any effort or visit takes up an entire morning or afternoon. With my presence here, letters and requests for instructions and guidelines are pouring in to the delegation from all our delegates. Since we're not rolling in money, we lack even the most indispensable staff. Manu Sota is worn out with the work I'm giving him. I hope that the economic question will be sorted out. I think that the negotiations with the English to unblock the sums belonging to the Basque government that are in London will reach a successful conclusion. With them, we'll be able to organize our staff a little more efficiently and respond to our people's desires. Although our difficulties are enormous, I hope and expect that they will be overcome with a spirit of sacrifice and a will to conquer.

DECEMBER 1941
MONDAY 1. ST. ELIGIUS. 335-30

By ten a.m., Father Ford, the highly respected chaplain at Columbia University, was waiting for us in the visitors' parlor of the archbishop's residence in order to take us in to see the archbishop.[231] The archbishop, who is the leading figure in the American Church, received us with true affection. A personal friend of Pope Pius XII,[232] with whom he worked in Rome for quite a few years, he receives the consideration of a true primate. He told me that my presence in the United States is a blessing for the Catholic Church. He spoke about the confusion that there was at the beginning about the Basques' position. Today, things are changing. He told me that we'll keep in contact. A cordial and important interview. President Roosevelt himself consults with this prelate on important issues. Inchausti and Manu Sota are astonished at the prelate's tone. They maintain that there's something behind the scenes that's motivating these ceremonies and welcomes. We'll know soon.

DECEMBER 1941
TUESDAY 2. ST. BIBIANA. 336-29

In the morning, I wrote letters and more letters, answering the abundant mail of recent days. First thing in the afternoon, to the delegation again. I received the English heads of the Chilean and Mexican propaganda

---

231 From 1939 until his death, Francis Joseph Spellman (1889–1967), a cardinal beginning in 1946, served as archbishop of New York and apostolic vicar for the U.S. Armed Forces.

232 Eugenio Maria Giovanni Pacelli (1876–1958) served as pope with the name of Pius XII between 1939 and 1958.

service. This completed the South American picture. They don't trust anyone but the Basques. They're happy about how our people respond all over. All these contributions, some large and others small, are building a sold scaffolding of prestige that will have political repercussions in the future. It's not I or the leaders, it's our people who are triumphing due to their enthusiasm and loyalty. Despite all this service, how many instances of ingratitude and incomprehension still await us! But that's how peoples are made, in contradiction and in sorrow. Later, these sacrifices are repaid a hundredfold. I'm very satisfied with all my compatriots.

DECEMBER 1941
WEDNESDAY 3. ST. FRANC. XAVIER. 337-28

I spent the morning working at home. In the afternoon, I went to the university, where I had agreed to meet Professor Hayes to visit Columbia's library. This library has three million volumes. The bibliography I can make use of is enormous. Much larger than the time I can use in consulting it. I don't know how I'll be able to meet all my obligations. Preparing my classes in English takes a lot of time. I have to definitively settle on the topic with Professor Hayes. Professor Hayes wants me to study the last hundred years on the Iberian Peninsula. That will give me an opportunity to frame appropriately the problems confused by the ignorance or the malice of the Spanish professors. The topic will be complemented with the study of the influence of the thought of the Peninsular peoples on the development of South American political ideas and South American life. The topic is enormously current, because it will lead us to an explanation of the current problems.

DECEMBER 1941
THURSDAY 4. ST. BARBARA. 338-27

Today I spent the whole day studying English and the matters raised by London. Long reports from Irujo and Lizaso that have to be studied with great care. The letter from the Catalan leader Py y Suñer is extraordinarily important.[233] I'm satisfied, because the Catalans are firmly establishing their national attitude, openly proclaiming their nationality. The serious problem before us is to combine this fundamental postulate with political

---

233 Carles Pi Sunyer (1888–1971) was a Catalan engineer, economist, writer, and politician active in the Republican Left of Catalonia (*Esquerra Republicana de Catalunya*, ERC). Between 1941 and 1945 he served as president of the National Council of Catalonia (*Consell Nacional de Catalunya*).

reality, not so much current reality as future reality. Will our national problem be understood and solved outside the context of the Iberian Peninsula? Will they obligate us to Peninsular solutions, naturally within the framework of the autonomous recognition of our nationality? Should we wait, or should we proclaim these postulates starting now? We're always running up against the lack of a clear explanation at high levels. Do they know what they want? Do they have a concrete plan?

DECEMBER 1941
FRIDAY 5. ST. SABAS. 339-26

In the morning, I continued studying and writing letters. I'd like to finish these first throes of correspondence soon, in order to dedicate myself entirely to study, but I don't know whether I'll be able to. In the afternoon, I went to New York to receive two journalists from the London *Daily Mail* for an interview. I told them as much as was proper, hiding details that might cause harm to others. In the evening, we were invited by Captain Gerrikaetxebarria to have dinner on his ship, the Honduran steamer *Corinto*. By accepting this invitation, I wanted to express my thanks in some way to our brave sailors for the magnificent work that they are doing on all levels in favor of our cause and that of the Allies in this war. We had a very pleasant time in a decidedly Basque atmosphere in the middle of the port of New York, surrounded by fog and constantly hearing the ships' foghorns. This whole picture had an attractive tint.

DECEMBER 1941
SATURDAY 6. ST. NICHOLAS. 340-25

I spent the whole day studying. Composing letters with instructions for the delegations, which are constantly asking for them, also takes up a lot of my time. Every issue raised requires extended study. I don't want to ever reverse course or have to correct what I've said. Everyone will be permitted to be mistaken on occasion except me. This is why I think and meditate about my words a great deal before I write them. The people in Mexico sent a satisfied answer after receiving my instructions. Monzón has arrived there safely now. His presence can be highly beneficial. They all have faith, and they all want to work. We run up against the lack of money. But everything will be sorted out with God's help.

Serious rumors are circulating today about Japan's intentions. Another fundamental element in this war. The Dakar problem will then come to the fore, with the American entry into the war. Then Franco, Vichy ...

DECEMBER 1941
SUNDAY 7. ST. AMBROSE. 341-24

After fulfilling all our religious duties, we waited for Manu Sota to arrive, like every Sunday. At church, we and the Intxaustis, with our six children between us, attract attention, since we fill almost half of the small chapel near the house. Today we invited the Pelans to lunch. The wife is the daughter of the mayor of Baiona [Bayonne], who distinguished us so much in those regions with his affection.[234] In the afternoon, a Dominican father arrived, one of the Paris group who were always very good friends of ours.[235] The conversation was very interesting. He gave us many specifics about the current situation of the Free French. At that moment, the news arrived of the state of war between Japan and the United States and England.[236] The entry of these Americans into the war will determine a fundamental change in the war. Now we're missing Spain, whose entry we won't have to wait long for. Everything is developing, step by step.

DECEMBER 1941
MONDAY 8. *IMM. CONCEPT*. 342-23

We celebrated the Virgin's feast day remembering our time in Euzkadi. I spent the whole day working at home. Now I miss my good assistants Secun and Ramón.[237] How well I worked with them taking dictation!

---

234 Jacques Simonet, a radical socialist, who was mayor of Baiona from 1935 on.

235 The Paris Dominicans, publishers of the journals *La vie intellectuelle* and *Sept*, unlike their brethren of the same order in Spain, adopted theological and consequently political positions, including with regard to the Spanish Civil War, in accordance with the more progressive social Catholicism they professed, bringing them closer to the positions of the Basque nationalists. The adoption by this group of French Dominicans of opinions unfavorable to the Spanish rebel faction was opposed by the order's Spanish journal *La ciencia tomista*, ultimately leading to the closure of *Sept* by the Dominican superiors on the pretext of a response to the publication's economic problems.

236 The Japanese attack on the U.S. base at Pearl Harbor took place on December 7, 1941. War was declared by a joint session of the U.S. Congress the following day.

237 Secundino Urrutia Rodeño and Ramón Sánchez Arana, employees of the president's

Now I work twice as much and get half as much done. Since we don't have money, we have to make up the lack with personal effort. But this impossible situation will have to be sorted out somehow. With my salary, I can't do more than just manage to live. Then this London dispute that's keeping our collective money frozen is regrettable and criminal. I don't know whether the English will finally realize it. But how difficult it is for them to understand things!

Our friend Intxausti is very concerned about the events in the Pacific. He has good reason to be, since he's at risk of losing a considerable fortune. God will help him as a reward for so many, many sufferings of his neighbors that he's known how to prevent.

DECEMBER 1941
TUESDAY 9. ST. LEOCADIA. 343-22

I went to the university starting in the morning. I visited Professor Hayes, who was dismayed by the course of events. The life of the university will also suffer a blow as so many students join the military. We settled on the program for my classes. The topic I will begin to discuss in my February lectures will have the title "History of the Iberian Peninsula in the Last Hundred Years." In October—if circumstances permit—I will alternate this course with one that will be titled "Influence of the Iberian Peninsula on South American Thought." With these topics, I will be able to explain the true Basque history and the influence of our national thought in South America. An abundant and very interesting topic. Only God knows where we'll find ourselves in October. Things are moving so fast that nothing can be predicted.

In the afternoon, I worked at the delegation, sending and reading a lot of correspondence.

DECEMBER 1941
WEDNESDAY 10. ST. MELCHIADES. 344-21

I spent the day at the university again today. I was invited by Professor Tannenbaum, one of the most notable and competent professors at Columbia.[238] We had lunch together at the University Club. This professor

---

office at the Basque government's Paris delegation.
238 Frank Tannenbaum (1893–1969) was a professor of Latin American history at Columbia University.

was sent to Mexico some years ago by the government in Washington to sort out the religious issue. He has great prestige and important friends. We talked about the program for my course, which he judged to be of great interest. In the afternoon, we visited the university's colossal library, which has more than three million volumes. It's a thing of grandeur. I registered as a professor with the right to take books home. Everything was marvelously organized. I paid attention to everything with a view toward the Basque university that we've always dreamed of making worthy, ours, and universal.

Afterward, I spent a good chunk of time at the delegation, examining various matters.

To the train and home around six.

DECEMBER 1941
THURSDAY 11. ST. DAMASUS. 345-20

Today I spent the day working and answering letters and more letters. I received a very interesting one from Basterretxea and Olivares Larrondo.[239] These two good and competent friends are acting in agreement, as in Paris, and always in a constructive spirit. They presented to me the plan for a worldwide association of Basques of all classes for cultural and fraternal purposes. They sketched out the creation of a journal that would have the purpose of dismantling the Spanish totalitarian atmosphere. They're in absolute agreement with what our friend Intxausti, Manu Sota, and I have in hand to launch one of these days, taking advantage of the *Gabon* celebrations.[240] It's curious how patriots often coincidentally light on the

---

239 José Olivares Larrondo, known as Tellagorri (1892–1960), was a writer and journalist. A founding member of Basque Nationalist Action (Acción Nacionalista Vasca, ANV), he directed the party's official publication, *Tierra Vasca*, until 1933. After going into exile in Baiona, he contributed to *Sud-Ouest* and to the Paris *Euzko Deya*. In 1940, he embarked for the Western Hemisphere on the *Alsina*. In Argentina, he contributed to the Buenos Aires *Euzko Deya*, to *Galeuzca*, and to numerous Latin American publications. In 1956, he was named director of the Buenos Aires *Tierra Vasca*, a post he occupied until his death. For Francisco Basterrechea, see note 148.

240 *Gabon* means "Christmas" in Euskara. On the Ludiko Euzko Alkartasuna or World Association of Basques (Asociación Mundial de Vascos), the president wrote to Irujo and Lizaso: "The name of the entity, which we desire to see bring together the allegiances of Basque entities, associations, and individuals of all kinds scattered throughout the world, has not yet been determined. . . . It responds to a need and at the same time to a remarkably shared concern expressed by various delegations. Culture and mutual aid will be its defining aspects, with the natural declarations in

same things even though they may be thousands of kilometers apart, a coincidence that can extend to the smallest details, as in this case. For this reason, our cause prospers, because it is served with loyalty and faith.

DECEMBER 1941
FRIDAY 12. ST. AUBERT. 346-19

In the morning, I stayed home. Very early in the afternoon, I arrived at the delegation, where I dealt with correspondence and marveled at what arrives every day. Later, I listened to the interesting report of a compatriot who left Euzkadi about two months ago. I'm satisfied by the spirit of our compatriots and especially of our prisoners. What a page of history is theirs! On the other hand, I'm saddened by the stories that are already being constantly repeated about the taste for luxury, spending, and amusement of the people with money, who believe that they've momentarily triumphed. People with money and without spiritual content. It seems like they are throwing themselves madly into amusements in order to forget a past full of remorse and in order to take advantage of the brief time left to them as they look toward the future. Like always, they live on the margins of the people, without caring about their sorrow. Once again, they're dancing on the volcano's rim. And they're laughing, because they know . . . that we won't kill.

DECEMBER 1941
SATURDAY 13. ST. LUCY. 347-18

I was at the delegation beginning in the morning, occupied with finishing the composition of the customary *Gabon* manifesto to my compatriots. I remembered the one composed last year in Antwerp. I signed it the same day that Álvarez—I had already forgotten—received permission from the German authorities to go to Berlin. And I dated the manifesto in London, to be more impudent about it. The good patriot Arrieta took it with him. I know that it was distributed in Euzkadi, and the recently

---

favor of the democratic cause and in recognition and support of the national cause.... "Each country will establish its own Council of the World Association of Basques. The president in each country will be a member of the Supreme Council, which Intxausti will head. ... It will be a magnificent auxiliary to the Basque government in its struggle, since it will reach previously distanced sectors who need to be given an intermediate stage on the path." Letter from José Antonio Agirre to Manuel Irujo and José Ignacio Lizaso, New York, December 3, 1941. GE-259-2.

arrived and escaped boy from Portugalete confirmed it to me yesterday. In this year's manifesto, I confirm our belligerent position in this war; I call on the Basques of all the Western Hemisphere communities to unite, chiefly those who were with Franco and have now repented; I greet our prisoners, as always; and I send another greeting to our illustrious priests, a glory of our religion and of our fatherland. I believe that it will be published all over.

DECEMBER 1941
SUNDAY 14. ST. NICASIUS. 348-17

After our visit to the church to fulfill our religious duties, Intxausti, Manu, and I took a walk, as usual. It serves us as a source of oxygen, given that the life that we're living these days is not the most observant of the rules of health and hygiene. Since I work all day in a room that isn't suitable for it, since it's our bedroom, or go to New York, a trip that's fatiguing to an extent I would never have believed, these Sunday walks do me a lot of good. They say that life moves fast here. It has to, because it's necessary to run around a lot, given the distances. But let's not confuse speed with work. Due to the same circumstances, not much work gets done. That's my impression. That makes the lack of immediate reaction to the Japanese attack understandable. I'm referring to material reactions. Now, if they make them work, they'll produce. I remember our men!

DECEMBER 1941
MONDAY 15. ST. FORTUNAT. 349-16

Throughout all these days, after my ordinary work, I've been studying and meditating on a plan of action for Euzkadi in these grave circumstances. The chancelleries won't take a step in support of Euzkadi's freedom until the Spanish diplomatic and political process has been exhausted in all its aspects and to its fullest extent. In other words, they'll first exhaust all the diplomatic resources of the oldest school of diplomacy to prevent Spain from entering the war on the side of the Axis. Afterward, they'll similarly exhaust all their efforts to get what was the Spanish Republican state to unite for joint action against Franco and his Axis friends. Only after this process will they study and potentially approve the problem of Basque and Catalan freedom. This is a terrible reality. Of course, our identity will always come out strengthened, and the

Basque national problem will be more firmly established, but days of great struggle await us. Nothing disturbs me, since we're moving forward toward victory every day.

DECEMBER 1941
TUESDAY 16. ST. EUSEBIUS. 350-15

Today I had an interesting interview with Mr. Fernández Artuccio, a Uruguayan and that country's special envoy to London and Washington to serve as a liaison and observer concerning these countries' relations with the South American republics. He was in London two months ago now. He could judge that we Basques have credit and capital with the Foreign Office. We talked about South America and about the problem of the Iberian Peninsula. He assigned us a predominant role in peninsular politics by way of the freedom of Euzkadi.[241] He confirmed

---

241 Hugo Fernández Artucio was a Uruguayan journalist of socialist leanings who published a book in the summer of 1940 synthesizing the denunciations of Nazi activities in Uruguay that he himself had previously broadcast on the CX14 radio station, part of the El Espectador network. Hugo Fernández Artucio, *Nazis en el Uruguay* (Montevideo: Talleres Gráficos Sur, 1940). He twice met with Basque representatives in London, with José Ignacio Lizaso on September 24, 1941, and with Manuel Irujo on the 26th of the same month. In the first interview, Artucio declared that his trip to London had "the aim of studying wartime conditions in England and learning about the plans and orientations of the English democratic parties." He informed Lizaso that democratic Uruguayans were perfectly well aware of the Nazi presence in South American and were "ready to offer the United States facilities of all kinds to prepare the necessary bases on our republic's coasts to enable its fleet to be in a position to come the aid of the South American republics." Irujo was told by the Uruguayan envoy that "the most efficacious contribution that you [the Basques] can make to the work of democracy is to cooperate with your communities in the Western Hemisphere to rouse those peoples, who are still asleep." Irujo ended his report on his interview with Fernández Artucio with the following commentary on his interlocutor: "From the terms in which he spoke, we deduced that he is a South American observer placed at the service of President Roosevelt's perspective, a position that corresponds exactly to that of Uruguay with respect to the United States." Report on the meeting between José Ignacio Lizaso and Hugo Fernández Artucio, London, September 24, 1941, and Manuel Irujo, "Conferencia con el Dr. Fernández Artucio," London, September 26, 1941. GE-259-1. It was not Fernández Artucio's first contact with Basque delegates. Several years earlier, in August 1938, in connection with the World Congress for Peace held in New York, the Basque representative to the congress, José Luis de la Lombana, had occasion to address the various delegates from parties of Marxist leanings, one of whom was Artucio, representing the Uruguayan Social Democratic Party. José Luis de la Lombana, "Informe de la actuación de José Luis de la Lombana en América,

the chancelleries' perspective that I was already familiar with, that they desire that an effort be made in favor of common action. My joint plan goes along these lines; it's bold and innovative in parts, and on the other hand, it has elements that are constructive and fit the desires of the English and the Americans. *Jaungoikoa*, Whom I have asked, as always, to guide my pen and my mind, will do what is best for Basque happiness.

DECEMBER 1941
WEDNESDAY 17. ST. LAZARUS. 351-14

I composed the action plan for Euzkadi and Catalonia. Our thinking was already known and beyond dispute: Basque and Catalan national affirmation and right of self-determination.[242] What was lacking was the program for action. Either a declaration of independence or joint peninsular action on the basis of those principles. The former will be difficult to get the chancelleries to approve without exhausting the latter. My proposal, which has gone to our London delegation and to the Catalans by rapid diplomatic channels—on the English plane—takes concrete form in a proclamation by which Pi Suñer and I, in the names of Catalonia and Euzkadi, affirming our right of self-determination and our democratic and social ideas, our adhesion as belligerents to the democracies, and our state of war with Franco, call on Spanish democrats of all persuasions to engage in a common struggle under the acceptance of those principles. Will the Spaniards understand it?

DECEMBER 1941
THURSDAY 18. ST. GATIAN. 352-13

At home in the morning, and by two I was already in New York. Today the English services visited me. A long conversation. Despite being the ones in charge, how slow they are to understand things! Today a bold deed was done, one that is a great help to the British Admiralty. Finally, one of our ship's captains—Etxabe from Somorrostro—has turned over the envelope with secret instructions from Franco's officials to the captains in wartime and in the event that Spain enters the conflict, as

---

13-VIII a 5-XI de 1938," Paris, November 24, 1938.

242 This manifesto may be consulted in Goiogana, Irujo, and Legarreta, *Un nuevo 31*, 418–39. Appendix 17 of the current volume includes a letter from the *lehendakari* to the delegate in Mexico explaining the document's arguments.

she is sure to do.²⁴³ Instructions that have served to confirm what Spain's decision will be. I've been talking to the English authorities about the Argentine danger, and in effect, one of the orders for these ships is to go to that nation.²⁴⁴ But we've already begun to become informed, and the British and American battleships will act for us later. My letter and proclamation from yesterday are on their way to London.

DECEMBER 1941
FRIDAY 19. ST. ZOSIME. 353-12

Today we were invited by Don Valentín de Aguirre for an early *Gabon* celebration. He hosted us in his Jai Alai restaurant with an excellent meal that did not fail to include some good lobsters, prepared the classic way, after starting off with a very good fish soup. Good Murrieta wine, of course—it had been a while since we'd tasted it—etc., etc. Afterward, to the delegation to prepare tomorrow's correspondence and business. I received new reports from London. This time it was Gondra's turn;²⁴⁵ he's a boy who's worth something. I read everything and prepared an answer. The bad thing is that letters take so long! Some days back, the English offered me the diplomatic pouch and sent letters to London for me. Now they've promised me another time. We'll see whether they arrive, since for the moment, I'm not receiving replies of any kind.

---

243 The first instructions for captains of Spanish-flagged ships were issued in late April 1941. They specified that upon receiving the agreed radio signal, "A group of drifting mines was sighted at 46°15' latitude north and 29°25' longitude west," the captains should open the sealed envelopes that had been secretly entrusted to them. In the event that half an hour after the first message, they received another one saying, "Avoid sailing through an area fifty miles around the point indicated in the previous alert," the captains should turn their ships toward Norwegian or South American ports, preferably Argentine ones. If none of these options was viable, they should head for a Spanish port. The messages, which would change their text several times as long as Franco nourished desires to enter the war in favor of the Axis, were to be broadcast forty-eight hours in advance of the date set for Spain's entry into the war. Ros Agudo, *La guerra secreta*, 118–20.

244 Argentina's non-alignment with U.S. aims concerning the policy to be followed with respect to the Axis powers, together with the frequently and strikingly ambiguous posture of the Argentine executive branch with regard to its attitude toward the war in progress, led many to believe that the southern country was just short of openly taking the Nazi and Fascist side. In this context, revelations like those found in the secret orders the *lehendakari* mentions increased the plausibility of theories linking Argentina to the Nazis.

245 Ángel Gondra Garro was secretary of the London delegation.

DECEMBER 1941
SATURDAY 20. ST. EUGENE. 354-11

I worked all morning. I went to New York and continued work at the delegation. We lack staff, because we don't have money. They think that we're potentates, seeing that we're functioning, and they don't really know that we don't even have the money available to keep a typist to take care of our correspondence. Manu Sota has to put a hand to everything, visits, typing, errands, and even food. He's a great cook by now. I hope that this situation will be sorted out. As things stand, we can't bear the fruit that we would be able to with a minimum of staff. Meanwhile, our money is blocked or inactive in London as a result of errors and mistakes on all sides. Good grief! God grant that everything get sorted out. They tell me that I'm too good, because I don't break things, tear things up, and dismiss people. They don't know what they're saying. There aren't many of us; we need everyone. And then, our people, even if they make mistakes, are good, honorable, loyal ...

DECEMBER 1941
SUNDAY 21. ST. THOMAS. 355-10

Like every Sunday, to church en masse. Afterward, our hygienic Sunday stroll, today a little harder than other Sundays, because it was extraordinarily cold. After lunch, Intxausti, Manu, and I went to the movies. Our wives, who are a whirlwind of activity these days, stayed home. Afterward, we passed the time pleasantly in Intxausti's living room, amid such good friends. Yesterday we were at Gamboa's house, where his wife María, as good and kind as always, wanted to give us an early Christmas with presents for the children and offering us splendid refreshments. I went very late, when our *umetxus*[246] had already lost all respect. We were expecting María today, but she wasn't able to come. We're starting to receive loving holiday wishes from our compatriots and from Americans.

---

246 *Ume* means "child" in Euskara, and *umetxu* is one of its endearing forms.

DECEMBER 1941
MONDAY 22. ST. FLAVIAN. 356-9

I worked all day. Mari is very busy preparing the house where we're going to live. We've been lucky, since it's cheap in comparison to the exorbitant prices that are the fashion here, it's appropriately small, since we can't allow ourselves the luxury of even a single maid, and it's comfortable. Mari has bought very cheap used furniture. She's very clever, and up to now, she's decorated the house quite well while spending very little. The cottage is located about a hundred meters from Intxausti, who hasn't let us get any farther away. The little neighborhood church is twenty meters away, the bus is nearby, and it's an extremely healthy location for the children. We've been very lucky, as in everything, thanks be to God.[247]

I'm impatient for them to finish setting up my modest office so I can work in my room and make a serious start on the book that several publishing house want me to publish.[248]

DECEMBER 1941
TUESDAY 23. ST. VICTORIA. 357-8

In the morning, I worked. Immediately after lunch, I went to New York, since I had received a call from the English services at the embassy and the Foreign Office and from the head of the American services. They arrived. They want to seriously establish a formal organization with the Basques throughout the Western Hemisphere. The actions the Basques have carried out have convinced them. They've sent us congratulations from London. Afterward, I worked on a proclamation in Euskara addressed to Basque sailors, to be sent to them by the Admiralty at the moment that Spain enters the war, which we will know from the instructions that Spanish-flagged ships will receive, in a code to which we already have the key. We hope that some captains will listen to us. The English expressed great satisfaction. Freedom is won with many small things.

---

247 White Plains was a small city of around thirty thousand inhabitants located twenty-five miles north of Manhattan; since the cost of living was lower than in New York, a number of Basque families in addition to Manuel Ynchausti's had settled there.

248 The book to which the *lehendakari* refers is the much-mentioned *De Guernica a Nueva York pasando por Berlín*, first published in Spanish by the Editorial Vasca Ekin in Buenos Aires in 1943. The first edition in English was titled *Escape Via Berlin* and was brought out by Macmillan in 1944.

DECEMBER 1941
WEDNESDAY 24. ST. DELPHINUS. 358-7

Today I went to New York in the morning. The big city had a holiday air, well prepared with all its decorations. I felt only nostalgia for the fatherland and those—my loved ones among them—who will spend these days in separation and insecurity.

I had lunch with the Uruguayan envoy Artussio, who invited Professor Halpak from the Sorbonne in Paris, a British citizen and an important player at the English embassy and Foreign Office. We talked about the problem of the Iberian Peninsula. They're interested in its solution. I expounded the same theory as always, my people's right of self-determination. On this basis, any arrangement that respects our national soul can be accepted. The English mentality understands this language; the Spanish mentality is another story. How much there still is to be fought! I've fired off the same orders to everyone: unity, firmness, forward movement, even if slowly and prudently. This is how we've conquered all difficulties, and this is how we will conquer them.

DECEMBER 1941
THURSDAY 25. CHRISTMAS DAY. 359-6

Yesterday we went to bed very late. We had to put the children's toys under the Christmas tree set up in Intxausti's house. This good friend doesn't do anything by half-measures, and despite the bad news arriving from the Philippines, neither obstacles nor prices exist for him.[249] He's rained down money buying all kinds of presents for children and adults. How we've remembered those who are suffering and in danger, especially in France, in Belgium, and in the prisons! We, thanks be to God, enjoyed ourselves seeing the children happy with their toys and participating for a few moments in their saving innocence. Manu and Ramón Sota were invited. The church very full. In the afternoon, we were invited by Professor Vignaud, whom I hadn't seen since Paris.[250]

---

249 The *lehendakari* is referring to the Japanese offensive against and occupation of the Philippines. The invasion began on December 10, 1941, and the occupation of Luzon, the largest island in the archipelago, began on the 22nd. The capital, Manila, fell on January 2, 1942.

250 Paul Vignaux (1904–1987) was a French philosopher and medievalist specializing in medieval philosophy. His Christian Democratic ideology brought him into contact with Basque nationalism and the Basque government. A fruit of this relationship

He's teaching philosophy near Chicago. We spent a pleasant holiday. Thinking about other, better ones . . .

DECEMBER 1941
FRIDAY 26. ST. STEPHEN. 360-5

I spent all day in New York taking care of delegation business. I'm starting to receive letters in which they let me know that the *Gabon* manifesto has been received. I've followed my annual custom. Here in this country of *arlotes*, they celebrate *Gabon* with a happiness and fervor that have moved me.[251] Every house has its Christmas tree, which they light up artistically. There are many in the yards, as well as in the streets and squares. In the stations, the large department stores, etc., the profusion of lights, music, and decorative arts is truly astounding. One feels the Christian happiness of these days of optimism and rejoicing. It's too bad that for us, the memory of our loved ones has unintentionally cast a shadow over the festivities. Here, despite the war, they've celebrated the holiday with great joy. So far they've only begun. God has given them a great deal of strength. For this reason, they will never leave their land . . .

DECEMBER 1941
SATURDAY 27. ST. JOHN, APOSTLE. 361-4

Today I went to New York early, like yesterday. After reading the correspondence—today it was Mexico's turn—I answered some letters. I'm very far behind on all my office work. Manu and I can't multiply ourselves. The interruptions are continuous. Visits, inquiries, Basques who ask for our card, matters that turn up unexpectedly. Prieto has been here for some days now.[252] He visited me three days ago. We had

---

was the biography he would write of Manuel Irujo, *Manuel de Irujo: Ministre de la République dans la guerre d'Espagne: 1936–1939* (Paris: Beauchesne Éditeur, 1986). An opponent of the French collaborationist regime, he went into exile in the United States, where, in addition to teaching at the University of Notre Dame in Indiana, he contributed to the Allied propaganda effort.

251 *Arlote* might be translated as "extravagant", and *Gabon*, as previously noted, means "Christmas."

252 Two matters brought Indalecio Prieto to New York in the second half of December 1941. On the one hand, he was concerned to resolve the problem of the *Alsina*'s passengers, stuck in Havana after having crossed the Atlantic, and arrange for them to continue their voyage to Montevideo and Buenos Aires, and on the other, he wanted to bring the Spanish refugees in Casablanca to the Western Hemisphere.

a long conversation. He's the same as always, a one-hundred-percent Spaniard. He's alarmed by our position, which he considers—what else?—exaggerated. Today he was invited to Gamboa's house. We continued our conversations, and I obtained the specifics I needed about the Spaniards' internal divisions. He and Negrín are the two prominent Spaniards who have true strength and with whom we'll have to fight

---

With regard to the former issue, Prieto submitted the following memorandum to the JARE: "Last spring, the French transatlantic liner *Alsina* left Marseilles headed for Rio de Janeiro, Montevideo, and Buenos Aires, with a large number of refugees of various nationalities, including Spaniards, on board. Prevented from crossing the ocean, the ship had to take refuge in Dakar, shifting later to Casablanca. The non-Spanish passengers were able to continue their voyage, some of them re-embarking in Cádiz and others in Lisbon, but the Spaniards, all enemies of Franco, had to stay in Casablanca, where they remained until leaving there a few weeks ago on board the Portuguese ship *Quanza*, sponsored by the Spanish Republican Aid Committee (*Junta de Auxilio a los Republicanos Españoles*) active in Mexico. Sixty-nine of the members of the expedition are currently in Havana; two of them have authorization to enter Chile, five Uruguay, and the rest Argentina. They have all been admitted to Cuba by the personal decision of President Batista and without limitations on the length of their stay, but they all wish to leave as soon as possible for the destinations mentioned above, where many of them have family and others have friends. Attached to this memorandum is the list of passengers in question, among whom, as will be seen, are Don Niceto Alcalá Zamora, first president of the Second Spanish Republic, and his four children. The majority of those included on the list are Basques by birth, as their surnames indicate, and some are officials of the Basque region's autonomous government. The difficulty posed for the travel of said passengers from Havana to Montevideo and Buenos Aires arises from the fact that at the moment and due to the exceptional circumstances of maritime traffic, there are no ships that call at Havana and go to South America. The only possible procedure consists in bringing the mentioned passengers from Havana to New York in order to sail from this port on one of the ships that make regular runs to Buenos Aires. However, for this purpose it is indispensable to provide the passengers with American transit visas. Their stay in New York would be extremely brief, since it would be limited to the days between the arrival of the Ward Line ship that would bring them from Cuba and the departure of the first American Republic Line packet boat, on which the Valentín Aguirre agency would have previously acquired their passage to their respective destinations. As a consequence of all this, the acquisition of those transit visas is desired, offering all guarantees that may be considered appropriate to this end." Where the second motive for his trip to New York was concerned, Prieto reported that he had written to Valentín Agirre, among other things, "I authorize you to arrange with Titan Shipping Company another, analogous expedition between the two mentioned ports on the ship *Nyassa*, if the news is confirmed according to which said ship will stop at the mentioned Moroccan port on its next voyage to Lisbon." Record no. 158, November 30, 1941, JARE record book for 1939–1942, books III and IV, http://www.cervantesvirtual.com/servlet/SirveObras/ace/.

in the future. But against peoples on the march, there's no fighting. Either you compromise, or you lose. For this reason, we look forward, with faith and security.

DECEMBER 1941
SUNDAY 28. HOLY INNOCENTS. 362-3

In the morning, after attending church, we walked a little. Later, we were Don Valentín de Aguirre's guests for lunch at a magnificent restaurant in New York. Prieto was at the lunch. We spoke only about trivial matters. Don Valentín went all out in our honor. Prieto felt himself obligated to invite us for tomorrow. It seems that he came to New York accompanying a Spanish socialist who is supposed to have brought from Africa, where he was interned, some interesting information regarding the German danger in those regions. What is certain is that they brought the socialist to Washington. As a result, rumors of all kinds have been going around. The English are making Prieto the Spanish leader. Others were saying that Prieto and Negrín have joined hands in Washington. Others . . . In sum, poor Spaniards! It's not how things are done, and it's not that easy. Unless it's a joke for the feast of the Holy Innocents . . .

DECEMBER 1941
MONDAY 29. ST. THOMAS OF CANTERBURY. 363-2

I arrived at the delegation in the morning and worked there until one. We arrived at Don Valentín's Jai Alai Restaurant, where Prieto offered us a good lunch. It had more of our flavor. After lunch, there was singing. Prieto doesn't get beyond "Boga boga."[253] If they knew this in Bilbao, there would be no end to the comments and murmurs. The Prieto-Agirre friendship has caused much concern, including among my fellow believers. They're short-sighted people who have such worries. Friendship, even with political opponents, is one thing, and the political struggle is something very different. We've never made a bargain with Prieto about anything. On the contrary, we're the ones who brought him down from the political pedestal that he ascended in Euzkadi with the help of those who criticize us. Today in Euzkadi, there's no room for the alien spirit of Prieto or Franco, but only for the Basque national spirit.

---

253 "Boga boga" is a Basque popular song harmonized by Jesús Guridi Bidaola.

DECEMBER 1941
TUESDAY 30. ST. SABINUS. 364-1

In the morning, I continued working at home. In the afternoon, I went to the delegation. Shortly afterward, the English arrived to continue studying the organization of propaganda and services in South America with us. The points of view I set out to them were accepted. They had some bad moments when I expressed my displeasure because I still have no news from London that they've received the letters that I sent for Manuel and Ortuzar and then for Manuel and Pi y Suñer in the English diplomatic pouch. In these times, anything is possible. It's frightening to think that in the middle of a war like this one, there might be enemies in the English and American diplomatic centers. And nevertheless, that's how it is. The English chiefs were very worried, but I'm even more so, since in the most recent letters, the whole Basque-Catalan action plan was laid out. They promised me that they would take good care to find out what might have happened.

I returned home. My good friend Inchausti is naturally worried about what's happening in the Philippines.

DECEMBER 1941
WEDNESDAY 31. ST. SYLVESTER. 365-0

Today brings an end to this year full of emotions and adventures. It ends well, thanks be to God. We spent the day at home in the morning, I dedicated to my ordinary tasks and Mari fully occupied in preparing the house. In the afternoon, I went to New York, and in the evening, we all gathered at Gamboa's house, where we were invited to spend *Gabon zar*.[254] Memories of so many things from the past are the mandatory topic at these gatherings of compatriots. We listened to the clock strike midnight on the radio and accompanied the sound with a private prayer that the upcoming year bring fewer misfortunes and instead clearly announce now the future in which we hope more firmly every day. Shortly after twelve, we left to take the train, which deposited us in White Plains half an hour later, on January 1, 1942.

---

254 *Gabon zar* means "New Year's Eve" in Euskara.

NOTES

[*In the upper margin*: 1941 came to an end, amid sorrows and hopes.]

Having begun in Louvain, the year ended in New York, after having crossed half of Europe at war, a sea full of dangers, and the Western Hemisphere from South to North. Here, I've been received by the overwhelming caring and affection of my compatriots and friends; there, we've left our mothers and our siblings in the uncertainty of a lengthy separation. Still further away are dear friends who are suffering behind prison bars for the horrible crime of loving their fatherland. I have only reasons to bless the good God who led me by His hand. My constant petition was nothing other than this, if it would be to His glory and for the good of my fatherland in freedom. I think about the victorious conclusion with security, but we will still encounter much work and sorrow along the way. 1942 will be a better year than the last one, despite everything. Let's hope for this with the same faith as always.

Marauette DIARY and Daily Reminder
A Page a Day for 1942

THURSDAY, JANUARY 1, 1942
1ST DAY-364 DAYS TO FOLLOW
NEW YEAR'S DAY

We made a happy start to the New Year. We attended high mass at our little church. At Intxausti's house, we celebrated the holiday in a worthy way. Manu and Ramón Sota were invited and also stayed for dinner. The Christmas tree was lit up; the little ones enjoyed it very much. We did not forget that there are many who cannot enjoy these holidays, so tied to the home, as we are doing. Separated families, dear friends in prison, others undergoing privations in exile. It consoles us to think that all these sacrifices will not be in vain. The year that is beginning will demonstrate it better.

FRIDAY, JANUARY 2, 1942
2ND DAY-363 DAYS TO FOLLOW

We continued our ordinary life. Mari busy with the little house to which we will soon move, and I working on my university classes, on the fatherland's business, and receiving visits and communications. Today, bad news was received at Intxausti's house, a telegram announcing the death of the younger brother of our friend's excellent wife.[255] Forced separation is such an evil in all ways that every day can bring news like this. I'm distributing my life: in the morning I work at home, in the afternoon at the delegation, and at night I keep working until something like three in the morning.

---

255 Ynchausti's brother-in-law's death was due to war wounds. "Don José Antonio de Aguirre en Nueva York."

SATURDAY, JANUARY 3, 1942
3RD DAY-362 DAYS TO FOLLOW

At home in the morning, and at the delegation offices in the afternoon. The English came by again today. For this reason, I was a little late getting to the party held at the Basque Center for our compatriots' children, with a distribution of refreshments and toys. A sword-dance group and a women's folkdance group [*hilanderas*] performed and did so very well. The abandonment of our national soul had been the reason that our dances had not been performed at this association for many years. Now, amid our vigorous rebirth, they've started again. They were very pleasing, and our compatriots, who were moved by it, enjoyed it a great deal.

SUNDAY, JANUARY 4, 1942
4TH DAY-361 DAYS TO FOLLOW

In the morning, I worked at home. In the afternoon, we closeted ourselves in the office at my new house—we still haven't moved there definitively—and I worked with Ramón Sota putting into English, and I putting into Basque and Spanish, some extremely interesting documents that are going to be broadcast from London by the BBC at the moment Spain enters the war on the Axis side. They're calls that I issue as president of Euzkadi to all Basque sailors to bring their ships to American or English ports.[256] Ramón Sota will do the same as a ship owner, in the name of the legitimate firm. Despite it being Sunday, we didn't rest a moment.

MONDAY, JANUARY 5, 1942
5TH DAY-360 DAYS TO FOLLOW

I continued working in the morning. In the afternoon, at the legation again. The English emissaries returned with two agents from the Intelligence Service specialized in radio. We pressed disks with my speech to all the Basques and Ramón's address to those of the firm. They came out magnificently. I believe that the fact that we're the ones who make the call, and we alone, has true importance. The call will go out constantly

---

256 These addresses were intended to invite the captains of Spanish ships to sail to Allied ports in the event that Spain entered the world war in favor of the Axis and they were ordered to go to ports in Spain or in territory controlled by Nazi and Fascist supporters.

for twenty-four hours from London to Basque sailors. At the request of the English—the specific request came from London—in addition to addressing our people in Euskara, I also addressed the Spaniards in Spanish. Imperialism, in the end . . . !

TUESDAY, JANUARY 6, 1942
6TH DAY-359 DAYS TO FOLLOW

In the morning, I helped Mari in arranging the house, because we moved there definitively this evening. Since we can't allow ourselves the luxury of even one maid, it's necessary to help my wife when she needs it. At the delegation in the afternoon, reading the correspondence, I learned an unpleasant piece of news. The Yankees have ordered their South American firms to expel Spaniards. And in Venezuela, they've expelled the Basques as <u>Spaniards</u>. Shameful and inconceivable precisely today, after listening to Roosevelt's speech.[257] But in the end, everything will be sorted out. How much these Americans still need to clean up!

WEDNESDAY, JANUARY 7, 1942
7TH DAY-358 DAYS TO FOLLOW

We slept well on the first night in our little house. Just the four of us: the novelty had a unique attraction. After more than a year and a half, we're living in our own house again. Completely modestly, but very happy. In addition, we can do no less than thank God and our good friends who have helped us so much at all times, starting with Intxausti, whose home has been ours for two months. Thanks to him, we've been able to spend my university salary on furnishing our house. Mari has done wonders. I don't know where she acquired the complete dining room for twelve dollars. Its former owner must have been left stunned. But we're in good health. Others are suffering quite a bit more.

THURSDAY, JANUARY 8, 1942
8TH DAY-357 DAYS TO FOLLOW

At home in the morning, I studied very intensively the subjects I will have to teach starting on February 1. Time passes and waits for no one. In the

---

257 The State of the Union speech to the U.S. Congress on January 6, 1942, in which the American president established the Allied and U.S. objectives in World War II.

afternoon, I composed a text addressed to President Roosevelt announcing Euzkadi's adhesion to the Washington accords.²⁵⁸ I emphasized that this adhesion is the consequence of a line of conduct followed at all times, upon leaving our fatherland, upon the start of the war, upon America's entry into the fight, now . . . I'm expecting the greatest contradictions here. One day, it will seem that they've recognized our independence; another day, they'll confuse us with Spanish supporters of Franco; another day, they'll do something else. I'm observing contradiction in many things. It's a country of true *arlotes*. That's how they surprised them.

FRIDAY, JANUARY 9, 1942
9TH DAY-356 DAYS TO FOLLOW

I continued my studies and preparation of topics for my classes. I went to bed at 3:30 this morning, and I'm still behind. The work of these days is tiring, especially without staff of any kind. In the afternoon, I have my English class first thing, and then, eating lunch like the Americans, I arrive at the delegation by subway, in order to take the subway, the train, and the bus again and finally arrive home. After dinner, I dry the dishes, helping with the washing-up, and then I start to pursue a more elevated profession, busying myself with my university topics until the wee hours of the morning. In the matter of washing-up, I'm a top performer, to the astonishment of Mari, who was expecting a catastrophe. I haven't dropped a single dish.

SATURDAY, JANUARY 10, 1942
10TH DAY-355 DAYS TO FOLLOW

In the morning, I worked at home for a while, as usual. Then I took the train and went to the university library. Manu Sota accompanied me to look for appropriate material on certain topics. Basque ones, naturally, since it's my intention to clearly set out the Basque actions that have been

---

258 The *lehendakari* is referring to the agreement signed by twenty-six nations on January 1, 1942, called the Declaration by the United Nations. The signatories—the United States, the United Kingdom, the Soviet Union, China, Australia, Belgium, Canada, Costa Rica, Cuba, Czechoslovakia, the Dominican Republic, El Salvador, Greece, Guatemala, Haiti, Honduras, India, Luxemburg, the Netherlands, New Zealand, Nicaragua, Norway, Panama, Poland, South Africa, and Yugoslavia—committed themselves to defend the Atlantic Charter, to employ all their resources in the war, and not to negotiate a separate peace with the Axis powers. The text Agirre mentions is found in appendix 22.

characteristic of Iberian history and have had an essential influence on it, to wit: Basque attitude toward the French Revolution and the invasion of the Convention's troops; the Basques and the first civil war, accurately determining its nature; also Basque participation in the emancipation of the Americas. After a pastry and a *café con leche*, to the delegation to continue with our affairs. In the evening, the Inchaustis and Manu Sota were invited to my house for dinner, in order to officially inaugurate it.

SUNDAY, JANUARY 11, 1942
11TH DAY-354 DAYS TO FOLLOW

A beautiful snow fell. Our little house looks like a classic illustration for Snow White. We're very satisfied with it, since it doesn't give us much work and especially because it's in this town of White Plains, which has one of the best climates in the United States. The children's health is improving a great deal, and that's the main thing. We have the little church about twenty meters away. This morning, because of the snow, there were fewer people. We then accompanied the children in the snow, where they played with sleds. We adults continued our walk on foot, talking about the plans to be carried out for Euzko Alkartasuna [Basque solidarity]. We had lunch at Inchausti's house, a mandatory custom every Sunday by now.

MONDAY, JANUARY 12, 1942
12TH DAY-353 DAYS TO FOLLOW

I started the week again at high speed. By the end of the week, I want to have the first two lectures for my course at Columbia completely finished. The material is abundant in general terms, somewhat scarce when more specialized work is desired. At all events, I believe that I can defend myself acceptably. I'm afraid that the translation into English may take me longer than necessary, and if my friends can't do it for me, I don't know how much money a proper translation will cost me. I don't have money for that. A modest salary doesn't cover more than just enough to live on. In the neighborhood, I'm the only one who doesn't have a car. The employers and the workers have one; at the little parish, each priest has his own. My turn still hasn't come. In the afternoon, I worked at the legation.

TUESDAY, JANUARY 13, 1942
13TH DAY-352 DAYS TO FOLLOW

Preparing my university classes is taking me a lot of time. I want to make a maximum effort now in order to get ahead and be more rested when the time comes for greater activity related to the war, which will involve Spain.

Each lecture takes me around thirty pages, all handwritten, which then have to be translated into English. All my good friends are helping me. Without them, I would be in quite a fix.

In the afternoon, as usual, I went to the delegation. Because of the war, correspondence is very delayed. It's been several days since we've received news from anyone. It seems that the censors hold on to the letters for several days, even if they don't examine them. I worked for four hours after dinner.

WEDNESDAY, JANUARY 14, 1942
14TH DAY-351 DAYS TO FOLLOW

This morning Intxausti came to my house, and we outlined in my office the content of a note that Intxausti will deliver in Washington shortly. It's a project for propaganda in South America in combination with the American services led by Nelson Rockefeller under the name of Inter-American Relations. At our request, Intxausti was given an appointment for one day next week. In addition to our relationship with the English, which covers all spheres of activity, we want this relationship with Inter-American Relations to enable the publication of a journal in South America and an information bulletin, needed now more than ever. The rest of the day as usual.

THURSDAY, JANUARY 15, 1942
15TH DAY-350 DAYS TO FOLLOW

We're working these days on a bold project in relation to the creation of Euzko Alkartasuna. We aim to launch the idea of the construction in Gernika of a grandiose monument in honor of democracy, since our democracy is the most ancient known. The money collected will be used for war purposes. In this way, donors will help the common cause and contribute to the construction of a monument that, in doing justice to the first population against which total war was introduced, will possibly be an occasion to affirm Basque freedom forever, since such a monument is inconceivable in a subjected land. We want to tackle the project in full force. We're enthusiastic. The program for the rest of the day, the same.

FRIDAY, JANUARY 16, 1942
16TH DAY-349 DAYS TO FOLLOW

Today was a work day entirely dedicated to preparing my lessons. I received a note from the university informing me that my first class will be on February 2, from 4:10 to 6:00 p.m. I've finished my first lecture, in which I situate the entire Spanish problem of the nineteenth century, studying the Portuguese, Basque, and Catalan problems alongside it. It will be the first time that these national problems are studied in an American university on their own terms. Without this prior study and exposition of the problem of the Iberian Peninsula, it's very difficult to understand the truth of history, and still more difficult to understand subsequent events. In the afternoon, I spend my usual period of time at the delegation, taking care of business with Manu Sota.

SATURDAY, JANUARY 17, 1942
17TH DAY-348 DAYS TO FOLLOW

I stayed in White Plains all day. I wanted to compose a paper for the English and the Americans and their respective state departments about the future of the Iberian Peninsula, indicating the relevant solutions. I primarily examined the nature and tendencies of the different political groups, in order then to reach conclusions based on the nature of each faction and not on its caprices. Intxausti visited me in the morning and told me about his meeting with Professor Chamberlain.[259] We'll go to Washington with him on Thursday to pay some important visits related to our problems and the problem of South America. I'll take advantage of the trip to do something in favor of Consul Guardia Jaén, who seems to have remained in Germany. His family is anxious about him,

---

259 Joseph Perkins Chamberlain (1873–1951) was a professor of administrative law and director of the Legislative Drafting Research Fund at Columbia University, as well as a member of private and governmental organizations for refugee assistance. At the time, he belonged to the American Christian Committee for Refugees and the President's Advisory Committee on Political Refugees.

especially since the break in relations and declaration of war between Panama and the Axis.

SUNDAY, JANUARY 18, 1942
18TH DAY-347 DAYS TO FOLLOW

Today we had the bad idea of taking the children to mass, especially Joseba. Since we don't have staff, we can't leave them home alone. In sum, Joseba didn't let us hear mass. He's a rebel of the first order. Of necessity, we have to go back to the system of taking turns.

At eleven-thirty, Intxausti and Manu came to the house, as they usually do on Sundays. We took a good walk in order to then sit down at Intxausti's table. Despite the Philippines disaster, which has brought our friend Intxausti so much economic ruin, his generosity does not decrease. In the afternoon, we had some refreshments at our house with Mrs. Elizalde, a relative of the Philippine commissioner in Washington. The weather was springlike today.

MONDAY, JANUARY 19, 1942
19TH DAY-346 DAYS TO FOLLOW

In the morning, I continued preparing my university lessons. The lack of some texts that I would have liked to consult prevents me from giving my first lessons a bit of originality, as I wanted. I believe that the subsequent ones will go better. In the afternoon, I followed my usual route: English lesson, delegation, subways, buses, train, and home to work from nine-thirty until two-thirty or three in the morning. Every day I go into Saint Patrick's Cathedral, dedicated to the patron saint of the Irish. Amid so agitated a life, this little spiritual calm helps. Many people don't know what they're missing because they're not fortunate enough to need it.

TUESDAY, JANUARY 20, 1942
20TH DAY-345 DAYS TO FOLLOW

I continued my ordinary life. In the afternoon, at the delegation, I greeted a group of sailors who came by with Captain Kobeaga, an excellent patriot. They behaved very well. It's very curious that Franco's ships are almost without exception crewed by Basques. I've said, "Franco's ships." They're the Basques' ships, and even if many of the outfitters don't deserve this name, it seems that they still have some sense of the honor of the race. These sailors serve us very well, and we know many things through them.

In the evening, Intxausti informed me that he has been told by Washington that I've been invited to the assembly of Christian politicians to study the future of Europe after victory.[260]

WEDNESDAY, JANUARY 21, 1942
21ST DAY-344 DAYS TO FOLLOW

I pursued my ordinary life all day. In the morning, I worked at home. In the afternoon, English and delegation. I returned to White Plains, and after dinner, Inchausti and I left for Washington. There weren't any tickets or beds on the ordinary train. We had to take the New Jersey line. We crossed the Hudson on a ferryboat and finally made it to the train. The number of people who travel is so large that there are almost never tickets. We don't know whether we'll have a room at the hotel on our arrival in Washington. They calculate that there are 400,000 more people in Washington than in normal times, due to the war. They've warned us accordingly. We left at one in the morning.

---

260 As the *lehendakari* says, the Basque refugees in New York were invited to the periodic meetings held by the European Christian Democrats who had taken refuge in the United States to prepare the future of Europe once the various strains of Nazism and Fascism were defeated. This is the reason for the long series of names of Catholic politicians with whom Agirre appears in contact in the diary. One fruit of these relationships was the manifesto published by a group of exiled Catholic intellectuals and politicians including the *lehendakari*. The preparation of Europe's postwar future also encompassed the Europeanist movement represented by Richard Caudenhove-Kalergi and his Paneuropean Union, a movement to which Basque nationalism also belonged. J. A. de Aguirre, Charles Boyer, et al., *Devant la crise mondiale: Manifeste de catholiques européens séjournant en Amérique* (New York: Éditions de la Maison Française, 1942). "Asteko berriak," *Euzko Deya* (Buenos Aires), no. 126 (October 30, 1942), 11. "Ante la crisis mundial. El manifiesto de los intelectuales católicos europeos," *Euzko Deya* (Buenos Aires), no. 129 (November 30, 1942), 6. "Intelectuales católicos de distintas nacionalidades europeas dieron a conocer un importante manifiesto: Los firmantes del documento se refieren al significado de la actual guerra y a los principios que deben regir la vida del futuro," *Euzko Deya* (Buenos Aires), no. 132 (December 31, 1942), 18. *Report of the Pan-European Conference Called at the Invitation of New York University Extended through the Research Seminar for Postwar European Federation* (New York, 1943).

THURSDAY, JANUARY 22, 1942
22ND DAY-343 DAYS TO FOLLOW

We arrived in Washington at 7:30 in the morning. The train traveled slowly on the route, which ordinarily only takes four hours. We arrived at the hotel. Although they had promised us a room for the night, we didn't have it yet. Professor Chamberlain visited us at the hotel to tell us that Mr. Duggan[261] will receive us tomorrow at the state department. He's Mr. Hull's political adviser for South American affairs.[262] He's his confidant and his most competent technocrat. We had lunch together with Father Parsons, a university professor in Washington and a confidant of Roosevelt.[263] Competent and influential, he's a very good friend of ours and well-informed about our problems.

In the evening, we had dinner with Ugarte, a counselor to the Philippine commissioner in Washington.

FRIDAY, JANUARY 23, 1942
23RD DAY-342 DAYS TO FOLLOW

We got a decent rest. At eleven, we attended the meeting called to set up a Catholic bloc to study the reconstruction of the world, and principally of Europe, after the war. The president of the Belgian Senate attended, among others. Chancellor Bruning and Don Sturzo were unable to come.[264] The next meeting will be next month in Washington. The American Catholic politicians will come. The project may have extraordinary scope. We were admirably received.

---

261 Laurence Duggan (1905–1948) was an "adviser on Political Relations" at the U.S. state department.
262 Cordell Hull (1871–1955) was a U.S. politician who served as Secretary of State between 1933 and 1944.
263 Wilfrid Parsons, SJ (1887–1958) was a professor at Georgetown University. Between 1925 and 1936 he was in charge of the journal *America*, published by the Society of Jesus. He was one of the prominent figures who backed Agirre's entry into the United States. Jean-Claude Larronde, *Manuel de Ynchausti: Un mecenas inspirado* (Milafranga: Bidasoa, 1998), 110.
264 Heinrich Brüning (1885–1970) was a German politician who belonged to the Catholic Center Party (*Zentrum*). He served as German federal chancellor between March 1930 and May 1932. He went into exile in the United States after the Nazis took power. For his part, Luigi Sturzo (1871–1959) was an Italian priest and politician. A founder of the Italian Popular Party, a direct predecessor of the Christian Democrats, he had to go into exile, first in London and then during World War II in the United States, once the Fascists came into power.

In the afternoon, Mr. Duggan received us at the state department. An hour and a half of a magnificent exchange of impressions. He agreed to call me back to Washington soon to continue studying the problems of South America and of the Iberian Peninsula with the department.[265]

SATURDAY, JANUARY 24, 1942
24TH DAY-341 DAYS TO FOLLOW

Today I devoted myself all day to finishing my second lesson or lecture at Columbia. Each of them consists of at least thirty pages. It's too bad that I don't have more leisure, because interesting work could be done. But my fatherland's problems have seized my spirit, and I consider everything else secondary. Yesterday's Washington visit and meetings have left us with pleasant memories. It's possible that we've made a start on the practical route. In the demoralized international order that we're suffering, it's necessary to be prepared for surprises of all kinds, both pleasant and unpleasant. But everything will move forward with work and faith. For the moment, we've now established the necessary contact.

SUNDAY, JANUARY 25, 1942
25TH DAY-340 DAYS TO FOLLOW

A Sunday like the previous ones, except that Inchausti went to New York to meet with Max Ascoli of Rockefeller's Inter-American Coordination Institute.[266] This institute works in accord with the state department. Inchausti came back full of enthusiasm. They received him too well, from what he says. Now these gentlemen are remembering how much

---

265 The University of Nevada, Reno holds photocopies of documents from various American archives concerning the residence and activities in the United States of José Antonio Agirre and other Basque nationalist politicians. These photocopies include a document that says, among other things, "810.00/91 "Memorandum of Conversation: Aguirre, M. de Ynchausti (New York) and Mr Laurence Duggan, Adviser on Pol. Relations. Conv of Jan 23, 1942 "Aguirre, accompanied by Ynchausti, called on state & left proposal of help by Basques in other American republics to create an attitude more sympathetic to the democracies. Duggan thanked him, said he should study memo & consult his colleagues." Reno 76.
266 Max Ascoli (1898–1978) was an Italian intellectual of Jewish origin. He served as professor of the philosophy of law at the University of Rome until he left Fascist Italy in 1932 to emigrate to the United States, where he was given a fellowship by the Rockefeller Foundation.

they've abandoned the South American terrain, where it's Spanish propaganda that does the most damage. Max Ascoli wants to see me on Thursday. They liked the project we presented to them a lot. Things are moving forward, although slowly. These matters aren't designed for the impatient. Sure of the end, we have to move forward slowly.

MONDAY, JANUARY 26, 1942
26TH DAY-339 DAYS TO FOLLOW

In the morning, I worked with Inchausti on drawing up a list of names of prominent Basque individuals for a vast organization in South America. Max Ascoli asked for it. I'm preparing a memorandum for Thursday with specifics on various options, especially with regard to our newspapers and journals, the information bulletins, and other projects in connection with the Ekin publishing house created in Buenos Aires. In the afternoon, after my English lessons, I went to the delegation. The English called again. They want to see me. They'll come tomorrow if they don't have to go to Washington. I hope that the business we're collaborating on will go better now. I continued with my Columbia lectures in the evening.

TUESDAY, JANUARY 27, 1942
27TH DAY-338 DAYS TO FOLLOW

I studied and prepared my Columbia classes all day. I received letters from Buenos Aires, London, Mexico, etc., in which they tell me about the various affairs of our delegations. Our men have a good spirit and great desire to work. It's too bad that our poverty of economic resources prevents us at the moment from quickly harvesting excellent fruit. The impression everywhere is of a great rapprochement by those who were separated from us, deceived by enemy propaganda. Everything is moving forward slowly here, including sorting out the economic issue, always so vital, but more so today. But we push every day.

WEDNESDAY, JANUARY 28, 1942
28TH DAY-337 DAYS TO FOLLOW

In the morning, I studied and worked on my lectures for my professorship. In the afternoon, after my English classes, I went to the delegation. The correspondence from the delegations continued. Today it was the turn of Cuba, Venezuela, Santo Domingo, Chile, Uruguay ... From Venezuela they sent me their impressions of the economic issues. They weren't pleasant. We haven't had good luck. We'll see whether things will get straightened out little by little.[267] I'm happy with the delegates' selflessness. They work well, they're enthusiastic, and they do it without asking for a cent. In these latitudes, they don't understand these generous attitudes. We do understand them. Without them, we would not have taken even one step forward.

THURSDAY, JANUARY 29, 1942
29TH DAY-336 DAYS TO FOLLOW

After studying in the morning and having my English class first thing in the afternoon, I went to meet with Max Ascoli, the director of the Office of the Coordinator of Panamerican Affairs, who had given me an appointment for four-thirty. I was accompanied by Intxausti, who had an interesting interview with the said gentleman on Sunday. His position is a very important one, since he directs the South American propaganda, or rather, he's the person who finances activities in those regions. Our projects were liked by all sides. Now, he told us, it's time to turn them into a dollar figure. Here everything is assessed in monetary terms. We agreed to submit the numbers to him. Very friendly and very refined, he nevertheless didn't entirely convince me.[268]

---

267 The *lehendakari* is again referring to the crisis at Pesquerías Vascas del Caribe, where there were accusations that some managers had made improper use of the company's funds when, in reality, the company failed because the Caribbean required other types of fishing and, in addition, because the Venezuelan market for fish was very limited.

268 The numbers the *lehendakari* mentions were submitted in a report dated February 6, 1942, which broke the request down into two major sections. Section A discussed a subsidy for the publication of the Buenos Aires *Euzko Deya* with the aim of putting 15,000 more copies of this journal into circulation and so doubling its print run. Section B discussed a provisional plan for establishing an information service. The increase in *Euzko Deya*'s circulation was assessed at 1,500 dollars a month, while the information service was substantially more expensive, 30,000 dollars. This service, the Basques promised, would be able to cover the following areas in South America: politics, economy, the Church, consulates, embassies, centers sponsored by the Falange or by other Spanish organizations, aristocratic circles (especially in Argentina and Chile), and the merchant marine. Report on a letter from José Antonio Agirre to Max Ascoli, February 6, 1942. Reno 76.

FRIDAY, JANUARY 30, 1942
30TH DAY-335 DAYS TO FOLLOW

Joseba was not very calm tonight. With his visits to our room and his complaints, neither Mari nor I got much sleep. I went to bed after three, as usual. In sum, I was very tired in the morning and stayed in bed. I'm drowning in things I'm behind on.

When Inchausti heard, he came with a big thermometer. He was very surprised when it read 36° [96.8° F]. This good friend thought that I was sick. His solicitude is admirable. I've never known a case of greater generosity to friends. For this reason, I stayed at home all day, working on my lesson for Monday, with which I will inaugurate my classes at Columbia.

SATURDAY, JANUARY 31, 1942
31ST DAY-334 DAYS TO FOLLOW

Prieto arrived in New York today. He came to sign in the J.A.R.E.'s name a shipping contract for a ship that will bring—this is what they want—eight hundred-odd refugees from France.[269] If they haven't left previously, our government comrades and some high officials from our administration will come on this expedition. Prieto called me to say hello, and we took advantage of an invitation from Marino Gamboa to talk. I took an interest in these trips, and Prieto promised me that all these dear friends will be on the final list if they haven't been able to get on another steamer first. I'm working these days on getting the exit prohibition lifted for Lasarte and Jauregi. May God help us all.

---

269 The purpose of the contract was to engage the steamer *Nyassa*, belonging to the Companhia Nacional de Navegação of Lisbon, to transport 804 refugee supporters of the Spanish Republic from Casablanca to Veracruz; settle the cost of various passages on the *Serpa Pinto*, also contracted in Casablanca; and pay the Compañía Naviera Dominicana for the passages of the Spaniards who were to be transported from Ciudad Trujillo to Veracruz on the *Presidente Trujillo*. With Valentín Agirre and Jon Zabal acting as intermediaries, the contract was signed for a sum of 350,000 dollars. Junta de Auxilio a los Republicanos Españoles, 1939–1942 record book, books III and IV, records 170, 171, 172, and 179, http://www.cervantesvirtual.com/servlet/SirveObras/ace/. For firsthand details on the *Nyassa*'s voyage see Antonio Ruiz de Azua, known as "Ogoñope," "Desde Marsella a Méjico: Alrededor del mundo," *Euzko Deya* (Buenos Aires), n. 132 (December 31, 1942), 5.

SUNDAY, FEBRUARY 1, 1942
32ND DAY-333 DAYS TO FOLLOW

Yesterday evening Manu Sota and the Intxaustis had dinner at our house. We spent a very pleasant and tranquil time together after the week's toil. Whenever we have some pleasant moments, we remember our relatives and friends whom we left on the other side of the sea, constantly exposed to all the inconveniences of a compromised situation. Communication is more difficult every day, and this increases the uncertainty and the pain of separation. Never until now has the world been able to realize just how hateful censorship is, and the other obstacles to freedom that dictators aim to establish on earth. We spent this Sunday rehearsing tomorrow's lecture at Columbia.

MONDAY, FEBRUARY 2, 1942
33RD DAY-332 DAYS TO FOLLOW

In the morning, I went to our delegation in New York, and from there I went to the university with Manu Sota. We had lunch at the University Club. At 4:10, I began my first class. All my friends came. With more impudence than skill, I read my first lesson in English for an hour and a half. I put the nerves of my friends and listeners to a definite test. A young Argentine lady gave me great comfort when she showed me her notes, faithfully taken down as I gave my exposition. I was very doubtful that they would understand me, and they understood me. It's a comfort like others. Now onward.

TUESDAY, FEBRUARY 3, 1942
34TH DAY-331 DAYS TO FOLLOW

In the morning, I prepared my lessons and my English. In the afternoon, I went to my English class. Afterward, to the delegation. The head of the English services visited me. Now they want me to go to Argentina. These English and Americans are incorrigible. Up to today, they've been going along believing that the Rio de Janeiro conference would be a success.[270] Now that they've seen the failure, they say that we Basques

---

270 The reference is to the Third Advisory Meeting of Foreign Ministers held in Rio de Janeiro in January 1942. At this summit, as at the two previous ones (Panama, September–October 1939, and Havana, July 1940), the countries of the Western Hemisphere determined their position with respect to World War II. The failure

can turn things around better than anyone, in Argentina no less. In any event, it's better that they consider us to be important and powerful people. What we are, we ourselves see better than anyone. They invited me to have lunch with them tomorrow. The political head will also come.

WEDNESDAY, FEBRUARY 4, 1942
35TH DAY-330 DAYS TO FOLLOW

In the morning, I worked for an hour. Afterward, I went to New York. I had lunch with the English. They're waiting for the report from Rio de Janeiro in order to organize a vast movement in South America with us. I spoke somewhat harshly to them about their slowness. Always late in all matters, they then have to put in twice the effort. It's too bad, because a lot of time is wasted with all these indecisions. Then I was at the university, where I took some notes and composed a letter for Ascoli about *Euzko Deya* in Buenos Aires with the budget to expand it, along with another one about the information service. We'll see what they answer.[271] Afterward, back home to continue working on my lessons.

THURSDAY, FEBRUARY 5, 1942
36TH DAY-329 DAYS TO FOLLOW

I received letters from South America, chiefly from Argentina, where the delegation's economic situation is deplorable and Aldasoro's personal effort has its limits. It's sad, but our people still have an egotistical concept of the public good. No one gives a cent. It seems that work is obligatory for those of us who lead the national cause even without means of any kind. Our equivocations are censured. Now, no one is capable of asking us whether we are in need of funds. And amid true indigence, we go forward. How little an idea these people have who believe—and I don't know on what basis—that we must have money!

FRIDAY, FEBRUARY 6, 1942
37TH DAY-328 DAYS TO FOLLOW

I continued my ordinary life today, like yesterday. Today I answered Aldasoro's letter from yesterday, which made a strong impression.

---

mentioned in the diary was Argentina's refusal to join the break in relations with the Axis that the United States promoted at the conference.
271 See note 268.

Sometimes our people frighten me by the sense of irresponsibility they have. They look to us as beacons of salvation, but no one believes that he has a duty to cooperate with the national effort. This will surely harm us more than once. I will soon have to address myself to everyone, calling them to order very harshly. I continue preparing my lessons. I thereby bother everyone, since Intxausti, Ramón Sota, and Marino Gamboa translate them for me. I have a great deal to thank them for, since pages are raining down, and I've worn them out. The professorship isn't mine; it belongs to everyone. That's how these compatriots have understood it.

SATURDAY, FEBRUARY 7, 1942
38TH DAY-327 DAYS TO FOLLOW

In the morning, I stayed home preparing my lessons and answering correspondence. In the afternoon, I went to the delegation. In the evening, the Columbia University history department held its annual meeting. A gala dinner with a speech by Professor Hayes, the department chair. He mentioned me at length, telling my fellow professors all my adventures. They forced me to stand up and respond to the enthusiastic applause of such good people. It was a truly kind act that called attention to those of us who unfortunately live far from our homelands and our hearths. They're at home, and they don't believe they're at war yet. But they're good people, truly.

SUNDAY, FEBRUARY 8, 1942
39TH DAY-326 DAYS TO FOLLOW

I spent Sunday as usual. Today I stayed home with the children while Mari heard the first mass. Manu Sota arrived, and I then went to church with him. We took a walk later with Intxausti, at whose house we had lunch, like every Sunday. In the afternoon, Manu and I retired to prepare tomorrow's lecture. We then greeted Father Couturier, a French Dominican, a good artist, and a good thinker, who is one of the Free French patriots.[272] Sundays are a true rest for me. For Mari also,

---

272 Marie-Alain Couturier (1897–1954) was a French Dominican and a theoretician of sacred art. He is considered to be the first person to introduce elements of secular art such as abstraction into ecclesiastical art. In this regard, and as an example, it is appropriate to note that it was due to his intervention that an artist like Henri Matisse decorated San Pablo da Vence and designed the liturgical vestments of its priests, in addition to the construction of the church of Notre Dame du Haut de

since without staff at home, she has to work a great deal. Up to now, her health has been excellent. May God keep it that way. The little ones are also very well.

MONDAY, FEBRUARY 9, 1942
40TH DAY-325 DAYS TO FOLLOW

The war news is dreadful. Imminent fall of Singapore, retreat in Libya, invasion of the Dutch East Indies, attack on Burma, etc.[273] 1942 will be a horrible year. I'm expecting anything. They laugh when I tell them that I expect to see the Americans fighting in Africa. Nobody could believe the extension that the conflict has attained. And that it will attain. We hear talk about India, North Africa, etc., battlefields that we never suspected could belong to this age.

Today I gave my second class at the university. They told me that I did better. Little by little, all this gets done, like the war. In the evening, to study until the wee hours, as usual.

TUESDAY, FEBRUARY 10, 1942
41ST DAY-324 DAYS TO FOLLOW

Today is Juan Mari's saint's day. We remembered the day and our relatives in Louvain. Despite everything, we were sure that Martín Lasa and his wife and children will have been invited out in Louvain and that they will have done everything possible to forget their troubles and the forced separation, always such a sad thing.[274] But in general, our people don't

---

Ronchamp and the Dominican monastery of La Tourette by the famous architect Le Corbusier. Deyan Sudjic, *La arquitectura del poder: Cómo los ricos y poderosos dan forma al mundo* (Barcelona: Ariel, 2007). In English, see Deyan Sudjic, *The Edifice Complex: How the Rich and Powerful Shape the World* (London and New York: Allen Lane, 2005).

273 The invasion of Burma began on January 15, 1942, with an offensive from the south. On the 20th, the troops stationed in Thailand converged on the attack. On the 31st, the Japanese conquered Ambon Island, a territorial acquisition they added to others in the Dutch East Indies, with the result that by February 10, the colony was expected to fall into Japanese hands. At the end of January, German troops in Libya were advancing as they maneuvered to conquer Cyrenaica; nevertheless, they did not get further than Tobruk due to a lack of supplies. Elsewhere, on February 1, the siege of Singapore began; on the 8th, Japanese troops crossed the Straits of Johore from Malaysia; and on the 15th, the British colony fell into Japanese hands.

274 Martín Lasa Ercilla (1904–1976) was a member of the Basque trade delegation in

lose their good humor. But worry for our families and friends grows as the war is prolonged and time passes. But God is good. We would never have thought we would be able to hold out this long, having left Euzkadi without money, without clothes, without the hope of resources of any kind. Only trusting that one day, we will conquer.

WEDNESDAY, FEBRUARY 11, 1942
42ND DAY-323 DAYS TO FOLLOW

Today I received a courteous letter from Cardinal Spellman in which he promises me that he will work on behalf of Lasarte and Jauregui. I received a letter from Monzón. He transcribed a telegram from Marseilles for me. Lasarte now has his permit. He talked about Picabea and Biguri.[275] I thought that they had their permits, but that's not the case. I'll get back to work. I also received a very courteous letter from Max Ascoli, the director of the Coordinator's office. It seems that our projects met with approval and that something will be done. The tone of the letter was encouraging. To wait a little, since he talked about sending me a definitive answer in a few days. God grant it, so as in this way to get out of the penury in which we're living.

Antwerp and a director of the Compagnie Maritime et Commerciale S.A., together with Juan Mari Agirre and Cesáreo Asporosa. In spring 1940, both Asporosa and Lasa had completed all the paperwork to emigrate to Venezuela, but the war situation and the immediate German occupation of Belgium in May of that year prevented both of them from emigrating. In addition, Martín Lasa was detained by the Germans as they occupied the country and was held until January 1941. In the postwar period, he became honorary Panamanian consul in Antwerp. Upon his death, *OPE* reported that he was the Basque government's delegate in Belgium and had been general director of commerce and supplies from that organization's founding in 1936. "Necrológica," *OPE* (Paris), no. 6,798 (April 29, 1976), 4.

275 Rafael Picavea Leguia (1867–1946) was a journalist, politician, and businessman. At the beginning of the Spanish Civil War, the *lehendakari* sent him to the French capital to create and lead the Paris delegation and the Basque government's foreign propaganda apparatus. For his part, Ramón Viguri Ruiz de Olano (1886–?) was a prominent supporter of the Spanish Republic and a parliamentary representative for Araba. On this and other topics see appendixes 18, 23, and 24.

THURSDAY, FEBRUARY 12, 1942
43RD DAY-322 DAYS TO FOLLOW

Today was the twenty-second anniversary of *aita*'s death. How the years pass, and what years! This morning Intxausti turned up at my house. He told me that I work too much and that we had to take the afternoon off. Today is Lincoln Day.[276] I agreed, and after lunch we went to see the *Normandie*.[277] An impressive sight. Like a great slaughtered whale, the *Normandie* is heeled over amid the ice of the small basin where it was anchored awaiting its departure with troops. The sabotage was colossal. The tranquility of these Americans is excessive, and their vigilance is non-existent. It was a sight comparable only to the one we then saw from the Empire Building.[278]

FRIDAY, FEBRUARY 13, 1942
44TH DAY-321 DAYS TO FOLLOW

I stayed home working all day. I prepared the topics for the following lessons. I took a bit of care with the upcoming one, because it deals with Euzkadi's situation in political and social terms and as a universally applicable example in the period ending in 1800. It will be the first time that a concrete Basque topic like this one is discussed at an American university. It's too bad that the war has drained the university of students.

Inchausti has come down with a sore throat and a bad case of the flu. May so excellent a friend get well soon!

---

276 Lincoln Day is celebrated on various dates in February or March, depending on the state or county that celebrates it.

277 The *Normandie* was a luxury transatlantic liner belonging to the French shipping company Cie. Génerale Transatlantique (CGT). At the start of World War II, it was detained by U.S. authorities upon arriving in the port of New York, and it was subsequently seized when the Germans occupied France. On February 9, 1942, it was being reconditioned for use as a troop transport when a spark from a welding torch started a fire. The fire was brought under control, but the large amount of water used to extinguish it caused the ship to capsize.

278 The Empire State Building was the tallest building in the world at the time. It was built between 1929 and 1931.

SATURDAY, FEBRUARY 14, 1942
45TH DAY-320 DAYS TO FOLLOW

I continued working on my lessons at home. I received a letter from Ortuzar answering the one I wrote to him ordering him to withdraw from the London dispute in order to liquidate our share as soon as possible. The letter has the positive side of his obedience and the negative side of his intolerable haughtiness. I'm not going to get into a debate, of which we've had plenty, harmful and unpleasant ones. Their responsibility is their problem! How unfortunate we are! Self-centeredness always getting in the way of our affairs. God grant that things get sorted out.

SUNDAY, FEBRUARY 15, 1942
46TH DAY-319 DAYS TO FOLLOW

We spent a quiet Sunday. We kept Inchausti company; he's still tired because of his fever. We also took advantage of the day to prepare some points for tomorrow's lesson. We ate lunch and dinner at Inchausti's house. Sundays are days of true rest, especially for Mari, who leaves behind all her kitchen obligations on this day. She works a lot and well deserves this rest. Like servants in our country. It's been very cold, so much so that because of the extreme temperatures, it hasn't snowed. The climate is definitely putting us to the test.

MONDAY, FEBRUARY 16, 1942
47TH DAY-318 DAYS TO FOLLOW

Today, simultaneously with preparing my class, I began to compose a plan for the meeting in Washington on the 20th. Toward the latter part of the morning, I went to New York. We had lunch at the University Club. Afterward, I read my third lesson at the university, on the historical topic of Euzkadi in 1800. The topic met with great approval. Perhaps it could be extended a bit later on, completed, and published as a pamphlet, when we have money, of course. Today we still can't allow ourselves any luxuries.

TUESDAY, FEBRUARY 17, 1942
48TH DAY-317 DAYS TO FOLLOW

I prepared the plan for the conference in Washington on the 20th. The idea is to hold an international conference in Buenos Aires this summer for Catholic politicians, writers, and academics from all countries to establish some norms of action that can enable Catholicism to take a position and act accordingly. In these times, it's a matter of great interest, due to the confusion that's evident. I'm sure that I'm going to frighten them, but in order for them to wake up here, it's necessary to give them a good scare. That's how everything is going, unfortunately. But it will all change.

WEDNESDAY, FEBRUARY 18, 1942
49TH DAY-316 DAYS TO FOLLOW

I've received a courteous communication from Max Ascoli inviting me to lunch next Thursday to talk about a range of political and non-political matters, as he puts it. I've accepted, to see whether our projects are starting to get definitively underway, even if I don't have the slightest confidence in any of it. Here things take time. Strange as it may seem, there are still elements that seem to be helping the enemy more than us. The spirit of egoism has done damage, and fighting it is costly. I was at the university.

THURSDAY, FEBRUARY 19, 1942
50TH DAY-315 DAYS TO FOLLOW

Today I worked at home in the morning. I received a telegram from Irujo in which he again rejects the offer I made him of a portfolio in the Basque government. It seems that the damned London dispute has stirred them up in such a way that they have neither the calm nor the serenity that are needed. I felt very bad about it. Knowing Manuel's temperament, I begged him to take a week to think over his refusal. As soon as he received my telegram, he replied repeating his negative answer. I wanted to give him a decorous way out of the National Council mess that's been so much debated. In the end . . .[279]

---

[279] With regard to these relations, Irujo began a letter dated from London on February 20, 1942, by telling the *lehendakari*, "I received your cable giving me a week to determine my position. I did not answer immediately out of respect for you personally

FRIDAY, FEBRUARY 20, 1942
51ST DAY-314 DAYS TO FOLLOW

I left White Plains at 7:20 a.m. From New York at 8:30, arriving in Washington at 12:30. Ramón de la Sota accompanied me. We had a room reserved at the Hamilton Hotel. As soon as I arrived at the hotel, I had a message from Mr. Lozada, who invited me on Vice President Wallace's behalf to have lunch with him.[280] An important interview. An hour and a half talking about our problem. The vice president wants to continue gathering information, and we will remain in contact. In the afternoon, I attended the Catholic group's meetings. I'm afraid that it will end in nothing, like many Catholic efforts. Due to lack of nerve. My plan for a conference will be examined at the next meeting.

SATURDAY, FEBRUARY 21, 1942
52ND DAY-313 DAYS TO FOLLOW

We got up and telephoned Lozada about whether I had to see Mr. Duggan from the state department this morning. Lozada told me that it's been impossible for him to discuss the matter. Instead, he told me that my interview with Vice President Wallace made a very good impression. He asked me to send him a report of parts of our conversation as a guide to the upcoming ones to be held with the vice president. At one, we took the train for New York, where we arrived at five. I picked up Mari and the children at Gamboa's house, and we returned to White Plains together. We asked after Inchausti, who is continuing to improve. I returned very satisfied with my trip.

---

and for your office and in order to consult about the matter with the men who, along with me, merged emotion and responsibility as long as your absence lasted... . But I believe that it's my duty to tell you, with as much affection as clarity, that the policy you have initiated runs the risk, in my view, of shattering your extraordinary prestige—which would be harmful enough in itself—and of losing for Euzkadi what may be a unique historical opportunity to resolve her national problem, which would constitute irreparable damage. I also believe that in the direction you are taking, you are not following the views of the majority of the Basques, nor of the best among them." The correspondence exchanged between Agirre and Irujo in the months following the *lehendakari*'s appearance in the Western Hemisphere can be consulted in Goiogana, Irujo, and Legarreta, *Un nuevo 31*.

280 Enrique Sánchez de Lozada was an advisor to the Rockefeller Committee on International Affairs. For his part, Henry Agard Wallace (1888–1965) was vice president of the United States between 1941 and 1945. As a contribution to the war effort, he participated in numerous missions to Latin America and Asia, and between 1942 and 1943 he acted as head of the Board of Economic Warfare.

SUNDAY, FEBRUARY 22, 1942
53RD DAY-312 DAYS TO FOLLOW
WASHINGTON'S BIRTHDAY

[*Crossed out in the upper margin*: Tomorrow, since it was celebrated on Monday]

After mass and breakfast, Manu Sota and I spent the whole day at home preparing the table of contents for the book that I'm planning to write this month with all the adventures of my journey. The people whom I tell about my adventures of the last year are constantly encouraging me to write a book. I don't know why the moment to write it—I believe—has arrived. We came up with six possible chapters, leaving for the last chapter the whole examination of the South American question, which is so much in fashion today.[281]

In the afternoon, before dinner, we invited Inchausti, who is quite a bit better from his illness. We had dinner at home.

MONDAY, FEBRUARY 23, 1942
54TH DAY-311 DAYS TO FOLLOW

I pursued my ordinary life. In the morning, I worked at home, pegging away at my English, which is quite feeble, despite my progress. I wasn't born to learn foreign languages. My pronunciation has horrendous defects. First thing in the afternoon, I went to New York for my English

---

281 In the end, the *lehendakari*'s book *De Guernica* was published with seven chapters and an epilogue. The chapters were "I. Guernica, soul of Basque democracy," "II. The agony of a heroic people," "III. In France, which went to war with a divided soul," "IV. In the whirlwind," "V. Hidden in German-occupied Belgium," "VI. Dr. Álvarez's diary in Germany," and "VII. Toward lands of freedom." The epilogue, for its part, was divided into the following sections: "Guernica's message for the Americas," "Those who deny that the war is ideological are the ones who cause ideological confusion," "Spain, a typical example of ideological confusion," "The democrats, and not democracy, are the ones who have failed," "Social question and communism," "The nationalities problem," "The shrinking of universal ideas," "The hope of those who are suffering need not be in vain," "Mission of the Western Hemisphere," "The third enemy front: the Latin Union," "The danger of Christian dictatorships," "Withered diplomacy and the Latin axis," "Hispanoamericanism versus Panamericanism," "The Iberian problem," and "Message of the Basques, who sing and suffer." Agirre, *De Guernica*, 269–334 and 347.

class. Afterward to the delegation, where I composed a note for the U.S. vice president, which I'm sending by way of Lozada.

I missed the train, and then in White Plains I spent a good while waiting for the bus in order to get home. I continued writing the book.

TUESDAY, FEBRUARY 24, 1942
55TH DAY-310 DAYS TO FOLLOW

I continued my ordinary life, studying my university lessons and writing the book. I didn't have class yesterday, because despite being at war, these Americans can't give up their tradition of having a holiday on a working day for Washington's anniversary, which was Sunday. I was at the delegation in the afternoon preparing various letters and dispatching various matters. There's a holdup in correspondence, surely due to censorship and to the fact that no one works here when it's a holiday, despite being at war. They're unbelievable, and a couple of bombardments would do them good.

WEDNESDAY, FEBRUARY 25, 1942
56TH DAY-309 DAYS TO FOLLOW

In the morning, I studied at home. First thing in the afternoon, I went to the university. On Wednesdays I'm in my university office from two to four for the purpose of receiving visits and inquiries. Today no one visited me. Afterward, to the delegation. I gathered background material on Guernika for the book I've started from the Paris weekly *Euzko Deya*, which gathered interesting testimonies in its day. Afterward, home again. Today I started on the catechism in Euskara with the little ones; they finally sent it to me.[282] Afterward, I continued my work, preparing my classes and then composing pages of the book.

---

282 The catechism in Euskara sent to the *lehendakari* was possibly a copy of the one published in Belgium for the instruction of the Basque children evacuated there during the Spanish Civil War. *Aurtxoen kristau ikastia* (Antwerp: Drukkerij De Vlijt, 1937).

THURSDAY, FEBRUARY 26, 1942
57TH DAY-308 DAYS TO FOLLOW

In the morning, I worked at home. In the afternoon, I had my English class and went to the delegation. Manu Sota received a letter from Aldasoro, in which, among various ideas, he reports that a good number of our sailors are getting jobs with the navigation services of the state of Buenos Aires. It seems that they're giving Father a high-ranking position in the Argentine executive. God grant it, in order to put an end to the Calvary of his distressing economic situation. I continued studying and writing. I have abundant material, but I don't know whether I'll end up with a good product. If I did, we could sort out many problems of patriotic exigency.

FRIDAY, FEBRUARY 27, 1942
58TH DAY-307 DAYS TO FOLLOW

Today I spent all day at home working, from morning till evening. I wrote letters, and I dedicated the rest of the time to the first chapter of the book. I finished it except for some paragraphs that I need to consult about. I've now entered the period that writers usually have in which they're full of enthusiasm about their works. Up to now, I've kept it quiet, but I think that the time has come to do something, especially hearing the advice of the people of different nationalities who have encouraged me to write down my adventures. If I thereby do a service to our ideal, God will help me in the enterprise, which is not an easy one in these lands with their difficult mentality.

SATURDAY, FEBRUARY 28, 1942
59TH DAY-306 DAYS TO FOLLOW

Today I finished the first chapter of the book, of which I don't know the title. It happens to a lot of people that they leave the title for last. They've warned me that publishers often change the titles and impose names. I'll continue writing, and God will say what will come. Every Saturday, we host a gathering at our house in the evening. It's the day of rest. The Intxaustis and Manu Sota came. We had a very pleasant time, since during the work we're busy with work and always in a hurry. I wrote various letters today, especially to Galicians (Castelao) and Catalans (Serra Moret) who are writing to me courteously and enthusiastically from Argentina.[283]

SUNDAY, MARCH 1, 1942
60TH DAY-305 DAYS TO FOLLOW

After being at our little church, we took a walk. Like every Sunday, we were invited to Intxausti's house today. Monsieur and Madame Pelan, a very nice French couple, were also invited. She's Basque, the daughter of the mayor of Baiona who treated us Basques so favorably in our first hours of exile. Later, Mrs. Elizalde, the relative of the Philippine commissioner, arrived. Sundays are pleasant and serve us as a rest. We received a letter from Don Constan, who is somewhat worried because Margari and Mother, who are in Bilbao now, wrote in a pessimistic mood.[284] They'll get things cleared up.

MONDAY, MARCH 2, 1942
61ST DAY-304 DAYS TO FOLLOW

Another week of work began. In the morning, I went to the delegation, reviewing the correspondence received. Then to the university. In my office for a while. I had lunch at the University Club restaurant. At one-thirty, I was already in my office preparing my class, which begins at 4:10 and lasts until 6:00. We're still at the beginning of the nineteenth century. Little by little, I'm getting better at this diabolic pronunciation, which I struggle with quite a bit, thanks be to God and to my practice of speaking in public. They understand me, and I'm happy.

---

283 Alfonso Daniel Rodríguez Castelao (1886–1950), a Galician politician, writer, painter, and visual artist and the most important advocate of Galician nationalism at the time. For his part, Manuel Serra Moret (1884–1963) was a Catalan politician and writer who held various prominent positions in Catalan politics, including the vice presidency and presidency of the Catalan parliament.

284 With regard to the return to Euzkadi by some of the *lehendakari*'s in-laws, a letter sent by Juan Mari Agirre to Martín Lasa on November 22, 1941, and kindly provided to us by the Lasa family in fact, says, "Doña María and Margari just received German permits. They'll leave during the first half of December."

TUESDAY, MARCH 3, 1942
62ND DAY-303 DAYS TO FOLLOW

In the morning, I was in White Plains doing some shopping. I ate lunch quickly, and as I ordinarily do, I took the 12:45 bus, which brings me to the train that leaves for New York at 1:08. Afterward, to my English class. Since I had time before class, I visited Saint Patrick's Cathedral, and then I had a cup of *café con leche*. Once my class was over, I went to the delegation. I don't understand the London business. They sent us some telegrams that are difficult to understand. I'm quite annoyed, because there's a lot of self-centeredness and too much ambition in the lawyers, who will end up with everything if we don't take care.

WEDNESDAY, MARCH 4, 1942
63RD DAY-302 DAYS TO FOLLOW

This morning Mari left for New York with Ana Belén by 8:30. They're going to observe triduum at the College of the Sacred Heart.[285] The children went to Intxausti's house, and I stayed home alone working.

I went to the university early and spent the afternoon in my office. Then to the delegation. I answered various urgent letters. We received the first issue of *Batasuna*.[286] It's good. Now they want to bring out a journal in Cuba. Our people are first-class individualists. They don't remember their duty to work in common in these times. But in the end, the thing is that they work.[287] I say yes to everything that means doing something.

THURSDAY, MARCH 5, 1942
64TH DAY-301 DAYS TO FOLLOW

In the morning, I was in my office again, working on correspondence. After lunch at Intxausti's house, I went to New York. I had my English

---

285 According to the *Diccionario de la Real Academia*, a triduum (*triduo*) consists of "pious exercises practiced over three days."
286 The journal *Batasuna* was published in Chile between December 1941 and April 1942. It arose out of the initiative of Eduardo Díaz de Mendibil and was directed by Bernardo Estornés Lasa. Five issues were printed, the first a single issue and the remaining four double issues.
287 The *lehendakari*'s lament was probably due to the fact that multiplying the number of publications would weaken the only Basque journal circulating at the time, *Euzko Deya* of Buenos Aires, which was already suffering serious economic difficulties as it was.

class. Afterward, at the delegation, I received a visit from Mr. Miller, the head of the English services. We had tea while he delivered a letter from London with lawyers' reports, etc. Ortuzar sent it. It put me in a very bad mood. It would be better for them to sort out their differences without causing this kind of scandal. I received a telegram from Max Ascoli. He's sick, so we have to put off tomorrow's meeting. We're going through a bad season, in all aspects.

FRIDAY, MARCH 6, 1942
65TH DAY-300 DAYS TO FOLLOW

We didn't celebrate my birthday today, in order to be able to work as on ordinary days. We'll celebrate it tomorrow, Saturday, when we're free from our occupations. Only my family remembered me. The poor people who are in Louvain also, although their letters haven't arrived yet due to the circumstances. My friend Inchausti had to do his usual. He gave me a precious Christ carved in wood. In the evening, we celebrated the saint's day *en petit comité* and invited the Intxaustis to have coffee with us. We drank it in the kitchen while Mari prepared tomorrow's menu and Ana Belén helped her.

SATURDAY, MARCH 7, 1942
66TH DAY-299 DAYS TO FOLLOW

The children gave me presents: two ties from Aintzane and a notebook from Joseba. They both saw themselves as doing a grand deed. The Intxaustis, Gamboa's family, Manu, and Ramón Sota came to the house to have lunch with us. We spent a truly pleasant day, among family. All who are suffering were very much in our thoughts, especially now with the bad war news, which will make the conflict much longer.[288] Manu and the Intxaustis stayed on in the evening, and we continued the party. They gave me a few things; they were all very courteous. It was a day on which we enjoyed ourselves remembering so many, many things.

---

288 Probably a reference to the Japanese victories in the Philippines and the Dutch East Indies around this time.

SUNDAY, MARCH 8, 1942
67TH DAY-298 DAYS TO FOLLOW

We pursued our ordinary Sunday life. I received a letter from Archbishop Spellman telling me that Jauregui's and Lasarte's departure case has been recommended to the Vatican Secretariat of State by the Vatican chargé d'affaires here, by way of the nuncio in Vichy.[289] It's an attention to be very grateful for. We've already had news that the exit permits for our two friends have been granted. God grant that the voyage will be quick and that there will be no need to fear more complications like what happened on the previous voyage of those who arrived on the *Quanza*. How much our poor people suffers!

MONDAY, MARCH 9, 1942
68TH DAY-297 DAYS TO FOLLOW

In the morning, I worked at home, answering some letters. In the afternoon, I went to the university to give my usual lecture. I'm improving little by little, but not as quickly as I would like. I received a letter from Pi y Suñer expressing his agreement with my proposal to issue a proclamation in the name of Catalonia and Euzkadi to achieve, if possible, a Peninsular entente that can serve as the basis for future action. In this way, we Catalans and Basques will get ahead of everyone and will have the right to make demands when the time comes. Staying on the defensive wastes time and loses the war.

TUESDAY, MARCH 10, 1942
69TH DAY-296 DAYS TO FOLLOW

I continued my labors at home. I've made some progress composing the book. I want to have more than 150 pages prepared this week, since time is pressing. In the afternoon, I went to class first thing and later to the delegation. Roberto de Etxebarria visited me to deliver a letter for Tomás from Teodoro, Iñaki, and Ángel.[290] They're in a good mood

---

289 Cardinal Amleto Giovanni Cicognani served as apostolic delegate in the United States starting in 1933, and Cardinal Valerio Valeri served as nuncio in France starting in 1936. Cicognani remained in his position until 1958, while Valeri was called to Rome in 1944.

290 Teodoro, Iñaki, Ángel, and Tomás Agirre Lekube were José Antonio's brothers.

and apparently received one of my letters in January, I suppose one from December. We were happy to receive news of how they spent the Christmas holidays. Their optimism and good spirits are something to be thankful for amid such painful circumstances. God will reward them for their good will and for taking a joyful view of life despite everything.

WEDNESDAY, MARCH 11, 1942
70TH DAY-295 DAYS TO FOLLOW

In the morning, I went to New York with Mari and the Intxaustis. They went shopping; I went to the delegation. Afterward, I ate lunch at the University Club. Then to my office in the history department. There I worked with Sota until four-thirty, when we left to go back to the delegation. Since the distances are so great here, one excursion immediately uses up the morning and the afternoon. Today I left a message for the president of the Belgian Chamber of Deputies inviting him to lunch. He was in Washington. He'll be back tomorrow. I'd like to see him on Saturday. He attends the Washington meetings with me. He's a very affable and cultivated man. He's Flemish.

THURSDAY, MARCH 12, 1942
71ST DAY-294 DAYS TO FOLLOW

Today I received a letter sent from Mexico by the Euzkadi communists and another one, which arrived on the same day, sent by the Basque communists in Santo Domingo. They reminded me of those telegrams from Oriol's mayors that were sent in series.[291] The topic was the same as always: their profound anti-Nazism, their love for democracy. Not the same as always, with the exception of the period of the German-Soviet Pact.[292] Also Basque national union, self-determination, etc., but now the 1931 Constitution and the Negrín government coming and going.

Roberto Echevarria was a Bilbao entrepreneur who had put down roots in New York, where he headed the Bilbao Contracting Company with agencies in Argentina, Colombia, France, Spain, and Venezuela.

291 José Luis de Oriol y Urigüen (1877–1972) was a businessman and politician, the leading political figure on the right in Araba during the Spanish Republic.

292 The German-Soviet Non-aggression Pact, also known as the Molotov-Ribbentrop Pact, was signed by the two countries' foreign ministers on August 23, 1939. In addition to affirming their mutual non-aggression, Germany and the Soviet Union used the pact to divide up the area of Eastern and Central Europe into zones of influence dominated by each power.

They're incorrigible. Slogans are more powerful than blood. How well Moscow makes use of them, working for Russia, which I'm damned if we're interested in!

FRIDAY, MARCH 13, 1942
72ND DAY-293 DAYS TO FOLLOW

I took advantage of the whole day to work. I'm now on the third chapter of the book, which will have about seven. I've made major progress, and I want to finish it by the end of the month. Then the corrections, the translation, etc., will take a lot of time. That's why I want to race ahead now. Sometimes what I write seems good to me; other times it doesn't. I'm not the one who should be the judge of it.

I spoke by telephone with Dr. Van Cauwelaert, the president of the Belgian Chamber.[293] We'll have lunch together on Monday to discuss quite a few things related to our countries and to the Washington meetings. Maritain has written us that he wants to join me. Don Sturzo also. They're two minds of the first order.[294]

SATURDAY, MARCH 14, 1942
73RD DAY-292 DAYS TO FOLLOW

I worked at home all day. Today we were visited by Valentín Aguirre, his wife, and their son-in-law Jon de Zabal. They had dinner at our house. The Intxaustis and Manu Sota also came, like every Saturday. We were amused by Don Valentín's witticisms as he told us various anecdotes from his life. He's a classic representative of these American

---

[293] Frans Van Cauwelaert (1880–1961) was a Flemish Catholic politician and university professor. As a university professor he taught psychology in Louvain, and as a politician he was active in the Flemish nationalist movement, holding various portfolios in the Belgian government before going into exile in New York as a consequence of World War II.

[294] Probably a reference to the correspondence exchanged by some European Christian Democrats exiled in the United States with the aim of reaching agreement of the terms of a manifesto ultimately published around this time. This manifesto was published in various formats, including as a book, José Antonio de Aguirre, Charles Boyer, et al., *Devant la crise mondiale: Manifeste de catholiques européens séjournant en Amérique* (New York: Éditions de la Maison Française, 1942). On the correspondence on this and other topics between Luigi Sturzo and Jacques Maritain see *Luigi Sturzo e gli intellettuali cattolici francesi: Carteggi (1925–1945)*, ed. Emile Goichot (Soveria Mannelli: Rubbettino, 2003), 427–32.

Basques who have established themselves by hard work and who, since they came over many years ago, have not really understood our national movement. Nevertheless, they preserve all our national characteristics, language included, better than those of South America. It's a typical case of patriotic maintenance after their fashion.

SUNDAY, MARCH 15, 1942
74TH DAY-291 DAYS TO FOLLOW

Like every Sunday, after mass we worked a bit on the book, which is advancing little by little.

As usual, we had lunch at Intxausti's house. Afterward, he also forced us to stay for dinner. Today we had some blackout drills, with sirens blaring. Even if it's very unpleasant, it's possible that a true blackout wouldn't be a bad thing for these slumbering Americans. Today María Luisa Elizalde had lunch at home with her two little ones. All the children were at the house of a friend of theirs in the neighborhood whose birthday it was. In the evening, I heard from Van Cawvelard asking me to postpone our lunch until Tuesday, since it's not possible for him tomorrow.

MONDAY, MARCH 16, 1942
75TH DAY-290 DAYS TO FOLLOW

In the morning, I went to the delegation early. Afterward, to the university. We ate lunch at the University Club. Of course, because of the war, they've closed one of the dining rooms, since part of the staff has been called up. The club is very pleasant and simple. The food is quite good. All kinds of characters and all kinds of nationalities are to be seen there. While I was giving my class, there was a horrible rainstorm; I had to wait for a bit, and we spent more than a dollar getting to the station. We keep a close eye on our money, the subway is our ordinary means of transportation, but today it was raining too much.

TUESDAY, MARCH 17, 1942
76TH DAY-289 DAYS TO FOLLOW

Today I had lunch with the president of the Belgian Chamber. It was an interesting conversation. The topic of South America is absolutely transcendental and has everyone worried. Now they're starting to realize here that it's useless to waste time. During our lunch at the Hotel Gothan, the parade for Saint Patrick, the patron of Ireland, was going by. More than fifty thousand Irish or descendants of the Irish marched down Fifth Avenue with their picturesque brass bands and their characteristic disguises. American and Irish flags. It's too bad that Ireland's position in this conflict is so strange, especially with America, to which it owes its freedom.[295]

WEDNESDAY, MARCH 18, 1942
77TH DAY-288 DAYS TO FOLLOW

I worked in the morning. After lunch, I went to New York. Directly to the university, where I spent about three hours in my office. Then to the delegation. I received the book that Tellagorri published in Havana, taking advantage of his stay there.[296] Tellagorri writes very well. I'll enjoy reading the book. Jesús Galíndez, our delegate in Santo Domingo, also sent me his book for me to write a prologue for it. I hope to please him. Galíndez is one of our strengths for the future. He's very well oriented. His book will be published by the Ekin publishing house in Buenos Aires.[297] Good luck to all of them! We received a visit from a

---

295 Despite having belonged to the Commonwealth since its independence in 1921, Ireland declared its neutrality in the conflict as soon as it began, due to its past and ongoing difficult relationship with the United Kingdom. Although the British were not pleased by the measure, it had its positive consequences for the United Kingdom, such as the use of the Irish Free State as a rest area for its troops and as a supply depot from which to acquire provisions. Irish neutrality was also convenient for Germany, since it prevented the majority of the island from becoming a potential site for Allied military bases.

296 Tellagorri was the pseudonym of José Olivares Larrondo. The book referred to in the text was *París abandonada*, illustrated by Néstor Basterretxea (Havana: La Verónica, 1942). See note 239.

297 Jesús Galíndez Suárez (1915–1956) was the Basque government's delegate in the Dominican Republic beginning in 1940, when he replaced Eusebio Irujo, who had left the post vacant upon departing for Venezuela. Galíndez remained on that Caribbean island from his arrival in 1939 until he moved to New York in 1946, summoned by the *lehendakari* to help him write the history he was preparing and to reinforce the delegation in that city. A tireless writer, professor, and politician, he composed numerous articles and books on both Basque and Latin American history, law, culture, and politics. His time in the Dominican Republic had a profound impact on him, and Rafael Leónidas Trujillo's dictatorship in that country was the topic he chose for his doctoral dissertation, which became the posthumously published book *La era de Trujillo* (Santiago de Chile: Editorial del Pacífico, 1956). He disappeared at the hands of agents of Trujillo's dictatorship on March 12,

representative of an Argentine-Basque firm. He was recommended by Aldasoro.

THURSDAY, MARCH 19, 1942
78TH DAY-287 DAYS TO FOLLOW

Today we were invited to Valentín de Aguirre's Jai Alai Restaurant. A good lunch as always. For me, it was a day of rest, since there were nearly three days when I went to bed at four in the morning. Afterward, we went with the Intxaustis to the magnificent Radio City Hall at the Rockefeller building.[298] Afterward, to White Plains. At eleven, we set out for Washington, as on this date in previous months. Intxausti accompanied me. The trip is very comfortable, since leaving New York at 1:00 a.m., one arrives in Washington at 7:30 a.m. The train goes slowly so that the passengers can sleep.

FRIDAY, MARCH 20, 1942
79TH DAY-286 DAYS TO FOLLOW

We arrived in Washington in very good shape. I visited Losada, the advisor to the Coordinating Committee for South American activities. He passed on to me excellent impressions from Vice President Wallace;

1956. The book mentioned by the *lehendakari* in this entry is *La aportación vasca al derecho internacional* (Buenos Aires: Editorial Vasca Ekin, 1942). The prologue that the delegate in the Dominican Republic requested from the *lehendakari* was not published, because the original arrived late at the publisher.

298 Once the diary's pages begin to reflect the *lehendakari*'s experiences in New York, the direct and indirect references to Nelson Rockefeller are numerous. This is due not only to the contacts maintained by the Basque leaders with the agents of this Republican powerbroker in the service of the Democratic administration (such as Max Ascoli and Enrique Sánchez de Lozada), but also to the fact that some of the offices frequented by the Basques amid New York's skyscrapers were located at Rockefeller Center. This building on Fifth Avenue housed, among others, the British propaganda services, the first U.S. intelligence agency, the COI, and the Éditions de la Maison Française publishing house, which published the Christian Democratic manifesto mentioned in notes 260 and 294 as well as the works of numerous French intellectuals exiled in the United States and aligned with this current of political thought. Even a habit as deeply rooted in Agirre as that of visiting churches to pray was influenced to a certain extent by the location of Rockefeller Center, since we have little doubt that his visits to Saint Patrick's Cathedral were due to the proximity of the two buildings, practically across the street from each other on New York's Fifth Avenue.

they were very laudatory, and God grant that they may be to the benefit of our cause. After lunch, I went to the Argentine embassy, where I talked about various matters with Secretary Uriburu,[299] who takes great pride in his Basque ancestry. At five, I entered the room where the Catholic intellectual elements were studying postwar organization and principles. At ten, the meeting ended. Intxausti arrived with Sebastián Ugarte, the counselor of the Philippine legation. We talked about interesting and current matters. I went to bed very tired.

SATURDAY, MARCH 21, 1942
80TH DAY-285 DAYS TO FOLLOW

I was expecting a visit today from Ortiz Etxague, the Washington correspondent of the Buenos Aires newspaper *La Nación*. A good friend of ours, he has constantly dedicated interesting columns to us. He advised Manu that he would come to see me and confirmed as much in a letter. I waited for him at the hotel in the morning, and he's surely absent, because I didn't hear anything from him. We took the train at noon and arrived in New York at four. Then to White Plains, where they were waiting for us. We had dinner at Intxausti's house. Since I'm invited to go on board the Chilean passenger ship commanded by our good compatriot Captain Atxurra tomorrow, we suspended our Saturday dinners today.

---

299 Probably Guillermo Uriburu, a passenger on the steamer *Uruguay* on the same voyage that brought the Agirre-Zabala family to New York. According to the manifest of foreigners filled out when the ship arrived in New York, Uriburu was traveling as a diplomat posted to the Argentine embassy in Washington and was thirty years old and single. He was directly related to former Argentine presidents José Evaristo Uriburu and José Félix Uriburu. List or manifest of alien passengers for the United States immigrant inspector at port of arrival, New York, November 4, 1941, Ancestry.com, http://content.ancestry.com/Browse/print_u.aspx?dbid=7488&iid=NYT715_6590-0576.

SUNDAY, MARCH 22, 1942
81ST DAY-284 DAYS TO FOLLOW

After mass, I left for New York. Once a good group had gathered, we went to Captain Atxurra's ship.[300] They received us with full honors. The Basque flag and the Chilean flag presided over the elegant dining room where we were hosted A magnificent meal, appropriate to a Basque captain. It was a very pleasant gathering. Captain Atxurra has a grand patriotic temperament. At the end, I said a few words in Euskara and in Spanish, for the Basques of Chile and for the Chileans who have always behaved so well toward us. Afterward, to White Plains. Since good fortune is never total, we found the house's basement flooded.

MONDAY, MARCH 23, 1942
82ND DAY-283 DAYS TO FOLLOW

I first went to the university in fulfillment of an invitation from Professor Chamberlain, who had prepared a panel with five other professors. The

---

300 "Ramuntcho Etxepherdia," a pseudonym of Ramón de la Sota, published the following account of this meeting between the *lehendakari* and Capt. Pedro Atxurra Madarieta in *Euzko Deya* of Buenos Aires on July 20, 1942: "Recently arrived from Washington, the president was given a grand banquet on board a Chilean steamer, the motor ship *Copiapó*, commanded by a native of Lekeitio, Captain Atxurra. It was an excellent banquet. Captain Atxurra is an *abertzale* [patriot] of refinement. A typical Basque sailor. He feels nostalgia for the age of sail, which is irremediably disappearing little by little. He commanded large sailing ships for years and today commands steamers with advanced features of all kinds. He always had a Basque flag on board all his ships. A flag that has waved in Australia, in China, in Europe, in the Americas. This same flag, now worn by the years and the wind, adorned the main dining room together with a Chilean one on the day of the banquet that this great Basque offered to President Aguirre. The meal was attended by, among others, the Basque delegate in America, Don Manuel de la Sota, and other members of the Basque delegation, Don Valentín de Aguirre, Don Marino de Gamboa and his wife and children, Jon de Zabalaundikoetxea, Jon de Argiarro, the head of New York passenger traffic for the Compañía Chilena, Don Alfonso Tondo, various prominent Americans, and this correspondent. "In his speech, the president charged Captain Atxurra to bring a greeting to the Basques of Chile, whom he hoped to visit during the upcoming summer, and another to the Chileans, who have known how to exercise a magnanimous spirit of aid to those Basques who have found themselves faced with the adversities of exile. "The president charged Captain Atxurra to act as an envoy of the Basques to thank Chile and its democracy in their name for the welcome given to all Basques suffering misfortune." Published by Iñaki Anasagasti on his blog http://ianasagasti.blogs.com/mi_blog/2009/08/saski-naski-newyorkino-y-el-lehendakari-aguirre.html.

conversation was truly pleasant. All these Yankee professors are very sympathetic and have an exemplary spirit of comradeship. Today we received a pleasant letter in which Aldasoro informed us that Father has been given a high-ranking position in the Argentine state-operated merchant marine with residence in New York. The news made us very happy. It seems that Ramón is sorting out his affairs, which are those of the delegation and of the fatherland. Ramón well deserves gratitude of all kinds.

TUESDAY, MARCH 24, 1942
83RD DAY-282 DAYS TO FOLLOW

I worked at home in the morning. Afterward, to my English class. Later, to the delegation. Today a Basque from the Philippines arrived with a message for me from our compatriots on those islands. I wasn't able to see him, because he came at a time when I was absent. It seems that he was one of the last to leave the Philippines. I received an invitation from Columbia University's South American groups to speak to them at their April meeting. They're very affectionate toward me, and some of them attend my class. We received a letter from Father confirming the appointment and announcing his upcoming arrival.

WEDNESDAY, MARCH 25, 1942
84TH DAY-281 DAYS TO FOLLOW

After working at home during the morning, I went to the university, as I usually do on Wednesdays. I was visited by the leaders of the South American graduate students, asking me to speak to them about the Basque problem. All these South Americans are generally doctoral graduates or professors at South American institutes or universities who come to the Columbia to pursue a specialization. In general, they're cultivated people who want to perfect their studies. Some of them come to my class with true assiduity. Since I'll start another class in October on the influence of the thought of the Peninsular peoples in South America, these contacts are of great interest. I continue writing the book in order to finish it in April.

THURSDAY, MARCH 26, 1942
85TH DAY-280 DAYS TO FOLLOW

I spent the morning at home working and answering some correspondence. With the censorship, letters take a long time to arrive. Especially those from Mexico, which to judge by the proximity shouldn't take more than a very few days. Since letters take so long, it may be that Basterretxea and Tellagorri haven't received my most recent one. They had left for Buenos Aires without my most recent news and observations. Besides, this is all so immense! This week turned out to be inventors' week. One of them turned up at the delegation with an advertising invention, and another one had a new fuse for aerial bombs. Every day, someone arrives with another novelty. We had a very delayed letter from Irala.[301] God grant that the people in Marseilles leave soon.

FRIDAY, MARCH 27, 1942
86TH DAY-279 DAYS TO FOLLOW

In the morning, I was in New York. I went to the delegation and then to fulfill my invitation from Prof. Max Ascoli, the director of the South American Coordination Council. Maritain came to the lunch. We talked about the current moment and the lack of understanding for foreign groups. The policy of distancing that is followed is not the best, because there's no one who isn't needed in the struggle. Everyone is needed, given the enormous proportions of the current conflict. Max Ascoli informed us that a profound change in political direction is necessarily in preparation. Without that, it's difficult to think about anything positive. We would never have believed that reactionary and egoistical sentiment was so deeply rooted in a people like this one.

SATURDAY, MARCH 28, 1942
87TH DAY-278 DAYS TO FALLOW

I went to the delegation in the morning. Later, to the lunch that was given for me by the Catalan groups, which are now going to form themselves into a delegation. They have a mandate from the National

---

301 The lawyer and politician Antonio Irala Irala (1909–1996) served as general secretary of the office of the president of the Basque government from 1936 until the late 1940s. On April 14, 1942, he succeeded in leaving France for exile in the United States, where he resumed his close collaboration with the *lehendakari*.

Council in London for this. I showed them the Basque-Catalan pact, as agreed with Pi y Suñer. We'll see when an opportunity arises for its publication. The Catalan movement in the Americas can be important if it is well-led. My trip can bear great fruit if I can make it this summer. The Catalans have notably improved in spirit. They're establishing their ideas, which are at the same time very deeply ingrained. Basque-Catalan action may be very important in the future.

SUNDAY, MARCH 29, 1942
88TH DAY-277 DAYS TO FOLLOW

Today was a day of true rest. Like every Sunday, Manu Sota came to White Plains. In the morning, we went over the book manuscript, which is getting written little by little, not as quickly as I wanted. The topic is a rich one, but it's all about the way to present to the American public, which is so peculiar. With the book, I want to present in an attractive way the problem of a people that deserves to live, because it has won that right the hard way. God will help me in the task, which is a hard one. I've already written almost two hundred pages.

MONDAY, MARCH 30, 1942
89TH DAY-276 DAYS TO FOLLOW

I have a week of vacation for Holy Week, which I want to make good use of by making major progress on my book. But invitations come one after another these days. Today it was Marino Gamboa, who gave a "cocktail party" at his house to celebrate the advertising launch of a perfume business here in America. His competitors have accused him of fascism. My presence at the gathering was able to lighten the atmosphere. Accusations of this nature have their humorous side at this point. But that's life. On this account, I lost several hours of work.

TUESDAY, MARCH 31, 1942
90TH DAY-275 DAYS TO FOLLOW

I worked at home in the morning. Then I went to my English class. Later, to the delegation. They invited me to a meeting tomorrow with the English head of propaganda at the embassy. We'll see what comes of it. There's a strange watchword abroad at the moment that nothing related to Spain should be touched. No one knows what's happening.

It seems that the Spanish ships have received orders not to depart. It seems that the English services should have acted more rapidly, but they aren't doing so. Is there some mystery behind it? We'll find out soon, because this situation can't last long.

WEDNESDAY, APRIL 1, 1942
91ST DAY-274 DAYS TO FOLLOW

In the morning, I was in New York with the head of liaison between the English and American propaganda services. A well-oriented man, he received me with all friendliness. We talked for an hour and a half about our problem, the Spanish problem, the South American problem, everything related to propaganda. He asked me to send him a brief summary of our conversation with special mention of whatever can be done in Argentina and Chile. I came away with a very good impression. He gives the problem of Spain the disturbing character that we assign to it. He knew Spain and the twenty-one South American republics. He didn't know Euzkadi, but he was familiar with the problem. I spent the rest of the day in White Plains.

THURSDAY, APRIL 2, 1942
92ND DAY-273 DAYS TO FOLLOW

In the morning, I attended Holy Thursday services at our little church. The services were very poor, without the solemnity of our country or anything close to it. The liturgy very simplified, with only the indispensable ceremonies.

We went to New York, having been invited to lunch at Gamboa's house. In the afternoon, we went out to Saint Patrick's Cathedral, where the Holy Week liturgies are splendid. Part of the time we were there, they were magnificently singing Holy Thursday Vespers. The monument was very fine to see and of a very sober elegance. The contrast with our little church was extraordinary. The children came home very tired after so much walking.

FRIDAY, APRIL 3, 1942
93RD DAY-272 DAYS TO FOLLOW

We attended the services, which continued to have the same stamp of liturgical poverty as the ones yesterday. I then worked all day, continuing to compose the book. The material is piling up, since it's very abundant. It's necessary to go along making a careful selection so that the book reflects our desires and at the same time does not become a slog for the Western Hemisphere reader, especially the American reader with his peculiar tastes. It surprised me that in a country like this one that's so respectful of the religious idea, today wasn't a holiday. It's the contradictions of this country, in which strange indifference is found alongside a profound religious spirit. The liturgical solemnities of our ever-more-beloved Euzkadi were much in our thoughts.

SATURDAY, APRIL 4, 1942
94TH DAY-271 DAYS TO FOLLOW

Today at Gamboa's house again. The Vichy consul, who behaved very well toward us with regard to the petition we made to him in favor of Lasarte and Jauregui, expressed to Manu Sota his great interest in making my acquaintance and said that if we could arrange a lunch or tea at a private house, he would find it a true pleasure to meet me. That's what we did, since Gamboa offered us his house. This is issuing invitations at someone else's expense. The consul, a former minister, repeated interesting things that were useful for getting exact information about matters that are always of interest with regard to the complicated and difficult French situation. Disorientation is the dominant mood.

SUNDAY, APRIL 5, 1942
95TH DAY-270 DAYS TO FOLLOW
EASTER SUNDAY

Easter Sunday. Day of the Fatherland. So many memories rush in. Here we spent the day among intimates, invited to Intxausti's house, where the Gamboas and their daughter Tere came after dinner. Given that it wasn't all the Basques or a good group of them, we celebrated *en petit comité*, remembering the day and those who must have remembered and even celebrated it both in exile and in prison. The children took excellent advantage of the good weather, running around with their bicycles. It was a good decision to live outside New York. The little ones' health is much improved.

MONDAY, APRIL 6, 1942
96TH DAY-269 DAYS TO FOLLOW

In the morning, I worked at home. Then to the university. There they came to remind me about my commitment to speak at the South Americans' dinner, which will be held at the International House building on Thursday the 16th. They want me to speak to them about the Basque problem, because there are many who desire to hear about it since they're not familiar with it, others are familiar with it but with great errors, and finally others are familiar with it and enthusiastic about it, but they're the smallest group. I was glad to attend, because I'm very interested in having these exchanges of impressions with representatives of these South American countries with which we will have much to do in the future.

TUESDAY, APRIL 7, 1942
97TH DAY-268 DAYS TO FOLLOW

I continued my ordinary life. I worked in the morning. I finished the report for the head of liaison with American propaganda. I'm going along repeating the same theme to everyone. By dint of repetition, it doesn't seem as attractive to me as it did at the beginning. It seemed very good to the mentioned head of liaison, a very intelligent Englishman, in our conversation. Now it's in writing, as he asked. The theme is the impossibility of conducting propaganda in the Iberian Peninsula without considering that territory as a plurinational geographical grouping. Speaking to each people in its own language, we'll understand one another.

WEDNESDAY, APRIL 8, 1942
98TH DAY-267 DAYS TO FOLLOW

For the last two days, I've been thinking about inviting the Argentine president's son, Mr. Ortiz. This evening I did it. In order to introduce him to a classic location, I took him to the Jai Alai. He enjoyed it very much, and we enjoyed it along with him. He was completely wrapped up in the events in Argentina. He was sure that blood would even run, but in the end, these South Americans are very hot-blooded, but I don't think that they'll shed it as Mr. Ortiz (the son) thinks, because it would be senseless under these circumstances. The dinner was very well served, and we all left satisfied. We remembered President Ortiz.

THURSDAY, APRIL 9, 1942
99TH DAY-226 DAYS TO FOLLOW

Today was a notable day. We held an intimate dinner at the Hotel Croydon attended by the new U.S. ambassador to Spain Prof. Carlton Hayes and his wife, Professor Chamberlain, Professor Tannenbaum, Rockefeller's architect Fayoux[302] and his wife, Intxausti and his wife, Manu Sota, and Mari and I. Professor Carlton Hayes's attendance was significant. For the sake of our friendship, he set aside all the diplomatic rules that are so current in that world. But he's a friend of ours. His judgment is very sensible, he knows us well, and he moves forward with a firm orientation. His wife is admirable, and his sympathy for us is very great. This intimate gathering may have truly important practical results for the future.

FRIDAY, APRIL 10, 1942
100TH DAY-265 DAYS TO FOLLOW

Today I worked at home all day. I began to compose a long report for Prof. Carlton Hayes, which he asked me for at yesterday's dinner. I'm summarizing recent political affairs, indicating the characteristics of each group and their leaders. I'm also indicating the solutions of the Peninsular problem, clearly determining the national significance of our claim to freedom, and finally noting that our problem is more a matter of the future than of the present. I think that it will be a long

---

302 Jacques André Fouilhoux (1879–1945), a naturalized American of French origin, was an important architect. One of his most important architectural activities was heading the consortium responsible for designing Rockefeller Center, along with his partners Max Abramovitz and Wallace Harrison. More immediately relevant to us, this French architect, together with Wilfrid Parsons and C. Gouverneur Paulding, was one of the American citizens who joined Manu de la Sota and Manuel Ynchausti in vouching for the *lehendakari* to the American authorities in order to obtain his U.S. entry permit. Larronde, *Manuel de Ynchausti*, 110; Sudjic, *La arquitectura*, 270.

but interesting paper. I don't think that they'll be able to give him such an exact account of the problem at the state department.

SATURDAY, APRIL 11, 1942
101ST DAY-264 DAYS TO FOLLOW

Today I worked at home in the morning. I continued putting together the memorandum I was asked for by my superior at the university, the current U.S. ambassador to Spain. Then I went to New York, having been invited by my compatriot Saralegui from Cuba.[303] We had a very good lunch at the Jai-Alai. Good cigars, very appropriate for someone from Havana. The conversation was interesting because it clarified some errors by our people or our sympathizers who think that we have abundant economic resources available from the JARE.[304] Fortunately, everything is being clarified, and our dignity and freedom continue to have no strings attached.

SUNDAY, APRIL 12, 1942
102ND DAY-263 DAYS TO FOLLOW

We pursued our ordinary Sunday life. After fulfilling our religious duties, we spent all morning going over the week's work. Like every Sunday, we had lunch at Intxausti's house. In the afternoon, we went to the movies, since the weather was bad for taking a walk. An odd and extremely exaggerated film about Gestapo activities in America. If I tell them how I didn't see all those things, they don't believe me. It's a bit childish to attribute all these diabolic machinations to the enemy. Later, the truth and disillusionment arrive. It's enough that he's a tyrant and a usurper of others' freedom.

MONDAY, APRIL 13, 1942
103RD DAY-262 DAYS TO FOLLOW

I went to the university beginning in the morning in order to give my class in the afternoon. In my classes, I'm continuing to study the history of the Iberian Peninsula in the time of Napoleon. I still haven't gotten to the Parliament of Cádiz.

---

303 Francisco Saralegui Arrizubieta was an important Cuban press entrepreneur, the co-owner of the journals *Bohemia*, *Carteles*, and *Vanidades*.
304 On the JARE see note 209.

Today our two little ones and Intxausti's four came down with chickenpox. All of them at once. When I got home, I found them covered by the rash and very bothered by the itching. It seems that they'll get over it quickly, according to the doctor's assurances. It hurts to see the children so disfigured with the spots and especially somewhat under the weather because of the fever.

TUESDAY, APRIL 14, 1942
104TH DAY-261 DAYS TO FOLLOW

An ordinary day, altered only by the illness of the little ones, who were enormously restless all day with the rash caused by the chickenpox. They spent all night very bothered and agitated. When I returned home, they were calmer. It seems that the infection is starting to run its course. I went to the delegation. A letter came from the press that is interested in my book and is recommended by Ambassador Carlton Hayes. They'll set an appointment any day. Manu will speak with them, and we'll see what they say. It's one of the most important publishing houses in the world. If I get it right, the success will be very great.

WEDNESDAY, APRIL 15, 1942
105TH DAY-260 DAYS TO FOLLOW

Since I have to go to the university on Thursday to give a talk to the South American graduate students, I took all day today to compose the report for Ambassador Carlton Hayes and continue my work on my book. The report for the ambassador analyzes the recent period on the Iberian Peninsula, examines all the political groups, and studies future solutions within the framework of the current international ideology. Naturally, the Basque national fact and the problems of its sovereignty are set out with all clarity. The Catalan case is also studied.

I'm making progress on the book, which will be at least 450 pages. I don't think that I'll be able to finish it by the end of the month.

THURSDAY, APRIL 16, 1942
106TH DAY-259 DAYS TO FOLLOW

In the morning, I worked at home. In the afternoon, I gave the announced talk to the South American graduate students at International House. In general, they're young South Americans with doctorates who are perfecting their studies at Columbia.

I discussed the history of Euzkadi, giving a historical survey of our fatherland from the most ancient times until today. At the end of my talk, there was an interesting question-and-answer session that was very instructive. Our problem is very well understood and always received with sympathy. The human value of all our institutions and Basque firmness on the side of freedom attract attention and produce admiration.

FRIDAY, APRIL 17, 1942
107TH DAY-258 DAYS TO FOLLOW

All day at home, and all day writing. I finished the report for Ambassador Carlton Hayes. I wrote about eighty large pages. I think that it's a complete report. And I hope that it clarifies a series of problems and situations that foreigners generally don't manage to understand unless they listen to someone who has experienced the situations, because it's frequently seen that even friends who want to explain things favorably say many inexact things, especially in this generous but picturesque country, where in order to make a narrative or a statement pleasant, they introduce a *txirenada* [slang term for a witty comment] without permission.

SATURDAY, APRIL 18, 1942
108TH DAY-257 DAYS TO FOLLOW

I continued working on the book all day, describing the odyssey of my final days in Germany. The material is abundant, and the biggest difficulty is summarizing it, in addition to choosing what's most interesting and instructive. Afterward, I'll narrate the episode of our two-month stay in Sweden. I won't do it in diary form like my time in Germany. In the evening, the Intxaustis and Manu Sota had dinner at our house, like almost every Saturday. It's usually the only time during the week, except for Sunday, when we abandon all the things we have to do and discuss whatever news has reached us. We have a good time, amid everything.

SUNDAY, APRIL 19, 1942
109TH DAY-256 DAYS TO FOLLOW

Although tomorrow is Aintzane's saint's day, we celebrated it today. Because of the chickenpox they had, only Intxausti's little friends were invited. All the little ones were well supplied with refreshments, and there were even presents. The children enjoyed it very much, and we also enjoyed it with them. Aintzane did the honors with her little friends, who also included an American boy, Lore, who was also hit by the contagion, since he belonged to the sick gang. Fortunately, they're all very well and spent a very happy day. For them, for their good fortune, neither sadness nor bad moments exist. At their side, everything is forgotten.

MONDAY, APRIL 20, 1942
110TH DAY-255 DAYS TO FOLLOW

I started the week again with my usual class at Columbia. One of the South American students who comes told me that his comrades at International House were very happy with the talk I gave to them on Thursday. They want me to visit them again. It can't happen right now, but I'll be very happy to do it later on, since these talks and these acquaintances are always of interest looking to the future. In my classes, I'm still studying the Napoleonic era. I'll probably finish this course with a study of the Cádiz Parliament and the Basque attitude toward them. There won't be time for more.

TUESDAY, APRIL 21, 1942
111TH DAY-254 DAYS TO FOLLOW

I worked at home in the morning. When I arrived at the delegation, I found Ricardo de Leizaola, who had arrived from his trip to London by way of Portugal. He had the boldness to try to get to Biarritz, where his wife and children are. He crossed the Portuguese-Spanish border, but he wasn't able to get beyond the first towns in Orense due to the difficulties encountered on the road. He brought me news from London. He returned on one of the ships in a convey of thirty-eight armed merchant vessels escorted by a schooner and by two English destroyers. Quite an adventure.

WEDNESDAY, APRIL 22, 1942
112TH DAY-253 DAYS TO FOLLOW

I spent the morning at the delegation. I then went to fulfill an invitation from Gurmendi, the Argentine industrialist who attended my talk at International House last week. Today Manu Sota went in my name to meet with one of the principal agents of the best American and English publishing house, which through the mediation of Ambassador Carlton Hayes has taken an interest in my book in preparation. Manu returned with a wonderful impression, believing that it's something serious and formal. They've given us three weeks to finish the book. We'll see whether we'll be able to submit it at least in part by that date. It will require a great effort!

THURSDAY, APRIL 23, 1942
113TH DAY-252 DAYS TO FOLLOW

Leizaola (Ricardo) told us his impressions of London and of our men's work. His observations are interesting, especially with regard to the spirit of the British population, which is certain of triumph. The destruction is severe, but as I supposed, it's not what people in the world imagine. There's a lot of exaggeration on both sides. His account of the voyage in convoy made quite an impression. His adventurous spirit had to acquaint itself with even this vivid experience, traveling in an escorted convoy at a time when the German submarine offensive is in full swing.

FRIDAY, APRIL 24, 1942
114TH DAY-251 DAYS TO FOLLOW

As a consequence of my talk at International House, a well-known couple, Professor Weil and his wife, invited me to have lunch with them at the Hotel Pierre where they're staying.[305] He's the author of the celebrated book about the Dreyfus trial in France that filled the pages of thousands of publications around the whole world. He was familiar with the Basque case as a historian and looked on it with extraordinary sympathy. He thought that our hour of reckoning had arrived in political terms. The conversation was truly interesting.

---

305 The historian Bruno Weil, author of the book *De zaak Dreyfus*, translated into Spanish as *El proceso Dreyfus* (The Dreyfus trial) and published in Buenos Aires in 1941, and his wife.

SATURDAY, APRIL 25, 1942
115TH DAY-250 DAYS TO FOLLOW

Since it was Saturday, I worked on correcting the translation that my friend Intxausti did for me of the memorandum to Carlton Hayes, which was then sent to an English typist for final polishing. I think that it's turned out well. We'll deliver it on Monday, and if Prof. Carlton Hayes is in Washington that day, as is very possible, we'll send it to him there. Afterward, I continued with my book and with the preparation of my university lecture for Monday. In the evening, we all had dinner together at my house.

SUNDAY, APRIL 26, 1942
116TH DAY-249 DAYS TO FOLLOW

This morning, I went over the memorandum again; since there are two copies, it's very possible that Ambassador Carlton Hayes will send one of them to the state department. Afterward, we pursued our ordinary Sunday life of rest with our morning walk and a very good and abundant lunch at Intxausti's house, where Eulogi, the cook from Lekeitio, has not lost "the evil culinary arts" of our excellent indigenous cuisine. These suburbs of New York are pleasant places for rest.

MONDAY, APRIL 27, 1942
117TH DAY-248 DAYS TO FOLLOW

In the morning, I worked at home in order to take the bus that gets me to the station for the 1:08 train. I went directly to the university to start my class at 4:10. We can't get past the end of the eighteenth century. The material is abundant, despite the lack of specialized bibliography. We're now entering the Napoleonic period. What precious research can be done in the future on Basque-French relations in this extremely interesting period!

TUESDAY, APRIL 28, 1942
118TH DAY-247 DAYS TO FOLLOW

After working at home in the morning and after my English lessons, I went to the delegation. I had letters from Aldasoro, from Telesforo in México, and from Cuba, where Delegate Garay told me about Saralegui's impressions and those of our compatriots in that country.[306] They're all animated, in good spirits, and eager to work firmly. This good desire is evident everywhere, and if we know how to develop and then coordinate it, it will bear exceedingly estimable fruit for the good of the cause. We need everyone, and even if many don't deserve praise, but rather the contrary, as a consequence of their previous cowardly attitude, it's impossible to reject them now.

WEDNESDAY, APRIL 29, 1942
119TH DAY-246 DAYS TO FOLLOW

We received a letter from Margari, written in Bilbao. Someone must have carried it, because the freedom of language indicates that it did not go through the censors. In the letter, she says that the disaster of that regime is such that anything we can imagine will fall far short. She says that it's difficult to get used to so much *sikiñeria* and so much *belarrimotz*.[307] It's truly significant that people like Margari, coming from Belgium, an occupied and needy country, have to inform us of this bad impression. Only God knows the discredit into which Franco's regime is going to fall when these circumstances have been overcome.

THURSDAY, APRIL 30, 1942
120TH DAY-245 DAYS TO FOLLOW

We had a reception at the university in honor of President Butler. Despite being over eighty years old, he received and greeted all of us at the entrance to the salon of our club at the university. Mari came with me to the reception. They honored us a great deal, and we were greeted by many professors who wanted to meet us. These Americans are atrociously nice. In addition, they're simple and generous. There's great camaraderie among the professors. A picturesque note was provided by

---

306 José Luis Garay Uribiarte, a native of Areatza, left in January 1938 for Cuba, where he acted as a liaison between the Basques resident on that Caribbean island and the Basque government. He emigrated to Havana through the mediation of a brother who was a priest, a vicar in Santa Clara, and of uncles and nephews who were also established on the island.

307 In Euskara, *zikineria* literally means "filth" and can also figuratively mean something like "nasty business" or "dirty tricks," while *belarrimotz*, literally "with short or cut ears," is a derogatory term sometimes used to refer to those not from Euzkadi or who do not know Euskara.

those old tailcoats of many professors and the evening gowns of these peculiar female professors or professors' wives.

FRIDAY, MAY 1, 1942
121ST DAY-244 DAYS TO FOLLOW

I dedicated the whole day to answering correspondence. I would need a bureau just to be able to respond to Manuel de Irujo. But he's not the only one. It's all our centers, our organizations, our isolated compatriots. They all want a reply, and they all expect one. I'm the one who has to pay the price. But my reply isn't much, because they well deserve something better.

Today we had a letter from Father in Buenos Aires. If he hasn't sent us a telegram by May 6, it's because he's leaving that day for New York. We're impatient to know that he's finally left.

SATURDAY, MAY 2, 1942
122ND DAY-243 DAYS TO FOLLOW

A letter arrived from Aldasoro with better news. Our poor compatriots from the *Alsina* have arrived, after so much suffering in so many countries, including the inhospitable sands of the Sahara. Our people are writing on this account some pages of sacrifice that are the prelude to happier days. Men of great moral temperament, tested by adversity, have arrived in Buenos Aires. It seems that they're all going to find positions. It's the least that they deserve after their odyssey. Aldasoro wrote to me satisfied. As always, he's known how to spend himself for his compatriots. They'll know how to thank him one day. I had great satisfaction from this news.

SUNDAY, MAY 3, 1942
123RD DAY-242 DAYS TO FOLLOW

The day passed calmly, like every Sunday. Today, I abstained completely from work of any kind, because I was very tired by the end of the week. This afternoon, we went for a car ride with all the children. We went to the beach. Very bad and very dirty. We remembered our beaches with their waters in continuous movement and change. We walked along the coast, and adults and children had fun collecting *magurios* along a cliff, taking advantage of the low tide.[308] We brought them home. They were very good. The weather was splendid. Truly restful, between the sun and the breeze.

MONDAY, MAY 4, 1942
124TH DAY-241 DAYS TO FOLLOW

Today at the university I received an announcement about the end of classes. I've been named a member of the tribunal that has to examine various graduate students for the degree of doctor of philosophy awarded by Columbia University. At the same time, they sent me the notice extending my position as professor in the history department for a year (until July 1943). This distinction given to me at a university that passes as the best in the world is really something to be grateful for. I'll never know how to thank these good professors sufficiently for the friendliness with which they distinguish me, without anything on my part to deserve it.

TUESDAY, MAY 5, 1942
125TH DAY-240 DAYS TO FOLLOW

Today, after studying in the morning, I had my English class and went to the delegation. As they had informed me, I had a visit from Mr. Dalles,[309] the head of President Roosevelt's Coordination and Information Office. The English are the ones who talked about us and introduced us. An interesting and very important conversation. In the end, we'll probably be able to coordinate our services with theirs and do useful work. I hope that this time, it's serious, since otherwise, time is wasted and a lot of energy for the common cause is squandered.

---

308 The word *magurio* in Euskara means "periwinkle."
309 During World War II, Allen Welsh Dulles (1893–1969) was an important member of the Office of Strategic Services (OSS), the predecessor of the Central Intelligence Agency (CIA), of which he would be the director years later. At the time, he was the New York head of operations for the Office of the Coordinator of Information (COI), itself a predecessor of the spy services just mentioned.

WEDNESDAY, MAY 6, 1942
126TH DAY-239 DAYS TO FOLLOW

I had an interesting conversation with Professor Tannenbaum at the university. We talked about the future of our problems and then about the future of Europe and America. He's a good friend of ours. I received a friendly letter from the ambassador to Franco, Prof. Carlton Hayes, my good friend. He acknowledged receipt of the memorandum and thanked me for it very much. He characterized it as important and congratulated himself for having met me before taking up his post in Spain. The English and American heads also indicated that they were satisfied with yesterday's meeting. They've announced an invitation for next week.

THURSDAY, MAY 7, 1942
127TH DAY-238 DAYS TO FOLLOW

In the morning, I continued my work at home. After my English lesson, to the delegation. Today I attended a concert by the Catalan pianist Villalta, a magnificent recitalist.[310] The Catalan community of artists, painters, musicians, and sculptors was there en masse. The Catalans are little by little making their unity a reality. They have interesting elements with which to do useful work. They're provided with valuable artistic elements that, if they knew how to take good advantage of them, could perform truly effective service for Catalonia's cause. Professor Villalta performed one of Father Donostia's compositions in our honor.[311]

FRIDAY, MAY 8, 1942
128TH DAY-237 DAYS TO FOLLOW

In the afternoon, I went to the delegation. This morning, we turned in the first half of my book to be translated. I'd like to have it finished by

---

310 Alexandre Vilalta (1904–1984) was a Catalan piano virtuoso. During the Spanish Civil War, he worked with the Generalitat, giving concerts in France and South America. At the end of the conflict, he moved to the United States, making his debut at New York's City Hall and giving concerts at Carnegie Hall in the same city, where he was acclaimed the pianist of the season. He remained in the United States until 1947, when he moved to Mexico.

311 José Gonzalo Zulaica y Arregui (1886–1956) was a Capuchin friar and a musician. Following the tradition of his order, he adopted the religious name of Fray José Antonio de San Sebastián and was known as Aita or Padre Donostia.

the end of the month. The work that comes up—letters, visits, reports, etc.—delays its completion. This evening was the banquet with which the Columbia history professors were honoring Ambassador Carlton Hayes. I attended. The ambassador congratulated me on the report I sent him and told me that he had sent the copy to the state department. He spoke a few words emphasizing the difficulty of his mission of preventing Spain from entering the war.

SATURDAY, MAY 9, 1942
129TH DAY-236 DAYS TO FOLLOW

I worked at home all day. On the Fridays and Saturdays that they leave me in peace, I work shut up in my office in order to try to get caught up on my correspondence, on which I'm always very behind. I physically don't have time for so many things, despite the fact that every day I hear the clock strike three in the morning as I'm working. How I miss my stenographers and typists in Paris and Euzkadi, my good old Secun and Ramón! Here I have to do it myself instead of dictating, losing time that I saved for other things there. They must also wish to be with me.

SUNDAY, MAY 10, 1942
130TH DAY-235 DAYS TO FOLLOW

During this morning's walk, my friend Intxausti told us about his interview with Ambassador Carlton Hayes. This good friend still thanked Intxausti for the fact that I was at the dinner at which the Columbia professors said goodbye to him. Having had some hesitation about going to that homage so as not to put him into a corner with my presence, in view of my significance and his for the post to which he has been appointed, I see that on the contrary, he's still thanking me for it. He liked the memorandum that I gave him a great deal and has once again said as much.

MONDAY, MAY 11, 1942
131ST DAY-234 DAYS TO FOLLOW

Today Ana Belén and Mari were invited to Ambassador Carlton Hayes's house by his wife. They came back enchanted by how they were treated as honored guests. If Franco knew! The ambassador's wife took some "photos" of Aintzane and Joseba to send to Mother and Margari, and for them to send them on to Louvain if they can. Those poor people will be very happy. The ambassador's wife and her husband the professor are both people of endearing friendliness and affection for us. We've found true friends in them.

TUESDAY, MAY 12, 1942
132ND DAY-233 DAYS TO FOLLOW

Today I pursued my ordinary life. I went to my English class. I'm now starting to think that I've gotten a little beyond my difficulties and clumsiness. I'm very clumsy with languages and with so many things. Afterward, at the delegation, I received correspondence from various locations, Santo Domingo among them. The young lawyer Jesús de Galíndez is carrying out his position as delegate very well there and has written a very interesting book on *La contribución de los vascos al derecho internacional* [The Basque contribution to international law]. He studies the figures of Vitoria and Bolibar in order to reveal how Vitoria and Bolibar are connected to the thought of the race.[312]

WEDNESDAY, MAY 13, 1942
133RD DAY-232 DAYS TO FOLLOW

I continued reading Galíndez's book. I physically don't have time to write a prologue for it that says anything of substance. This new Basque intellectual, full of future promise, well deserves it. But my prologue will be pedestrian, stealing a little time from all these rather urgent tasks. I also received letters from Ireland, from good old Don José Camiña and from my dear friends Manu de Egileor and Elías de Gallastegi, who were answering other letters from me. They're well and full of spirit. May God help us all![313]

---

312 Francisco de Vitoria (1486–1546) was a Dominican theologian considered the founder of international law.

313 José Camiña Beraza (1878–1953) was an important Bilbao capitalist who had to go into exile during the 1936 war due to his Social Christian ideas, which were opposed to the rebels, and established himself in Donibane Lohizune. He succeeded in fleeing to Ireland before the German occupation of France and remained there until the end of World War II. For his part, Elías Gallastegi Uriarte (1892–1974) was a nationalist leader and the chief mover behind the newspaper *Jagi-Jagi*. Opposed to Basque participation in the Spanish Civil War, he succeeded in going into exile in Ireland, where he remained until the end of World War II. Finally, on Manu Egileor see note 40.

THURSDAY, MAY 14, 1942
134TH DAY-231 DAYS TO FOLLOW

Today we had lunch at the Rockefeller Center Club at the invitation of Mr. Dabaks and Mr. Thomas, the organizational head and secretary of President Roosevelt's committee chaired by Colonel Donovan.[314] The conversation was very interesting and important. It seems to me that we're going to do something positive, because these men want to work firmly, leaving diplomatic niceties behind. It's about time! They've become convinced that the danger is in waiting and leaving things alone while the adversary is working every day with tenacity and without scruples of any kind.

FRIDAY, MAY 15, 1942
135TH DAY-230 DAYS TO FOLLOW

We received a letter from Venezuela explaining the pleasant consequences of the celebration of the Day of the Fatherland, the festivities for which were attended by the British minister and his wife, among others, and by distinguished Venezuelans. Our men are behaving very well everywhere. They're working with enormous faith and enthusiasm. Many of them are simple people, but for this very reason, their work attracts more attention. I'm going to congratulate them with all enthusiasm so that they continue with an effort that has efficacious repercussions on all sides.

SATURDAY, MAY 16, 1942
136TH DAY-229 DAYS TO FOLLOW

The young lady who is translating my book paid us a visit. She's very satisfied, offers grand compliments. Since we're well forewarned against all such things by now, we want to wait for the end. She says that the book will attract great interest because "it's divine." These affirmations

---

314 William Joseph Donovan was the creator, at President Roosevelt's request, of the first U.S. general intelligence agency independent of the military spy agencies, the Office of the Coordinator of Information (COI). He also led the COI's successor, the Office of Strategic Services (OSS). The name that we have transcribed as Mr. Dabaks, on the other hand, given that the *lehendakari* describes him as head of the COI, the same description applied to the person whose name we have transcribed as Mr. Dalles in the entry for May 5, 1942, seems to refer to Allen Dulles, at the time the COI's New York head of operations. The Thomas mentioned must be Gregory H. Thomas, also a top COI official in New York. Months later, after the creation of the Office of Strategic Services (OSS), he moved to the OSS's Madrid station.

in the mouth of a Peruvian young lady, one of those who are generally so refined: she has a certain delicacy that I'm not sure is best for making a severe critique of the book. But in the end, it's better to hear things of this sort than other, more unpleasant ones. I worked the rest of the day.

SUNDAY, MAY 17, 1942
137TH DAY-228 DAYS TO FOLLOW

Today Manu Sota was absent from our classic Sunday gathering. He went to spend the "weekend" with some French friends. We went for a walk. Ricardo Leizaola is here with us; he hasn't yet returned to Venezuela, because he hasn't finished sorting out his affairs involving the Caracas newspaper. The English are slow, very slow. It's too bad that many services and other, worse or more serious things are forfeited because of their slowness. Accustomed to hit the mark and triumph, they put their trust in time. Very well, but hammering away every day is safer.

MONDAY, MAY 18, 1942
138TH DAY-227 DAYS TO FOLLOW

I stayed at home working all day. I'm declining invitations of all kinds, which are multiplying these days. Committees for aid to China, banquets and luncheons for aid to Russia. Many interesting, prominent figures from all countries attend these events, but I have to finish the book, which I wish was the book of Euzkadi! I'm now getting to the last chapters, which are always the most difficult, and at the end I want to firmly attack the topic of the dangers of the third front, that is, the intolerant and dictatorially-inclined Latin countries.

TUESDAY, MAY 19, 1942
139TH DAY-226 DAYS TO FOLLOW

Teodoro's saint's day. May God help him to be what we will all wish in life. Today I received a courteous letter from Professor Chamberlain. He invited me to lunch to introduce me to Mr. Bridgewater, the head of Columbia University Press, who wants to commission me to write a book on the history of Euzkadi for one of the university's special schools. It's a very important commission. I'll see about doing what is most advantageous with respect to the fatherland, since this book would constitute a very interesting element of propaganda.³¹⁵ Little by little, we're penetrating into this people's greatest esteem.

WEDNESDAY, MAY 20, 1942
140TH DAY-225 DAYS TO FOLLOW

Today is *ama*'s saint's day.³¹⁶ I suppose that the message of congratulations that we all signed and sent her a month ago will have arrived or will be on the point of arriving. May God preserve her health and protect her, along with the rest of the family, until the day we can all reunite with the triumph of justice. Today I did one of my usual fine jobs. I had an examination at the university as part of a tribunal with five other professors. Well, I got it into my head that the 20th was Thursday and didn't go to the examination. This afternoon, I went to the university to inform myself about the examination "tomorrow." Professor Tannenbaum, laughing out loud, told me that it was held today and that from now on, I'm a true professor. There's always one . . . like me.

THURSDAY, MAY 21, 1942
141ST DAY-224 DAYS TO FOLLOW

Today we put some points on the scoreboard. Captain Cobeaga sent us the agreed telegram to let us know that the instructions for Spanish-flagged Basque merchant ships have been changed. The English and American services have set about capturing the new instructions. Each of them wants to get there first, but the Captain won't do it, only to the person I indicate. For this reason, we're on the agenda of the English and American services. The zeal and patriotism of our people are estimable; they put their lives on the line to provide us successes like these, colossally transcendent and important ones.

---

315 The composition of a book on the history of Euzkadi, initially a Columbia University commission, became one of the *lehendakari*'s most cherished cultural projects. José Antonio Agirre felt that the project should be a collective work by Basque historians, with the *lehendakari* reserving direction and authorship for himself by virtue of his position as president. Writers of the stature of Jesús Galíndez and Ildefonso Gurrutxaga collaborated on the work, and a manuscript was completed and sent to Buenos Aires for publication, but even so, the book never came out.

316 Perhaps the celebration of his mother's saint's day and the desire to pay her homage led the *lehendakari* to give his book *De Guernica* this date, even though he says in the entry for May 27, 1942, that he was "working on the book to see whether I can finish it once and for all."

FRIDAY, MAY 22, 1942
142ND DAY-223 DAYS TO FOLLOW

The Americans informed us that our joint work should start quickly. That a bank account will be opened so that we don't lack resources for our travels and those of our friends. It seems that this is serious. With elements and support, the activity of the Basques in the Americas can be singularly important. They've finally understood this. President Roosevelt's Donovan Committee is the organization that we've seen working most effectively up to now. We'll see whether our activities get started properly and successfully.

SATURDAY, MAY 23, 1942
143RD DAY-222 DAYS TO FOLLOW

I worked hard all day to get to the next-to-last chapter of my book, the name of which I still don't know. They change the titles here, and it's necessary to comply with what the agencies decide. The agencies' scheming is usually enormous. Since it was the agency that asked for my book, and not me asking them, I hope that they'll move somewhat quickly to get it published. So that I could work in peace, they took Joseba to Intxausti's house. When he's home, it's impossible to work calmly.

SUNDAY, MAY 24, 1942
144TH DAY-221 DAYS TO FOLLOW

Pentecost. As I did a year ago, as I've done many times, I asked God that the Spirit of truth, which is wisdom and right judgment, descend on all my compatriots, so that each one at his post may know how to carry out the mission that has been commended to him. We went for a walk and rested, commenting on the fact that next Sunday, Father will be with us, after so many uncertainties about whether they would or would not grant him the appointment that he was so anxious for in order to be near his grandchildren. May God help him, and may he arrive with all good fortune.

MONDAY, MAY 25, 1942
145TH DAY-220 DAYS TO FOLLOW

Today was my lunch with Professor Chamberlain and Mr. Bridgewater, the member of Columbia's press council. They're commissioning me to write a book about Basque history, especially the Basque movement for freedom. He said that our case is a sympathetic one and that it's necessary for Americans to know about it. They want the book to be four hundred pages typed, which they reckon comes to almost six hundred pages printed. In sum, these Americans are formidable. I wish it would occur to them to make us free! Because we will be. But today we can't complain. Everything is moving little by little toward that end for which our people has suffered so much sorrow and given so much blood.

TUESDAY, MAY 26, 1942
146TH DAY-219 DAYS TO FOLLOW

I forgot to mention that my university classes ended last Monday with the start of the examination period. Due to the nature of my class, lectures, I didn't have to examine anyone, fortunately. Next year, if things keep going as they have up to now, it will be a different matter.

Today Mrs. Elizalde invited us to dinner at the Chinese restaurant on Seventh Avenue. We ate Chinese food, including the famous *pan-tzit*, which is certainly unique. Mrs. Elizalde thereby fulfilled a promise she made a while back to take us to a classic place. Intxausti and his wife also came. We enjoyed ourselves a lot amid subjects of Chan Kai-chek.

WEDNESDAY, MAY 27, 1942
147TH DAY-218 DAYS TO FOLLOW

Since my university classes are over, I stayed home all day, working on my book to see whether I can finish it once and for all. It's always the end that's the hardest in work of this kind. Afterward, right at the end of the afternoon, I went to New York to have dinner with the English consul, Mr. List, who wanted to meet me. He's a typical Englishman, very friendly, but very English. The conversation was interesting. He reminisced a great deal about his years in Bilbao between 1919 and 1923. Afterward, he served as consul in various countries, both in Europe and in the Americas. His impressions of London—where he was in November—were of great interest.

THURSDAY, MAY 28, 1942
148TH DAY-217 DAYS TO FOLLOW

I worked at home in the morning. I prepared the summary of the Euzkadi history that they're going to commission from me. I touched on the most important points, relating Basque historical events to those of worldwide scope wherever possible. I'll ask all our scholars for information and documents, because given how little we have available here and given the summer of travel I'm expecting, it will be a bit difficult for me to be able to finish so extensive and important a work by myself. At the delegation in the afternoon, a representative of Nelson Rockfeller's coordinator visited me to talk about South America, requesting information on the Basques.

Index

A

Abaroa Rodríguez, Enrique 173, 174, 177, 182
Abramovitz, Max 278
Abreu, Pedro 85, 86, 91
Agirre Barrenetxea-Arando, Teodoro 31
Agirre Cerda, Pedro 195
Agirre Esquibel, Valentín 201, 202, 203, 209, 225, 230, 231, 248, 266, 269, 271
Agirre Etxebarria 199
Agirre Guisasola, José Urbano de 185, 186, 188
Agirre Lekube, Ángel 42, 264
Agirre Lekube, Encarnación 56, 100, 110
Agirre-Lekube, family 30
Agirre Lekube, Ignacio 30
Agirre Lekube, Iñaki 264
Agirre Lekube, José Antonio (Álvarez Lastra, José Andrés) 7, 8, 9, 10, 12, 13, 15, 19, 27, 35, 41, 43, 44, 46, 56, 63, 69, 72, 76, 80, 81, 100, 119, 135, 156, 159, 160, 181, 184, 190, 191, 195, 199, 221, 231, 243, 244, 245, 257, 269, 271, 293
Agirre Lekube, Juan Mari 8, 10, 30, 81, 109, 122, 123, 162, 190, 204, 252, 253, 261
Agirre Lekube, Teodoro 94, 264, 292
Agirre Lekube, Teresa 9, 66, 144, 167
Agirre Lekube, Tomás 9, 66, 148, 161, 264

Agirre Zabala, Aintzane 76, 97, 104, 105, 108, 109, 115, 117, 121, 124, 126, 127, 129, 132, 138, 139, 140, 141, 143, 147, 150, 152, 162, 186, 200, 206, 263, 282, 289

Agirre-Zabala, family 38, 41, 118, 190, 270

Agirre Zabala, Joseba 97, 98, 99, 102, 104, 105, 108, 109, 112, 115, 116, 117, 121, 124, 125, 126, 127, 128, 129, 132, 138, 139, 140, 141, 142, 143, 145, 147, 150, 152, 155, 159, 161, 162, 186, 200, 206, 210, 242, 248, 263, 289, 294

Aizpuru, Luis 182

Aketxe de la Hera, María 41, 261

Alba, duke of. *Véase* Fitz-James y Falcó, Jacobo

Alcalá Zamora y Torres, Niceto 167, 230

Aldasoro Galarza, Ramón María 9, 26, 47, 77, 145, 155, 156, 165, 166, 167, 169, 171, 172, 173, 174, 177, 179, 180, 181, 182, 184, 185, 186, 190, 210, 211, 212, 250, 260, 269, 272, 284, 286

Alembert, Jean le Rond d' 18, 20

Alfonso XIII 34, 42, 50

Algar, James 162

Altuna, Ignacio Manuel de 16

Álvarez, Antonio 10

Álvarez del Vayo Olloqui, Julio 165, 210, 213

Álvarez Lastra, José Andrés. *Véase* Agirre Lekube, José Antonio (Álvarez Lastra, José Andrés)

Alvear Pacheco, Máximo Marcelo Torcuato de 188

André, Marius 55

Araujo, Rómulo 9, 10, 12, 20, 23, 28, 38, 40, 41, 44, 45, 47, 49, 50, 51, 52, 53, 63, 72, 73

Archanco Zubiri, Pablo 9, 182

Argiarro, Jon 271

Arias Madrid, Arnulfo 79, 80, 81

Arin, Eugenio 182

Arin, Juan 182

Arin, Pedro 182

Armstrong, Samuel 162
Arrieta (Basque refugee who acted as a courier for the lehendakari's 1941 Gabon message) 221
Arrigorriaga Larrazabal, Luisa 7
Arrigorriaga, Rodolfo 7, 65
Arrigorriaga, Trini 8, 66
Arteche, Pedro 180
Artigas, José Gervasio 183
Ascoli, Max 245, 246, 247, 250, 253, 256, 263, 269, 273
Asporosa Aristondo, Cesáreo 8, 100, 152, 253
Atxurra Madarieta, Pedro 270, 271
Augustin of Vienna 14
Aunós Pérez, Eduardo 166
Aznar Sarachaga, Santiago 136, 137
Aznar Zubigaray, Manuel 52, 53, 54

B

Baldomir, Alfredo 185
Barbieri, Antonio María 185
Barrena (Basque resident in Uruguay) 182
Basaldua Ibarmia, Pedro 156
Basterrechea y Zaldibar, Francisco 144, 156, 220, 273
Basterretxea Arzadun, Néstor 268
Batista Zaldibar, Fulgencio 147, 230
Beebe, Fort 162
Beotegi, Juan 198, 199, 200
Berdyaev, Nikolai Aleksandrovitch 165
Berthier de Sauvigny, Emmanuel de 9, 66
Bigeard, Georges 8
Bikuña Hormaza, Miren 154
Bismarck, Otto von 13, 14
Bolívar, Simón 45, 55, 79, 198, 290
Borbón, Juan de 34

Borgioli, Dino 160, 161
Branden de Reeth, baron Albert van den 10, 66
Brena, Tomás G. 184
Bridgewater (head of Columbia University Press) 292, 295
Brüning, Heinrich 244
Butler, Nicholas Murray 205, 208, 285

C

Caffery, Jefferson 161, 178
Camiña Beraza, José 290
Casado López, Segismundo 196
Castelao, Alfonso Daniel Rodríguez 261
Castillo, Ramón S. 170, 187
Caudenhove-Kalergi, Richard 243
Cauwelaert, Frans Van 266, 267
Chamberlain, Joseph Perkins 241, 244, 271, 278, 292, 295
Chiang Kai-shek 32, 295
Chotek, Sophia 84
Chouy Terra, Alberto 185
Churchill, Winston 125, 145, 146, 147, 151
Cicero, Marcus Tullius 27, 28, 29, 33, 34, 36, 39, 50
Cicognani, Amleto Giovanni 264
Columbus, Christopher 53
Companys i Jover, Lluís 28, 195
Constantino Arrigorriaga, Antonio 7, 65
Constantino Carral, Florencio 7
Couturier, Marie-Alain 251
Cunchillos Manterola, Santiago 9, 182

D

Degrelle, Léon 49
Demarbaix, Edouard 8, 66
Despradel, family 43

Despradel Pennell, Roberto Luis 11, 14, 27, 28, 29, 31, 32, 33, 36, 37, 38, 39, 47, 49, 50, 51, 55, 65, 66, 72, 78, 80, 84, 85, 88, 90, 91, 96, 97, 105, 122, 126, 127, 130, 135, 160, 199

Díaz de Mendibil Rotaeche, Eduardo 105, 262

Disney, Walt 162

Donostia, Father. *Véase* Zulaica y Arregui, José Gonzalo

Donovan, William Joseph 209, 291, 294

Dreyfus, Alfred 283

Ducattillon, Joseph Vincent 165

Duggan, Laurence 244, 245, 257

Dulles, Allen Welsh 287, 291

E

Echevarria, Roberto 264, 265

Egileor Orueta, Manu 20, 290

Elizalde, María Luisa 242, 261, 267, 295

Elorriaga (president of the New York Basque center) 209

Emo, E. W. 14

Enrique (chauffeur of the Dominican legation in Germany) 32, 52, 57, 96, 105, 108

Enriquillo (Dominican Indian chief) 35, 74

Erezuma, Eulogia 284

Espinosa de los Monteros y Abellán, Eugenio María 24

Estévez y Romero, Luis 35, 76

Estornés Lasa, Bernardo 262

Etxabe (captain in the merchant marine) 224

Etxepherdia, Ramuntcho. *Véase* Sota MacMahon, Ramón de la

F

Ferguson, Norman 162

Fernández Artucio, Hugo 223, 228

Fernández Cuesta y Melero, Raimundo 163, 164

Ferro, António 69, 190, 191

Fitz-James Stuart y Falcó, Jacobo 188
Ford, George Barry 207, 215
Fouilhoux, Jacques André 278
Franco Bahamonde, Francisco 24, 53, 73, 131, 163, 184, 187, 191, 196, 208,
    210, 218, 222, 224, 225, 230, 231, 242, 285, 288, 289
Franz Ferdinand, archduke of Austria 84

G

Galíndez Suárez, Jesús 199, 268, 269, 290, 293
Gallart, Mr. and Mrs. (Jewish refugees) 151
Gallastegi Uriarte, Elías 290
Gamboa Aurrecoechea, Joaquín 10, 66, 148
Gamboa Ibargaray, Teresa 276
Gamboa Urcelay, Marino 8, 200, 201, 204, 205, 209, 213, 226, 230, 232, 248,
    251, 257, 263, 271, 274, 275, 276
Garate, José María 7
Garay Uribiarte, José Luis 284, 285
Garmendia, Dionisio 180, 182
Gay y Forner, Vicente 59, 60, 61, 83
Gerrikaetxebarria (captain in the merchant marine) 217
Gil Borges, Esteban 41
Godoy Alcayaga, Lucila. *Véase* Mistral, Gabriela
Gómez Báez, Máximo 56, 57
Gondra Garro, Ángel 225
González Roa, Edmundo 7, 65
Gorgolini, Pedro 74, 75
Gorriti, Rodolfo 189
Gracia Colás, Juan 81
Guani, Alberto 182
Guardia Jaén, Carlos Alfonso 7, 65
Guardia Jaén, Germán Gil 10, 12, 35, 44, 45, 46, 47, 48, 49, 50, 51, 56, 73, 79,
    80, 81, 82, 84, 85, 86, 87, 88, 95, 96, 122, 123, 241
Guardia Jaén, Mrs. 10, 66

Guerra, María Arrigorriaga, widow. *Véase* Zabala Aketxe, Mari (Guerra, María Arrigorriaga, widow)
Guisasola, Ricardo 180, 182
Guridi Bidaola, Jesús 231
Gurmendi (Argentine industrialist) 283
Gurrutxaga Ansola, Ildefonso 293
Gustavus II Adolfus of Sweden 97
Gustav V of Sweden 116, 124

H

Halpak (professor at the Sorbonne) 228
Handley, Jim 162
Hansson, Per Albin 134
Harrison, Wallace 278
Hartmann, Paul 13
Hayes, Carlton Joseph Huntley 205, 212, 216, 219, 251, 278, 280, 281, 283, 284, 288, 289
Hee, T. 162
Herrera, Luis Alberto de 185
Hess, Rudolf 94
Hitler, Adolf 24, 28, 29, 30, 36, 39, 59, 76, 107, 113
Hörbiger, Paul 14
Hormaeche, Aitor 180
Hull, Cordell 244

I

Ibargaray Artaza, María 200, 226, 276
Irala Irala, Antonio 7, 273
Irazusta Muñoa, Jon Andoni 195, 197, 198, 199, 200
Irazusta Muñoa, Rosario 198
Irizar, Javier 181
Irujo Ollo, Andrés 184
Irujo Ollo, Eusebio 268

Irujo Ollo, Manuel 26, 28, 77, 105, 191, 199, 202, 216, 220, 223, 229, 232, 256, 257, 286

Iturbide, Julio V. 146, 180, 181, 185

J

Jackson, Wilfred 162

Jannings, Emil 87

Jauregui Lasanta, Julio 137, 248, 253, 264, 276

Jones (former British vice consul in Bilbao) 154, 191

Justo, Agustín Pedro 188

K

Keyserling, Hermann, count 165, 166

Kobeaga (captain in the merchant marine) 242, 293

Krüger, Stephanus Johannes Paulus 35, 87

L

Lacroix, L. Luis Perú de 45

Landaburu Fernández de Betoño, Francisco Javier 21, 81, 96, 123, 136, 137

Landau, brothers (Jewish refugees) 150

Larrauri, Ana Belén 200, 262, 263, 289

Lasa Ercilla, Martín 8, 252, 253, 261

Lasa, Javier de 8

Lasarte Arana, José María 136, 137, 204, 248, 253, 264, 276

Lasarte, Elpidio R. 185, 186

Le Corbusier, Charles-Edouard Jeanneret-Gris 252

Leizaola Sánchez, Jesús María 63, 136, 137, 198, 202, 212

Leizaola Sánchez, Ricardo 212, 282, 283, 292

Lekube Aranburu, Bernardina 95

Leturia Mendia, Pedro 45

Liebeneiner, Wolgang 13

Lincoln, Abraham 254

List (British consul) 295

Lizaso Ilarraza, José Ignacio 8, 66, 191, 195, 204, 216, 220, 223

Lombana Foncea, José Luis de la 223

López Mendizabal, Isaac 9, 182, 184, 210

Lore (American boy, friend of Aintzane and Joseba Agirre) 282

Luske, Hamilton 162

M

Madariaga Astigarraga, Juan 144

Madariaga Rojo, Salvador de 58, 59

Maeztu Whitnay, Ramiro de 23

Magaz y Pers, Antonio 187

Malin, Patrick Murphy 204

María (assistant hired by the Agirre-Zabala family in Río de Janeiro) 178

Maritain, Jacques 164, 266, 273

Martí, José 31, 35, 39

Matisse, Henri 251

Matsuoka, Yosuke 57, 59, 62

Mauriac, François 39

Maurois, André 164

Maurras, Charles 55

Méndez (employee of the Spanish embassy in Germany) 86

Mendivil, Javier 185

Mendizabal (Basque from Sopuerta resident in Puerto Rico) 198

Mendizabal, Vidal 209

Mikolei, E. 10, 66

Millar (head of the British services in the United States) 263

Miquelarena Regueiro, Jacinto 46, 47

Mistral, Gabriela 178

Mitre, Bartolomé 57, 186

Monzón Ortiz de Urruela, Telesforo 86, 144, 167, 204, 211, 212, 217, 253, 284

Mounier, Emmanuel 165

Mugica (Tolosan resident in Río Grande) 181

Mujica, José Tomás 182
Mussolini, Benito 19, 75
Mussorgsky, Modest Petrovich 163

N

Napoleon I 279
Nardiz Bengoetxea, Gonzalo 136, 137
Navarro, Nicolás E. 45
Negrín López, Juan 165, 195, 213, 230, 231, 265
Noldan, Svend 26

O

Olazabal Gómez, Juan 65
Olivares Larrondo, José (Tellagorri) 220, 268, 273
Olivera, Ricardo 11, 14, 65
Olivier, Maurice 204, 205
Orbe Urquiza, Jesús 10
Orbe Urquiza, Pedro 10
Oriol y Urigüen, José Luis de 265
Ortega y Gasset, José 58, 59, 166
Ortiz Echagüe, Fernando 270
Ortiz Lizardi, Roberto Marcelino 186, 187, 277, 278
Ortiz (son of the president of Argentina) 278
Ortuzar Peñeñuri, Luis 202, 211, 232, 255, 263
Oshima, Hiroshi 59, 62
Otegui, Adrián 182

P

Pacelli, Eugenio Maria Giovanni. *Véase* Pius XII
Parsons, Wilfrid 244, 278
Pascal, Blaise 39
Pastoriza, Andrés 27, 83, 90, 133
Paulding, C. Gouverneur 278

Paysé Reyes, Héctor 184
Paz, José Clemente 186

Pelan, family (daughter and son-in-law of the mayor of Bayonne, Jacques Simonet) 218, 261
Peñaflorida, Munibe Idiaquez, Francisco Xavier, count of 16
Persson, family 104, 125, 127, 129, 132, 136
Persson, Mr. 104, 110, 112, 113, 114, 117, 122, 125, 126, 128, 129, 131, 132, 133, 134, 135, 136, 137
Persson, Mrs. 117, 124, 126, 127, 132
Petterson. *Véase* Persson, Mr.
Philip II 187
Picavea Leguia, Rafael 136, 137, 253
Pi Sunyer, Carles 216, 224, 232, 264, 274
Pius VII 45
Pius XI 187
Pius XII 215
Plutarch of Chaeronea 12, 13, 16, 17, 18, 19, 39, 88, 89, 90
Prieto Tuero, Indalecio 163, 195, 229, 230, 231, 248
Primo de Rivera y Orbaneja, Miguel 187
Princip, Gavrilo 84

R

Raguer, Hilari 187
Regules, Dardo 185
Reynold, Gonzague de 17, 39, 40, 42, 43, 49
Ribbentrop, Joachim von 59, 156
Roberts, Bill 162
Roca, Julio A. 188
Rockefeller, Nelson Aldrich 209, 240, 245, 269, 278, 296
Rodó, José Enrique 78, 79, 87
Rodríguez Larreta, Eduardo 184
Rojo Lluch, Vicente 165

Romains, Jules 164

Rommel, Erwin 67

Roosevelt, Franklin Delano 52, 122, 145, 146, 147, 204, 209, 214, 215, 223, 237, 238, 244, 287, 291, 294

Ros Agudo, Manuel 116

Rousseau, Jean-Jacques 16, 17, 18, 19, 20

Ruiz Guiñazú, Enrique 188

S

Saint Francis Xavier 136

Saint Ignatius of Loyola 139

Saint Paul 167

Salazar, António de Oliveira 69, 70, 190, 191

Sánchez Arana, Ramón 218, 289

Sánchez Coello, Alonso 139

Sánchez de Lozada, Enrique 257, 259, 269

Sánchez Lustrino 160

San Martín, José de 57

Santoro, Cesare 28, 29, 43

Saralegui Arrizubieta, Francisco 279, 284

Sassmann, Hans 14

Saterfield, Paul 162

Schipa, Tito 160, 161

Serra Moret, Manuel 261

Serrano Suñer, Ramón 163, 164

Shakespeare, William 192

Silva Freitas, José Sebastián da 8, 66

Simonet, Jacques 218

Solaetxe, Alejandro 199

Sota Aburto, Manu de la 7, 26, 65, 126, 160, 194, 195, 200, 201, 202, 206, 207, 208, 210, 214, 215, 218, 220, 222, 226, 228, 229, 235, 238, 239, 241, 242, 249, 251, 258, 260, 263, 265, 266, 270, 271, 274, 276, 278, 280, 281, 283, 292

Sota MacMahon, Ramón de la 200, 207, 209, 228, 235, 236, 251, 257, 263, 271
Spellman, Francis Joseph 215, 253, 264
Stalin, Iosif Vissarionovich Dzhugashvili 122
Steinhoff, Hans 87
Stevenson, family 169
Stevenson, Mrs. 154
Stevenson, Ralph Corwallis 15, 16, 153, 154, 155, 156, 157, 159, 166, 167, 172, 191
Sturzo, Luigi 244, 266
Sun Yat-sen 32

T

Tamara, Sonia 205
Tannenbaum, Frank 219, 278, 288, 293
Tellagorri. *Véase* Olivares Larrondo, José
Thomas, Gregory H. 291
Toja, Pedro 209
Tondo, Alfonso 271
Torre Larrinaga, Eliodoro de la 136, 137, 202, 204
Trias i Peitx, Josep Maria 204
Trujillo y Molina, Rafael Leónidas 268
Txantxote (individual from Bergara) 143

U

Ugarte, Sebastián 244, 270
Unamuno y Jugo, Miguel de 58, 59, 69, 73, 166
Uraga, Juan 180
Uriarte, Juan Domingo 180, 182
Uribarri, Mario Pablo 180
Uriburu, Guillermo 270
Uriburu, José Evaristo 270
Uriburu, José Félix 270

Urquijo Ybarra, Julio 17
Urrutia Rodeño, Secundino 218, 289
Urrutxua Arano, Txomin 199

V

Vaca (Colombian resident in Berlin) 47, 48
Valeri, Valerio 264
Vargas, Getúlio 158
Vignaux, Paul 228
Viguri Ruiz de Olano, Ramón 253
Vilalta, Alexandre 288
Villalaz (Panamanian ambassador to Germany) 11, 14, 30, 38, 47, 49, 50, 51, 52, 63, 65, 66, 67, 73, 74, 75, 80, 81, 82, 85, 86, 88
Viñas Calixto, Joaquín 9
Vitoria, Francisco de 290

W

Wallace, Henry Agard 257, 269
Washington, George 259
Weil, Bruno 283
Wilhelm, Swedish prince 104

Y

Ybarnegaray, Jean 46, 47
Ynchausti, family 202, 205, 206, 218, 249, 260, 263, 265, 266, 269, 281
Ynchausti, Manuel 7, 26, 27, 65, 83, 84, 86, 88, 98, 101, 103, 104, 110, 111, 112, 113, 114, 116, 117, 118, 123, 124, 132, 133, 134, 144, 151, 152, 153, 155, 156, 157, 160, 161, 162, 163, 165, 166, 168, 171, 172, 173, 174, 189, 192, 193, 194, 195, 197, 199, 200, 201, 202, 206, 207, 209, 214, 215, 219, 220, 221, 222, 226, 227, 228, 232, 235, 237, 239, 240, 241, 242, 243, 245, 246, 247, 248, 251, 254, 255, 257, 258, 261, 262, 263, 267, 269, 270, 276, 278, 279, 280, 282, 284, 289, 294, 295
Yoldi, Tomás 182

Yrigoyen, Hipólito 188

Z

Zabala Aketxe, Constantino 148
Zabala Aketxe, Ignacio 41
Zabala Aketxe, Manu 154
Zabala Aketxe, Margari 41, 106, 112, 123, 261, 285, 289
Zabala Aketxe, Mari (Guerra, María Arrigorriaga, widow) 41, 44, 45, 52, 53, 54, 56, 58, 63, 76, 77, 79, 80, 81, 82, 85, 86, 91, 92, 93, 94, 95, 98, 99, 101, 102, 104, 105, 108, 109, 111, 112, 117, 119, 122, 124, 125, 126, 127, 128, 129, 130, 132, 134, 135, 136, 137, 138, 139, 140, 144, 145, 147, 148, 152, 153, 155, 157, 159, 160, 162, 163, 164, 165, 168, 181, 186, 190, 192, 193, 196, 197, 199, 200, 204, 206, 227, 232, 235, 237, 238, 248, 251, 255, 257, 262, 263, 265, 278, 285, 289
Zabala Aketxe, Santiago 41
Zabala Aketxe, Vicente 148
Zabala Arrigorriaga, Constantino 7, 8, 65, 71, 105, 144, 148, 174, 261
Zabala (Basque resident in Uruguay) 182
Zabala, Bruno Mauricio de 183
Zabala, Carmen. *Véase* Zabala Aketxe, Mari (Guerra, María Arrigorriaga, widow)
Zabal, Jon 202, 248, 266, 271
Zalduondo, Carmen 200
Zerega Fombona, Alberto 11, 14, 23, 30, 33, 38, 40, 49, 50, 55, 65, 93, 94
Ziaurritz Aginaga, Doroteo 96, 123, 136, 137
Zubillaga (Basque resident in Puerto Rico) 198
Zulaica y Arregui, José Gonzalo (Father Donostia) 288
Zweig, Stefan 166

www.ingramcontent.com/pod-product-compliance
Lightning Source LLC
Chambersburg PA
CBHW031615160426
43196CB00006B/140